ADVENTURES OF THE BATMAN

EDITED BY
MARTIN H. GREENBERG

MJF BOOKS

NEW YORK

Published by MJF Books
Fine Communications
Two Lincoln Square
60 West 66th Street
New York, NY 10023

Adventures of The Batman

Library of Congress Catalog Card Number 95-76047
ISBN 1-56731-077-X

Cover painting: Steve Stanley

Manufactured in the United States of America

MJF Books and the MJF colophon are trademarks of Fine Creative
Media, Inc.

10 9 8 7 6 5 4 3 2 1

Contents

ADVENTURES OF THE BATMAN

The Batman Memos

STUART M. KAMINSKY

MEMO FROM: David O. Selznick

TO: All Executives, Selznick International Studios

DATE: December 14, 1942

Follow-up projects to *Gone With the Wind* and *Rebecca* are moving much too slowly. Submit reports immediately on status of projects. Did we ever get the copyright on *Mein Kampf*? What about the ghost novel? Is Ben Hecht wrapped up? And what about the Batman story discussed at the Friday meeting? Is there something there? Is it a hoax? Harry, what about the rights? Is Walter back from Gotham City? Did he bring the clips? Ed thinks Errol Flynn would be willing to play Batman, but it would take a trade with Warners and they might want too much. Let's get some action on this one before MGM picks up on it. Fleming says he would consider directing but I think it's more a Woody Van Dyke project, which means another deal with MGM. Ivan, where is the report on Joan Teel? Have your people found her? We have four more weeks of

The Batman Memos

shooting on the Leslie Howard movie. Jess tells me she has two more scenes that can be shot on the last day. If you don't turn her up, we'll have to have a fast rewrite. Has anyone gone to the police with this? Ivan, if you don't turn her up by the 6th, go to Murchison in the Los Angeles Police Department and ask him to make some discreet inquiries. Or should it be discreet? What does publicity think about letting the information get to the press? Good promo for the Howard movie? Bad taste? Feedback on this one. What's going on with Phyllis Walker name change?

MEMO TO: David O. Selznick

FROM: Walter Schlect, Story Development and Rights

DATE: December 17, 1942

Batman is the real thing. I interviewed Gotham City's Police Commissioner Gordon, who's high on the guy and suggested I talk to Bruce Wayne, one of the town's social and business leaders. Wayne is into textiles, construction. Inherited a bundle and keeps his investments local. Wayne's a little stuffy, lives with a kid about sixteen whom he calls his "ward." Setup seems odd to me but so does the whole setup in Gotham. Wayne claims to be able to make contact with Batman and says he can get Batman to let Wayne represent him. Wayne didn't seem too interested in the whole deal but he said he'd be willing to talk. I've attached some newspaper pictures of Batman and his kid sidekick, Robin. We've got nothing in color but I've had Sheila in art fill in. I've also asked Dr. Benjamin Pinesett at U.C.L.A. to send you a psychological profile on Batman based on the clips and interviews attached. I billed the trip and profile to my department. A copy of the billing report is attached.

Stuart M. Kaminsky

MEMO TO:	David O. Selznick
FROM:	Ivan O'Connor, Security
DATE:	January 3, 1943

Nothing to report on Joan Teel. Check of her apartment indicates she hasn't moved out. Clothes are still in the closets. Food in the refrigerator. I've talked to Lieutenant Murchison of the Los Angeles Police Department as you requested. He is making inquiries.

MEMO TO:	David O. Selznick
FROM:	Benjamin Pinesett, M.D., Ph.D. Professor of Psychiatry, The University of California, Los Angeles
DATE:	January 4, 1943

At the request of Mr. Walter Schlect of your story department and based upon (a) biographical information provided by Mr. Schlect, (b) newspaper and magazine clippings also supplied by Mr. Schlect, (c) photographs, and (d) interview transcripts provided by Mr. Schlect, I can draw some tentative, but only very tentative, conclusions about Batman. I would be happy to interview Batman if and when he is available for a more conclusive study at my usual fee. As you will note, the bill enclosed takes into account that Mr. Schlect informed me that the report was needed urgently and his insistence that the report be no more than three pages. I therefore worked on it over the New Year weekend. I will also include a few observations concerning the disappearance of Joan Teel, which Mr. Schlect also mentioned to me and for which he supplied me with studio biographical information and a private investigator's report.

It is my opinion about Batman that we are dealing with a case of infantile fixation combined with a Messianic complex. The two often accompany each other as your experience and mine with actors will bear out. Whoever this man is he is fulfilled only by wearing a Halloween costume. Fortunately, this need to hide his identity behind a costume is combined with a belief that his intervention is necessary to protect the city of Gotham from criminals. I say "fortunately" because under other circumstances such a man might well become a transvestite or join the Ku Klux Klan or, to put a better light on the situation, he might join an institution or organization that would allow him to wear a uniform—the police, the postal service, hospital service. However, such institutions would not allow him to preserve his identity. That the man is, in lay terms, mentally disturbed is self evident. What disturbs me even more is that the entire community of Gotham City including the Police Commissioner has embraced and supported this delusion, allowing "Batman" to not only feel that he is above the law but give him structured support for such a delusion. It is possible that such an unstable personality will eventually lose the distinction between right and wrong. Untreated and unchecked I would say institutionalization is inevitable. What disturbs me even more is that he has enlisted a young man in his delusion. The damage may already be great for the young man.

Note that Batman is garbed in the dark vesture of a bat, a night creature. Note the shape of the costume, the cowl as helmet, the dark phallic imagery is undeniable. In contrast, Robin is identified with a vulnerable bird, a bird of light hues. The relationship is dangerous.

My recommendation is to enter into no negotiations or correspondence with this man other than to suggest that he seek professional consultation which, I am sure at this point, he will not seek.

As for the Joan Teel situation, I'd suggest you place a call to her parents' home in Dixon, Illinois. It is not unusual for a 20-year-old girl in her first pressure situation—a 20-year-old girl who has been nurtured, supported, and given awards and prizes by parents and those surrounding her in a small, isolated community—to find the pressure too great and simply return to the "womb."

MEMO FROM: David O. Selznick

TO: Walter Schlect, Story Development and
                 Rights

DATE: January 7, 1943

Our boys are dying around the world. I think they could use a Messianic hero. The whole country can use one and F.D.R., while he fills the emotional need, doesn't address the physical. I've called Bruce Wayne in Gotham City and said the same thing to him. I think I've persuaded him and he is willing to make the trip to Los Angeles to discuss the project and to bring with him a letter of consent from Batman. Wayne has even indicated an interest in investing in the project and serving as consultant. Danny has talked to Errol Flynn. He is *definitely* interested. I'm not sure what our alternatives would be. Gable is an Army private.

Ty Power is a Marine private. Hank Fonda is a sailor, and Van Heflin has just been drafted.

MEMO TO: David O. Selznick

FROM: Ivan O'Connor, Security

DATE: January 7, 1943

Joan Teel did not return to Illinois. Dead end here. Lieutenant Murchison of L.A. police is checking girlfriends, boyfriends. So far, nothing. Might turn into a touchy one. Check of unidentified DOAs and hospitals has also turned up nothing.

MEMO TO: David O. Selznick

FROM: Harlan Turkbekian; Turbekian, Zimmer and Kitt, Attorneys

DATE: January 8, 1943

We'll have to move cautiously on this one. I'm not sure the signature "Batman" on a contract will be legally binding since, we assume, Batman has another, legal identity. We have done our own profile on Bruce Wayne of Gotham City. He is, indeed, a man of both substance and, apparently, integrity. In spite of his considerable business interests, there has never been a major suit brought against him or any of his companies. If Bruce Wayne is willing to sign a contract or letter of indemnification holding him responsible should "Batman" bring suit or contest any movie, book, play, or story based on his exploits, we feel it safe and reasonable to proceed. It is also my opinion that in case of litigation Selznick International could claim that Batman's exploits are in the public domain. In that case, however, you might be compelled to present a past exploit of Batman drawn from newspaper and other accounts rather than create a fictional tale. Ross Zimmer and I will both be available after Friday for further discussion on this.

As for the Joan Teel situation, her departure, whether by her choice, "act of God," or circumstances beyond her control, releases Selznick International from any financial obligation should you decide to replace her or alter your working script. The situation is much the same as the Warner Brothers/Bette Davis case last year.

MEMO FROM: David O. Selznick

TO: Myron Selznick

DATE: January 10, 1943

Proceed with Flynn negotiations for Batman picture. I've just met with Bruce Wayne. Like most successful businessmen he has eyes like our father. He looks as if he has a secret that puts him one up on the rest of the world. That's fine with me. He brought a letter of release from Batman that I have sent to Turbekian. One sticky point. Wayne wants script approval for Batman. I don't like it but I don't see how we can get around it. I think we can live with it. Let's see if we can get Ben Hecht on a treatment and script right away. Keep the cost down in case we can't get script approval from Wayne and have to pull out. This means no signing for Flynn though talk seriously to him. How about Thomas Mitchell to play the police commissioner? Villains: Alan Hale, Basil Rathbone? Love interest—this is a sticky one. Who does Flynn want to work with? We don't need a big one but I'd still like Lana

Turner, Ida Lupino, or Phyllis Walker. How about Jennifer Jones as the new name for Walker?

I've got a favor to ask. Can you find a spot for Alice Feigner in your office? She's a good worker, fast typist but less than brilliant. She burst in when Bruce Wayne was in my office and said there was a call on the phone from someone who claimed to have kidnapped Joan Teel. Whoever it was hung up before I could pick up the call. I had to tell Wayne about the situation. He seemed interested but we went on with the negotiations. Nothing was lost but I'd appreciate finding a less sensitive position for Alice.

MEMO FROM: David O. Selznick

TO: Ivan O'Connor, Security

DATE: January 14, 1943

The Teel situation is getting out of hand. As you know, I've had two calls from a man who claims to have kidnapped Joan Teel. A woman did come on the line weeping and claiming to be Teel. I couldn't tell if it was Teel. Since talking to you I've discussed the situation with our attorneys. There are several possibilities here. Teel may be a part of this attempt to extort money from us. It isn't likely but we both know situations in which normally decent people have been tempted by love, sex, or confusion to do things they wouldn't normally do. That's the basic plot of half of the pictures Warner Brothers makes. If the threat is legitimate, it's from someone who doesn't know the picture business. He seems to think we'll lose millions on the Howard picture if she doesn't come back to it. I did not disillusion him. He wants $150,000. I see no alternative but to pay it. You are at liberty to discuss this with Lieutenant Murchison and get back to me this afternoon. If I'm in conference, give me a memo.

One more point. Let's dispense with the services of Dr. Pinesett. His fees are too high and his advice is about as far off as Tojo is from Washington.

Letter to David O. Selznick
From Bruce Wayne, The Beverly Hills Hotel
January 15, 1943

Dear Mr. Selznick:

It was a pleasure meeting you. As I told you, I admire your work and am particularly fond of *Gone With the Wind*. Your invitation to have me meet Miss DeHavilland was and is most gracious. I've decided to remain in the Los Angeles area for a while on business. You can reach me here. There is a chance that Batman will be joining me briefly. I mentioned the missing young actress to him and he, as do I, felt great concern and offered his services should they be needed.

I have spoken to my attorneys and instructed them to prepare a contract of indemnification as you requested. I assure you I am not in the least offended by this request. On the contrary, I think it a matter of sound business practice.

I look forward to hearing from you.

Sincerely,

Bruce Wayne

REPORT TO: David O. Selznick

FROM: Lieutenant Tom Murchison, Los Angeles
Police Department

DATE: January 19, 1943

Ivan O'Connor tells me you plan to pay $150,000 to the supposed kidnappers of Joan Teel. I think this is a mistake. At this point we don't even know for sure she's been abducted. My advice is to stall, then set up a meet with the supposed kidnappers with me and two of my men ahead of you at the site. The decision is yours but I think our chances of getting Miss Teel back are better if we act rather than if we rely on the good graces of kidnappers.

This whole situation is complicated, as you know, by the reports of sightings of a man dressed like a black umbrella at Miss Teel's apartment last night. The custodian swore the man wearing a black hood and black wings came out of the Teel apartment. That's not the strangest costume I've seen around this town over the past thirty years but it rates right up there with Barrymore in his birthday suit and a top hat.

I tried to reach you by phone but couldn't get through. I'd prefer you destroy this letter after you read it.

Sincerely,

Tom Murchison, Lieutenant,
Los Angeles Police Department

MEMO FROM: David O. Selznick

TO: Ivan O'Connor, Security

DATE: January 19, 1943

The Teel situation is taking too much of mine and the studio's time. I'm concerned for Miss Teel's safety and the fact that you and Lieutenant Murchison have made so little headway in finding her. I'm willing to take your advice and *not* have Murchison set a trap for the kidnappers when the money is delivered. I am concerned, however, that the kidnappers insist that I personally deliver the money. What's to keep them from kidnapping me and making an even greater demand?

No, at his next call I intend, as you suggested, to tell the kidnapper that an emissary, you, will be delivering the cash. I'll tell him that this is the only way I will deal with the situation. Then, God help us, I hope they agree and that we deliver the money and get her free, after which I want you and Murchison to find this person.

MEMO TO: David O. Selznick

FROM: Ivan O'Connor, Security

DATE: January 21, 1943

This is to confirm our telephone conversation this morning and your instructions. I will pick up the package from you on Wednesday night, your office, take it to the tiger cage at the Griffith Park Zoo at midnight and trade it for the merchandise agreed upon.

MEMO FROM: David O. Selznick

TO: Janice Templeton

DATE: January 21, 1943

I've just come into my office this morning and discovered that someone has been through the copies of my recent memos and papers. No one is to go through my papers without my direct approval.

MEMO TO: David O. Selznick

FROM: Janice Templeton

DATE: January 21, 1943

I have checked with the night janitors and with night security. Both sources report no one entered your office during the night. I've also checked with the secretarial pool. No one entered your office and I assure you I did not. I am most distressed and should you wish my resignation it will be on your desk within an hour of your so informing me.

I hesitate to add this but feel I must. One of the night janitors, Baylor Riggs, who has been on several occasions reprimanded for intoxication while at work, reported that a "big fat black owl, big as a man" was prowling around the building after midnight. It is possible Mr. Riggs may have seen someone but security and his supervisor doubt it.

MEMO FROM: David O. Selznick

TO: Janice Templeton

DATE: January 21, 1943

I value your service very highly and have no intention of asking for your resignation. These are both difficult and interesting days for all of us and I rely upon your discretion and judgment and expect that you will continue to participate in our creative growth in the future. I would

Stuart M. Kaminsky

appreciate your arranging for locks for my files this afternoon. One set of keys only. I'll carry them with me.

NEWS ITEM: *THE LOS ANGELES TIMES*, January 24, 1943

—A large bird reportedly escaped from the Griffith Park Zoo some time after midnight last night, according to reports of an overnight caretaker at the zoo and a patroling police car.

In spite of the reported sightings, zoo officials report that no animals are missing from the zoo.

Dr. Leon Santucci, a veterinarian with the zoo, speculated than an eagle attracted by the caged animals may have flown down from the Hollywood Hills. "It's happened before," said Dr. Santucci. "Not often but it has happened."

The caretaker, Oliver Palmer, reported the sighting of the bird near the large mammal cages. According to Palmer, "the bird seemed to be attacking a man with a suitcase." Palmer says he shouted and tried to come to the assistance of the attacked man, but both bird and man were gone when he got there.

Another explanation of the strange events came from Lieutenant Tom Murchison of the Los Angeles police who was in the vicinity of the zoo after midnight on an unrelated matter. Murchison said that he saw two men emerging from the zoo, approached them and determined that they were "a couple of drunks playing games in the zoo."

Zoo officials promised a complete investigation and a tightening of zoo security though zoo officials said it is difficult to get sufficient help with so many men and women serving in the armed forces or engaged in work vital to the war effort.

The Batman Memos

MEMO FROM: David O. Selznick

TO: Tom Murchison

DATE: January 23, 1943

I have destroyed your note to me as you requested. I ask that you do the same after reading this. I am pleased that Miss Teel is free and unharmed after her ordeal and imprisonment in Ivan O'Connor's basement. I'm not sure how Batman figured out that Ivan O'Connor was involved in her abduction, but I'm glad he did or O'Connor would have gotten away with the money and, in spite of his protests, might, as you have suggested, not have allowed Miss Teel an opportunity to tell her story. If possible, I would like to keep the entire episode as quiet as possible which, my lawyers tell me, means making a deal for a reduced sentence and a plea of guilty by O'Connor. Please work with our attorneys on this. As you know, Mr. O'Connor's departure leaves an opening in our security section. I would be pleased if you would consider the post.

Letter to David O. Selznick

From Bruce Wayne, The Beverly Hills Hotel

January 25, 1943

Dear Mr. Selznick:

Batman and I truly appreciate your hospitality but he informs me that he would like to withdraw his offer to participate in a film based upon his endeavors. He informs me that his decision has something to do with the handling of the abduction of Miss Teel and the subsequent handling of the case. Batman does not believe that he is sufficiently prepared to deal with Hollywood at this point. Should a time come when he feels differently, he assures me that you will be the first to know.

Please give my regrets to Miss DeHavilland. Should she or you ever get to Gotham City, please consider staying at Wayne Manor.

Sincerely,

Bruce Wayne

MEMO TO:	David O. Selznick
FROM:	Harlan Turbekian; Turbekian, Zimmer and Kitt, Attorneys
DATE:	January 26, 1943

I have copies of the reports, memos, and data you forwarded to me along with your very persuasive conclusions concerning the identity of Batman. I and my associates are not certain that we have sufficient evidence that Batman indeed broke into your office though the circumstantial evidence is certainly overwhelming. We will, as you instructed, hold the documentation concerning Batman's identity until such time as you wish it or wish, as you indicated, to turn it over to another production company.

Daddy's Girl

WILLIAM F. NOLAN

From Robin's Casebook...

It was a solo night job.

Bruce had gone to Washington to deliver a lecture on the economic affairs at a business convention, and had asked me to stay here in Gotham. My job was nailing the Tomcat, a very sharp jewel thief who was hitting all the wealthy West Side mansions in the hours past midnight, one each night, and cleaning them out. There were a lot of very angry Gotham City citizens demanding his arrest, but the police had never been able to catch sight of him let alone arrest him. Nabbing the fellow, with Batman gone, was my responsibility.

"As you know, a prowling cat tends to follow a pro-scribed route," Batman had reminded me. "So all we have to do, in order to figure out where our Tomcat will prowl next, is to counter-triangulate the area of his previous robberies, feed in the fixed coordinates of his probable strike area, and we'll have it narrowed to a one-block target."

When Batman pulls off stuff like this he reminds me of Sherlock Holmes— but ol' Sherlock never had a Bat-computer to work with. Ours produced a one-block area readout, mansion by mansion, so all we had to do was to set up a stakeout in that area and wait for the Tomcat to show.

"Up to you to nail this Tomcat's tail to the fence," he told me.

"Don't worry, I'll make him yowl," I promised.

So here I was on my solo night job. I'd come in the Batmobile, but had sent it back to the Batcave; I didn't want our catman to spot it in the area. The directional computer took it back without any problem—like sending a good horse home to the stable.

Now I was on the hunt, hugging the tree shadows along Forest Avenue, using the InfraBatscope to scan the buildings for possible Tomcat activity. A full spring moon was riding above Gotham City, painting rooftops and sidewalks with glimmering sliver. A lovely night for action.

I was glad to be out here under the sky on a hunt instead of being stuck in Washington the way Batman was. Despite all the years of crook-catching the thrill of the hunt had never diminished. On a night like this my blood raced and my whole body was on alert—every muscle tensed and ready for combat. For a true crimefighter, what else was there to live for?

That was when I saw him—the Tomcat, clawing his way up a vine toward the roof of a mansion, a big Victorian structure set well back from the street and almost buried in trees.

I muttered "Gotcha!"—heading for the mansion's black iron fence. I was up and over, sprinting for the tall side of the house rising ahead of me like a white iceberg under the moon. I moved over the grass, shadow-quick, without sound, and he had no idea I was coming for him.

I scrambled up to the roof, reaching it just in time to spot Mr. Tomcat crouched next to a skylight, trying to jimmy the lock with a crowbar. He was a tall string-bean of a guy, all in black, sporting a black stovepipe hat and black leather gloves—and he had a sharp, beaked profile that reminded me of the Penguin. Apparently he figured nobody was home since he sure wasn't trying to be subtle about getting inside.

I padded across the roof, smiling, sure of the game. Bagging this particular feline was going to be a cinch.

I was wrong. When I was just two feet away from him he whipped up his head, let out a venomous cat hiss, and lunged at me with the heavy crowbar—which wouldn't have given me any trouble if my right foot hadn't snagged on a loose shingle, throwing me off balance.

The Tomcat's crowbar slammed into me across the chest, and I went crashing, head first, through the glass skylight. I felt myself falling through space. Then, a big crash, and darkness.

Pitch-black darkness.

What I saw next was a delicate white face floating above me—the face of a beautiful young woman with round, dark, startled eyes like the eyes of a fawn in the forest.

"Hello," she said in a voice as soft as her eyes. "Does your body flesh hurt?"

An odd question. "My...body flesh?" Things were coming into focus around me. I was in a large bedroom, her bedroom most likely, since it was all pink and flouncy. And the young lady was also in pink, the kind of wide-skirted lacy Victorian dress you'd wear to a costume ball.

Daddy's Girl

I tried to sit up. "Ouch!" I groaned, clutching my side. "It *does* hurt."

Which is when I realized I was wearing white silk pajamas. My cape and mask and clothes were gone! This was serious, since no one in Gotham City was ever supposed to see Robin without his mask. Batman was going to be plenty sore at me for this!

"Who are you?" I asked the girl.

"Sue-Ellen," she said softly.

"Sue-Ellen who?"

She flushed. "I don't have a last name. Sometimes I don't even feel like a real person. I mean, real people have last names—and Father has never told me what mine is."

"It would be the same as his," I pointed out.

"But I don't know that either. I just call him Father." She blinked at me. "What's your name?"

"I'm...I'm not authorized to reveal my true identity." Her eyes were wide. "Are you with the FBI?"

"No. But I *do* fight crime."

"Is that why you were wearing a mask?" She had long blond hair framing the oval of her face; the moonlight from the window made it shine like a halo.

I adjusted the pillow, sitting up straight. "Haven't you seen my picture in the papers?"

"I don't ever see newspapers. Or magazines either. Father won't allow them in the house."

She'd caught me in full costume—and Robin had been on TV plenty of times. "You must have seen me on television?"

"We don't have television here," she said. Then she smiled for the first time and she was radiant. I was stunned by her pale beauty.

This surreal conversation was getting nowhere; it was time to end it. "I must leave now," I told her. "How long have I been here?"

William F. Nolan

"About ten hours. But you can't leave. Nobody ever leaves this house but Father. And he's away now. Far, far away."

"No, really," I said, "I must go. Just get me the clothes I had on when you found me."

She shook her head. "I want you to stay here with me. You're the first flesh person I've ever known, except for Father."

"Look, Sue-Ellen," I said, sliding my legs over the edge of the bed. "I really appreciate what you've done for me—fixing up my rib and all—but I have to leave immediately." I stood up. "Even if I have to walk out of here in a pair of silk pajamas."

"Gork will stop you," she declared. "I told him that you should stay." And she snapped her fingers.

A huge seven-footer appeared in the bedroom door. He had a flat gray face and eyes without pupils and wore a seamless gray uniform. He looked strong—but I was sure I could handle him.

"I'll have to clobber your big pal if he gets in my way." I told the girl. "Tell him to move back from the door."

"Gork is my friend. He does what I ask. He won't allow you to leave."

I was in no mood to argue the point. I just lowered my head and charged. Hitting him was like slamming into a brick wall. And trying to punch him was hopeless. My blows had no effect.

Then Gork put his hands on me. Like two steel meat hooks.

"Don't hurt him, Gork," said Sue-Ellen. "Just put him back in bed."

The big lug did that. And he tucked me in like a three-year-old. All without changing expression.

"You can go now," the girl told him.

Daddy's Girl

He shambled out of the room.

"He's not human, is he?"

"Of course not," she said. "No one in this house is human, except for me. And Father—when he's home."

"What *is* Gork?"

"Mostly, he's made of metal. When I was very young Father got interested in the science of robotics. He's quite brilliant, and has many interests. He began to experiment with metal people. Robots. That's what Gork is—and he's identical to a dozen others that Father had constructed to take care of me. But Gork is the only one I really like." She moved very close, leaning over the bed. "May I touch your face?"

"Uh...sure, I guess so."

She reached out with tentative fingers to explore the planes of my face.

"It's warm—just like mine. The robots have cold faces, like wet fish." She gave me one of her radiant smiles. "I'm a flesh person, too. Just like you are."

This whole situation was totally bizarre; I couldn't figure it out.

"I need to talk to a friend," I told her. "Could I use your phone?"

"We don't have any phones here. Father says they'd just distract me—that I'd use them to try to call other flesh people." She giggled. "But that's silly because I don't know anyone but you and you're right here. I don't have to call you."

I looked at her intently. "Is it true...that I'm...the first boy you've ever met?"

"I said so, and I never lie."

"Where did you go to school?"

"Here. In this house. The robots taught me."

"You mean...you've never been to an outside school?"

"I've never been to an outside anything," she declared. "I've just been *here*, in Father's house. For my whole life."

I was shocked. "Are you saying your father has kept you prisoner?"

"Prisoner?" She frowned at the word. "No...I'm not a prisoner...I'm Daddy's girl. This is where he wants me to be—where he brought me as a tiny baby after Mother and Father quit living together."

"What happened to your mother?"

"I don't know. I never saw her again. Anyhow, after she left, Father told me I was 'too precious' to have the world 'pollute' me. He said he'd keep me here, always, safe from the 'harshness' of the world, that he didn't want me 'tarnished.' Father uses words like that all the time. He's a lot smarter than me."

"Did you ever get to play with other children?"

"Oh, no—never. Father had robot children made for me to play with. I never saw any real ones. I just grew up here—with the robots." She brightened. "I've even learned to make robots myself now. I'm very good at it, too."

"Who *is* your father?" I was angry at what the man had done to his daughter. "Tell me who he is."

"I've told you, I don't *know* his name. He's just...Father."

I walked over to her dresser. "You must have a picture of him...a photo. I want to see his face."

"He doesn't like pictures. There aren't any."

"What does he do for a living? How does he earn the money for all this?"

"He works in the circus. As a clown. I guess he always has. That's where he is right now, with a circus, way off in Washington. You know, the D.C. place."

Daddy's Girl

"Yes, that's where my friend is now—the one I need to contact."

She nodded. "Then maybe Father will see your friend there."

Something was very wrong. I sensed it—a rushing chill inside me, a prickly feeling that this crazy father of hers was a threat to Batman. I had no evidence to back it up, just a gut hunch. But it was strong.

I *had* to find out what was happening in Washington.

"When you found me," I said urgently to Sue-Ellen. "After I'd fallen through the skylight...I was wearing a wrist chron."

She looked confused.

"Like a watch," I said. "Where is it?"

"The robots took it away with your other clothing."

"I *need* it, Sue-Ellen! Badly."

"All right, I'll have Gork fetch it."

And she did. The big gray robot handed it to me, then shambled out again.

The Batchron was a communication device, featuring a mini-TV. I punched in the coordinates, and the face of a worried-looking newscaster flashed to life on the tiny screen. He was speaking with gravity: "...and the shocking attempt on the President's life was averted by Gotham City's Caped Crusader in a daring action when Batman suddenly appeared at the circus, throwing himself directly in the path of the killer clown, and managing to wrest a lethal dart-weapon from his grasp. Had just one of the deadly venom-coated darts struck the President he would have died instantly. In the subsequent melee the killer escaped from the circus tent, but Batman was unhurt..."

I switched it off. Sue-Ellen and I were staring at each other. "That clown...on the newscast," she said. "They only showed him from the back—but I'm sure it's Father."

William F. Nolan

"Then your father attempted to assassinate the President of the United States."

"I'm sorry," murmured Sue-Ellen softly, head down. "That's very wrong, isn't it?"

"Very," I said.

"I wonder why he'd *do* a thing like that," the girl said. "But then...he's not a very nice man. I have tried to love him, but I just can't. Gork has been much kinder to me than Father."

I was beginning to suspect a terrible truth about Sue-Ellen's father. But I needed to have her verify it.

"Describe him to me," I asked. "What does your father look like?"

"If you mean his features, I'm not sure. I mean, not really. He's always in his clown makeup. I've never seen him without it."

I nodded. "And what about his hair? What color is it?" My voice was intense.

"It's green," she said. "An ugly green color...and he always wears red on his lips."

I was right. Sue-Ellen's father was our old enemy, the Clown Prince of Crime himself....

"Surprise!" An oily voice from the doorway.

I looked up—and he was there, with his demonic smile distorting that dead-white face, the face of total evil.

"Joker!" I glared at him. Sue-Ellen drew back, as if from a snake. He ignored her, his eyes blazing into mine.

"Ah...it's Dick Grayson," he said slowly. "A known friend to Batman and Robin."

"And proud of it," I said tightly.

"Well, it seems your friend foiled me again," said the Joker. "I intend to make him pay for what he did to me in Washington!"

Daddy's Girl

We were face-to-face at the bed. His breath was foul, like rotten meat. "You're big at making empty threats, Joker," I told him. "But when the chips are down you always lose. Batman and Robin have defeated you time and again—and one of these days they'll put you permanently out of business."

"Never! My brain far surpasses the range of normal men."

"At least we both agree on that," I told him. "You're anything but normal."

During this entire exchange, from the moment her father had appeared in the room, Sue-Ellen had been silent, intent on the play of words between us. Now she spoke firmly, her small chin raised in defiance.

"Father, you are being very unkind. This is my first flesh friend and I don't like the mean way you've been talking to him. I think you should apologize."

"Apologize!" The Joker's laugh was bitter. "I'll apologize to no friend of Batman's. That bat-eared fool has been a plague in my life—continually thwarting my plans."

"If you have acted as wickedly in the past as you acted in Washington," declared the girl. "Then your plans *should* have been thwarted."

The clown glared at her. "What do you know of good and evil...of profit and gain...of besting authority...of the sheer power and joy in being a master of crime?"

"I know it's nothing to be proud of," she snapped. "From what I've learned here today, I would say you belong in jail."

"If Batman were here you'd see how he'd deal with your father," I told Sue-Ellen. "He'd put him out of action fast enough!"

"Oh, he'll be here," smiled the Joker. "I will see to that! I'll lead him to this very house...and there will be a pres-

William F. Nolan

ent waiting for him...a present from the Joker to the Batman."

"What do you mean?" I demanded.

"I don't know what odd twist of fate brought you to this house," he said, "but I shall make good use of you. When Batman arrives—and I shall summon him personally—he shall find his society friend, Dick Grayson, waiting for him..." A fiendish cackle. "...with a cut throat!"

And he held up a long-bladed knife. Light trembled along the razored edge.

"And you, dear daughter," he said, turning to Sue-Ellen, "shall slice his throat neatly from ear to ear and we shall leave him for his bat-friend to find." His eyes glowed hotly. "It will be simply *delicious*—watching Batman's shock when he encounters Grayson's corpse!"

"How utterly *horrible*!" exclaimed Sue-Ellen. "You're a monster! You can never make me do such a..."

Her voice faltered. The Joker was standing above her, staring into her eyes. The tone of his voice was soft and compelling: "You shall obey your father in all things...You will do exactly as I command...You are Daddy's girl...Daddy's girl...Daddy's girl..." And his eyes burned like glowing coals in the dead white of his face.

"I...am...Daddy's...girl," Sue-Ellen murmured in a drugged voice. Her hands fell to her sides. She was blank-eyed and rigid, a victim of his dark powers.

That's when I jumped him, driving my right fist into the white of that grinning face—but before I could deliver a second blow I was jerked violently backward. Two gray-skinned house robots held my arms in a literal grip of steel. I was helpless.

"Don't try to fight them," said the clown. "They are far more powerful than any human." He reached into his

Daddy's Girl

striped coat and produced a small, jell capsule. "When she uses the knife on you," he said. "You'll never feel a thing."

And he snapped the capsule in two under my nose. A wave of sleeping gas spun me into blackness.

From the Batman's Casebook...

I had just returned from Washington—more enraged than ever at the Joker. His vicious attempt on the President's life was yet another act of total madness. I was grimly determined to run him into the ground in Gotham City.

When no word from Robin awaited me upon my return I was concerned as to his whereabouts. Cruising the West Side in the Batmobile, I scanned each section of the street, but found no sign of him. Where could Robin be?

Then, abruptly, the Joker's grinning face appeared directly ahead. The image was being beamed down from the sky above me—from the Joker's Clowncopter. I could see him at the controls as he hovered over me with his mocking devil's smile. He fired a burst from his laser nosecannon, blasting apart the road, and I veered sharply left to avoid a smoking crater. (More work for the street department.)

It was a short chase. The Joker brought his machine down on the roof of an old Victorian mansion on Forest Avenue, and I followed him through an open roof door.

The house was silent and lightless. The Clown Prince of Crime was hiding somewhere inside this gloomy building, and I was determined to find him. The silence seemed to deepen as I moved through the darkness, hunting from room to room, gliding down the main staircase.

William F. Nolan

I padded softly along a dimly lit hallway toward an open door just ahead. This was the main ballroom, immense and ornate, moonlight tinting its polished oak floor.

Then I gasped. Someone was spread-eagled on a table in the middle of the cavernous chamber. I moved closer.

And fell back in agonized shock. It was Robin! Unmasked, and dressed in white silk pajamas—spattered with blood! His head was twisted at a sharp angle—and his throat had been cut from ear to ear!

A searing white cone of light stabbed suddenly down from the ceiling and an amplified wave of ghoulish laughter crashed through the room. The Joker's laughter! Taunting, demonic, triumphant...

"He is dead, Batman. Your meddlesome little friend, Dick Grayson, is no more."

"Damn you, Joker, I'll tear you apart for this!" In a red rage, fists doubled, I swung around, raking the darkness for a glimpse of him. My fingers itched to close on his windpipe; I wanted to choke the life out of his foul body, to see his eyes bug and his tongue protrude from his swollen red lips...

"No use looking around for me, Batman. I'm in my second-floor study, enjoying this splendid show on my monitor screen."

I looked up. A shielded scanner rotated with my movements, providing the Joker with his image of my agony. Then the tall entrance door to the ballroom banged shut like an exploding cannon.

"There's no way out for you," the Joker informed me. "That door is steel-ribbed and the walls are rock solid."

"What's your game, Joker?"

Daddy's Girl

"Simple. I intend to leave you with your dead friend. No food. No water. Just you and a slowly-rotting corpse. I shall savor your death, Batman. Indeed, I shall."

And, again, the cackle of demonic laughter from the wall speakers.

I sprinted for the door, throwing my full weight against it, but the door held fast. The Joker was right; I was trapped like a fly in a web.

I slumped against the door, the full horror of Robin's death assaulting me. Tears ran down my cheeks behind the Batcowl, and I slammed the wall in pained frustration. Indeed, it seemed the Joker would have a good show.

Then, just beyond the viewing range of the scan unit, from the deep corner shadow, I saw a small white hand beckoning to me.

I didn't want to alert the Joker so I put on the act he was hoping for: I groaned aloud, turned in a hopeless circle, then staggered to the corner to beat both fists against the wall.

A young woman with frightened eyes was crouched there. Looking up at me, her words tumbled out in a desperate whisper.

"Your friend is alive," she said. "The figure on the table is a robot—to fool Father. He thought I was hypnotized, but I wasn't, I just pretended. Gork helped me. He's a robot, too. We modeled the machine boy after Dick Grayson. I made the face myself!"

Relief that Robin was still alive flooded through me. I leaned close to the girl. "Who are you?"

"I'm Sue-Ellen, the daughter of the person you call the Joker. He tried to force me to kill your friend, but I could never do that. I *love* him!"

"Where have you hidden him?"

William F. Nolan

"Below...in the basement. He's still unconscious from Father's sleeping gas. But the two of you can get away through a secret passage leading to the street."

"But how do I get out of this room?"

"Behind you...there's a trapdoor in the floor. It was bolted shut from below but I got it open."

"Where are you, Batman?" The Joker's taunting voice boomed from the speakers. "Come, come, this will never do." The tone became harsh. "Step back into the light or I shall be forced to send down some of my metallic friends to drag you out of that corner. And they won't be gentle about it. Now, do as I say!"

Sue-Ellen was gesturing to me; her voice was urgent: "Quickly! He'll send his robots if we don't hurry."

And she tugged open the trapdoor, revealing a square of pale yellow light from the basement below us. A twist of sagging wooden stairs led downward.

"This way," whispered the girl. "Follow me."

I slipped through the trapdoor, closing it behind me, and followed her rapidly down the stairs.

From Robin's Casebook...

I woke up, blinking, acrid powder fumes in my nostrils. Batman was leaning over me; he'd used a reviver vial from his utility belt to bring me around.

"You okay?"

"Yeah...a little dizzy is all." I gripped his arm. "How did you get here, Batman? And where's Sue-Ellen?"

The girl stepped forward, taking my hand. Her fingers felt warm and strong. "Here I am." She was smiling; my personal angel.

"I don't understand. I thought the Joker had—"

"Never mind what you thought," said Batman. "By now the Joker knows that his daughter tricked him. He'll

Daddy's Girl

be sending down his killer robots." He reached out a gloved hand. "On your feet. We need to get out of here."

I stood up. A bit shaky, but otherwise I was fine.

Then: wham!—the basement door crashed open.

Sue-Ellen screamed: "They're here!"

A half-dozen giant, gray-faced robots were pouring through the door, straight at us.

"Maybe this will slow them down," shouted Batman, tossing a Batpellet at the advancing tinmen. They staggered back as the pellet exploded into yellow fire.

"This way!" cried Sue-Ellen, taking the lead down a narrow rock-walled passageway. It was damp and cobwebby and smelled of dead rats.

The tunnel was as black as the Joker's soul—but we kept running full tilt behind the girl. Then we could make out a faint glow at the far end.

"That's the street light from the corner of Forest and Troost," Sue-Ellen informed us. "You're almost out."

But "almost" wasn't good enough; the robots were gaining fast. In another couple of seconds they'd catch us for sure.

"Do something, Batman!" I pleaded. "Or we're goners!"

The Caped Crusader spun around and flipped out another belt vial. Whoom! The whole roof caved in behind us, trapping the robots in rock and mud.

Then we were at the tunnel exit. Sue-Ellen stepped back. "Go quickly," she said.

I hesitated. "But we're taking you with us."

"Oh, no you're not!" rasped an oily voice—and the Joker leaped toward us, a gleaming .357 Magnum in his gloved hand.

Batman didn't say a word. It was time for action, not talk. He ducked under the Joker's gun arm to deliver a smashing blow to the clown's pointed chin.

William F. Nolan

The Joker fell back, dropping the Magnum. Then he pressed a button on his coat—and the Clowncopter, blades whirling, dropped to the pavement between us like a giant cat. Instantly, the Joker hopped to the controls, roaring the chopper skyward; it whip-sawed away over the trees.

My voice was intense: "Can we catch him in the Batcopter?"

"Afraid not," sighed Batman. "I left it on the roof. No doubt our green-haired friend disabled it. He wouldn't risk a pursuit."

We turned toward the girl. She was crouching inside the tunnel, peering out at us from the darkness.

"Come on, Sue-Ellen," I said. "Time to go."

She shook her head, "I can't."

I moved quickly to her. "But why not? You...you've said that you love me."

"I do...I really truly do," she declared. "But—"

I stopped her words with my lips.

"A kiss!" She gasped in delight. "I've never had one of those before."

"Sue-Ellen, I want you *with* me," I told her. "To share my life. I've never met a girl like you. I want to marry you."

Tears welled in her eyes. "Oh, that sounds...so wonderful. But it can't ever happen. Because..."

"Because why?"

She stepped forward into the light from the street lamp. "Because I'm dying."

Sue-Ellen was pale and her hands trembled; a crimson thread of blood ran from the corner of her mouth.

"Father made certain I'd never be able to go out into the world," she told us. "He gave me...injections. So long as I stayed indoors, in the house, I was all right.

Daddy's Girl

But...those injections changed the chemistry of my body. I can't survive...on the outside. My coming out...set off a kind of...chain-reaction inside my body and nothing can save me now. Not even your love."

"But there must be an antidote," I gasped.

"No...too late..." She was moaning out the words. "Father was brilliant. He wanted to make sure that I'd always be...Daddy's girl."

She reached out, slowly, to clasp my hand. Her fingers were already turning cold. "Goodbye, Dick Grayson," she whispered. "Goodbye, my love!"

And she was gone.

I lowered her body to the ground.

Batman gripped my shoulder. "Dick, I...I'm sorry."

I'd lost the sweetest girl I'd ever known.

I loved her. Very much.

And I always will.

The Origin of The Polarizer

GEORGE ALEC EFFINGER

How ironic, Bertram Waters thought, that I, one of the most promising researchers in the field of plasmonics, should be denied Ivy University's facilities because of something as trivial as money. Until he'd found a job with Jennings Radio Supply in the summer of 1957, Waters despaired that he'd ever be able to complete his graduate studies at the college. He had a tedious job as a stock and shipping clerk, but he realized that his meager wages wouldn't entirely cover his expenses. He was already exploring other means of augmenting his income.

Waters was a brilliant young man who had grown frustrated with his poverty and the stubborn ignorance of Ivy University's bursar. His coworkers at Jennings knew little about him because he rarely spoke except as required by his duties. In his presence, one was always aware that his powerful brain was constantly observing, cataloging, evaluating, and deciding. He was a tall, slender man, strong, but not in a bulky way. He had black hair with a sharp widow's peak, a narrow, straight nose, deep dark eyes that people unfailingly described as "magnetic," and promi-

The Origin of The Polarizer

nent cheekbones that gave his face a long, somewhat sinister appearance. He had one affectation—a carefully trimmed mustache of the sort film stars had worn fifteen or twenty years earlier. Someone had once remarked, quite accurately, that Bertram Waters looked like Satan as played by Errol Flynn.

The shipping department was a wire cage separated from the rest of the Jennings warehouse. During the summer, there had been two employees to handle the stock and two in shipping. Now that school had begun again, however, three of the young men had quit their jobs, leaving only Waters to keep up with the never ending stream of orders. Again and again, he would grab the next purchase form, run to the warehouse and pull the stock, then run back to the shipping department to box it, address it, and get it ready for delivery. Mr. Jennings promised every day to hire more help, but as the year slipped from late summer into autumn, Waters was still all alone, doing the work of four men.

One day, while Waters was eating lunch alone and reading Vance Packard's new bestseller, *The Hidden Persuaders*, Joe Sampson, the deliveryman, came into the shipping cage. Waters and he were not really friends—Bertram Waters did not encourage friendship in anyone—but sometimes in odd moments they talked about the few interests they had in common. Both were ardent baseball fans, for instance, and they often discussed the chances that the Gotham City club might follow the Brooklyn Dodgers and the New York Giants to the West Coast.

Today, however, the subject wasn't baseball. "It never fails," complained Sampson. "Whenever I have to make a big delivery on one end of town, the next one will be clear over on the other side. What do you have for me after lunch?"

Waters put down his book and his fried egg sandwich. He glanced at a clipboard hanging on the wire enclosure near him. "Just one," he said. "Another big order from Bruce Wayne."

"Jeez," said Sampson, "that guy again! Well, I guess he can afford it."

"That's what I hear," said Waters.

"He's one of Jennings' best accounts. I know for a fact that he gets as much electrical gear as some of the biggest factories and scientific outfits in Gotham City. What do you think he does with it all?"

Waters wasn't terribly interested. He only shrugged and picked up his book again.

"I hope he's around when I drop the stuff off," Sampson went on. "That butler of his never gives me any trouble or anything, but when the Wayne guy himself is there, he always gives me a healthy tip."

"Uh huh," said Waters absently. He kept on reading.

"Listen, pal. How about if I give you a hand filling the Wayne order? The sooner you get done, the sooner I can run it out to his mansion. Then I'll be done for the day. And I'll tell you what: if he slips me a few bucks, I'll come back here and split it with you. What do you say?"

Waters sighed. He was sure now that although he hadn't finished eating, his lunch break had come to an end. "Fine." he said. "Take one of those order form pages and find the electrical components in the bins. Bring them here to my desk because I have to check them all off."

"Whatever you say." Sampson slid the top sheet of paper free of the clipboard. Before he went to collect the parts, he switched on the maroon plastic AM radio above Waters' desk. The radio had been forgotten and left behind by one of the shipping clerks who had quit his job at Jennings to go back to school. Waters never turned it on because he hated pop music, and the radio did not receive Gotham City's FM classical music station. "Jeez, I'm getting sick of this song," said Sampson, listening to Pat Boone crooning "Love Letters in the Sand." Nevertheless, he left the radio on and went off in search of the electrical components Bruce Wayne had ordered.

Waters marked his place and closed *The Hidden Persuaders*. He watched Sampson wander off toward the vacuum tubes. "There should be a higher law," he muttered. "Something that would bring to justice all the double-digit IQs like Sampson." He took a deep breath and let it out, then stood and took the second page of the Wayne order. He began pulling boxes of resistors. He could tell that, once again, Wayne had ordered a small mountain of them.

Half an hour later, Sampson returned with a puzzled look on his face.

"This guy wants *two thousand* tubes," he said. "What can anybody do with two thousand vacuum tubes?"

"He can build a radio the size of your garage," said Waters irritably. "Maybe he has a crazy passion for Chinese music."

"Anyway, we're all out of some of these." He showed the order form to Waters.

"You can substitute for most of these tubes. Where it says 2A3, you can use a 2A3W, and it will be even more reliable."

"Yeah, easy for you to say, Waters. I haven't memorized the code numbers of every tube in the world."

Waters just stared at Sampson until he got himself under control again. "There's a big yellow chart on the wall, right in front of you," he said in a dangerous tone of voice, "and it gives all the tube numbers and all the permissible substitutions. It's probably been there since

George Alec Effinger

before you were born. You've seen it every time you've come into the cage."

Sampson grinned sheepishly, "I guess I never really noticed it before."

"That figures," said Waters sourly. "All right, I'll finish the vacuum tubes. You work on the resistors."

Sampson swapped pages with him and started to leave the shipping department. Then he stopped and turned back to Waters. "I always forget," he said. "What do the colored bands on the resistors mean again?"

It was all Waters could do to keep from punching him. "Forget it!" he said. "I'll finish the whole thing by myself. You just sit there and listen to the radio and don't touch *anything*."

Sampson shrugged. "All right, if you say so." He sat down and began munching on Waters' unfinished sandwich. "Listen," he said happily, "they're playing 'The Banana Boat Song.'"

Late that afternoon, Bruce Wayne bent over his work in the Batcave's superbly equipped laboratory. In addition to being in top physical condition to fight criminals on the streets of Gotham City, Wayne also found it necessary to keep current with all the latest advances in such fields as chemistry and electronics. What he had read in recent scientific journals had persuaded him that it was time to make improvements on the Batcave's Crime Data Analyzer. Wayne was convinced that he could build a new computer that could store and process information with even greater speed and efficiency.

New technology meant learning new techniques, but Bruce Wayne—the Batman—was never dismayed by such a challenge. As the day wore on, he worked with intense concentration, unaware that both Dick Grayson, his ward, and his faithful butler, Alfred, were concerned about him. Alfred, in particular, was unhappy that his master had eaten little of his lunch and then hurried back to his experiment. He was worried that Wayne might be overtiring himself.

At four o'clock, Dick Grayson entered the Batcave and greeted the older man. "Gosh, Bruce," he said, "I'm sorry that I couldn't get out of that social engagement. I would much rather have been here, helping you with our project."

Wayne looked up, startled. "Hello, Dick. How was the matinee concert?"

"I've never heard the Gotham Philharmonic sound better. I explained to everyone that you had an important business matter that prevented you from accompanying me. But now I'm ready to get to work. Oh, and Alfred said to tell you that dinner will be served promptly at six."

Wayne glanced at his wristwatch and reacted with surprise. "I had no idea that I'd been working here so long."

Grayson came closer to the workbench to see what Wayne was doing. "Tell me, Bruce," he said, "what is that board? It's plastic on one side, and copper on the other. Is it going to be part of the new BATIVAC Crime Computer?"

Wayne smiled. "Yes, Dick. This is the prototype of the sort of printed circuit I've devised for the BATIVAC."

Grayson looked bewildered. "Printed circuit?"

"The printed circuit board will make building the BATIVAC much simpler. The plastic board will become the base onto which we will mount the necessary electrical components. After the board is properly processed, the remaining copper on the other side will serve as the 'wiring.' It will save us many hours of tedious wiring and difficult soldering. The BATIVAC will consist of hundreds of these printed circuit boards, and if a component or a circuit should fail, it will be much easier to remove the entire board and replace it with an identical one."

Grayson examined the unfinished circuit board in admiration. "This is wonderful, Bruce," he said, "but I suppose you won't be needing me and my soldering iron anymore."

Wayne laughed. "Oh, there will still be plenty of connections to make, Dick," he said. "We'll place the components on the plastic side of the board, with their leads pushed through properly spaced holes. Then it will be a simple matter to fasten them down to copper pathways on the other side with a bit of solder."

"What about the excess copper?"

Wayne indicated the copper-clad side of the board. "I'm just about to remove it now. I've masked the outline of the circuit I want with a resistant ink. Now I merely dip the board into this pan of ferric chloride solution, which will etch away all the excess copper. When it's finished, I'll rinse the board in clear water and remove that resistant ink with lacquer thinner. All that will be left on the copper side is a map of the circuit I designed."

"Wow, Bruce," said Grayson excitedly. "No more fumbling with copper wire!"

"Exactly, Dick. And this process will enable us to build our equipment more quickly and will reduce the overall size of it, too. We've entered the modern age of miniaturization. The BATIVAC will require several thousand vacuum tubes, and without miniaturization, it would take up much of the area of the Batcave."

Grayson understood the possibilities immediately. "Maybe later we could build a smaller version of the BATI-VAC for the crime lab aboard the Batplane. And think of

The Origin of The Polarizer

the new miniature devices we could carry in our utility belts."

"First things first, Dick," said Wayne, amused by his ward's enthusiasm. "And I think I've worked hard enough for tonight, although the sooner the BATIVAC is finished, the sooner all of Gotham City can sleep more securely."

It would be many days before the BATIVAC was completed, but both Bruce Wayne and Dick Grayson knew that there was no point in working to exhaustion. Together the two left the Batcave and went upstairs where Alfred had prepared them both a light but nutritious snack.

It was already after five o'clock when Bertram Walters drove the Jennings Radio Supply delivery truck up the long, curved driveway leading to Wayne Manor. Joe Sampson had said something that got Walters thinking, and when he'd finished locating all of the electrical components to fill Wayne's order, Waters had volunteered to make the delivery himself. Sampson had only shrugged, thankful to be going home early. He hadn't questioned why Waters would do him such a favor.

What Sampson had said was that Bruce Wayne bought as many electrical supplies as some of the largest factories in town. What did he do with it all? It seemed like too great a quantity for a mere hobbyist, someone who enjoyed puttering around in his basement workshop building homemade burglar alarms and electric-eye garage door openers. Unless, of course, Wayne were an electronics genius, just as Bertram Walters was. That seemed highly unlikely, too. Wayne was very well-known in Gotham City, but his reputation was as a wealthy playboy and socialite, not as a new Thomas Edison.

George Alec Effinger

Waters switched off the truck's engine, opened the door, and jumped down to the gravel drive. He had a few not-so-innocent questions for whoever came to the door, and if the answers to those questions suited him, Waters might soon be embarked on an entirely new career—one that promised to be much more lucrative than his current job. Holding a clipboard and a box of vacuum tubes, Waters rang the doorbell and waited.

"Yes?" The man who opened the front door wasn't Bruce Wayne, whose photograph Waters had seen often enough in the newspaper. This must be the butler that Sampson mentioned, thought Waters.

"Jennings Radio," said Waters, trying to sound bored.

"Yes, of course," said the butler. He paused and examined Waters briefly. "Another gentleman usually delivers Mr. Wayne's orders."

"Yeah?" said Waters. "Well, today he didn't."

"Indeed, sir. Shall I sign?" he took the clipboard holding the invoice and packing list from Waters.

"Right. Top copy is yours."

The butler was shrewed enough not to return the clipboard until he'd examined the invoice thoroughly. "Pardon me, sir," he said at last, "but unless you have quite a few more parcels in your truck, this order is incomplete."

"Yeah, well, the stuff's on back order. It should be in tomorrow. I'll make a special trip out just as soon as it comes in."

"Thank you," said the butler. "I'm sure Mr. Wayne will be most appreciative."

"Uh huh. So tell me, this boss of yours, does he do a lot of electrical work around the house or what?"

The butler permitted himself a tiny smile. "Oh no, I wouldn't say that. Everyone knows that Mr. Wayne cer-

The Origin of The Polarizer

tainly doesn't need to attend to his own wiring difficulties."

"Well, he sure orders enough junk. All those vacuum tubes and everything."

"I believe, sir, that Mr. Wayne is planning to build a television set. He finds that sort of thing relaxing."

"Then he's not some sort of brilliant inventor, huh?"

Again, the butler favored Waters with a brief smile. "Oh, my goodness, no. He finds the plans in those home mechanic's magazines, but to be brutally honest, he's never yet finished a project. Now, good day to you, sir." He closed the great oak door quickly and firmly.

Well, Mr. Wayne, you have a clever and quick-witted butler, thought Waters, as he headed back to the delivery truck. A television set with two thousand tubes! You'll be able to tune in Mars if you want. But Waters was sure now that the components from Jennings Radio Supply would never form the inside of a television receiver. There was only one private citizen in all of Gotham City who would use such a great quantity of sophisticated electronic gear, and at the same time be so cautious about hiding the fact—the Batman!

Mr. Wayne, thought Waters as he drove the delivery truck to his own apartment, you'll receive the remainder of your order tomorrow, but first I want to put my own stamp of approval on every single part. And then I'll be ready for you when we meet at last.

Several weeks later, Bruce Wayne and Dick Grayson were putting the finishing touches on the newly completed BAT-IVAC, the Batman Algorithmic Tabular Integrated Vector Analzyer and Calculator. They had both enjoyed constructing the mammoth machine because the practical

George Alec Effinger

experience had taught them a great deal about the latest developments in electronics and data processing. There still remained the task of entering Batman's vast library of crime information. However, much of that was stored on punch cards for use with the non-obsolete Crime Data Analyzer, and the cards were also compatible with the BATIVAC. New information would have to be recorded on still more punch cards, and that job fell to the reliable Alfred, who, it should be obvious, was far more than a butler to his ever-vigilant masters.

Shortly before midnight, the red warning light far underground in the Batcave began flashing, indicating that the Bat-Signal was blazing through the night sky over Gotham City, invisible to Wayne and Grayson. They changed into their costumes as they raced to the Bat-mobile, as they had on innumerable occasions in the past. "I wonder what dangers we'll face tonight, Batman," said Robin.

"We'll learn soon enough," replied the Caped Crusader. "We'll report first to Commissioner Gordon. There are no urgent calls on the emergency radio frequency, so whatever the trouble is, no citizens or police officers are in a life-threatening situation."

"I suppose we can be grateful for that, but there are certainly plenty of other ways for crooks to cause trouble without using deadly force. And I'll bet we've fought every one."

Batman laughed ruefully. "Yet every time we think we've seen it all, Robin," he said, "some misguided mastermind comes up with an entirely new avenue of attack.

"We've been shot at, gassed, and trapped in burning buildings. The one thing we'll never have to worry about is being *bored* to death."

The Origin of The Polarizer

They drove at high speed through the rain-slicked city streets. It was late enough that there was little traffic about. Just before they reached police headquarters, Batman glanced at Robin. "Something's been bothering me about the Bat-Signal, Robin," he said. "Have you noticed it, too?"

"It seems to be flickering, Batman. Do you think it needs repair?"

"That's what I thought at first, but observe it carefully. The flickers aren't occurring at random."

"Gosh, you're right! It's a message in Morse Code! Let's see: B-A-T-M-A-N-! Y-O-U A-R-E H-E-L-P-L-E-S-S A-G-A-I-N-S-T T-H-E- A-W-E-S-O-M-E M-E-N-A-C-E O-F T-H-E P-O-L-A-R-I-Z-E-R-! But who or what is The Polarizer?"

"Perhaps the commissioner knows," said Batman. He had an ominous feeling that although the city's law enforcement chief had not seen fit to give the matter top priority, the case would soon prove to be one of the most bizarre and dangerous in the Batman's long career.

Leaving the Batmobile in a parking place reserved for police vehicles, the Dynamic Duo went inside to meet with the police commissioner. They hurried into the building and up to the commissioner's office.

"We got here as quickly as we could, Commissioner Gordon," said Batman.

"Good evening, Batman, Robin," said Gordon. He looked slightly perplexed. "Is there something I can do for you?"

Batman and Robin exchanged glances. "We came as soon as our warning light in the Batcave notified us that you'd activated the Bat-Signal, Commissioner," said Batman.

Gordon stood up behind his deck and looked levelly at the costumed crimefighters. "I don't know what you

George Alec Effinger

mean, Batman," he said. "I haven't turned on the Bat-Signal this evening. You know that the control switch is right here on my desk. I haven't used it, and I haven't been out of this room at all tonight, so that no one else could have used it, either. And even if the Bat-Signal had been operated without my knowledge, how could that help a crook in his criminal activity?"

"Hmm," said Batman. "It may be just an electrical problem, but perhaps it's something much more sinister. I think we'd better go up to the roof of Police Headquarters and examine the Bat-Signal itself."

When they all arrived there, the rooftop was deserted, but the Bat-Signal was still flashing its message in Morse Code across the clouds over Gotham City. "What does it mean, Batman?" asked Commissioner Gordon.

"I'm not sure, Commissioner," said Batman. "It seems to be a taunting threat, but I don't know of any criminal who calls himself The Polarizer. Perhaps it's just a demented hoax, but until we know for certain, we'll have to stay on guard."

"Look, Batman!" called Robin. "I've found a note."

"Is it in Morse Code, too?" asked Gordon.

"Let me see it," said Batman, taking the paper from Robin. "No it's in plain English. It's addressed to me. 'Dear Batman: Sorry I couldn't wait around to meet you in person, but while I lured you here, I've been robbing Shattuck Brothers Jewelry. For quite a while I've been admiring a sapphire and diamond necklace in their display window. Don't worry, though—we'll meet in person soon enough. At that time, you'll learn what it means to pit your meager skills against my power!' It's signed 'The Polarizer.'"

Commissioner Gordon took the note from Batman and studied it for a moment. "He sounds quite mad."

The Origin of The Polarizer

"Yes, that may be so," said Batman. "But he certainly knows enough about electricity to control the Bat-Signal from some remote location. And he has a strange sense of humor, as well, to use the Bat-Signal itself as a diversion to lure us here while he committed his robbery elsewhere. Somehow, I have no doubt that The Polarizer has made good on his boast. It's time for Robin and me to investigate the break-in at the jewelry store."

With Batman and Robin otherwise occupied at Police Headquarters, it was relatively simple for The Polarizer to break into the Gotham Ritz Jewelry Exchange. "Ha ha," he gloated, "even if those costumed fools decipher the Bat-Signal's message and find my note, they'll rush off in the wrong direction!" Although all the most elegant and luxurious jewelry had been put away in a safe for the night, there was still a large quantity of expensive merchandise left in the Jewelry Exchange's glass showcases. The Polarizer moved from one to another, stealing only the most exquisite and valuable pieces. I must hurry, he thought, aware that silent alarms must be sounding in a nearby police station. I can't afford to be greedy. I'll take only enough to pay my expenses for another year of graduate study.

When he estimated that he'd taken enough, he climbed back out through the plate-glass window he'd shattered only a few minutes before. He paused a moment to glance down the street in both directions, but he saw no one. He turned and sprinted down a narrow alley, where he'd parked the Jennings Radio Supply delivery truck. Already he could hear the howling shriek of sirens as police patrols began to converge on the neighborhood.

George Alec Effinger

The Polarizer threw his bag of loot carelessly into the back of the delivery truck and climbed in, pulling down the overhead door behind him. Hurriedly, he stripped off the stark black and white costume and the grotesque mask that hid his features. He had become Bertram Waters once again. Kittlemeier did a great job with this suit, he thought. I wonder if he could give me some advice about hiring henchmen. I could've gotten away with a lot more jewelry if I'd had a henchman or two. But you can't just put an ad in the Help Wanted section of the newspaper for somebody like that.

Waters hid his loot and The Polarizer's costume in the false bottom of a toolbox filled with needle-nose pliers and vacuum-tube extractors. The suit was close-fitting yet comfortable, and hadn't restricted his movements in the least. It was midnight black leather on the right side and snowy white on the left, separated by a jagged lightning bolt blazing diagonally down from the right shoulder to the left hip. He wore a white P in a black starburst on his chest, black gauntlets and high black boots, and a grimacing leather mask also divided into black and white halves.

When Waters was satisfied that everthing was safely stowed away, he pushed up the truck's sliding door and jumped down to the street. Once again behind the wheel, he turned the key in the truck's ignition and headed across town toward his own apartment. He would be many blocks from the crime scene before the police arrived.

Rain began to fall again, and Waters felt a damp chill in the air. He realized that he was driving too fast, fleeing in fear as though the Police might suspect the driver of a battered delivery truck to be Gotham City's most audacious jewel thief. He smiled at his own nervousness and slowed down, telling himself that it would be foolish to be stopped now for speeding. "I left no clues behind," he told himself, "There were no witnesses, and not even Batman will be able to find me."

Waters pulled the truck into his apartment building's parking area, then carried the toolbox holding the stolen gems and the costume of The Polarizer up to his apartment. He felt a peculiar excitement as he unlocked his front door. He had done it! He'd planned and executed a simple crime, taken enough valuable jewelry to pay for his needs, and gotten away cleanly. Now he could quit his boring job at Jennings Radio and take up again his studies in plasmonics.

Yet there was an intoxicating headiness about it all, and Waters realized that his ideas had changed. He'd planned at first to commit only one or two small thefts, just to pay for his further studies and enable him to get along without a regular job. But why should he limit himself? Tonight's crime had been so easy! Surely with a little more preparation, a large-scale robbery would be just as easy. Waters looked forward to working out the details of The Polarizer's second strike.

And there was one further matter that he did not want to let go of: the matter of Batman. It seemed likely to Waters that Bruce Wayne were one and the same, but Bertram Waters' scientific training required clear and unambiguous proof. He could not abandon his new life of crime until he knew for certain whether his hypothesis was true or false.

He took a cold bottle of Coca-Cola from his refrigerator, turned on his boxy, small-screen Muntz television, and sat down on his living room couch. As the opening theme of *Maverick* filled the room, Waters lifted the bottle in a toast. "Here's to you, Batman," he said. "Here's to your defeat and your unmasking…at the hands of The Polarizer!"

George Alec Effinger

Three days later, the entire punch card library had been fed into the BATIVAC, and Bruce Wayne and Dick Grayson were busily adding further information to the computer's memory. Grayson sat at the keypunch machine, while Wayne sat near him at the computer console's keyboard. "We must explore even the most unlikely hypothesis," said Wayne thoughtfully. "I don't think The Polarizer is one of our old enemies in a new guise, but we have to investigate that possibility nevertheless."

"I've recorded every detail of The Polarizer's *modus operandi* on these cards, Bruce. At least, as much as we could learn from our first encounter with him."

"We never actually saw The Polarizer, Dick," Wayne reminded him. "All we have to gone on is the Bat-Signal message and the unsolved thefts from the Gotham Ritz Jewelry Exchange. Does any of that match the known methods of the criminals in our Crime File?"

Grayson got up from the keypunch machine. "Let me feed these last few cards into the BATIVAC, " he said, "and then we can let it sort all the information. Our answer will appear on the teletype."

"Good," said Wayne. "I hope the computer tells us something we can use. I haven't mentioned it before, Dick, but there's something about The Polarizer's attitude that worries me."

His young ward finished his task and looked up. "I think I know what you mean," he said. "It's almost as if The Polarizer were watching over our shoulders, right here in the Batcave. Of course, that's impossible."

Before Wayne could say any more, the BATIVAC began its operation. There was a loud hum of machinery and whirring of fans, as well as the rapid riffling of the punch

The Origin of The Polarizer

cards. "I'll have it select all those criminals in our files who have the necessary knowledge and skills to use the Bat-Signal to send a coded message," said Wayne.

They waited and watched as the BATIVAC considered each past villain in turn. More than half an hour later, the computer had produced a stack of punch cards eighteen inches high. Grayson collected them from the output tray and returned them to the input tray. "What characteristic do you want to look for next, Bruce?" he asked.

Wayne considered the problem carefully. "If The Polarizer was known to us before, under another name, then his card must be in that stack. But many of those cards belong to criminals who are dead or in prison or can otherwise be accounted for. So next we should eliminate—"

Just then, the teletype started chattering. "How can it be typing, Bruce?" asked Grayson, startled by the machine. "We haven't even finished the sorting routine. It couldn't possibly have the answer yet!"

Wayne moved quickly to the teletype, which had once again fallen silent. He ripped the yellow paper free and read the single paragraph that had been typed on it. "Batman, it is time that we met in person. I am at this moment robbing the payroll of the Gotham *Daily Gazette*. Your friend, Vicki Vale, is waiting to photograph us together. Please don't keep us waiting! (Signed) The Polarizer."

"Come on, Bruce!" cried Grayson. "This time, innocent people may be in danger!"

"Right, Dick," said Wayne. "And now we have something else to bear in mind."

"What's that, Bruce?"

"We must face the possibility that The Polarizer has guessed our secret identities. He may have deduced the truth after learning that Bruce Wayne recently ordered a

George Alec Effinger

large quantity of electronic equipment. He may only be toying with us."

As if to underscore Wayne's suggestion, there came a rapid series of loud popping sounds from the BATIVAC, Grayson hurried to remove a panel from the back of the computer. "Bruce!" he cried. "The vacuum tubes! They're exploding! The BATIVAC—and our entire Crime File—may be useless now!"

They looked at each other in grim silence for a moment. "Don't worry about the Crime File," said Wayne. "I kept a duplicate set of punch cards as a backup. But we've got to put an end to The Polarizer's mischief. He's the cause of this, I'm sure of it."

As he and his young ward quickly completed their transformation into Batman and Robin, they each gave some thought to this new demonstration of The Polarizer's electronic wizardry.

"How could he get the teletype to print out that message?" asked Robin, as the fearsome Batmobile raced through the streets of Gotham City. "And how could he destroy the vacuum tubes in the computer? No one but Alfred and the two of us have ever been near the BATIVAC."

"We don't have the answers yet," said Batman in a low voice. "But we can't rest until we have them all. The Polarizer has discovered that we are somehow vulnerable, Robin, and therefore he's become a serious threat to our effectiveness as crime fighters in Gotham City. Our very future is at stake."

A crowd of spectators had already formed on the sidewalk outside the Gotham *Daily Gazette* building, drawn by the piercing alarm sounding in the newspaper's payroll office. The Polarizer, in his bizarre mask and black-and-white costume, pushed his way through the onlookers. He was carrying a heavy sack of stolen money and a box with several switches, meters, and a large antenna. He seemed to be in good spirits.

Vicki Vale, the famed photographer, accompanied him, snapping one picture after another. "Turn this way, sir," she called to The Polarizer. "And look menacing!"

"Ah, but my dear Miss Vale," he added, "I don't *feel* menacing today. I feel exhilarated and happy and full of all the warmest wishes for you and all mankind. Look at this lovely day. The sky is clear and the sun is bright, I've stolen enough money to indulge even my most fantastic whims, and soon I shall defeat this city's most cherished heroes. What more could any man ask?"

"Time for one more picture?" asked Vicki Vale.

The Polarizer nodded pleasantly. "I'm not going anywhere until Batman and Robin get here."

"You sound confident, Mr. Polarizer," said a man in the crowd.

"I *am* confident," he replied. "After all, I know something the Caped Crusaders don't know."

"What's that, you cowardly masked hoodlum?" shouted another spectator.

"Please," said The Polarizer. "Let's not start hurling personal insults. I only meant that I understand the full significance of my Terror Ray, and Batman and Robin couldn't even imagine the danger they're facing."

"They'll beat you," cried the first man, "Terror Ray or no Terror Ray!" The Polarizer only chuckled pleasantly.

A few moments later, the powerful thrumming sound of the Batmobile's engine signaled the arrival of the Dynamic Duo. Batman surveyed the scene and spotted The Polarizer. Vicki Vale was beside him, still clicking off one roll of film after another. "Robin," said Batman in a

George Alec Effinger

low voice, "we can't fight him here. An innocent bystander in this crowd might be injured."

"Gosh, you're right, Batman. What are we going to do?"

"Everyone, please move back!" called Batman in a loud, clear voice.

"Don't worry about them, Batman," said The Polarizer cheerfully. "They're in no danger from me. It's you who has to worry."

"Look out, Batman!" shouted someone in the crowd, "He has a Terror Ray!"

The Polarizer shook his head sadly. "Now, see that?" he chided. "You've given away my little surprise."

"Come on, Robin," urged Batman. "There's no such thing as a Terror Ray. That box he's holding looks like a remote-control unit of the type commonly used by model airplane hobbyists who fly radio-operated planes."

"Right, Batman! Let's get him!"

They ran toward The Polarizer, who dropped the sack of money and turned his attention to his Terror Ray box. He flipped two switches and turned a dial all the way to the right. "All right," he said, picking up the sack again, "I suppose this isn't really terror. But 'Consternation Ray' just doesn't have the same ring, don't you agree?"

Loud explosions came first from Robin's utility belt, and then from Batman's. Flames licked up, threatening to burn them, and they quickly unfastened the famed belts and dropped them to the ground. "Robin," said Batman without panic, "get the fire extinguisher from the Batmobile."

"But The Polarizer is using this diversion to make his getaway!" Robin said.

Indeed, the Radio Wizard had already loaded the stolen payroll into a brand-new Ford Edsel convertible

The Origin of The Polarizer

parked illegally at the curb, and was getting behind the steering wheel. He put the Edsel in gear and drove away.

Vicki Vale had run to the edge of the sidewalk to photograph The Polarizer's escape. Robin held her back. "Please, Miss Vale," he said, "there are potentially dangerous materials in some of the compartments of our utility belts. Until we have the fire under control, we have to ask you to stand back for your own safety."

·"I understand, Robin," said the glamorous red-headed photographer. "But you *will* catch him, won't you? I want to get a picture of that egotistical maniac being brought to justice."

"We'll get him," said Batman grimly, "but we'll have to do it without our utility belts. Come on, Robin. To the Batmobile!"

As they sped off in pursuit, Batman thought over what little they knew about The Polarizer. "I'm beginning to understand how he's managed to wreck our equipment," he said. "And just as he may have applied logic to guess our secret identities, he may also have unknowingly revealed a clue to his own."

The fleeing Edsel appeared ahead of them, racing recklessly through Gotham City's afternoon traffic. "Look, Batman," said Robin. "We're beginning to shorten the distance between us. His car's engine sure doesn't have the power of the Batmobile. The license plate on the Edsel will probably give us no useful information. No doubt he's also stolen that car."

"Nevertheless, make a note of it, Robin. I think the Batmobile will catch up to him soon. In addition to being much slower, he's not a very good driver."

Robin grinned in anticipation. "I can't wait to see if he's immune to a right cross!" he said.

George Alec Effinger

The Polarizer steered the stolen Edsel onto the new Gotham Crosstown Expressway. He glanced into the rearview mirror and saw the Batmobile following some distance behind. Don't worry, Batman, he thought. Or should I say, Bruce Wayne? I'm not trying to evade you in this traffic. Indeed, I fully intend to let you catch me, but not until we reach the place I've chosen. And then I've got one final surprise for you!

He reached out and switched on the car's AM Radio, hoping to find a station broadcasting a news report of his daring daylight payroll robbery. As The Polarizer tuned the radio from one end of the band to the other, all he heard were the raucous and simpleminded pop tunes he hated so much. He felt it was horribly unfair for a genius such as he to be immersed against his will in the cesspool that was American culture in 1957.

The money he had stolen—the money that he would *continue* to steal—would help to shelter him from those demeaning influences. With money, he could live and work in a world unmarred by the cheap trash that passed nowadays for music and art and literature. He wanted to surround himself with the finer things, and carry on his own sophisticated research in the field of plasmonics. He had no desire to inflict harm, or to hurt people or wreak vengeance. He wanted only to be left alone with an awful lot of money.

He left the expressway and headed out beyond Gotham City's suburbs into a wooded, hilly area. "Only a little farther, you hapless heroes," he muttered. Beside him on the seat was the homemade remote-control unit. The Polarizer glanced over at it and reassured himself that all of its telltale lights were burning green. The unit was functioning perfectly. There was still one more switch to throw, but the time for that hadn't quite arrived.

The road wound around in sharp hairpin turns, leading up to the heights where The Polarizer planned to prove to Batman and Robin that they could never defeat him. "Shall I let them die?" he asked himself. "Or shall I let them live, knowing that I can take their lives any time I wish?" He decided to leave the matter in the hand of Fate. Once again he glanced into the mirror, and saw that the Batmobile had surged ahead on the empty road and was now following close behind. In another minute it would overtake the Edsel.

"It's time to say goodbye, Batman," said The Polarizer. He saw that the road was now little more than a broad ledge along the sheer rock wall to the left. On the right, there was a sharp drop leading down into a steep, rocky gorge. The Polarizer shrugged and flipped the final switch. He could hear the muted explosions behind him, as many of the elements of the Batmobile's electrical systems burst and shattered.

He watched the Batmobile swerve dangerously close to the edge of the cliff, and then, as Batman struggled to maintain control, it came to a halt across the middle of the road. Thick black smoke poured from beneath the Batmobile's hood and from underneath the chassis. The Polarizer braked the Edsel to a stop far enough away so that the costumed heroes wouldn't be able to capture him easily. He let the engine run, but got out of the car, carrying the remote-control unit and the bag of money.

"You've faced many ingenious foes, Batman," The Polarizer called, "but none so clever as I. Who else has been able to manipulate you at will? Who else has discovered the means to defeat you through your own oversight?

George Alec Effinger

Who else has been able to prove that you are, in fact, Bruce Wayne and Dick Grayson?"

Robin looked at Batman in surprise. "Batman, you were right! He knows our identities! But what does he mean about an oversight?"

"Quite simple, Robin," said Batman. "It must have occurred to him that Batman must need to purchase large quantities of electronic components and other materials in order to build his many crime-fighting aids. Think how much time we spend maintaining the Batplane and the Batmobile in top working order, as well as keeping them up-to-date with all the latest instruments and weapons."

"Of course, Mr. Wayne," said the Polarizer. "It would take someone with a personal fortune as large as yours to pay for all that."

Robin shook his head. "Then The Polarizer had some way of knowing which wealthy individuals in Gotham City were always buying electronic components and other parts."

"Yes," said Batman. "I think that behind that hideous mask is someone who, until a short time ago, worked for one of the city's major supply companies."

The Polarizer laughed. "I salute you, Batman. You're quite as shrewd as legend has it. But you must give me some credit, as well. After all, I certainly don't wish to draw unwanted attention to myself. If I did work for such a company, I wouldn't be foolish enough to quit just as I began my career as The Polarizer."

"Perhaps not," said Robin. "But I don't understand how you've wrecked the BATIVAC and the Batmobile."

The Polarizer laughed again. "Forgive me for keeping that a trade secret," he said.

"It's simple enough, Robin," said Batman. "Before delivering the components to us, he merely rigged them

The Origin of The Polarizer

all with small amounts of plastic explosive, which he could detonate at will with his remote-control unit. In that way, he seemed to reach down into the very Batcave itself. As for the Bat-signal, that was even simpler. He didn't need to destroy anything, but merely control one or more key components from a distance, to make the Bat-signal flash in dots and dashes."

"And now I must leave you here," said The Polarizer. "Replace the tens of thousands of components in your computer if you wish, although it would take years to examine them all one at a time, to guarantee that each one is safe. And remember, you rely on other complicated hardware, too. Someday, perhaps, every electronic system in the Batplane will fail when you're flying over the ocean at 25,000 feet. You will never be able to trust your sophisticated machinery again." He threw back his head and laughed. It was a sound that was not altogether sane.

"I'm not frightened." said Batman. "We'll soon have you out of circulation. I placed a Bat-Tracer on your car back at the *Daily Gazette* building. When you drive home, it will let me know exactly where you are. If you abandon the car when you get back to Gotham City, then you'll be very conspicuous on foot. The police department will pick you up in a very short time."

The Polarizer laughed again. "Why, I'll merely destroy your tracer the same way I destroyed the Batmobile," he said.

"I used a Bat-Tracer that I constructed more than a year ago," said Batman. "That was before you began sabotaging the electronic components. Your remote-control unit will have no effect at all."

The Polarizer stared at his enemies for a few seconds, realizing that Batman had spoken the truth. If the Dynamic Duo were stranded on this little-traveled hill-

George Alec Effinger

side, so was he. He dropped the remote-control unit to the ground, and began running up the road, still clutching the bag of money.

"After him, Robin!" shouted Batman. While the Boy Wonder sprinted after The Polarizer, Batman took a rope Batarang from the damaged Batmobile. He flung it with practiced skill, and the Batarang looped through the air and twisted its rope around the bag containing the *Daily Gazette's* payroll. When the Batarang returned to Batman's hand, he gave a hard yank on the rope, and the bag pulled free of The Polarizer's grasp.

"What?—" huffed The Polarizer, short of breath. "We're going to end this adventure the old-fashioned way," said Robin. He struck The Polarizer hard in the solar plexus, doubling him over. Then Robin landed a single massive blow to the point of The Polarizer's chin, and the costumed villain went down in a heap.

"Need any help, Robin?" called Batman, who had put the payroll money safely inside the Batmobile.

"I think he's under control. I'll just tie him securely to be sure—"

The Polarizer had regained his breath, however, and rolled away a short distance. He staggered to his feet, obviously confused and in pain.

"We're placing you under arrest," said Batman. "I've already called Commissioner Gordon on the radio in the Batmobile, and the police will be here in a few minutes."

"No jail," muttered The Polarizer, panting for breath and backing away across the shoulder of the road. "I won't go the jail."

Robin tried to wrap him with his strong silken cord, but again The Polarizer retreated. "You might as well give up now and make it easy on yourself," said Robin.

The Origin of The Polarizer

"There's a nice, warm cell waiting for you in Gotham City Jail."

Behind his mask, The Polarizer's eyes grew large. "I told you," he said, "I won't go to jail." He held his hands out in front of him, as if he were trying to ward off something terrifying.

"Robin," said Batman quietly, "obviously this man is mentally disturbed. Don't say or do anything to upset him further."

The Polarizer made a cackling sound. "Disturbed, am I? Are you calling me mad? Is that what you say about all the villains who defeat you? Well, I'm not mad. Is it mad to refuse to be locked up in some horrible penal institution?

"Be careful, you're near the edge!" warned Batman, but it was already too late.

The Polarizer had backed up as he delivered his final speech, and finally his foot slipped over the unguarded brink. He tottered there helplessly for the space of a heartbeat, and his terrified eyes flicked from Batman to Robin. Then, suddenly, he was gone. He did not utter a sound as he fell, but Batman and Robin both heard the sickening dull thud as The Polarizer's body hit the rocks far below.

"Should we go down after him, Batman?" asked Robin.

"I don't see his body," said the solemn Caped Crusader. "But I don't think anyone could have survived that fall. In any event, the police team will scour the area when they get here."

Batman and Robin moved away from the edge of the cliff. They sat in the Batmobile while they waited for the Gotham City Police units to arrive. "He must have been a brilliant man," mused Robin. "After all, he did figure out our secret identities, but they're safe again now."

George Alec Effinger

For a few moments, Batman seemed lost in thought. When he spoke up, there was a sadness in his voice. "How ironic, Robin," he said, "that such a genius should have forgotten one of mankind's oldest proverbs: A sound mind in a sound body. The Polarizer couldn't hope to defeat us because he had followed only half of that ancient advice. It wasn't enough for him to wreck our modern devices because in the end it was that centuries-old piece of wisdom that conquered him. Wisdom, Robin! When all is said and done, the greatest force on Earth is still the human mind.

—With thanks to Doug Wirth

Batman in Nighttown

KAREN HABER and ROBERT SILVERBERG

When the masked and caped figure walked into the black-and-white marble entry hall of the Wayne mansion thirty minutes before midnight, excitement ripped through the mass of party-goers.

"Can you imagine! It's Batman. Someone call the police," Alice Chilton said in feigned alarm. Resplendent in her gilded Indonesian dance garb, she strode forward to get a better look at him.

"Oh, no. Don't call the police," Mara Osuna said. "Call Channel Five news. I think he's exciting." And, sinuous in a black spandex cat costume, she too prowled closer, gliding through the splendid ballroom with barely concealed eagerness.

Trial attorney Carlton Thayer, done up as a British Redcoat, raised his glass in mock tribute. "Somebody's got to deal with crime," he said. "Certainly the courtrooms can't handle it all. I say, more power to him."

"He's just a damned vigilante," Alice Chilton retorted. "We can't have people taking the law into their own hands. Even if they are wearing blue silk gloves."

She turned to their host, who was standing quietly to one side, a bemused expression on what was visible of his face.

"What do you think, Bruce?"

Bruce Wayne had been watching the doppelganger of his crime-fighting alter-ego with amusement, and perhaps with a little perplexity. He swung about now and smiled at his aunt.

"I don't know if this Batman is a criminal or a saint," Wayne said. "But I do know that he's late. Alfred, see if our unexpected guest would like a drink."

"Very good, sir," the butler said in his clipped British accent. "And perhaps the gentleman would like me to take his cape as well? No?"

"Batman" shook his head.

When the newcomer accepted a glass of champagne, Wayne lifted his own flute in a toast.

Clever, he thought. And a damned close replica. If that's how I look, the effect is even better than I'd hoped. The cape is very good.

"Batman" moved into the main ballroom, joining the assorted demons and sprites, witches and warlocks. Wayne tracked him for a moment in deepening fascination.

It was a little dreamlike, he thought. As though I'm standing outside my own body, looking at myself arrive at a party. He admired the stranger's audacity. Did he know whose house he was at? Probably not. Or perhaps he knew very well, Wayne told himself. Who is he? I'll find out at the unmasking.

Wayne circulated through the party, playing the part of host to perfection. Initially, the young millionaire had regretted his offer to let the masked ball be held at Wayne Manor. But Aunt Alice had been so persuasive, wheedling

Karen Haber and Robert Silverberg

until he gave in. He certainly owed her a favor. Dear Alice. All those holidays, home from prep school, which he'd spent in her warm, gracious company. After his parents' murder, Alice Chilton had been very good to him. An "aunt," yes. Though not a blood relation, she was almost a second mother. The least he could do was provide a place for her Women's Auxiliary Charity Ball. Besides, he wanted to deflate his growing reputation as a hermit. And so the cream of Gotham society, bewigged, bejeweled, and by now pretty well inebriated, was crammed into his mansion, awaiting the toll of midnight to unmask.

With a quick motion of his hand, Wayne reached behind his own mask—a grinning, red-faced devil—and wiped the sweat from his jaw. Through the mask's narrow eye-slits, he peered at his jeweled Rolex. The time was 11:40 p.m. Only twenty minutes to go. He adjusted his sleek red tuxedo. Perhaps he should have come as Batman, too. But that would have been too easy.

"Swell party, Wayne," said a brown-cowled figure sporting an owl mask, with a long, thin cigar poking bizarrely through its mouthpiece. The tones were the bass rasp of Police Commissioner Gordon. "Nice to see the old mansion lit up like this."

"All for a good cause," Wayne said. "I don't mind, as long as nobody breaks the Ming vase. Or," he said, staring meaningfully at the Commissioner's stogie, "uses the Egyptian urn for an ashtray."

Gordon exhaled a large, malodorous cloud of smoke. Wayne coughed.

"Is your life insurance paid up?" he inquired pleasantly. "I'd hate to see your lung x-rays."

"And I'd hate to see the bill for this party," Gordon said. "But it's not my problem, I guess. How long have you been back in town now, anyway?"

"Six months, Commissioner."

"Gstaad lost its appeal?"

Wayne forced a debonair chuckle. "The world is filled with all manner of delights and distractions, yes. But occasionally one needs to come home."

The gray eyes behind the owl mask fixed him with a shrewd gaze.

"I don't know, Bruce. If I had the money and time, there's plenty of places I'd be happy to call home besides Gotham City."

With a shrug, he moved off.

A good man, Wayne thought. A good cop, too. Perhaps too good. He had a deep streak of keen curiosity, Gordon. Way too much curiosity. Did he suspect the truth?

Wayne walked across the ballroom toward the door.

"Don't just walk right by me like that," said a throaty female voice.

Wayne turned. Ellen Harring was standing by the window, her white-gloved hand resting coquettishly upon her hip. Her blond hair fell loosely down her back, gleaming like a dazzling cascade in the lamplight. She was dressed as a houri, all golden veils and shimmer.

Very apt, Wayne thought. Since his return to Gotham City, Ellen had found one pretext after another for coming by, leaving messages, indefatigably pursuing him with social hunting skills burnished by long use. Each time she made a move, he managed to extricate himself. One step forward, two steps back. For a time, he'd found it amusing, but the *pas de deux* was becoming all too intricate. Now she walked toward him as though oiled, all fluid motion.

She hooked her arms around his neck and leaned forward until her chest rested on his.

Karen Haber and Robert Silverberg

"Why don't you come tell me all about your erotic weapon collection?" she crooned.

Wayne smelled bourbon on her breath. Gently, he freed himself from her grasp.

"You'd miss the prize for prettiest costume," he said. "We can't have that."

She seemed unperturbed by his amiable coolness. Her expression was all too frank, her eyes all too explicitly intense. He cast around for escape. And found it as the mysterious blue-caped figure in the bat mask moved past them.

"Why don't we ask Batman about his exploits?" Wayne suggested, stepping back to include the stranger. "Even a costumed vigilante could use a beautiful assistant like you, Ellen."

She turned to gape just long enough for Wayne to slip past her and out through a hall door into the servants' quarters.

Safe.

Wayne leaned against the plain white wall and shook his head. A shame, really. So attractive, Ellen. He could feel the heat of her against him even now. But her kind never let up. If he invited her into his world, into his bed, he knew that eventually he would regret the decision. It would all end badly, with him prying her fingers, one by one, away from his life. And he had no time, no room left for any sort of serious entanglements on that level. Europe had cured him of such things.

He moved through the dim passage, his footsteps echoing on the concrete floor, and emerged from behind a bookshelf into the gaming room. Here, the noise of the party was muffled by teak paneling and thick russet carpeting. Two amber-shaded swag lamps cast warm circles of light on the greensward of an enormous pool table. A footman in white powdered wig and purple waistcoat was making an intricate carom shot, studied intently by his challenger, an imposing sultan in flowing black robes and an enormous, bejeweled turban.

"Super soiree, Bruce," the footman said as he watched the sultan ponder his next move.

"Harry—still hanging out by the pool table. I should have know." Wayne paused. Even in prep school, Harry Thornton had never been able to resist a pool game. Fifteen years had only honed his appetite.

The sultan looked up. It was Wayne's accountant, Jim Weatherby. He gestured broadly with his cue stick toward the scattered balls on the table.

"Got any tips?"

Wayne nodded. "Sure," he said. "Don't play Harry. He's a semiprofessional pool hustler." He gave them a half smile and moved on, restless. Surrounded by this swirling horde of friends and acquaintances, he was still alone, concealing his agitation, his alienation, behind clever patter and the aloofness that wealth conferred.

Wayne had come back heartsick from Europe, tired of the gambling tables and rich widows. He was weary of the same faces seen at the same spas, those hungry faces avidly scanning the crowd. All of them looking for the same thing. Fresh meat. He'd done his own share of predatory stalking, and with no little success. Long ago, he'd learned that his trim body, dark hair, and blue eyes were quite acceptable to women of all shapes and sizes. Of course, the money helped. And he'd inherited one of the largest fortunes in Gotham City.

But now he hunted different prey. He'd come back home to search for meaning. To do something useful. To avenge the past. It made little difference to him how Batman was perceived, whether as vigilante or folk hero. All he knew was that he felt alive and connected with the world when he was wearing that blue-caped costume, and hollow and remote when he was not.

He slipped through the door into the library.

Three generations of Wayne bibliophiles had amassed a collection of rarities that filled two stories' worth of bookcases. The room, rich with its smell of antique leather binding and musty pages, its graceful cherrywood railings and ladders, was one of Wayne's favorites. He'd hoped to take a few minutes here, alone. But he saw now that the library was already occupied. Somebody wearing a blue silk mask and cape was wandering about by the far shelves, nineteenth-century French literature. The Batman masquerader.

For an eerie moment, Wayne felt as if he were looking into a mirror. As though he were a stranger standing across the room, watching himself. Then he shook off the dream image. With an effort, he managed a jocular tone, a tight grin, as he said, "Well, so how's the crime-fighting business these days?"

The impostor turned, nodded. He looked tense.

"Could be worse," he said in a tenor voice that perhaps was roughened a little around the edges by drink.

Wayne moved closer. He could see now that the outfit he wore was virtually an exact replica of his own Batman suit. "Nice costume," he said. "Who does your tailoring?"

"This little thing?" "Batman" shrugged. "Oh, I just picked it up someplace. Midnight blue has always been my favorite color."

"And mine."

"Want to switch costumes?" the impostor said. "I wouldn't mind being in your shoes for a while. Even if they are red. It'd be worth it, to find out what it's like to be a millionaire."

There was a wistful tone to his comment. And just a hint of menace.

Wayne was growing impatient to discover whose face lay behind that mask.

"You wouldn't like being in my shoes. Since I have an unusually shaped foot," he said, "all of them are hand-made. They aren't likely to fit anybody else."

He stared at "Batman," his annoyance growing. This joke was rapidly losing its charm. How dare some gate-crashing creep show up in, of all costumes, this one.

"I think I need a refill," the impostor said. "Excuse me."

His cape rustled like dry leaves as he brushed past Wayne and walked out of the library.

Slowly, the grandfather clock in the entry hall struck, twelve dolorous notes.

On the twelfth tone, the lights went out.

At first, the conversations and music continued. But as the darkness extended its hold on the party, the convivial noise began to ebb into silence. What had seemed like a gag was starting to feel odd. Disquieting. Aside from an occasional nervous giggle from a guest, an unbroken hush prevailed.

Alarmed, Wayne groped along the wall toward what he hoped was the door. Where were the auxiliary lights? The generator below the house should be working...

"My pearls!!" a woman shrieked.

In the dark, other cries joined hers.

"My watch!!"

"Thief!! Stop him!!"

"Lights!! We need lights!"

Wayne found the library door and began working his way toward the basement stairs. He'd have to throw the circuit breakers himself. If that didn't work, the next step

Karen Haber and Robert Silverberg

was to find some hand lamps. Where was Alfred when he needed him?

Then he heard the hum of the auxiliary generator, and the lights came on, flickered uncertainly a moment, grew brighter again, and this time held. Wayne breathed easier. Better head off a major panic, he thought.

"Relax, everyone," he said. "Nothing to worry about. That was a little prank I thought you'd enjoy."

Laughter and applause met his words. With a bow, he moved toward the front door.

A small knot of people gathered there, Ellen Harring and Alice Chilton among them. Wayne's aunt was close to tears.

"Bruce, it's ghastly," she said. "Do you know what's happened? Someone's stolen Ellen's pearls. And Harry's watch. And even the brooch from Jim's turban."

Wayne pursed his lips. "You mean all of that stuff was real?"

"Of course," Ellen said sharply. "How could you think otherwise?"

"And you wore them to a costume party?"

He wanted to shake her.

Commissioner Gordon shouldered brusquely into the group, his mask pushed up off his face, its yellow owl eyes goggling the ceiling weirdly.

"Anybody get a sense of who the thief was?" he demanded.

"None."

"Nope."

"I heard something," Harry said. "Like a woman walking by in a satin dress. Then a yank at my sleeve, and my watch was gone."

"Somebody must see very well in the dark," Wayne said.

"Yes, with eyes like a cat," Gordon added.

Or the sonar of a bat, Wayne thought. Quickly, he glanced around the room, but saw no sign of a blue half-mask, ribbed cape, or golden utility belt. The bogus Batman had vanished. Of course.

A cold breeze drifted into the room, lifting the edges of Wayne's tuxedo jacket, setting Gordon's brown corduroy feathers dancing.

Wayne swung around. In the dining room, a leaded window yawned open, permitting a narrow rectangle of night sky to break the symmetry of the beveled glass wall.

Escape route, he thought. And precious minutes had already been devoured by chitchat. He had to get out of here.

He clutched his brow dramatically.

"Damn! The quotes are coming in from Tokyo." He turned to the group. "Auntie, I've got to run upstairs for a while and check the ticker. Would you see to the guests and close down the party?"

"Of course, Bruce. But what about the robbery?"

Wayne shrugged.

"That's Commissioner Gordon's department. I'm sure he'll handle it well."

He hurried up the stairs, ignoring the shocked looks on their faces.

Hurry, damn it. Through the door by the guest rooms, down the staircase to the back door, and out into wintry November darkness.

A car motor rumbled to life. Wayne recognized the sound and scowled. It was his car. Where was the alarm? That damned "Batman" was not only good at robbery, he was skilled at hot wiring as well. And the front gate was open. Even if Wayne reached the remote controls, he'd never close it in time.

Karen Haber and Robert Silverberg

The cave, he thought. Get the new motorcycle. Change into costume. No. No time. Go as I am.

He took the stairs in twos, grabbed the keys to the cycle, and leaped onto the powerful Harley.

The cycle roared to life, its headlight a white beacon spilling light on the path to the front drive. Wayne switched on the tracer. A small red light pulsed on the schematic map set next to the odometer. His quarry was heading out of Wayne's imposing suburb through the newer, cheaper neighborhoods toward the freeway.

Wayne frowned. If he'd had more time he could have radioed the police and told Gordon to put some cars in pursuit. Now he'd have to go it alone, chasing his own car into nighttime Gotham.

The wind cut through his red silk suit like sharpened icicles. The chill glow of streetlights flickered through the bare branches of the oak trees that lined the boulevard. Wayne reached behind, pulled goggles out of the cycle's side box, and strapped them on.

He began to feel more confident.

Cutting across Elm Street, he detoured through the parking lot of the First Episcopal Church and jumped its hedge, shearing seconds off his ride. The schematic showed his quarry entering the freeway. Wayne pressed harder on the accelerator.

Dark streets whizzed past, punctuated by patches of frozen water reflecting light onto the slick pavement. Houses went by in a blur—large, dark shapes looming behind carefully manicured hedges.

Motor screaming, the Harley hit a wet patch of leaves and fishtailed. Desperately, Wayne fought for control as the cycle skidded around and began to go off the road.

"Brake. No, don't brake, stupid. Steer into it," he muttered.

The cycle kept sliding. A massive oak, its limbs knotted with age, loomed on the right. Wayne braced for bone-crunching impact. Break collarbone at least, he thought. Hospital casts. Eight weeks to heal...

A patch of dry pavement caught the front wheel. With a whine, the bike pulled out of the skid at the last moment and righted itself.

Wayne sighed with relief. He glanced down, checked the map. His car was still on the freeway. In a moment, so was he, the wind screaming past his ears, trying to rip the back off his red tuxedo.

Exits flashed by: Hawken Street, Euclid, Morton. Ahead, the lights of downtown twinkled in their concrete and steel firmament.

The tracer showed his quarry at the Main Street ramp.

More lights, red and blue, caught his attention—a police car behind him. The mournful howl of the siren chased its way up his vertebrae. Belatedly, Wayne remembered that motorcycles were illegal on the freeway.

"Damn!"

No time now for playing tag with a squad car. And no utility belt, no bag of tricks to aid him. Have to tell Alfred to pack a spare in the cave.

He checked the gas tank. Three-quarters full. Good. The Harley could easily outpace any V-6 engine on open road. Once they were in the city, well, Wayne would worry about that later. They had to catch him first.

At the exit, he downshifted nimbly and squeaked through a yellow light turning red. The squad car was right behind him, tires squealing. He cut around a stalled car, sped between a double-parked delivery truck and a sedan, and made a hard right down an alley.

The police siren faded into a faint whine. Wayne glanced over his shoulder. The alley was empty, save for shadows. His pursuers must have gotten stuck behind the truck, trapped by the slow reactions of the driver. Good. Better speak to Gordon about upgrading driver training for his rookies, Wayne thought, grinning.

The red dot on his map turned onto Market. Came to a halt.

Wayne dialed up the address.

225 Market, just past the corner of Hayes.

Odd neighborhood. Just a few bars, grocery stores, and car-parts places. Wayne pulled the Harley out onto Market, searching his memory. No record of any fences in this neighborhood, as far as he knew. They were all in the East End.

He parked the cycle at the corner of Hayes and walked the two blocks, past locked, barred storefronts and shuttered windows.

There was his car: a low, dark shadow by the curb. Silent—the motor had been cut off. No sign of movement within, although the smoked-glass windows were difficult to see through. Wayne yanked the driver's door open. The gray Spencer was empty.

A trickle of music, bluesy and lonesome, pulled his attention from the car. Where was it coming from? He turned toward the dilapidated brownstone behind him.

Up two stone steps and he was in the hallway of an old flophouse. A row of tin mailboxes set into the wall bore tattered nameplates, all of them sad. faded ribbons save for the third box from the end. A new label had been glued to box 405 with red tape.

Club Astarte, it said.

In this dump? Must be an after-hours bar, Wayne thought. Moves its location regularly to avoid the cops. Probably operates without a liquor license and cleans up, charging five bucks a drink. Wouldn't Gordon enjoy being along for this one?

I'm beginning to miss him, he thought.

He climbed the stairs, each step squeaking, four flights up toward the growing sound of a bass guitar pulsing rhythm, women laughing a bit too shrilly, a horn player worrying a note.

Fourth floor. Dark as hell, he thought. Where's that music coming from?

He rounded a corner and saw light spilling through the cracked transom above the door to room 405. Club Astarte. Wayne pulled his devil mask down over his face and leaned against the door. It gave.

The room was filled with smoke and the cloying aroma of stale beer. Pink spotlights cut weakly through the murk. There was no band. No live music of any kind. Men and women sat slumped at tables, or moved slowly to taped music or their own internal drumbeat, leaning against each other on the tiny dance floor. They ignored him.

Maybe a man in red silk and a devil's mask comes in at this time every night, Wayne thought.

He shouldered through the crowd, searching for a sign of his quarry.

A long hallway, garishly painted green and orange, led back toward the bathrooms. One of them was in use. He leaned against the wall, waiting.

A woman in a short blue dress ran by, giggling tipsily. She disappeared into the empty bathroom.

The other bathroom door flew open. Wayne tensed.

A second woman, short, with a cloud of red hair, strode out of the john. She was wearing a tight, black, low-cut dress that showed a little too much. She stopped in her tracks when she saw him.

Karen Haber and Robert Silverberg

"Hey, devil," she said. Her smile was an unambiguous invitation. She lit a cigarette and inhaled, green eyes taking shrewd measure of him. When he failed to respond to the invitation, her eyes narrowed. She gestured, indicating his costume.

"What is this," she asked. "Mardi Gras?"

"I thought it was a bar," he said.

The redhead leaned back against the wall and crossed her arms. Smoke tendrils snaked around her head like a halo.

"First the guy in the cape," she said. "Now you with the red tux." She gave him a look of blunt approval. "Not bad. How about a peek behind the mask?"

"I'm shy."

"Want a drink?"

"Maybe later."

He started to move past her.

Mockingly, she rubbed her shoulders, shivering.

"Brrr. I thought you devils were supposed to be hot stuff. Guess you're just interested in buying souls. And Ricky is probably selling."

Her words stopped Wayne in mid-step. He turned to face her. "Ricky?" he asked.

She laughed, a high jagged sound. Her pupils were huge.

"Suddenly you're interested," she said. "Yeah, Beelzebub. It's Ricky you want, is it? Then keep going down that hall until you can't go any farther. That's my personal philosophy, too. See ya later, Satan."

She winked at him broadly and headed back to the other room.

Wayne followed the hallway. It came to an end in a flat, purple wall.

No exit? What did she mean, then?

He frowned and pushed against the wall. It swung back smoothly, spinning on recessed hinges.

Hidden doors were always useful for quick exits during police raids, he thought. I should have known.

He walked through into a dim corridor. The wall closed behind him.

Halfway down the hall, light glimmered under the crack of a door. He pressed his palm against the door and felt it move. Pushed harder. Hinges grating, the door opened.

Inside, a man with three days' growth of beard and a sour expression looked up from a desk littered with small plastic bags and a pile of ledgers. So there *was* a fence on Market Street. Wayne bit back a smile.

The fence sighed. "Not another one."

"Are you Ricky?" Wayne pitched his voice low.

"Who's asking?"

"The redhead sent me."

"Donna?"

"Who else?"

The fence's face relaxed into something midway between a scowl and a grin.

"Okay then," he said. "That last comedian made me jumpy. Comes in here with that goofy cape and wants to sell big jewels. Jerk. I only work in computer parts."

Wayne nodded. "So he left?"

"A minute ago. Weird son of a bitch. Wouldn't take off that bat mask."

"Which way?"

"Huh?"

Wayne grabbed a handful of the fence's shirt and pulled him halfway over the desk toward him. Between tightly clenched teeth, he asked again.

"I said, which way did he go?"

Karen Haber and Robert Silverberg

"T-that way." The fence pointed to a dark staircase across the hall. Shoving hard, Wayne released the man and dashed out the door. The stairs led down into blackness.

Grappling in his pocket, Wayne pulled out the infrared goggles from the cycle and slapped them on. Gray shadows were transmuted into hellish red and black geometry. He bolted down the stairs. One flight. Two flights.

Below him, he could hear the sound of footsteps running. He quickened his pace, using the handrail for balance. He missed a stair, started to fall, recovered, and kept going.

Three flights.

But he was still too far behind. Wayne bent one knee, grabbed the banister with both hands, vaulted up, over, and down to the final row of stairs, landing on the balls of his feet.

Thank God for that acrobatic training in France, he thought.

Wayne could see the front door swinging wildly. In three strides he was through it and on the street.

The Spencer had come to life again, motor rumbling. Wayne reached for his belt. A shame to have to slash my own tires, he thought. His hands closed on his red silk cummerbund.

He looked down.

And remembered that the only person wearing a utility belt was the man he'd been chasing.

Before he had time to curse, the Spencer moved. Tires squealed as the sleek, dark sedan pulled away from the curb, accelerating from zero to ninety in thirty seconds.

Wayne pounded down the sidewalk to the alley, kicked the cycle into overdrive. He was beginning to get annoyed.

It took fifteen minutes to trail his car back onto the highway, heading out of town.

Giddy with fatigue, Wayne watched the red blip move across the screen of the schematic monitor. He's going back to my house, he thought. Probably wants to drop off the car and have a drink. When I get there and ring the front doorbell, "Batman" will invite me in for a nightcap. Offer me a bed. Show me the gun collection.

The map shifted to a new quadrant as the Spencer took the exit back to Oakhurst. Wayne pressed the accelerator harder, and roared down the exit ramp and onto Oakdale Avenue. Trees flew by, street lamps, empty intersections. He was five minutes from Wayne Manor. Then the blip turned east on Vanderheel and continued on toward Huntington.

Where in hell was this clown going?

The red blip turned down Radison Drive. Pulled into number 211. Stopped.

Alice Chilton's house.

Was she in on this? Sweet, gray-haired Mrs. Chilton setting him up in his own home? Wayne was ready to believe anything.

He gunned the motor and made it to his aunt's driveway in two minutes.

The Spencer sat abandoned in the cul-de-sac near the front door. It was empty and the driver's door hung open. Out of habit, Wayne paused to shut and lock the door. Not that it would do him any good.

His aunt's taste in architecture ran to mock-Tudor. Wayne had always thought her house was attractive and inviting. But not tonight. Now each window was shuttered against him. The front door was dark. Odd. Alice usually left her light on all night.

Karen Haber and Robert Silverberg

He tried the front entrance. Locked. Well, no surprise there. But precious minutes would be wasted if he jimmied it open. Besides, what if it was armed? He imagined the look on his aunt's face as she came down the stairs to discover the host of the costume ball breaking into her house at a quarter to two in the morning?

Maybe he should ring the doorbell.

Surely she was home, in bed, the party an hour or so behind her. And if she wasn't in bed, if she was in league with this fraudulent Batman, it might shake her up to receive a visitor while she was busy counting the loot.

But the doorbell could also act as a warning.

Wayne sighed. Better try the windows.

He worked his way two-thirds around the house before a pantry window creaked open. He struggled through it, landing lightly, with practiced grace.

Tight fit, he thought. Better spend a few more minutes in the weight room.

The kitchen was dark. Wayne held his breath, listening. Footsteps, along the squeaking floorboards of the second story. Was it his aunt? The intruder menacing her? No time to guess. Move.

Lunging out of his hiding space, he made for the front stairs. Even in gloom, the house was familiar. The smell of freshly cleaned carpet and cedarwood summoned memories.

Christmas. New Years. Laughter.

Grimly, Wayne shoved the thoughts away.

On the second floor, he paused by an open doorway. This had to be his aunt's bedroom. Pink curtains and bedcovers. How she loved that color. The scent of her cologne hung in the air. The Indonesian dance costume was neatly folded over a chair. The room was empty.

A prickle of suspicion halted him in his tracks. Where was she, so late at night?

Moving past the open door, he walked down the hall. The first door he came to was a utility closet. The second, a study, empty save for a walnut antique desk and red easy chair. The third was a pastel-hued guest bedroom. Apparently, a guest had been using it for some time.

The pink chaise lounge was covered with scattered newspapers. Dirty clothing lay in wadded heaps on the yellow rug. The bed was unmade. Empty beer bottles huddled on the nightstand. The room smelled like an old ashtray that someone had forgotten to clean.

A pile of photo albums lay on a yellow bed pillow. Wayne flipped through them. Instead of photographs, each page held a newspaper or magazine clipping. The subject of each clip was the same. Batman. At the back of the last album were several sketches of a Batman costume.

Who would be living with Alice and keeping a record like this? Someone who also came to masquerades, uninvited, impersonating a masked vigilante?

Frustrated, Wayne threw the books down on the bed. The house was empty. His quarry had gotten away, possibly stopping to pick up his accomplice, the gracious Mrs. Chilton.

He was at the landing between floors when a harsh beam of light snapped on. He froze.

"Isn't it a bit late for trick or treat?" said a rusty tenor voice.

The light pinning Wayne down came from a flashlight. Behind its glare, he could just make out the pointed ears of a Batman mask.

"Who are you?" he demanded. "If you've hurt Alice in any way..."

Karen Haber and Robert Silverberg

"Hurt Alice?" The impostor sounded astonished. Then he laughed. The sound had a high, thin tone that climbed swiftly toward hysteria. "Are you nuts? Why would I hurt Alice? You're the one who's breaking and entering."

"I'm not the only one. You have no right to be here."

Again, the laugh.

"I have every right to be here," "Batman" said. "But that doesn't matter. You've made it so easy for me, Wayne. Very thoughtful. I should thank you."

"What do you mean?"

The flashlight beam was pulled back. Now Wayne could see a snub-nosed pistol pointing directly at him.

"Eccentric millionaire robs his own guests at fancy masked ball. Breaks into home of noted philanthropist to rob her as well. Discovered and shot in the act. It's perfect."

The madman's tone was gloating, triumphant.

Wayne played for time.

"Who are you?"

"Just call me Batman. Soon, everybody will."

"How did you get in here?"

"What difference does that make? I remind you, I'm holding a gun on you."

"But you really don't want to use it."

"Oh, but I do."

"Batman" tensed, took aim.

"No! Don't!" cried a woman's voice.

As he fired, a blurred figure cut in front of Wayne and fell back against him, propelled by the force of the bullet, knocking him to the ground. Aunt Alice.

"Damn you!" the false Batman cried. "See what you made me do!" He fired again, wildly, and bullets tore through the silk wallpaper above Wayne's head. Then he turned and fled upstairs. The light retreated with him.

For a moment, Wayne lay there, stunned, with Alice slumped against him. She'd taken the bullet meant for him.

Come on, man, move.

He set her gently against the wall, groped his way to the hall light switch, and flicked it on. She half lay, half sat, eyes closed. A dark red stain was widening across the front of her rose-colored nightgown.

Tenderly, Wayne knelt and touched her face. She stirred, opened her eyes.

"Bruce? Dear boy, is it you?"

"Yes. Don't try to talk."

There was a trickle of blood at the corner of her mouth. Wayne's insides turned to ice.

"Let me call an ambulance..."

"No time. Did you catch that phony Batman?"

"Dammit, Alice..."

He tried to set her down, but she clung to his lapels with surprising determination.

"Hush. I'm done for. That's all right. As long as you catch him. He came rampaging in here..."

She paused, coughed raggedly, bringing up blood.

Wayne cleaned her lips with the edge of his sleeve.

"Alice, let me get a doctor."

"Hush, dearie. Almost through. Catch him, Bruce. I know you can do it."

Wayne stared at her, astonished.

"What do you mean?"

Alice gave a feeble chuckle. "Don't play innocent with me, boy. You never could. It takes the real thing to catch an impostor." She leaned back and closed her eyes. Her voice was barely a whisper. "This crime fighting—good job. Parents would be proud."

She opened one eye, feebly touched his face.

"But what about love, Bruce? Don't forget love."

With a sigh, she was gone.

Wayne put his head against her shoulder, tears slipping from beneath clenched lids.

What about love? The little he had known of it lay lifeless in his arms, gone forever.

He pressed his lips to his aunt's forehead and set her down gently, taking care not to touch the seeping wound in her chest.

Tears turned to rage.

The Batman impostor would regret this evening in spades before Wayne was through with him.

He raced up the stairs.

"Batman" was in Alice's bedroom, opening the French windows that led out to the deck. Night wind caught the sheer curtains, swirling them about the gunman, ensnaring him long enough for Wayne to cross the room.

His first blow knocked the impostor against the doorframe. His next doubled him over. "Batman" wobbled, taken by surprise. Then he straightened up.

"You can't hurt Batman," he cried, and smashed his fist into Wayne's collarbone.

Wayne staggered backward, the wind knocked out of him. The impostor tore loose from the curtains and dashed past, through the bedroom door and out into the hall.

Come on. Get up. You're not going to let a phony Batman get the best of you, are you?

Gasping, Wayne half ran toward the stairs.

"Batman" was on the landing. In a moment, he'd be out of the house. Free.

Wayne bent at the knees, jumped, and catapulted himself over the railing. He came down two steps in front of the masquerader, cutting him off.

Savagely, Wayne launched a flying kick and caught the gunman in the shoulder, knocking him into the wall.

"Who are you?" he demanded.

"I told you," the impostor said, gasping for breath. "Batman."

The words were maddening. How could he be so crazy? With renewed fury, Wayne pulled him to his feet and flung him against the banister.

"There is only one Batman," he said coldly. "You're either a lunatic or an impostor. And a murderer!"

"Liar!"

For a moment, the gunman struggled in Wayne's grip. Then, seemingly exhausted, he relaxed, hanging his head.

That's better, Wayne thought. He pulled one hand back to wipe sweat from his chin.

With a violent heave, the impostor butted Wayne under the chin, shoved him aside, and ran down the stairs.

Got to stop him before he gets to the car, Wayne thought. He took the stairs in threes, praying for balance. For time.

The impostor had pulled the front door open.

From five stairs up, Wayne leaped. He tackled "Batman" hard, knocking him to the floor. Desperately, they struggled. The impostor seemed to have endless reserves of mad energy.

He kicked Wayne in the knee. Then he punched him savagely, a sharp blow to his kidneys.

Gasping, almost paralyzed, Wayne fell back. He heard the sound of footsteps moving up the stairs. Now what?

"I'll prove to you I'm Batman," the impostor shouted. His voice was high, wild.

Still immobilized by pain, Wayne opened his eyes. "Batman" was pulling a cord out of his utility belt. It glittered oddly.

Karen Haber and Robert Silverberg

"Sure," he said. "You think I'm just Joey, Alice's son. But I'll prove it to you. I'll prove it to everybody. I'm really Batman."

Alice's son? Wayne winced. Now he remembered. Her eldest son. Suffered from delusional episodes. Institutionalized years ago. Wayne had forgotten all about him. The whole world had. But Alice must have brought him home.

"I'm going to escape by swinging out the door," Joe Chilton announced. "That should convince you. Only the real Batman could do that."

He prepared to lasso the crystal chandelier with his glittering rope.

"You fool," Wayne cried. "Don't! Wait!"

The cord hooked around the light fixture. Faceted crystal teardrops danced and tinkled crazily. There was a flash. A pop. Joe Chilton screamed and kicked convulsively, like a puppet being jerked upward by its strings. A plume of smoke rose from the chandelier, and then the light went out. "Batman" tumbled forward, over the banister, down to the first floor, landing with a thud. He didn't move.

Slowly, painfully, Wayne pulled himself to his feet. His kidneys throbbed. His knee felt like it was on fire. With one hand on his lower back, he limped over to where Chilton lay, taking care to avoid the dangling rope. He didn't have to touch Chilton to know the truth. He was dead. Electrocuted. That shiny rope was metal cord.

The impostor lay on his back, his blue silk cape rayed out under him. The missing jewels lay by his side, jarred out of his pocket in the fall.

Again, Wayne had the uncomfortable sensation of looking at himself, dead. His head swam strangely. He felt a chill.

Batman in Nighttown

I'm alive, he told himself fiercely. I'm Batman, and I'm alive.

Taking hold of the blue silk mask, Wayne yanked it upward. For one eerie moment, he almost expected to see his own face revealed. The face behind the mask was sharply featured, though, with high cheekbones and sandy hair. It didn't even remotely look like him.

But the suit was a good copy.

Straightening up, Wayne lifted his head toward the stairs where his aunt lay and blew her a kiss.

Then he picked up the phone and called the police.

Masks

GARFIELD REEVES-STEVENS

A s if in a dream only one man can know, he tastes the dirt of the alley he crawls through, the filth of it mixing with the hot taste of his own blood and the cold taste of his own defeat. Laughter, mad and maniacal, peals from the dark brick walls, diminishing even the heaven's thunder and the white-noise hiss of the night-storm's downpour. In this place, at this time, the Batman's reign is ending.

And the Joker laughs.

Like a dying animal, propelled by instinct unknowing of reality, Batman drags himself across the rain-slicked paving stones of the nameless Park Row alley. His trembling fingers search for gaps between the stones. His breath coalesces in small pale clouds, smeared by rain. His failing muscles contract, and he pulls himself forward another few inches. Another few useless inches. For in this place, at this time, he has nowhere left to hide.

The laughter is like bullets.

Batman hears footsteps behind him, splashing,

spritely, like a dancer in the rain. He recognizes their childlike rhythm.

The Joker skips toward their final confrontation.

Batman rolls against the soaking ground. There is a dull metallic clink as his bullet-pocked emblem slips from his chestplate to fall into a puddle of mud and garbage, lost forever, the bat eclipsed.

The Joker howls.

Batman heaves himself against a formless mass of rain-decayed debris. The Joker stands before him, long face curtained by the sheet of rain that falls from the wide brim of his hat. But clearly through that curtain, blood-red lips curl in glee and wild eyes glow with madness fueled by genius beyond measure.

"Caped Crusader," the Joker sings. His laughter is hysterical.

Batman wills his battered arm to obey him, sends it to the belt, fifth compartment, second layer, feels for a familiar shape. But the Batarangs are gone, expended uselessly an hour ago as the rain began to pour. His hand fumbles to the third compartment, first layer. But the ampules are exhausted. All the compartments, all the layers, all are empty. Everything used up except for the binary chemicals in his hollowed heels. But his broken legs lie unmoving, and his last remaining weapons are forever out of reach.

The Joker steps closer, kicking playfully at a puddle. "World's greatest detective," he sniggers as if it were the punchline to God's greatest joke. He raises his arm.

Batman narrows his eyes against the rain that streams across his cowl, forcing himself to focus on the Joker's hand. But he sees nothing with eyes still blurred by the beating he has endured.

"Dark Knight," the Joker screams as his hand lifts

higher, a maestro's command for the final crescendo. A volley of lightning streaks down in answer to the night's new ruler and the monstrous arcs strobe over the alley.

In the flashes Batman sees others standing where shadows had hidden them. But his technology is spent, his body has betrayed him, and he is helpless.

The Joker leans forward, chortling with delight. "Stupid little boy!" It is the final insult. The ultimate joke. The Batman revealed as he always feared he would be.

Batman's lips tremble with the cold, with shock, with loss beyond anything he has felt before. He cannot form the words he needs to say, the apology he must make for the failure his life has been.

The others in the shadows point at him and stare.

The Joker laughs again and brings his other hand up to clap against the raised one, purple gloves meeting with a thunder of their own. "Hit it, boys," he merrily commands and the lightning fades before the onslaught of the searchlights that burst into life atop the surrounding buildings. The tableau is fixed, the mask of night removed from the Batman's defeat.

The sudden brilliance brings physical pain. Batman hears the whirr of motor-driven cameras and sees the light-forged outlines of television camera crews moving forward in the rain.

"Ladies and gentlemen of the press," the Joker intones, then breaks into mindless giggles. "You may wonder why I've asked you here today."

Batman senses the madman moving to stand at his side but can do nothing. Then suddenly he knows what the Joker plans to do. Everything else was nothing compared to the final defeat that faces him.

"What the Joker promises . . ." the Joker announces. He bends down beside the fallen man in black.

Masks

Batman feels cold cloth-covered fingers on his face. At first they are gentle, almost a parting caress, and then they are an unrelenting pressure, pushing hard against his bloodied cheek and deep beneath his cowl.

". . . the Joker delivers!"

The cowl separates from the Batman's face, pulling, cutting, ripping skin, lifting away, crushed in a purple fist.

Batman's cry of rage, of pain, of loss, is incomprehensible.

The cameras whirr.

"Look on my works, ye mighty," the Joker shrieks as the dark cowl bursts asunder in the light, "and *despair!*" And the reporters gasp as they peer beneath the Batman's mask and at last see that Batman is revealed as . . .

Batman's waking scream of anguish echoes in the dark shadows of his lair. He is drenched in sweat. His body trembles. No sleep for ten days. Because of the nightmares.

Because of the Joker.

Further sleep is impossible this night and he knows he approaches the threshold where even his superbly trained body will exhibit sleep-deprivation deficiencies. He arises and cloaks himself in cowl and costume.

This time, the Joker's science is beyond him and he has only one chance to free himself from the effects of the Joker's latest weapon. He must return to where it began. He must return to where the answer may yet lie. He imagines the Joker's laughter in his lair, and it chills him.

The Batman must return to Arkham.

Sunlight filters in through the wind-tossed leaves of ivy crowded too closely around the leaded glass window of

Garfield Reeves-Stevens

the chief psychiatrist's office. Dr. Bartholomew seems not to notice. The grounds of Arkham Asylum are always rich and dense and overgrown, never in control. The grounds of Arkham Asylum are like its inmates.

The psychiatrist studies the charts spread over his desk. A man cloaked in black waits in the corner of the office, beyond the window's shaft of sunlight, wrapped in his webbed cape, protected by his mask. There is impatience in his stillness.

Bartholomew looks up, adjusting his glasses, twin round circles of glass turning white in the glare from the window. He is bald, pink, featureless, with pursed lips like a cupid's. His finger taps a gas chromatograph printout. "I've seen a compound something like this before."

The Batman steps into the sunlight. His costume stays as dark as always, swallowing the light. "The Joker's venom."

"Ah, yes," Bartholomew says. He smiles himself, nodding his head nervously. "I've conducted autopsies on victims of that. Extraordinary chemical. Brilliant man."

The Batman's silence encompasses the room.

"All things considered, of course," Bartholomew adds quickly. He looks back to his charts.

"You know how the Joker venom works?" Batman asks.

"The textbook explanation," Bartholomew says without looking up. "Absorbed through the lungs, carried by the bloodstream into the brain. Direct stimulation to the portions of the amygdala controlling emotional responses. In the case of Joker venom, the stimulation leads to an unrestrained feeling of . . . good spirits. Well-being. Uncontrolled laughter as a sequela. Incredible knowledge of neurochemistry. Quite impressive."

"Victims die of cardiac arrhythmia and suffocation."
The Batman's voice is as dark as his cape.

Bartholomew stares up at him for a long time. "We all
die, Mr. Batman. At least the Joker's victims die happy."

There is the sound of creaking leather as Batman closes
his fists, considering his reply. "How is this compound
similar to the Joker venom?" he asks at last, fists opening
back into hands for the moment.

"By 'this,' you mean the compound to which you were
exposed when you last fought the Joker?"

"Yes."

Bartholomew leans back in his red-leather-covered
chair. The old wood complains. He takes off his glasses
and rubs the bridge of his nose, gazing up at the age-
darkened patterned plaster of the ceiling. "According to
my analysis, this new compound has the same general
molecular structure as Joker venom so I would assume it,
too, would be absorbed into the bloodstream through the
lungs and then be able to cross the blood-brain barrier."

"To stimulate portions of the amygdala."

"Exactly." Bartholomew studies what little he can see
of Batman's expression beneath the mask. "Have you
had bouts of extreme and . . . inappropriate emotional
responses since your exposure to the compound?"

"Yes."

"Care to provide details?"

"No."

Bartholomew smiles, a nervous tic. "General parame-
ters, perhaps?"

"Disruptive dreams."

"Nightmares?"

"They could be called that."

Bartholomew leans forward, hunching over his desk,
hands clasped together. "That a mind like his should

be locked away here, and not turned loose at MIT or DARPA or . . ."

The Batman looms over the desk. The shadow of his cowl falls across the little man.

"The compound is stimulating other areas of the amygdala than those affected by Joker venom, Mr. Batman—the portions that control your reaction to senseless fear, to danger, to personal threat."

"The things I fear, Dr. Bartholomew, are not senseless. They are precise and specific. How could any compound trigger such exact stimuli?"

Bartholomew waves his hand, the fluttering of a frightened bird. "You don't understand, Mr. Batman. The Joker has gone far beyond our understanding of biochemistry and psychology. It is your brain that provides the details of your nightmares. What the Joker's compound does while you're asleep is trigger the release of enormous amounts of chemicals and hormones just as if you had been badly frightened. Your sleeping mind, having to deal with this terrible feeling unleashed as the fear chemicals spread through your system, creates an extremely detailed dream of the thing you fear most in order to 'explain,' if you will, the feeling and its intensity." Bartholomew smiles and holds it. His teeth are small, pearl-like, perfect. "You see, the genius of the Joker has made it possible for one compound to affect each person differently. Each individual exposed to it will experience his or her own worst nightmare." He claps his hands in delight. "Oh, I must ask him if we might write a paper on it together. Has he written other papers before, do you know?"

"Will it wear off?"

Bartholomew grudgingly looks back at his charts. After a moment, he sighs. "Technically, yes. But practically, no."

"Explain."

The nervous smile appears again. "The compound should take about six months to be fully metabolized by your body."

"So in six months the nightmares will stop?"

"Oh, dear me, they'll stop sooner than that, Mr. Batman." He holds his smile. "If you don't develop an antagonist for this compound within another two to three weeks, you'll die. Of exhaustion, insanity . . . whatever." Bartholomew shakes his head as he folds up his charts. "Bloody genius," he whispers to himself. "Incredible."

The Batman's outspread hand descends on the doctor's desk, covering over the papers there. "I want to see him."

Bartholomew at last looks shocked. He answers in outrage. "Mr. Batman! You of all people should know that's impossible. Here at Arkham our goal is to help our patients over their past troubles. To point them toward the future as fully functioning, well-adjusted citizens able to—"

The black glove becomes a fist. "Now."

Bartholomew stands, all five feet four of him. He glares back at the eyes burning within the black mask. "As his psychiatrist, I cannot permit it. A confrontation with you could destroy everything Arkham has achieved with him in his long years of therapy."

"Between his escapes. His crimes. His murders."

"One must have hope, Mr. Batman."

"I *will* see him."

"No, you will *not*. I forbid it. And I can have an injunction drawn up to keep you away from him. And away from Arkham." Bartholomew straightens the charts on his desk, tapping them into perfect order. "Besides, he specifically asked that you not be allowed to bother him."

"Because he knows," Batman says.

"Knows what?"

"That he's the only one who can help me."

Bartholomew takes a clipboard from the side of his desk. "Perhaps you should have thought of that last week before you beat the poor man senseless and dragged him in here again. No wonder he's afraid of you." The little man marches to an ornate wooden door. "Now, if you'll excuse me, Mr. Batman, I have my rounds."

Batman stands helplessly by the window, staring out at the setting sun, seeing darkness grow among the thick bushes and gardens and high stone walls. Arkham's darkness. Like its grounds, like its inmates, rich and dense and uncontrolled.

Night is falling. The time of dreams. He makes the only decision he can.

"You know, Harv," the Joker says, "you're not *half* the man you used to be." Deep in the ancient cellars of Arkham, the Joker's laughter echoes down the long, dark corridors. From one of the other high-security cells, something wails in answer.

The other patient in the recreation lounge turns slowly away from the ceiling-mounted television. The half of the patient's face not corroded by acid smiles calmly. The other half, what little remains within it that is recognizably human, drools. The two-faced man reaches down the side of his leg and pulls out the slim shining needle of a commissary spoon, filed to a deadly point.

In one hand, he holds the weapon ready to strike. With his other hand, he expertly flips a silver dollar into the air and snatches it in flight. Then he studies the coin in his open palm and the half smile goes away. The man with two faces slips the weapon back into his sock, gets up, and leaves the lounge.

The Joker cackles. "Hey, Harv!" he calls out to the departing patient. "I think you've *flipped!*" He chokes with laughter, pounding his hand against the side of his chair.

Then he realizes that he is alone.

And not alone.

"Who's there?" the Joker asks the shadows in the hall outside the lounge.

One shadow answers.

"You're not supposed to be here," the Joker says happily. "Yet."

Silently, the Batman closes the door to the corridor behind him.

"I need your help." Batman says the words as if he were spitting out poison. "I want the antidote."

The Joker slaps his hands to the balls of his cheeks. "What? No buttering me up? No asking me about the wife and kids? Just, 'Gimme the antidote,' as if . . . as if . . . I mean nothing to you?" He wipes a single heartfelt tear from his eye. "And here I thought we had something special between us, a certain *je ne sais quoi?* A, how you say, give-and-take relationship."

The Batman waits.

The Joker holds two fingers to his lips to cover a giggle. "You know. I give you the antidote. And you . . . *take* me away from all of this."

"There is no negotiation."

The Joker shrugs and sits back down to watch the television. "Then there is no anti—"

The Joker's feet dangle above the floor as Batman jerks him into the air by the collar of his Arkham-issued white shirt. But the white-faced man rolls his eyeballs back, sticks out his tongue, and hangs limply, offering no resistance. Batman heaves the man across the room.

The Joker stretches out on the floor where he has landed and rests his head on his hand. Then he thrusts out his bottom lip. "Whatsa matter, Batikins? In the old days you could have held me up like that a good three or four minutes without breaking into a sweat." He narrows his eyes in concern. "Say, are you getting enough sleep?"

"Get up," Batman says.

"You're not thinking too clearly, Batpal. If you beat me silly—well, sillier—what are you going to do with me then? Take me away to . . . Arkham? Naa, a tad redundant. You going to kill me? Naa, what would the ACLU say? You going to torture me to reveal the secret of the antidote? Maybe slip toothpicks under my nails until I—"

A black hypodermic needle glints as Batman fills it with a clear ampule from his belt.

The Joker stands, grinning. "Would it make a difference if I just said no?"

Batman snaps the hypo into the barrel of his gas pistol.

The Joker carefully undoes the buttons of his institutional shirt, offering his pale chest as an easy target. "If I have an antidote to the nightmare compound, don't you think I also have an antidote to your truth compound? And don't you think I loaded myself with it because I knew you might try something like this?"

Batman takes aim.

"Go ahead, Batchump. All it'll do is put me to sleep for a day or two. A day or two during which you *won't* sleep. And by the time I wake up, you can bet that pink toad, Bartholomew, will have an injunction against you *and* have transferred me someplace you'll never find me. Not in the time you'll have left."

Batman hesitates.

The Joker smiles. He lowers his voice, twitches his lips. "So what you got to ask yourself, punk, is, 'do I feel lucky?' "

Batman lowers his pistol.

"Oh, wipe that silly frown off your face," the Joker says as he slowly buttons his shirt again. "You get me out of here tonight and the antidote's all yours."

Batman holds his pistol uselessly at his side. He looks away, shakes his head to clear it. "I . . . I can't help you escape."

The Joker waves his hand. "Of course you can. It's easy. I do it all the time myself."

"No," Batman says.

The Joker checks his reflection in the television screen and rubs his hands through his hair until it all stands on end like a green cloud. He smiles at his perfection and turns away from the television. "Think of it this way: If you don't help me, inside two weeks you'll have your own cell here and inside a month you'll be dead. Then I'll escape anyway but there won't be anyone who'll be able to bring me back."

He holds up a finger. "But, if you get me out of here tonight, I'll give you the antidote, and things will be back to normal, or abnormal in your case. I'll be free, like I'm going to be anyway, but you'll still be around to hunt me down and give my poor life some meaning in these dark and dangerous days." He holds out his hand. "Whaddaya say, B.M.? Is that a deal or is that a deal?"

Batman stares at the Joker's mad eyes. He breaks down his pistol and replaces it in his belt.

The Joker waves his hand toward Batman. "C'mon, shake on it?"

Batman's hands stay at his side. The Joker reaches out to his own hand, rips it off from his wrist, and holds the stump up to Batman's face. "See? Nothing up my sleeve . . ." He cackles.

Batman snatches the fake hand from the Joker and hefts it in his own. "Gas or explosive?" he asks.

The Joker smiles as he stretches his arm and pushes his real hand through the cuff of his shirt. "Remember who you're dealing with here, B.M. Of course, it's explosive. It's a *hand* grenade." When his laughter subsides, he adds, "Pull out the thumb, count to five—or is it two?—then toss and run. That's the only way to smuggle things into Arkham, you know. By making them look like things that already belong here."

Batman disables the explosive hand, turns his back on the Joker, and goes to the door. He opens it silently and checks the hall beyond with a narrow sliver of mirror from his belt. "Come here," he says and the Joker goes to him. "We do it my way, understand? No one gets killed. No one gets hurt."

"Didn't anyone ever tell you that a thing worth doing is worth doing well?" the Joker protests. "I've got a reputation to maintain and an Arkham breakout without a few gratuitous deaths will never make the eleven o'clock—"

Batman's hand goes around and tightens on the Joker's throat. "Or we could both end it here and now. Together."

The Joker pats Batman's cheek and for once he doesn't laugh. "You forget, Batman. Nothing ends in Arkham. Nothing."

Batman's cape moves with the beat of an immense batwing as it flows through the air and envelopes the Joker in blackness.

"My way," Batman says again, and then the two of them, the Batman and the Joker, move out into the tunnels of Arkham, into the shadows where nothing ends.

Together.

The moonlight and sudden night air on his face remind
the Joker of birth. The swift flutter of Batman's cape as it
withdraws fades to nothing, and the Joker stretches out
his hands and arms to steady himself and finds he is on
Arkham's south wall, fifteen feet up, tottering on the
rough-edged stones.

"Jump," says Batman but the Joker cannot see him.

Behind the Joker, the dark mass of Arkham is silhouet-
ted against a night sky of low clouds faintly underlit by
the distant glow of Gotham City's lights.

"A perfect escape," the Joker says wistfully. "Without
a single death. How amazing. How disappointing."

"Now!"

With a snicker, the Joker throws himself from the wall
without knowing where or how he will land, or even if.
But Batman catches him, saves him, lowers him gently to
the ground.

"That's it," Batman says.

The Joker turns away and brushes his hand against the
ancient stones of Arkham's walls. He has never touched
them from the outside. "So quickly?" he asks.

"My way," Batman says.

"I wish you had let me see more of it." The power of
Arkham resonates beneath the Joker's fingertips, calling
him back.

"I wish you had seen less as it is."

The Joker nods and takes his hand away from the wall.
His smile widens. "Perhaps that's our secret," he says and
turns back to Batman, a living shadow against the dark
surrounding forest.

"Our secret?" Batman asks.

"If we saw less, if we knew less, then we would not
need to be what we are, don't you think?"

"If we saw less, if we knew less, then we would be less."

"Of course," the Joker says. "Of course, you're right." And he laughs and he screams and he swings his fist at Batman's face.

A fraction of a second too late, Batman blocks and the Joker's blow connects with the top of his cowl. He flips backward, landing in a crouch, balancing on both feet and one hand. The other hand holds a Batarang. Dried leaves crackle beneath him as he shifts his weight. Behind him, the forest is dark and silent.

"Have you guessed?" the Joker asks, turning his body to provide the smallest target. "Has it taken you this long?"

The subtle crunching of the leaves is silenced.

"You haven't?" The Joker's laughter stops in amazement.

"There is no antidote?" Batman asks.

"Right again, B.M." The Joker chuckles. "For getting me out of Arkham, your reward is a few more weeks of sleepless nights, and an end to dreaming. You know what happens when you're prevented from dreaming?"

The Batarang sings through the air. The Joker arches back and the weapon sparks against the stones of Arkham and buries itself in the ground.

"The dreams build up inside you—" the Joker laughs, "—until they burst out while you're awake." He dives and rolls away as a second Batarang slices the air above his head, dying against the stones.

"Only then," the Joker says as he comes back to his feet and clasps his hands together, "they're called hallucinations. And because of my nightmare compound, they'll be hallucinations of the things you fear most as well." He pulls his arms apart. Two hands move grotesquely with one wrist. "Just like your dreams." He pulls a thumb from his second false hand.

Batman's arm snaps down and a billow of smoke erupts at his feet just as the Joker's second hand-grenade flies at him. The Joker twists and dives away. The explosive hand detonates. The Joker hears the grunt of a man who has lost his breath.

"Just like your *dreams*," the Joker cries into the night. He pulls a button from his shirt, scrapes a nail across it, counts to three then tosses it into the air. The button flares with four seconds of magnesium light. Long enough to see the stark outline of a man crawling away on the ground, seeking shelter beneath the trees.

The Joker pounces. He feels the explosive huff of breath burst from Batman's lungs. Batman's arm comes back to drive an elbow into the Joker's side but the countermove is slow and the Joker is on his feet again without being touched. Slowly, the Batman rolls over.

"It's only been ten days without sleep, B.M., but already your reflexes are off. You let me jump on your back! You couldn't block my punch. You're decaying in front of me."

The Joker laughs.

Batman sits up, hands at his belt. The Joker flicks another flare button and the unstable chemical bursts into metal flame and adheres to Batman's emblem. Batman's hands leave his belt and swirl his cape around him as he rolls on the forest floor to extinguish the flame. But by the time the flare is spent, the Joker's foot has found the Batman's head, again and again.

A final kick goes into the side of Batman's chest, just beneath the lip of his body armor. The Joker falls back, laughing with the memory of the satisfying give he had felt as a rib collapsed.

Batman moans, face down in the dead leaves and dirt.

The Joker sniggers as he catches his breath. "Whaddaya say, B.M.? You want to spend the last days of your life fighting hallucinations till you drop and die? Or would you rather end it? Here and now?" The Joker pulls the rest of the buttons from his smuggled shirt. Ignited in the proper positions, in the mouth, on the eyes, there are enough buttons to kill.

Batman rolls over. Blood glistens at his mouth, bubbling at the corner of his lips as he wheezes with each breath. The Joker drops to his knees at the Batman's side. He holds the fistful of flare buttons in his hands. "Tell the truth. Haven't you always wanted to go out in a blaze of glory?"

"Here and now?" Batman asks. His voice is weak, confused.

"That's the idea," the Joker says. He holds the buttons in the open palm of his hand.

"No," Batman says.

The Joker picks out the first button. He shrugs. "All good things . . ."

"Not here," Batman coughs. He tries to get up, can't make it, falls on his side with a sigh, hand going to his side. "Not now."

The Joker scratches the surface of the button and begins his count. "Count of two," he says. "Or is that five?"

The Batman's arm snaps up toward the overhanging trees. The Joker hears the hiss of a Batarang, the twang of a silken rope, the creak of a tree branch.

The button flares. The rope tightens on the suddenly stretched branch and the stretched branch straightens. Batman lifts up into the air, roaring in pain and defiance, until he is upright, holding himself on his rope above the ground.

His feet snap closed on the Joker's hands. The Joker's real hands.

Wrapped by white skin, pressed in against the others resting there, the button flares.

The Joker howls.

Batman shouts in triumph as his protective boots push in on the Joker's flaming hands. The blinding white glow of the raging magnesium shoots out from between charred fingers like a captured sun. Thin strands of glowing white smoke stream into the Joker's red-rimmed mouth as he takes in another desperate gasp of air to scream and scream and . . .

. . . there is nothing to wake to.

The chemical ignition is spent. The Joker twitches spasmodically. Batman releases his feet and drops to the ground, stumbling as the pain of his shattered rib burns through him.

The Joker babbles deliriously on the floor of the forest. The ruined flesh and bones of his hands are fused together. The skin of his hands is no longer white.

Batman limps over to stand above the Joker. He coughs out blood but the injury is still not enough to stop him. Never.

"You're wrong," Batman says hoarsely. "It does end in Arkham. For you."

With one arm clenched against his side, Batman snaps his rope from the tree branch and ties the Joker's legs together. Then he drags the writhing man around the great stone walls of Arkham to the thick twisted iron bars of the main gate. The Joker screams as he is pulled across the hard ground, but not in pain.

The gates swing open before the man from the shadows

and the gibbering burden he pulls. All the lights of Arkham blaze through its windows like eyes searching for something that has been missed.

The Joker lies on the cold stones of Arkham's front plaza. Batman leans beside him. A black blade slices through the rope that binds the Joker's legs, but he cannot move. His hands are locked before him, beyond any sensation.

"*Nothing* ends in Arkham," the Joker gasps. His throat burns with the aftertaste of the smoke from his own charred flesh. "*Nothing!*"

Batman's cowl becomes a sudden black shadow over the Joker as a searchlight hums into life on Arkham's roof. Then another, and another, until the mask of night is removed from the Joker's defeat.

Batman steps back and lifts his head. The Joker squints through the blinding light and sees the outlines of others who have been waiting. One of them is the man with two faces. But they wait no longer.

"It's time it ended," Batman calls out to the watchers of Arkham. He looks down at the Joker and suddenly the Joker knows what Batman plans to do. Everything else was nothing compared to the final defeat that faces him.

"Time to see you as you really are," Batman says. He bends down and his black gloves are like claws as he digs into the soft white folds of the Joker's flesh. He grabs at the outthrust cheeks, slips long fingers into the grimacing mouth, squeezes them like talons to get a good grip, a sure grip.

The Joker isn't laughing.

And the Batman pulls against the flesh. And pulls against the blood. Until the watchers of Arkham gasp as they peer beneath the Joker's mask and at last see that the Joker is revealed as . . .

The Joker's waking scream of anguish echoed down the dark corridors of Arkham. The viewing panel on the door to his cell slipped open.

"Ten days," Bartholomew said. "Been like this for ten days." The chief psychiatrist slipped off his black-framed glasses and pushed his hand through his graying hair. "Ever since you brought him in."

Beside the doctor, Batman stepped up to the viewing panel. In the cell, the Joker flopped on the padded floor, arms firmly held against him by the straitjacket he wore. He cackled softly to himself. The words he said were unintelligible. A thin trickle of drool at the side of his grinning mouth fed a growing dark stain beneath him.

"I finished my analysis of the chemical compound he had packaged in that shipment of sandbox sand," Batman said.

Bartholomew whistled softly and turned to look at the costumed man beside him. They were almost the same height. "Johns Hopkins told us they'd need two more weeks to even finish the preliminary spectroscopy on it."

Batman didn't acknowledge the awe in the psychiatrist's voice. "It's molecularly similar to his Joker venom."

Bartholomew shuddered. "Hideous stuff."

"Absorbed by the lungs," Batman continued. "Crosses the blood-brain barrier. Direct stimulation to the amygdala."

Bartholomew nodded. "Causing the victim's sleeping mind to create its worst nightmare."

The Joker sat up slowly in his cell, becoming aware of his audience at last.

"Exactly," Batman said. "The children of Gotham wouldn't have had a chance if that sand had made it into the toy-store distribution network."

"Neither would you," Bartholomew said, "if the Joker hadn't inhaled the dose he tried to use on you."

The Joker pulled himself up on his cot, then stood. He seemed to make an effort to adjust his straitjacket. He wiped his spittle-covered chin on his shoulder. He was making himself look presentable.

"Do you know what the prognosis is?" Bartholomew asked Batman. He held his pen ready to make a note on the Joker's chart.

"His system should metabolize the compound within six months," Batman said.

Bartholomew snorted with surprise and slipped his glasses back on. "How unfortunate," he said. "Because if the effects of that compound prevent him from dreaming much longer, I'm afraid he's going to be driven quite mad."

In his cell, the Joker began to laugh. Batman said nothing.

Then the Joker shivered once, and turned to stare at those who stared at him.

"I wonder what it is?" Bartholomew asked Batman. "I wonder what a man like the Joker would fear most?" He shook his head. "I wonder what he dreams?"

The Joker lurched toward the door of his cell and Bartholomew stepped back. "Don't ask me you baby-faced moron!" the Joker cried. He bashed his head against the padded door. "Ask him! The lunatic in the cape!" He clenched his eyes shut. "C'mon, Bats! You know, don't you? You know what I dream!!" He howled in a staccato burst of laughter. It wasn't funny.

Bartholomew blinked at the Joker's outburst, then scribbled on the chart he held. Beside him, Batman's gloved hand reached up to the side of his cowl and pulled it down imperceptibly. It was an almost unconscious habit he had developed over the years. Something he did just before he was to go into action, making sure his mask was firmly in place. Protective. Concealing.

Bartholomew stared into the Joker's blazing eyes. "Is that true, Batman? Do you know what the Joker's nightmare is?"

Batman didn't answer so the psychiatrist turned to him. "Do you?"

But Batman was gone. Swallowed by the shadows. Cloaked by the darkness. Protected by the concealing mask of night.

Bartholomew shook his head again as he peered down the dimly lit basement corridor. He turned back to the man in the cell.

"How can he know what you dream?" the psychiatrist asked.

The Joker leaned up against the viewing window and dropped his voice to a whisper.

"Because, he dreams it, too," the Joker hissed. "He dreams it, too."

The laughter that followed almost burst Bartholomew's eardrum.

Outside, within the beckoning shadows of Arkham's stone walls, Batman returned to the night, haunted by the sound of that mad laughter, driven by a dream only two men know.

Bats

HENRY SLESAR

I have always resisted the temptation to keep a diary. In my privileged position, a journal of my experiences would undoubtedly be of incalculable value, both commercial and historic, but it would also reveal secrets entrusted to me by the person to whom I owe my loyalty and my devoted service, to say nothing of my weekly salary. My name is Alfred Pennyworth, and I am Batman's butler.

It was only when that estimable person seemed lost to me (indeed, to the whole world) that I found myself in need of the cathartic that a diary often provides. I had a desperate yearning to share my pain and grief with someone, but my sacred vow of silence regarding Batman's secret identity left me with only one confidante: myself. And on that unhappy evening when I returned from the Pine-Whatney Clinic where Batman was languishing, I inserted a sheet of paper into a rather cranky portable typewriter (a sad reminder of Master Robin's school days) and made the first entry, beginning with an account of my visit to the hospital, an experience still vivid in my mind.

Bats

I have just returned from the Clinic, and Commissioner Gordon was kind enough to permit me a glimpse of Batman in his private room, in what he later described to me as his "antiseptic prison." I was impressed with the security arrangements the Commissioner had made to avoid any public disclosure of the fact that the legendary figure was a patient at the institution located in a secluded suburb of Gotham City. I was even more impressed by how zealously he had guarded Batman's concealed identity. Under the circumstances, he could easily have satisfied a long-standing curiosity concerning the face behind the Batmask, but the Commissioner did the honorable thing. The sedated man I saw in that hospital bed with those pitiful guard rails not only wore a hospital gown, he also wore his mask.

I had arrived in a disguise of my own. I came as an emissary of good will, from my employer, the wealthy Bruce Wayne, to offer whatever financial assistance necessary to provide Batman with the best of medical care. The ruse was of my own devising, but I soon learned from the Commissioner that I wasn't the first to extend a helping hand. Hundreds, even thousands of people, stricken by the news of Batman's breakdown, had volunteered their aid. It was a touching tribute from a grateful citizenry, and I felt a bit ashamed that my own offer was merely a subterfuge. Even though Batman's medical expenses were eventually paid by "The Wayne Foundation," Bruce Wayne was actually paying for his own care. Mr. Wayne, you see, is not only my employer and Commissioner Gordon's friend; he is also Batman's everyday identity.

It was during my visit to the Pine-Whatney that I learned the true details of the event that led to Batman's hospitalization. To this point, all my information had come from the lurid accounts in the press, including that ignominious headline that defaced the front page of the Gotham City Post:

BATMAN GOES BATS!

There have been many lies blazoned about Batman. But the shock of those words was heightened by my realization that the announcement may well have been valid. I was only too painfully aware of the troubled condition of Batman's mind ever since the death of Robin. His grief was understandable, of course, and while I am not a qualified psychiatrist, I have read enough in the field to know that his reaction may have been magnified by feelings of guilt. Robin's safety had always been Batman's first priority in all of their adventures, and Robin himself always recognized the perils he faced as Batman's partner in crime-fighting. Nevertheless, Batman may well have blamed himself for the loss of that brave young man.

There could not have been a worse time for Batman to fall into this "slough of despond," to quote Reverend Bunyan. Whether it was an evil conjunction of stars, or because the underworld had been emboldened by Robin's death, Gotham City was undergoing its worst crime wave in decades. The number of profit-motivated felonies, with all of their attendant violence, had risen sharply. A dozen banks had been robbed in a three-week period, two of them on the same day. The city's best and best-guarded jeweler had been plundered of almost ten million dollars worth of gems. Five payroll robberies had succeeded, in plants where the security systems had been vaunted as unassailable. Worst of all, a dozen innocent people had been slain or injured during the commission of these

offenses. Despite their audacity, the police seemed helpless to prevent them or to apprehend their perpetrators.

I was privy to the abysmal depth of the law's frustration when Commissioner Gordon came to dine with Mr.
Wayne only a few days before his breakdown. As I served
their meal, I overheard him express his anxiety in no
uncertain terms.

"I've never seen anything like it." he said, savagely
attacking his *ris de veau*. "These hoodlums are acting as
if there simply isn't any police deterrent in this city.
Sometimes," he added gloomily, "I think it may be my
fault, that perhaps I should offer the Mayor my
resignation."

Mr. Wayne murmured some placating response, but I
could see that his mind wasn't really on the conversation.

"There's organization behind it all," Commissioner
Gordon said. "But we just can't determine where the lead-
ership is, even though we've rounded up all the usual
suspects."

Mr. Wayne smiled thinly at this echo of Captain
Renault's line from *Casablanca*. It was the last smile I saw
on his face for a very long time.

"What about Federal assistance?" he asked. "Two of
the banks that were robbed were Federal institutions."

"I spoke to my friend from the FBI, Randolph Spicer.
He offered his aid but he seems as baffled and helpless as
I am."

"You've been under a lot of pressure, Commissioner,"
Mr. Wayne said. "Your wife's long illness, and the problems you've had with your daughter..." (Barbara Gordon
was a handful, and Commissioner Gordon would have
been even more upset if he knew of her secret life as
Batgirl.)

"Yes," the Commissioner sighed, "I haven't been myself lately. And, for that matter, neither has..." He stopped, as if reluctant to complete his thought. Both Mr. Wayne and I reached the same conclusion, but since I was only the butler, I allowed Mr. Wayne to express it.

"Neither has Batman?" he asked lightly.

"Not that I blame the man," Gordon said. "He's obviously still in mourning for poor Robin. And I haven't been upholding my part of our bargain lately. He always relied on me for briefings, and I haven't been in touch with him for weeks...."

Of course, the Commissioner, unaware of Mr. Wayne's other identity, didn't know he was "in touch" with Batman at that very moment. If there was an anticipatory gleam in Mr. Wayne's eyes, I failed to detect it in the candlelight; he merely regarded Commissioner Gordon in solemn contemplation and said nothing.

I recalled that last encounter when I faced the despondent Commissioner again, this time in the cold white confines of the Pine-Whatney Clinic, and heard his pathetic description of Batman as he had been discovered just twenty-four hours before.

"It was in Wellman's department store," he said. "An alarm had sounded, signaling that a robbery was in progress. I personally dispatched a dozen officers to the scene. Somehow, they got to the wrong floor, and the criminals who were ransacking the company safe escaped with half a million dollars in cash receipts.... But this time, despite my respect for this mourning period, I decided to use my hot line to reach Batman. I told him what was happening, and he responded."

"But wasn't it too late?" I ventured. "Since the criminals had already escaped?"

"Batman isn't all brawn and acrobatics, you know. He has a keen intelligence, especially when it comes to crime detection. I hoped he might have some idea about tracking the culprits to their hideout. But—well, you heard what happened."

I confessed to a mistrust of the newspaper count.

"It was accurate enough," Commissioner Gordon said ruefully. "A woman on the Lingerie floor of Wellman's screamed at the sight of the costumed man who was wandering aimlessly down the center aisle. A saleslady approached him, recognizing him as Batman, and asked if he needed help. He looked at her blankly and muttered something incoherent. Then he sat down on the carpet and put his head in his hands and...wept."

I couldn't exhibit my heartbroken reaction without revealing my close connection to the Caped Crusader. Instead, I merely clucked in sympathy and, fighting tears of my own, asked the Commissioner about the current state of Batman's health.

"He's coherent again," Gordon told me. "But he has no recollection of the 'fugue' he suffered. He's refused to remain at the Clinic for treatment, but he *has* agreed to enter intensive therapy at once."

I expressed my gratification, and inquired about the sort of treatment indicated.

"I've asked my own therapist to take him on as a patient," Gordon said, "and she's agreed."

"She?" I said, with a raised eyebrow that didn't escape his notice.

"Yes," Gordon said. "*She* happens to be one of the most eminent psychiatrists in Gotham City. Her name is Dr. Letitia Lace, and she was recommended to me by Randolph Spicer of the FBI. She was enormously helpful to me during my wife's serious illness...."

Henry Slesar

"But what about...well, Batman's actual identity? Won't that be...compromised by psychiatric treatment?"

"Dr. Lace has agreed to respect his desire for anonymity. And even if his identity is...well, spontaneously revealed, you can be sure she'll protect his secret. Professional confidentiality and all that."

This time, I couldn't conceal my look of skepticism, but the Commissioner merely shrugged.

"Who knows, perhaps it would do Batman good to stop playing a dual role. Maybe he's suffering an identity crisis. Perhaps if he was one person, he could lead a more normal life, settle down, marry perhaps..."

"Oh, dear," I said, trying to envision a woman in the Batcave. Batman has always resisted commitment because of his dedication, and it has cost him the love of several remarkable females. But right now, I was worrying about the *new* woman who was about to enter Batman's life.

Of course, I wasn't present when Batman first stretched his magnificent costumed frame on Dr. Lace's leather couch, and began psychoanalysis. This account, however, may be considered quite veracious, since it came to me from Batman himself, whose memory is as formidable as his musculature.

The first thing that must be said about Dr. Letitia Lace was that she failed utterly to inspire confidence in her patients upon their first encounter.

The reason was simple enough. The doctor, in parlance, was a "dish." She made a serious effort to disguise her pulchritude by wearing almost shapeless lead-gray suits, but her curvacious figure insisted upon reshaping them into voluptuous lines. Her hair was as black as a raven's wing, and she wore it severely, but the style only emphasized the striking violet of her eyes and the perfection of her features. The eyes, by the way, were shielded by thick-rimmed spectacles, but Batman's own sharp vision detected the plate glass within the frames.

Batman, however, harbored no prejudices and was willing to give Dr. Lace the benefit of the doubt, even when she began their session with a shocking question.

"Can you tell me why you have no respect for the American legal system?"

"Now wait a minute—" Batman said.

"Taking the law into one's hands is opposed to everything our criminal code stands for. Who gave you the right to be judge and jury over your fellow men?"

"Listen, doctor, there are some things you must not understand—"

"I understand vigilante justice," Dr. Lace said cooly. "And can you deny that it *always* leads to a breakdown of constitutional guarantees? That it denies due process, harms the innocent more than it punishes the guilty, that it leads to anarchy and even fascism?"

Batman started to sit up, indignation stirring, but then he decided he was being deliberately baited and relaxed.

"I happen to agree with you," he said disarmingly. "I don't believe in vigilantism either, Doctor. That's why I was officially deputized by the Commissioner of Police many years ago. I don't judge criminals; I try to apprehend them, and then turn them over to the proper authorities. I'm simply another sort of police officer. Does that answer your question?"

"One doesn't see many police officers in cowls, skintight bodysuits, and capes shaped like batwings."

"I have a reason for this costume."

"Would you care to tell me what it is?"

Henry Slesar

Batman hesitated. It had been a long time since he had experienced the necessity of explaining himself.

"When I first decided to dedicate my life to fighting crime, something happened—something you might call ...symbolic." He smiled wryly. "You know all about symbols, don't you, Doctor?"

"Go on."

"A large black bat flew into the open window of my study.... Do you like bats, Dr. Lace?" She didn't reply. "I don't suppose you do. Most people are terrified by bats; they inspire us with superstitious dread, even though the majority of them are harmless creatures, quite useful in the ecological balance."

"Is that what you wanted to do? Inspire superstitious dread in people?"

"Not 'people,' Doctor. Only criminals."

"Like the ones who killed your parents?"

"I see you know something about my background."

"Not your background," Dr. Lace said. "Your legend, Batman. It *is* a legend, isn't it?"

"Are you implying that it isn't true?"

Batman was conscious of the psychiatrist's shrug even though he couldn't see her from the couch.

"I think you're determined to create a mythology," she said. "Isn't that apparent from your behavior? My only question is whether the myth was created to help you in your 'career,' or to rationalize away some secret iniquity of your own."

"You think I'm hiding something?" Batman asked, amused.

"I have no idea," Dr. Lace confessed. "That's why we're here, to find out what might be happening beneath the surface of your life. The Batcave of your mind, you might say."

"And just what do you think that might be?"

"If I had to venture a guess, which would be very unprofessional—"

"You're among friends."

"I'd say guilt was a possibility. The guilt you may have felt the night your parents were shot down by that street-corner holdup man.... You didn't do much to save them, did you?"

"I was only a boy. What could I have done?"

"You could have died with them," Dr. Lace said. "But you survived.... This coldblooded killer let you live. Isn't that the truth of the situation?"

Batman frowned.

"Yes," he said. "He heard the sound of a police whistle after the shots were fired, and ran away."

"And what did you feel after it happened? After you realized that both your parents were dead? Pain, rage, the desire for revenge?"

"I felt all those things. That's when I made my vow to conduct my life the way I have. I spent every waking moment from that night on in training my mind, my body—"

"Did it help? Did all the dedication, all the criminals you apprehended, ever make up for the guilt you felt when your parents died?"

"I can't answer that."

"Can you answer this? How well do you remember that night? What you saw, how you acted, how you felt?"

Batman hesitated.

"Not much. Only the darkness. The sudden appearance of the holdup man, demanding my mother's necklace. My father's resistance. The gun going off...twice. That's all I can recall."

"Never mind," Dr. Lace said softly. "All the details are still in your mind, deep within your subconscious. I'll extract them all, through hypnosis. Then we'll see if they have any relevance to this new guilt you're suffering, the one that caused you to weep in public...."

"New guilt?" She didn't reply, but Batman easily read her thoughts. "You mean Robin, of course."

"Yes," Dr. Letitia Lace said. "Robin. What did the press call him?"

"The Boy Wonder," Batman said.

"Yes. The Boy who died fighting for others...unlike the boy who *lived*, while others died...."

Well, it was apparent from Batman's account of this dialogue that he was dealing with a formidable personality, fortunately in a beneficent cause. I must confess that, for the first time since I became Batman's confidante, I realized that he was subject to the same human weaknesses that separate the rest of us from the gods. I should have accepted this sign of his humanity, yet I couldn't escape a sense of disappointment.

I can give an even more detailed report of what occurred at Batman's next session with his psychiatrist, simply because every word was transcribed.

It was Batman's first hypnotherapy. He was concerned about the procedure, of course, worried about what he might reveal about himself (meaning Bruce Wayne) under hypnotic influence. Dr. Lace assured him that hypnotic subjects will not behave in any manner antithetical to their convictions, nor reveal secrets they consider sacred. Batman wisely required her to provide more assurance than that. He asked that she record the entire session on audio tape.

In the following transcript, I have edited out those statements employed to initiate the trance state.

DR. LACE: I want you to go back to the night of your parents death. I know the journey will be painful for you, that you would rather not make it, but you won't be able to help yourself. You will be the boy you were then, and you will be walking home with your parents. Are you on that dark, dark street now? Tell me what you see.

BATMAN: We're talking. We've just seen a movie, and we're talking about it. I liked the movie. They aren't so sure. My mother thought it was too violent.... Wait! There's someone.

DR. LACE: Someone where?

BATMAN: Under the lamppost. He's pretending to be tying a shoelace. I can tell he's waiting for us.

DR. LACE: You're only a boy. How do you know?

BATMAN: I'm not sure. I always seem able to...know things about people. What they're thinking, what they're about to do. Their eyes tell me things. This man's eyes... he's frightened. He's terribly afraid. And that makes me afraid—

DR. LACE: Why?

BATMAN: Frightened people are dangerous.... Gosh, Dad, that man has a gun!

It was at this point that Batman's voice altered on the tape. One could swear it was the voice of a boy not yet in his teens. It was uncanny, and a bit unnerving.

DR. LACE: Go on. What happened then?

BATMAN: He said—it was a stickup! It didn't seem real. It was almost like the movie we had just seen.... He said he'd take the necklace my mother was wearing. He grabbed her, and my father cried out for him to leave her alone.... That was when he fired the gun.... My father fell...and when my mother shouted for the police, the holdup man shot her

too.... I ran to my parents, but I knew that there was nothing I could do, that they were both dead, that they had died
instantly...

DR. LACE: And the holdup man? Where was he?

BATMAN: He ran away. A patrolman heard the shouts...he
blew his whistle and came running.... The rest of that
night...is just a blank.

DR. LACE: Then we must dig even deeper, Batman. You
must travel back even farther into your subconscious....

The tape ran silently for the next five minutes while, I
assume, Dr. Lace attempted to deepen the hypnotic state,
but when she resumed her questioning, Batman was still
unable to recall more than he had already related about
that fateful night.

Even as Batman struggled to regain his emotional sta-
bility, the world outside Dr. Lace's office seemed to go
stark staring mad!

It was the *Gotham City Post* that orchestrated the madness. Its editor, Samuel Leaze, had thirsted for Batman's
blood ever since that irresponsible tabloid had tried to
increase their circulation with scandalous rumors about
Batman. First, there was a story implying that Batman had
deliberately allowed the Catwoman to escape the clutches
of the law because of a romantic involvement. Then they
had printed gossip trash about Batman and Catwoman.
But the final straw was the reprehensible item in a gossip
column implying an illicit relationship between Batman
and Robin. Batman had been outraged, of course, but he
was in no position to sue, as Leaze well knew. It was actually some members of the Batman Fan Club who took
revenge. When the newspaper launched a hot-air balloon
as part of a promotional stunt, they amended the written
message on the balloon to read: THE GOTHAM CITY POST—

NOTHING BUT HOT AIR. The editor, in an attempt to eradicate the offensive words, accidentally set himself adrift in the balloon and had the humiliating experience of being rescued by—Batman himself. The episode only made Samuel Leaze despise Batman all the more.

From the day of Batman's breakdown, not a single issue of the *Gotham City Post* appeared without a front page headline about Batman's "hopeless" condition. With no regard for the truth, the *Post* quoted "informed sources" and "hospital spokesmen" and "intimate associates" who reported that Batman was on the brink of total insanity. Distressed as I was to read these stories, I still had faith that the public would discredit these shameless falsehoods. To some extent, my faith was justified—until the "Batty Batmans" appeared.

I'm sorry to repeat that dreadful vulgar phase, but it became common currency in Gotham City, and not just by the *Post*. All the local media, the national press, the television newscasters employed the phrase. Soon, broadcasters all over the country were dispatching ENG crews to our fair city in the hopes of capturing an exploit of "Batty Batman" for the consumption of their audience. It was surely the darkest period of Batman's life, to say nothing of my own.

The first appearance took place at the opening of a new shopping center in downtown Gotham City, an event hardly significant to the advancement of mankind, but one that attracted several thousand people, lured by the promise of free handouts and free entertainment. Indeed, they assumed that the caped figure that swooped into their midst on what appeared to be genuine Batwire was part of the entertainment program. I was stunned to see the front-page photograph of that moment, and to read the accompanying headline.

Henry Slesar

BATMAN BECOMES FATMAN!

Indeed, the headline was justified. The caped figure swinging at the end of the wire was definitely on the stout side. Batman's usually skin-tight body suit bulged with excess poundage, including a pot belly worthy of another legendary figure, St. Nicholas. And yet, there was no attempt to conceal the fact that the bulges and belly were false; that they were the result of cotton wool and feather pillows, that it was all someone's idea of a jolly mad masquerade—and that "someone" seemed to be Batman himself!

It was an imposter, of course; I felt absolutely certain of it as I hastily brought the morning paper to the door of Mr. Wayne's bedroom and knocked gingerly. It had to be a prank perpetrated by the promoters of the new shopping center, or perhaps even the *Gotham City Post*. But a terrible shock awaited me. When Mr. Wayne failed to respond to my knock, I let myself into his room and saw his sleeping figure in the bed. The first thing I saw, draped over a chair, was his Batman costume, flagrantly displayed. But what startled me was the sight of wads of cotton wool lying on the rug, along with pillows that had obviously been used as padding. Badly shaken, I left the newspaper and closed the bedroom door behind me.

I said nothing to Mr. Wayne about what I had seen, and he made no comment to me, not even after perusing the morning newspaper. Indeed, he had been virtually incommunicado since starting his therapy with Dr. Lace, almost as if reticence had been prescribed as part of his treatment.

Then, just two days later, another "Batty Batman" appeared.

You may be familiar with the Gotham City Park monument that has been the children's favorite for more than fifty years. In life-size stone carvings, it depicts many of the beloved characters from *Alice's Adventures in Wonderland*. During clement weather, it is always garlanded by climbing, laughing, happy youngsters.

The weather wasn't clement on the Sunday that marked the one hundredth and twenty-fifth anniversary of the Lewis Carroll classic. Despite the persistent drizzle, a small ceremony was held at the base of the *Alice* monument. There was an unexpected celebrity in attendance. Just as the Mayor and a dozen other political luminaries gathered to pay tribute to the author and his creation—and to provide the press with a photo opportunity—Batman appeared triumphantly on the top of the monument, standing on the stone shoulders of Tweedledum and Tweedledee. Only it wasn't the Batman they all knew and loved. Because this caped crusader wore an enormous top hat that carried a price tag in its ribbon, clearly the hat worn by the Mad Hatter of Tea Party fame. Flinging back his cape, he spread out his arms to the crowd and cried out:

"Happy anniversary from...Hatman!"

He laughed wildly, the shrill, humorless laughter of the deranged, and as swiftly as he had appeared, disappeared again. With Batman's customary alacrity, he was out of sight before the photographers present could capture anything more than a blurred image of his departure.

The next morning, I stared at that image on the front page of the *Post* and shuddered. My "imposter" theory was weakening. Despite the lack of photographic detail, I recognized the hat. It had been a trophy of one of Batman's most famous exploits, his capture of Jervis Tetch, the "Mad Hatter" who had terrorized Gotham City before Bat-

Henry Slesar

man ended his career. The hat had been locked away in Batman's private museum, but when I descended to his subterranean lair, there it was, lying carelessly beside the computer bank, still damp with rain....

In all my years of service, I had never ventured either advice or criticism to Batman, but I was sorely tempted now. It was obvious that he had gone from depression to dementia, and I had to discuss the matter with someone, no matter how obliquely.

Commissioner Gordon was the only logical person with which to share my concern. I decided to use the same ruse that gained me entry into Pine-Whatney Clinic, my master's concern for Batman's welfare. However, it was hopeless; the Commissioner was far too busy to take my call, and it was understandable. The criminals of Gotham City, showing their disdain for "Batty Batman," were intensifying their assault on public property. Commissioner Gordon was undoubtedly frantic, especially since the press was exhorting Mayor Paul Donovan to demand his resignation. Indeed, that action seemed inevitable.

Then another thought occurred to me. Perhaps it might be useful if I spoke privately with Batman's psychiatrist, Dr. Lace. Her fees *were* being paid through Mr. Wayne's bank, and that might provide enough excuse for a conversation.

Rather than risk another rejection by telephone, I made a personal visit to Dr. Lace, making sure that my timing didn't coincide with Batman's own scheduled daily visit. But there was still a surprise awaiting me. As I arrived, I saw someone else leaving Dr. Lace's quiet brownstone, a man whose face was immediately recognizable. It was Mayor Donovan himself.

I was still pondering this odd coincidence when I rang the doorbell. Dr. Lace's nurse-receptionist, a cold-eyed matron with the inappropriate name Mrs. Bonny, looked at me suspiciously. However, when she communicated my message to Dr. Lace, the psychiatrist amiably agreed to see me.

Her first question was why Batman's benefactor, Mr. Wayne, hadn't made this call himself. Wasn't it odd to send a butler in his place?

"Mr. Wayne is indisposed," I explained. "He contracted a virus of some sort." I didn't blink at the lie; there was actually some symbolic truth in it.

"Well, I hope your Mr. Wayne realizes that there is very little I can reveal about this case. It wouldn't be ethical."

"He understands that you have to respect your patient's confidentiality," I said. "But he's very concerned about this new development, these bizarre public appearances.... You are aware of your patient's...eccentric behavior?"

"I'm aware of it," the psychiatrist said coolly. "But why do you assume all 'eccentric' behavior is abnormal? Hasn't it occurred to you—that Batman may be merely expressing a long-supressed sense of humor?"

"I never thought Batman's humor was 'supressed,'" I replied, just as cooly. Then, fearing that I was revealing too much, added quickly: "It seems odd that he would turn prankster so shortly after suffering a tragic loss..."

"The normal mourning period passed some time ago," Dr. Lace said. "This may simply be Batman's way of expressing his renewed zest for life, by playing games with his identity."

"That's exactly what worries me—Mr. Wayne, I mean. The game seems so pointless! Fatman! Hatman! Who knows what's next?"

I was soon to find out. The telephone on Dr. Lace's desk chirped quietly, and she picked it up. Her lovely face darkened as she heard Mrs. Bonny's voice. When she hung up, she said: "I'm afraid you'll have to excuse me. I have a patient in trouble."

It was only after I left Dr. Lace's office that I learned that patient was Batman himself. Fortunately, I passed a blaring car radio on the street, and heard the news bulletin. Batman had been spotted perched on a thirty-story ledge of Gotham City Towers, and police and fire brigades had been dispatched with ladders and nets in case of a suicide attempt.

I was horrified, of course. Batman was frequently referred to as a superhero, and many myths circulated about his superhuman powers. Whatever supreme qualities he possessed, he had earned by rigorous training of his body and mind. He had already demonstrated that that mind was all too vulnerable, but so was his body. I sped to the site of Gotham City Towers.

Speed was impossible, however. Every street within a twenty-block radius of the skyscraper was clotted with people and vehicles. It was an irresistible attraction: not just a potential jumper, but a jumper who was surely the most famous individual in Gotham City. Perhaps now they would learn if their "superhero," like Superman, could fly; or perhaps their thirst for gore would be satisfied by the sight of Batman's crushed and bleeding body. As you can see, I entertained the most morbid thoughts as I finally came within viewing distance of Gotham City Towers. There, as promised, was Batman, sitting nonchalantly on the ledge, holding a white object in his blue-gauntleted hand.

I didn't know what the object was until Batman, apparently satisfied with the size of his audience, got to his feet and lifted it to his lips. Then his voice boomed out through the bullhorn, chilling me to the very marrow.

"Ladies and gentlemen! Introducing... *Splatman!*"

I knew what was going to happen next, but my mind refused to believe it. Batman stood on his toes, fanned out his batwing cape and dove gracefully into the air. For a single breathtaking moment he was poised in midair, almost as if he really could fly like the nocturnal creature he emulated—but gravity won the contest. A collective scream of horror and dismay rose from the crowd as Batman plunged toward them from that great height. The police and fire squads, their rescue equipment still aboard their respective vehicles, looked on helplessly. As for myself, I could only close my eyes and pray for my master's immortal soul.

Suddenly, time seemed to stop!

I didn't realize what had happened until another astonished cry from the spectators caused me to open my eyes and see Batman suspended above the ground as if caught by a stop-motion camera. His precipitous flight to oblivion had been halted abruptly. The almost invisible batwire tied to his leg had stopped him less than six feet from the pavement; a man of lesser strength would have had that leg torn from its socket by the sudden impact. Batman merely laughed at the "success" of his practical joke, and leaped lightly to the ground. Then, with a farewell wave to the stunned crowd, he hurried to the waiting batmobile and was soon tearing down the street, his wild laughter fading with the roar of the engine.

There was a videotape of the event on the six o'clock news that night, and the facetious commentary by the newscasters indicated that they shared the same opinion as the rest of the world: Batman was certifiable.

It wasn't the only item on the telecast. There was also a related story on the upsurge in crime in Gotham City, and a taped interview with Mayor Donovan, who stated

Henry Slesar

flatly that he still had complete confidence in Commissioner Gordon; there would be no request for his resignation. Even though I was relieved for the Commissioner's sake, there was still something about the development that troubled me.

That night, I decided that I would risk my entire relationship with Batman by breaking a sacred rule. I was going to ask Mr. Wayne a direct question about the situation.

I couldn't sleep that night. I was sure sleep would never come until I had unburdened myself. I tossed aside the bedclothes, slipped on a robe, and went to Mr. Wayne's door. I didn't bother to knock; I simply walked into the room. It was in darkness, illuminated only by the pale moonlight that fell across his sleeping figure. He stirred slightly as I approached, and for a moment, I almost lost my nerve. Then I spoke softly.

"Mr. Wayne?"

There was no answer, but my determination was so great I decided to waken him at all costs. I touched his shoulder lightly and realized...*I wasn't touching flesh!*

Swiftly, I drew back the covers and saw that I had been deceived by a cleverly constructed dummy, an artificial man so lifelike that it even contained a breathing mechanism. Then I recalled the time when Batman, threatened with disclosure of his dual identity, had created a "Bruce Wayne" robot to take his place while Batman performed his deeds. Now, Mr. Wayne was using the dummy to fool me, the one person in the world entrusted with his most important secret! I was so baffled that I spoke the word aloud to the darkness:

"Why?"

Of course, madness was the Great Explainer of all mysteries, but the least satisfying. Even madness has method in it, and what lunatic reasoning could Batman have for this deception of his loyal servant? Irrational as it sounds, I felt a tinge of anger, and that emboldened me to make still another clandestine trip to the cave beneath Wayne Manor.

I detected nothing out of the ordinary—if "ordinary" can describe the Batcave, a combination of computer room, laboratory, museum, and central headquarters. I understood enough of Batman's methods to know that his starting point is often at his liquid-cooled Cray computer console. Its workings were a mystery, but on one occasion Batman, in another location, had needed some stored data in a hurry, and had instructed me in the technique of "booting" the device. I did so now, and I was in luck. There was a program still in memory, and it asked:

Do you wish to see list again?

I hesitated, then punched the Return key. There on the screen, appeared the following:

```
PENTOTHYL DIAZINE
CHLOROPAM E.
ALPRAPROXIDE
TRITOPHENOZENE
```

I was unfamiliar with the names, but they sounded like pharmaceuticals, perhaps prescribed by Dr. Lace? Surely Batman couldn't take them *all*, although that might explain his erratic behavior. I had little time for speculation, because I heard the distinct whine of the Batcave elevator and realized that Batman was coming down!

I confess to a moment of sheer panic. Batman never denied me free access to the Batcave, but I would be hard pressed to explain why I was tampering with his computer. I decided to hide. The first place of concealment that met my eye: the back seat of the Batmobile.

It was not the most fortuitous choice because Batman went straight to the Batmobile and climbed into the driver's seat. A touch on the dashboard, and the camouflaged door of the Batcave opened, the Batmobile engine growled, and with a burst of speed that made my ears ring, we roared off into the night

You can imagine the trepidation I felt, clad in robe and pajamas, at the mercy of a man who was almost certainly mentally unsound. After the department store break down, the emergence of Fatman, Batman, and Splatman, I could no longer deny that "Batty Batman" was the correct appellation for the former superhero of Gotham City. Who knew what lunatic visions were driving him now, or me, for that matter?

The ride lasted no more than twenty minutes, but it seemed an eternity until the powerful vehicle slowed to a purring halt and grew silent. It was only when Batman left the Batmobile that I ventured to steal a glance at my surroundings. We were in the suburbs, in a parking lot behind a looming square structure with only one or two lighted windows.

Finally, I made out a sign that read:

PINE-WHATNEY CLINIC
Physician Parking Only
Violators will be prosecuted

That sign was innocuous beside the one I discerned on the tall wire fence surrounding the building.

WARNING!
ELECTRIFIED FENCE
DO NOT TOUCH

Then, as if once again demonstrating the loss of his reasoning powers, I saw that Batman was preparing to scale that very fence!

As I watched in horrified fascination, he removed an instrument from his belt that appeared to be a small snub-nosed revolver. He aimed it at the roof of the building and fired a tiny grappling hook attached to a length of batwire. It draped right across that electrified fence, evoking a shower of sparks, but Batman began his climb just the same.

To my great relief, nothing happened. It took me a moment to realize that Batman's rubberized boots and gloves were acting as insulation.

Then Batman disappeared into the darkness above the roof of the Clinic, and I was left alone to ponder the mystery.

Why did Batman return to the Pine-Whatney, the clinic he had once called "that antiseptic prison?" Was there some sub-conscious desire to seek help for his pathetic mental state? Why was he using stealth? Most of all, was there *any* rational explanation for his behavior?

I decided that my best course of action was to leave the Batmobile and make my way back home. It was probably the worst decision of my life. When I unfolded my frame from the back seat, a space never intended for passengers of my size, I lost my balance and fell forward toward the dashboard. I reached out to steady myself and my hand slammed into the Batmobile horn!

That sound, in the stillness of the night, was as penetrating as the wail of an air-raid siren and caused as much alarm among the residents of the building. I heard shouts that rose to a chorus so cacophonous that I felt sure it came from the throats of the inmates. Then some of the voices became discernible, and what they were saying was alarming indeed.

"We got him! We got Batman!"

I didn't know *who* was celebrating this victory; I hoped it was merely some hospital authority, but there was something distinctively malevolent about the tone. When I saw the two white-coated figures emerging from a back door, my instincts sent me back to my hiding place in the rear of the Batmobile.

Once again, I found myself an involuntary passenger. The two men chortled over finding the Batmobile, but their delight was tempered when they discovered they couldn't start the motor. No one but Batman could, of course; its ignition would respond only to the palmprint of Batman at the wheel. But that didn't prevent them from pushing the vehicle down a ramp and into a garage beneath the hospital. Then they took the stairway to the upper floor, leaving me to my anxiety and indecision.

My indecision didn't last long. I couldn't leave under the circumstances; I simply had to know what had become of Batman. I tried to tell myself that he was in compassionate custody; that this was a hospital, a place of healing, and the people who "got" him had acted out of humanitarian motives. Still, I couldn't shake a feeling of dread. I left the Batmobile and followed the route of the two attendants to the upper floor.

I climbed eight flights in all, pausing at each landing to open the door barely a crack, looking for a scene of activity.

It was on the topmost floor, when I was almost entirely breathless from fatigue and apprehension, that I heard the raised voices. I entered a dimly lit corridor and made my way to the source of the sound. It was apparently some kind of medical conference room, and judging from the medley I heard, there were at least a dozen men in heated discussion. The thought of eavesdropping was frightening, but, as my old grandfather used to say, in for a penny, in for a pound. I put my ears to the white door and listened.

"You're sure he can't use any of his tricks on us?" a grating voice asked. "He's smarter than a dozen foxes, you know."

"Don't worry about it," another man replied. "We've got him in our camisole. He's helpless as a baby."

It took me a moment to deduce that a "camisole" was what they used to call a "straitjacket."

"All right, then," the first man said. "Bring him in and let's find out how much he knows."

There was the sound of half a dozen chairs being scraped back on a hard wooden floor, and then an excited murmur that must have been produced by Batman's entry. I could no longer resist the opportunity of peering into that room. With agonizing slowness, I turned the knob and opened the door a fraction of an inch, enough to catch sight of my poor master strapped into a white restraining garment, being unceremoniously shoved to the head of a long conference table around which sat what appeared to be a strange convocation of doctors in their hospital whites and patients in their robes and pajamas.

"Go on, Batman," the grating voice said, its owner not in my line of sight. "Tell us how you got here."

"Maybe he missed the place," another voice said, and there was a rumble of unpleasant laughter.

"I didn't want to miss this meeting," Batman said, in a clear, steady voice. "There hasn't been a conference like this since Appalachin."

Henry Slesar

The reference meant nothing to me, but it caused a stir among the seated figures.

"We all know you've got bats in that belfry of yours, Batman," another voice said. "This is a hospital, remember? We're doctors."

"And patients, I see," Batman said dryly, confirming my own suspicion. "Do you let the inmates run this asylum, too?"

"Why are we listening to this maniac?" someone else said. "Let's give him a healthy dose of Alpaproxide and throw him into a rubber room."

"No," the grating voice said loudly. "Let's here what he has to say. Go on, Batman. What's all this crap about Appalachin? That's in the mountains, ain't it?

Strange grammar for a physician, I thought.

"Yes," Batman said. "It's in the Catskills. Back in 1957, it was where the biggest crime boss meeting in history was held. Also the most embarrassing, since it was broken up by the police."

"And is that what you think *you're* doing, Batman?"

I gasped at this implication.

"I knew this conference was going to take place because I overheard *your* boss making the arrangements. Where is the Big Boss, anyway?"

I didn't expect them to answer Batman's bold challenge, but someone did. Astonishingly, the voice was female. Even more incredible, it was a voice I recognized!

"I'm right here," Dr. Lace said composedly. "But I can hardly believe you 'overheard' anything, Batman, since you were well under the influence of a hypnotic drug at the time."

Batman's smile was wide beneath his mask.

"Sorry, doctor. Whichever delightful concoction you introduced into my system had no effect whatsoever. You see, I made sure I was immunized against all your hypnotics some time ago. At the beginning of your treatment, as a matter of fact."

"That's impossible!"

"The nice thing about Alpaproxide and Chloropram and the rest of those drugs—they can all be nullified by one compound. Of course, I had to be my own guinea pig before I could offer the same remedy to your other patients—like Commissioner Gordon, and Randolph Spicer of the FBI, and of course, your latest victim, Mayor Donovan."

"Hey, what is this?" The grating voice was harsher than ever. "What's going on here, Doc? I thought you said Batman was completely under control?"

"He was!" Dr. Lace said, and I detected a nervous quaver in her voice. "You know what he's been doing, acting like a complete lunatic, just as I ordered..."

Batman laughed, without a hint of nervousness.

"I enjoyed those little charades you devised for me, Doctor. It was fun carrying out your 'hypnotic' suggestions. Almost as much fun as becoming your patient in the first place."

"Wait a minute!" one of the others cried. "Are you kidding us? You *didn't* have a nervous breakdown?"

"Sorry to disappoint you," Batman said. "I simply thought it was the best way to find out if what I suspected was true—that Commissioner Gordon and others were being strangely influenced *not* to do their jobs. I've known Gordon a long time, and he never gave so many wrong orders, or followed such wrong leads, or reacted so wimpishly to a crime wave. I knew there was something wrong with his attitude, and I began to wonder if that 'attitude' wasn't being formed by somebody else."

"He is lying!" Dr. Lace said defensively. "The man was an emotional wreck when he came to me."

"Actually, you *did* do me good," Batman said with a grin. "You took my mind off my problems, Doctor. You gave me something to look forward to—like seeing all these illustrious gang bosses locked up in Gotham City jail."

"I've heard enough!" the harsh voice exploded. For the first time, I saw its owner, a huge man with barrel chest and hands like two sides of beef. I recognized Tough Teddy Thomas, once the most notorious crime figures in the country, long believed to be part of the asphalt in the Gotham City thruway. "This guy made a jackass out of you, Doc! He was the one playing games, not you! Only I'm making sure the game is over—"

To my horror, he drew a revolver from a shoulder holster, aimed it point blank at Batman, and fired! The force of the bullet sent Batman flying back against the wall of the conference room, and then limp as a rag doll, he slid to the ground and rolled over on his face.

Before my very eyes, Batman had been executed.

The stunning event electrified the assembly. Suddenly, chairs were pushed back and overthrown. The air was thick with cries and imprecations, and then there was a mad rush for the exit. The doors of the conference room were slammed open so precipitously that I was momentarily concealed behind them. Even when I could no longer remain hidden, my presence went completely unnoticed by the mobsters. Then I realized the reason. I was dressed just like most of the hoodlums posing as hospital patients, in robe and pajamas. They assumed I was one of them!

When the room was emptied, I hurried to Batman's side, certain that I could do no more than pay my last respects. I was already in tears, deeply regretting that I could never tell the fallen hero how sorry I was not to have trusted him from the beginning, not to have understood the elaborate game he had been playing to defeat this terrible criminal conspiracy. It was painful to realize that all his valiant effort, his willingness to humiliate himself for the greater good, was all in vain, that the villains had escaped leaving Batman to History.

Then I heard the sirens, and realized that Batman had foreseen this possibility, that he had arranged for police action before his arrival—but would they be in time?

"Don't worry, Alfred," Batman said. "I've wired all the exit doors shut with Batwire. The only way out of this building is through the garage, and they'll run into quite a number of squad cars there."

I could only gape at Batman as he rose to his feet and began to work his way out of the camisole.

"I've heard Houdini could do this in four minutes," he said lightly. "Let's see if I can beat his record."

I must record that he did not. Batman was free of his restraint in four minutes and fifteen seconds. The cloth garment hit the ground with a metallic thud.

"It's a bullet-proof shield," Batman explained. "I slipped it into a camisole before I allowed myself to be captured. Just to be on the safe side."

"You *wanted* to be caught?" I gasped.

"I thought it was the best way to get a confession from Dr. Lace." He removed the tiny tape recorder attached to his belt, and smiled. "Now I have it."

I must have collapsed suddenly, because the next minute was lost to my memory. I found myself in a chair, with Batman administering to me with a glass of water.

"I'm sorry," I said. "The truth is, I thought it was entirely my fault that you were captured."

Henry Slesar

"I'm the one who has to apologize to you, Alfred," he said. "I simply couldn't confide in you or anyone else about what I was doing; I couldn't afford to ruse the slightest suspicion about the state of my mental health."

"Then—it was all a ruse? From the beginning?"

"Only a game," Batman smiled. "There was definitely a method in my 'madness.'"

"Yes, sir," I said. "I understand perfectly. And I'm sure everyone in Gotham City will deeply appreciate the sacrifices you made."

"However," Batman said amiably, "no matter what the news media say about all this, don't be surprised if some people persist in believing that I really *am* 'bats.'"

Of course, it was the truth. It's human nature, I suppose, to believe the worst of others. To this day, there are people who think Batman is some schizophrenic with delusions of grandeur. There are others who think Batman is only a figment of someone's fevered imagination. Batman doesn't mind. He's willing to let the criminals of this world continue to live in fool's paradise, until that dark night when they see the black shadow of batwings against the circle of the yellow moon.

The Sound of One Hand Clapping

A Batman and Robin Story

MAX ALLAN COLLINS

The Joker sat on his playing-card throne behind a grotesquely grinning desk and frowned. His frown was as exaggerated as his (currently absent) trademark grin, and it reflected both emotional and physical pain: to summon a frown from a face frozen into a grin by a long-ago acid bath required effort, and concentration.

On those rare occasions when the Joker was depressed, when there was no news of earthquake devastation, school bus collisions, or toxic-waste spills to cheer him— he had to work hard at his despair.

"What is the *point* of it all?" mused the white-faced, green-haired, purple-jacketed psychotic. "Where is the *joy* in my life?"

He stood.

And paced.

And spoke to himself: "The pointlessness of my existence is no laughing matter."

He returned to his throne, his frown as down-turned as his usual crazed grin. He shook his elongated head, and wrung his purple-gloved hands.

The Sound of One Hand Clapping

The dreary castle from which this melancholy monarch ruled was a run-down, deserted toy factory near the slum area called Crime Alley. Jester Novelties had closed down years before, and stood condemned, even as was its current occupant by every local, state, and federal law enforcement agency you might name.

But the surroundings within the old factory were considerably more cheerful. On this rainy Gotham night, the clown prince of crime rested moodily on an oversize throne sculpted in his own harlequin image. The interior walls of the condemned factory were gaily, if not sanely, appointed with oversize playing cards—jokers, one and all—and bright yellow wallpaper smattered with hearts, spades, clubs, and diamonds.

No, it was not his castle that depressed him; it was his kingdom itself that had dimmed the demented devil's droll disposition—a kingdom of the mind in which a jester ruled.

"The boss is really depressed," whispered Kennison, a heavyset stooge in a long flasher topcoat and a black knit beret. "I'm afraid the boss is havin' a mid-life crisis."

"Th-th-that's only part of the problem," whispered back a second stooge, one "Bobcat" Goldman, a disheveled nervous wreck in tattered sweatshirt and tennies. "Th-th-that letter the Penguin sneaked outta stir to the boss—braggin' up the *joys* of bein' in love—has really, like you know...bummed him out."

Even now, the sour, self-pitying Joker stood behind his desk, reading the letter for perhaps the thousandth time. The Penguin had met his true love—Dovina—through the mail, a lonely heart's club friendship that blossomed into romance and impending wedlock.

"If that tuxedoed twerp can find happiness," the Joker pondered aloud bitterly, "why not *moi?*"

The Joker looked skyward, summoning his considerable powers of self-pity. He gestured to himself theatrically, a fourth-rate actor putting the ham into Hamlet.

"Here I stand at the midpoint of my life—and what have I to show for it?"

Kennison took a tentative step forward. "You've had a brilliant career, boss!"

"Well, that's true," the Joker said absently, as he casually plucked up three hard balls, not unlike those used in the game of croquet, and began to juggle.

"Y-y-yeah, Joker," Bobcat said, with a stupid nervous grin. "You've had a *wonderful* life!"

"Also true," the Joker admitted, juggling with lazy skill. "But who do I have to *share* it with?"

Kennison glanced at Bobcat and gestured with two big open hands and risked saying, "Us?"

It was a risk not worth taking.

"Precisely my point!" the Joker sneered, and savagely hurled the hard balls at the two stooges, who scurried away into the darker recesses of the warehouse-room, one hard ball bouncing off the head of the wincing, whimpering Bobcat.

"Where is the female companionship that could give my life resonance?" the Joker asked the sky—or, to be more precise, the skylight. "Where are the progeny who might carry my great tradition into the future?"

The Joker's long legs flashed like swords in a duel as he exited his inner sanctum and moved down a hallway, where framed portraits of famous comedians—from Eddie Cantor to Steve Martin—hung askew. His two stooges fell into step behind him—but at a safe distance.

"Boss," Kennison said, "you gotta cheer up—we gotta get back to work—"

The Sound of One Hand Clapping

"W-w-we haven't pulled a job in weeks," Bobcat said. "We're *broke!*"

The Joker glanced back at them with tragic self-pity as he entered the dark protective womb of his viewing room.

"Leave me to my solitude," the Joker said. "Perhaps Rodney will show me the way out of the slough of despond."

The Joker settled himself into a plush seat in his personal theater and summoned the image of Rodney Dangerfield on the giant television screen before him. As Rodney tugged at his tie, complaining of the lack of respect he received, the Joker remained unamused.

"I told my doctor I wanted a second opinion," said Rodney. "He said, 'Okay—you're *ugly!*'"

"Bah!" the Joker said, and he shot the screen with his remote control. "Even the great Rodney gives me no relief."

But the clown of crime, in turning off the VCR, had inadvertently filled the screen with another image, courtesy of a local news broadcast.

The image of a beautiful woman.

A woman in a black leotard, her face white, her lips bright red, her cheeks dotted with bright red circles, her long-lashed eyes dark and hauntingly sad.

This image—apparently that of a street mime—struck the Joker hard, like a loose board in a wooden sidewalk, leaving him awestruck. His mouth yawned open like a skillet awaiting eggs.

"Oh my," he said.

On the screen, a plump, middle-aged, balding blond male newscaster stood, microphone in hand, in front of a massive modern building.

"...Bellew, Eyewitness News," he said, "on the scene at the Gotham City Civic Center..."

Max Allan Collins

The image suddenly shifted as, amazingly, that sweet haunting slip of a girl was shown grabbing two rock musicians by their wrists, shocking them senseless.

"...where the criminal known as the Mime has attempted to disrupt a rock concert—"

A still photo filled the screen now, of a beautiful, pale, dark-haired woman.

"The Mime is believed to be, beneath the greasepaint, Camilla Comeo, heir to the Ortin Fireworks fortune."

Then the screen was filled with file footage of Camilla and several other mimes as they gracefully performed on stage.

"Cameo's acclaimed mime troupe reportedly exhausted her inheritance and was disbanded, after government funding for the arts was withdrawn."

Then the screen was filled with the image of the taxi whose windshield had been spider-webbed from a gunshot.

"The recent shooting of a taxi driver in a noisy traffic jam is also believed to be the work of the Mime, whose crimes are thought to be a protest against the cacophony of sounds that litter the urban landscape."

The Joker, starry-eyed, was no longer frowning; he was smiling at the screen, a smile enormous even for him. His hands clasped to his heaving bosom, he said breathlessly, to no one in particular and to the universe in general, "She's—she's beautiful—beautiful...."

On screen, the newscaster continued to speak into his mike, while behind him the lovely sad Mime, hands cuffed behind her back, was led off by the cops.

"The Mime has made *no* public statement," the newscaster said, "but her captor *has*."

The Joker cringed at the next image that filled the screen: a tall, muscular figure in cape and cowl.

The Sound of One Hand Clapping

"Miss Cameo," the Batman said, "is a gifted artist who has suffered a great deal of stress. It is my hope she will be given suitable medical treatment."

Enraged, the Joker, his nostrils and eyes flaring, thrust an accusatory finger at the screen.

"You!" he cried. "*You!*"

"The Dark Knight," the newscaster was saying, "is often thought of as a cold avenger, but his compassion here is evident. Goodnight for..."

"Compassion!" the Joker screamed. He fired his remote control at the big-screen TV, killing it with a KLIK! "Compassion my lily-white ass!"

He stalked out into the hallway, where his two stooges cowered at the sight of him. He lifted them each off the ground by the back of their collars, holding them up like puppies plucked from a cardboard box; they looked back at him with confused looks befitting plucked-up puppies.

"The most beautiful, sensitive soul in creation has been incarcerated!" he explained at the top of his voice. "And it's the cape cretin's doing!"

He dropped the pair to the cement floor, and looked up at nothing in particular, and stretched out his arms and hands and began to laugh: HA! HA! HA! HA! HA! HA!

Between laughs, he made a pledge: "*I* will rescue her! I will *woo* her—and *win* her!"

The stooges looked at each other and shrugged.

The next morning, on the street outside the Gotham City jail, the costumed vigilante who had earned the trust of a city spoke to the police commissioner who regarded him as a friend and ally. At Batman's side was Robin, the colorfully attired youth who accompanied him into battle.

"The staff psychiatrist agrees with you, Batman," said Commissioner Gordon. "Ms. Cameo's being transferred to Arkham Asylum for observation."

Max Allan Collins

Indeed, even as Gordon spoke, a jail matron was turning over Cameo to a pair of cops near a squad car.

"Good," Batman said. "If nothing else she'll be able to find some peace and quiet."

Her makeup washed unceremoniously away in the city jail shower the night before, the Mime—a.k.a. Camilla Cameo— sat in the backseat of the squad car; but now she would meet the world minus the whiteface mask she so loved to hide behind.

Soon the jail, Batman, and the city had been left behind, as the squad car cruised a quiet, shady country road on the way to the secluded asylum. Camilla Cameo sat stony-faced behind the wire mesh. The young cop looked back at her and said to his older partner, who drove, "She's a quiet one."

"Hey, don't knock it," the older cop said with a smirk. "It's what I look for in a broad."

The country solitude broke apart with the sound of a siren—RRRREEEEEE—and the young cop glanced curiously out his window. A helmeted cop on a motorcycle was drawing up alongside the squad car, waving them over.

"What the hell's that all about?" the older cop, behind the wheel, asked.

"Must be an emergency or a change of plans or something."

Camilla Cameo, behind the wire mesh, winced, and covered her ears at the piercing siren.

The squad car drew to a stop.

The motorcycle cop dismounted, placing his hand on his helmet, to remove it as he walked toward the squad car. The young cop leaned out his window, concerned.

"What's the problem, pard?"

The cop's helmet came off and his white face and red lips and green hair were revealed; he bent down and grinned at the two true cops seated within, and reveled in the beauty of Camilla, who wore an exaggerated expression of wonderment.

"Why, there's no problem, officers," the Joker said cheerfully. "Life is wonderful this sunny morning—don't you agree?"

He showed them the gun in his hand, which was no joke.

"Hands up, now," he said. "You're about to release your charge into my protective custody, gentlemen."

A bright red convertible rolled up alongside the squad car, driven by Kennison with Bobcat riding shotgun.

Bobcat helped Camilla out of the squad car and into the convertible while the Joker trained his automatic on the two dismayed cops, whose hands were raised. In the Joker's other hand now appeared a small, round, red object that might have been a Christmas tree ornament, but wasn't.

"And now, before we go on our merry way, and just to brighten up your morning, gents, so that you might start out the day with a *smile*..."

The Joker tossed the red bulb in the front seat between the two men, and it began to sizzle and smoke.

"...here's a little party favor for you. Ciao."

As if in joyful appreciation of the Joker's gracious gesture, the cops began to laugh uproariously. Tears rolled down their eyes, as their faces bobbed in a cloud of gas.

Camilla, sitting alone in the back of the convertible, looked with wide, bewildered eyes toward the Joker, who stood beside the car near her, pulling apart the Velcro stays of the cop uniform to reveal his "normal" attire.

"They seemed depressed, my dear," he explained, running a hand through his green mane, which had been matted down unattractively by the helmet. "I thought a smidgen of laughing gas might cheer them up."

Bobcat squealed away on the motorcycle, while the Joker slid into the back of the convertible, easing an arm around the confused Camilla's shoulder; Kennison drove them away.

"I know you must feel positively *naked* without your makeup, my sweet," the Joker said, heady with the closeness of her. He leaned toward a shell-like ear to confide: "I myself would never *dream* of going out in the world sans pancake, lipstick, and rouge,"

As the car roared back toward the city, the Joker gestured expansively, while Camilla silently recoiled.

"You will soon see, my sweet, that I've provided for your every need. Your smallest whim shall provide meaning to my meager existence!"

Camilla said nothing.

The Joker said, charmingly, "You may call me 'the Joker'—or 'Joker,' for short. Shall I call you 'Camilla'? or 'the Mime'? Or simply, 'Mime'?"

Camilla said nothing.

Several silent minutes later, the Joker was escorting the shell-shocked young woman regally to the door of his condemned castle, his two stooges tagging along.

"Well," he said, working the key in the lock, "you're shy. I can understand that." He opened the heavy wooden door, which swung open creakily. "For the nonce, we'll make it 'Ms. Cameo.'"

Camilla took in the surroundings with wide eyes—the motif of playing cards, toys, and clowns clung to the walls, even the furnishings. She stared hollowly at Harpo in a gigantic framed photo of the Marx Brothers as the Joker escorted her through his palace, gesturing solicitously.

The Sound of One Hand Clapping

"You'll be my guest until you've had a chance to reorder your, uh...affairs."

With pride, the Joker swung open a doorway, gesturing within. The young woman, walking zombielike, entered. It was a bedroom, a feminine bedroom decorated in black-and-white harlequin masks in keeping with the Mime's style. Prominently on one wall was a mammoth portrait of her pasty-faced host, signed "with gobs of love—Joker." On the theatrical dressing table, light bulbs framing its mirror, were several framed Joker portraits of varying sizes and coy poses.

"We've taken the liberty," the Joker said shyly, "of preparing this suite for you—hope it suffices...."

The Joker stood behind her, both hands on his heart, while Camilla sat at the dressing table, compulsively applying her mime's makeup.

"My dear," he said, "I don't mean to be forward—but I must speak my heart."

Camilla continued to apply her makeup, fingers gouging her cheeks.

"Since the moment I first gazed upon you—why, it seems like only yesterday—well, actually, it *was* only yesterday...."

Her face was white now. She stared at herself in the mirror.

"But, be that as it may, I must say that I do admire you so...your style, your grace, your poise, your very essence."

Now, as she looked in the mirror at herself, the Mime once more, she saw the Joker's grinning face beside hers, and there was reflected in her eyes the horror of recognizing that there was, indeed, a similarity.

"Is it my imagination, my dear, or were we *made* for each other?"

Max Allan Collins

The Mime said nothing.

The Joker moved gently away, gestured with one hand in the air, as if painting a picture, his other hand resting on the nearby shoulder of his blank-faced beloved.

"We have so much to discuss—the arts, philosophy.... 'What is the sound of one hand clapping?' 'If a tree falls in the forest, is there...'"

The Mime spoke.

She said, "AIEEEEEEEEEE!!!"

The Joker reared back, stunned.

The Mime rose from the dressing table and leaned into him, her tiny hands clenched.

She said, "Will—you—please—*shut*—up!"

She forcibly pushed the shocked Joker out the bedroom door and into the hall.

"But my dear," he said. "My love..."

The door slammed in his face.

The Joker, confused, shrugged pitifully to himself and spoke to the closed door.

"Was it something I said?" he asked.

Once again gloom descended upon the king of jests. He sat moping on his throne while his nervous stooges stood before him.

"She won't come out of her room, boss," Kennison said.

The Joker leaned forward and with utter sincerity asked, "Tell me, boys...and be brutally frank: do I *talk* too much?"

"Oh, *nooooo!*" Kennison said. "Are you kidding?"

"O-o-oh, no, *no*, boss!" Bobcat said.

Lying through their teeth.

The Sound of One Hand Clapping

"Perhaps," a thoughtful Joker posed, "I moved too quickly."

"Y-y-you gotta court her, boss," said the Bobcat. "G-g-get her a nice present or something."

The Joker snapped his fingers gleefully. "A present! Yes! What *better* way to express my esteem?"

"W-w-what are you going to get her, boss?" Bobcat asked.

The Joker smiled.

The sleek, black custom car glided along the Gotham City shoreline. Behind the wheel of the Batmobile was the Dark Knight himself, his face thoughtful behind the mask. Next to him, Robin wore a puzzled expression. If Batman looked foreboding in his dark attire, the Boy Wonder in yellow cape, with his red-breasted vest and emerald-green sleeves, gauntlets, and trunks, looked strangely festive.

"What do you suppose possessed the Joker to spring Camilla Cameo?"

"It's a mystery to me, Robin," Batman said, wheeling the machine into two parking spots in the lot of the Sprang Marina. "Their facial complexions may be similar, but their complexions as criminals couldn't be more dissimilar."

The night was cool and the moon reflected off the rippling water of Gotham Bay like the bat signal hugging in a dark sky. The pair jogged along a gravel path toward the docks. The police radio had said the Mime was sighted at the marina.

"You mean," Robin said, jogging, "the Joker breaks the law for fun and profit, while the Mime is a sort of social protester?"

"Yes," Batman said, "but it's also a clash of styles."

Max Allan Collins

Robin and Batman came to a stop on a buoyant walkway and looked out at a maze of similar boardwalks; the
vast moonlight-bathed marina was filled with pleasure
craft.

"The police call mentioned the Mime," Robin said,
"but not the Joker."

"Perhaps once the Joker got Camilla out of the authorities' hands," Batman said, surveying the scene, "they
went their separate ways."

"Or maybe somebody spotted a mime," Robin
suggested.

"A possibility," Batman admitted. "Lots of street performers around an area like..."

"Batman! Look..."

Running down one of the dock walkways, with boats
in the nearby background, was a slender figure.

The Mime.

"I'll handle this, Robin. Keep an eye out for the Joker
and his pals!"

With impossibly long strides, the Dark Knight streaked
down the gravel path to the boardwalk where the Mime
ran with easy grace.

"Camilla," he called, "stop!"

But this mime was not Camilla, though Batman did
not yet know as much. This mincing mime was male, his
back to his pursuer, hiding a grotesquely grinning face
under a wig that resembled Camilla Cameo's hairstyle.

"Stop!"

The Joker hopped onto the deck of a craft, a good-size
boat outfitted with sail and a motor. He nodded to Kennison and Bobcat, lurking in the shadows, holding on to a
rope that extended upward.

The deck appeared empty when Batman hopped
aboard. No sign of the Mime. The Dark Knight stood on
the deck of the ship and looked around.

The Sound of One Hand Clapping

But not down: beneath him, spread out on the deck, under his feet, was the heavy crosshatch of a fishing net.

"Camilla?" Batman said.

The Joker's two stooges yanked hard on their rope.

Batman, caught in the sack of a fishing net, was pulled bodily up off the ground.

Still in the Camilla-like wig, the Joker peeked up from a trapdoor in the deck to look gloatingly at the netted Batman.

Exasperated, Batman hung in the fishing net and suffered the Joker's taunts.

"Batman, Batman, Batman...you should've *known* there'd be a Joker in the deck!"

The Joker climbed out of his hole and leaned over, with mock sympathy, to smile at the upside-down Batman, the fierce scowl of his square jaw turned into a bizarre grin.

"You must be lonely," the Joker said, "hanging around the marina on a dark night like this."

"You only *think* you've caught me, Joker."

"My! What a good imagination I must have!" The Joker yanked off his wig and walked to the wheel of the craft, a faithful stooge at either side. "Well, boys, let's head for home. I think we've caught the limit!"

Robin, who had witnessed this from a distance while running along the boardwalk to intercede, found himself standing at the end of the dock, cape flapping, fists raised in midair, watching with infinite frustration as the boat headed out, an unjumpable distance away from him.

The Joker stood, hands clasped, bending forward, listening at Camilla's bedroom door.

"My dearest one," he said tenderly, tentatively, "I have a surprise for you...a gift...a very *special* gift."

Max Allan Collins

Within the bedroom, Camilla—the Mime—stood with her back to the door, captured by curiosity.

The Joker's voice from behind the door was supplicant. "And if it doesn't convince you that I'm your soulmate, if it doesn't touch you, move you...I'll gladly step out of your life—*forever.*"

Hesitant, Camilla exited the bedroom; the Joker bowed grandly to the supple figure in black and white face.

"Ah—accompany me, my love, if you would," he said, offering his arm. "And I must say you look *lovely.*"

The Mime pulled away, looking at him with suspicion and obvious dislike. The Joker ignored the reaction and gestured theatrically. He walked along and she followed, reluctantly.

"Now," he said, "consider that your run-of-the-mill suitor might have brought you chocolates—or perhaps said it with flowers."

In his main chamber, the Joker gestured with both hands as the Mime approached with puzzlement and even fear a huge package wrapped in colorful playing-card wrapping paper and a large red bow.

"Instead," the Joker said, "I've given you something much more...*personal.*"

The Mime stared at the package, which was much taller than she.

"Open it, precious..."

She began to tear off the wrapping paper, haltingly at first, but soon with the enthusiasm of a small child on Christmas morning. Curiosity made the eyes in the white face seem larger than life.

Shortly, her present was revealed; an unconscious Batman strapped to a chair, a big red ribbon and bow around him; a brightly painted Joker face could be seen carved

The Sound of One Hand Clapping

into the high back of the chair, rising above its slumbering occupant.

The Joker touched the shoulder of the shocked Mime, who viewed the unconscious, bound Batman without her usual expressiveness; her masklike face was blank.

"My gift of love," the Joker said, with a sweeping bow. "Our mutual nemesis!"

Camilla stood frozen.

The Joker placed a gentle gloved hand on her shoulder. "Shall I kill him for you, now, my sweet?"

She did not reply; ever so gently, he turned her to face him, gesturing grandly with one hand.

"You see, we really must decide quickly—he's a resourceful one."

Camilla touched her lips with one hand, confused, while the Joker walked to the desk before his joker-throne.

"We tranquilized the beast, my love...and we removed the porcupine's quills." The Joker displayed Batman's utility belt, lifting it from the desktop. "But even weaponless, he's troublesome—he won't remain groggy long."

Camilla stared at her present, which seemed to be coming around slowly.

"So, my precious...help me choose an artistic, a colorful means of demise for my love offering."

While the Joker gloated within his crumbling castle, Robin prowled the back streets of Gotham in the Batmobile, watching the dashboard computer screen on which a street map glowed and a dot blipped.

As long as they haven't tossed out Batman's utility belt, the youth thought, *I can track the signal.*

Within minutes Robin was stepping out of the Batmobile, facing the entrance of the tumbledown building
that had once housed the Jester Novelty Company.

Inside, the Joker held up a small gas canister with an oxygen mask attached; his two stooges smiled their approval.
Batman himself, fully awake now, wore a faint, wry smile.
The disturbed, frightened Mime wore an exaggerated
expression of dismay.

"Might I suggest, my sweetness," the Joker said, "a
lethal dose of my laughing gas?"

The Mime blinked.

"I think the Joker likes you, Camilla," Batman said.

The Joker, unable to contain his excitement, painted
the air with his hands, while Batman listened, unim-
pressed, smirking.

"Imagine it, my love—the bat boob is convulsed with
gales of laughter...laughing till his heart bursts—his face
frozen in a grotesque, eternal grin!"

At this the Mime recoiled.

But the Joker, caught up in himself, in his love for the
Mime and his hatred for Batman, failed to notice. He
approached the Mime, touching her shoulder tenderly.

"And all for you, my dear—for your *love*."

The Mime screamed silently, but the Joker did not hear,
or see, for that matter.

"For my...dare I say it...future *bride*."

The Mime slapped the Joker.

Hard.

The sound rang out like a rifle shot.

The Joker touched his face with splayed fingers and,
with the expression of a child who has suddenly had a

The Sound of One Hand Clapping

nagging question answered, said, "The sound of one hand clapping!"

The Mime sat on the floor, huddling, despair-ridden. The Joker hovered over her, trying to keep his distance at the same time. He was crushed, truly dumbfounded by her rejection. He did not notice, behind him, that Batman had struggled to his feet, despite being tied in the chair.

"I don't understand," the Joker said pleadingly. "I gave you a present! Why, I'd have shared it all with you—made you my queen!"

With those words the king of comedy was crowned, as Batman, still tied to the chair, bent forward forcefully and conked the clown with the upper portion of the high-backed throne, hitting the Joker hard on the top of his head with his own grinning image.

The Joker, stunned and sitting on the floor with his knobby knees pointing north and south, respectively, winced as Batman, bound in the chair but on his feet, sneered down at him.

"Oww!" the Joker said, rubbing his head.

"You're no king," Batman said. "Just the court fool."

The mad jester's nostrils flared and his eyes filled with rage as he pointed a long purple finger up at Batman.

"Get him!" the Joker cried.

But the Joker's two stooges were busy.

Robin had come up behind them, tapping them on the shoulder to ask, "Excuse me—shouldn't you get me first?"

For a moment, they looked stupidly, blankly back at him.

The Joker was on his feet again, fiercely commanding his boys, "Get the brat! I can handle that caped clod with—"

"Both hands tied behind my back," Batman sneered, just waiting for the Joker, chair or no chair. The Mime, standing once more, took all of this in, not quite sure what to make of it.

Robin ran down the hallway where the gallery of framed comedians hung off-kilter. He smiled, the two stooges in close pursuit.

"You guys are really wearing me out," he said over his shoulder.

Robin dropped to the floor, saying, "Mind if I stop for a rest?" while Kennison and Bobcat tried to put on the brakes. Both of them tripped over Robin and hit the floor hard, with twin WHUMPS! Robin, resting on his stomach, stifled a yawn.

Then the Boy Wonder stood over the pair of dopes, his arms folded, and said, "Gee—I guess you hoodlums are a little worn out yourselves. Take five, why don't you—years."

In the main chamber, the Joker stood before Batman, his purple fists pumping the air before him, ready to defend the honor of his ladylove.

Batman conked him with the chair again.

The Mime stifled a smile as the groggy Joker staggered, regrouping to try again. Purple fists pumping.

Only to be conked once more.

Knocked goofy, the Joker sat on the floor, counting the planets and stars that revolved before his vision.

And the Mime broke her silence with laughter worthy of the Joker himself: "HA! HA! HA! HA! HA! HA! HA!"

"I think she liked that," Robin smiled, as he untied Batman.

Tears streaked the white makeup off her face as she roared with glee, her laughter echoing through the old factory.

"Yes," Batman said, rubbing his arms where the ropes had been, "but I know something she *won't* like."

The Sound of One Hand Clapping

"What's that?"
"Her new home."

The next morning, within the sprawling, stern gothic structure of Arkham Asylum, a guard escorted a wide-eyed, shell-shocked Camilla Cameo—once again stripped of her mime's makeup—down the asylum hall. Walking along beside her was a frequent resident of the facility, a man whose whiteface could not be washed off.

"You'll like it here," the Joker was assuring her. "I'll put in a good word for you with my *therapist*, you'll make friends...there's plenty to do..."

Camilla said nothing.

But she wore a big, wide smile, not unlike the Joker's.

Only Camilla's seemed rather glazed.

Belly Laugh
or
The Joker's Trick or Treat

JOE R. LANSDALE

BATMAN'S JOURNAL

(Entry, October 28th)

Sometimes I start to believe my good press.

In my mind, late at night, before sleep claims me, I actually think of myself as the Caped Crusader, the Dark Knight, and all those ridiculous names the tabloids give me. I am fast and sure and perfect. The world's greatest acrobat, the world's greatest detective. There's nothing I can't do.

Then I awake and the world sets me straight. Creeps like the Joker step out of the light and into the shadows.

The Joker escaped from Arkham Asylum two weeks ago, and I've been looking for him without success. Waiting for him to strike. Dreading whatever craziness he might have planned this time out.

And last night it happened.

Judge Hadley's dead.

I wasn't there when Hadley died, but Jim told me what

he saw, and I can imagine how it must have been for the Judge last night. He's walking along, feeling all right, fresh from a quick dip in the pool, then he becomes aware of the trouble as his feet turn to goo in his shoes. He falls down and flops, his ribs poke through his skin, turn to paste, and flow away. His heart and lungs push through his chest, throb inside his robe, go to mush. His brain oozes out of his ears like oily oatmeal, then there are no ears and no skull, just a blob of white and gray.

The mess pops and gurgles momentarily, makes the robe in the midst of the puddle pulse as if full of rats. Then all movement ceases. The moonlight catches the goo and a little moon-made rainbow rises above it. A white-gloved hand reaches out and drops a party hat into the mess. Painted on the hat is the green-haired, red-lipped, white-skinned face of the Joker.

And the Joker laughs.

Spare me a vivid imagination.

Here's how I found out. It was yesterday, just after noon. Gordon's office.

Jim got word to me, and I went over there, sat in a chair with a loose spring, and looked at him. It was a bad view. His clothes were rumpled, his face unshaven. The corners of his mouth drooped like crumbling masonry. His hands clutched the arms of his chair as if he were strangling small throats. There was a drop of sweat dangling from the end of his nose. His forehead was wet. The room wasn't hot.

I didn't feel so good myself. Felt small and worn and ancient inside my cape and cowl. Even a little foolish. It had been that kind of year. My last case, the mess with Subway Jack, had taken a lot out of me. And now Gordon had something to say to me, and I knew what it was before he said it.

"The Joker."

Gordon got a tape recorder out of his desk drawer, took a tape from the plastic evidence bag, slipped it into the machine, said, "Listen."

(click)

Well, pilgrim, that old wind is howlin' around the asylum, and the rain is hittin' the nuthouse walls like whips. Lightnin's popping outside the windows like six guns, but it isn't botherin' me, nosirree. Day I get bothered, well, that'll be the day, pilgrim.

I'm sittin' here lookin' just the way Batman made me. White-faced, green-haired and red-lipped. No Stetson. No pony. Sittin' here in the hoosegow, right where Batman put me. And I been looking at the rain and lightnin' through barred windows. And I'll tell you, Mr., I'm tired of it. And know what, darned if I don't get me a plan to break out of this here hoosegow, like in the cowboy pictures.

Gonna break out and ride away.

Hear me, Sheriff Batman?

Pretty soon there's gonna be a showdown at high noon, and you and me and are gonna slap leather, and when the smoke clears, you and your bat ears are gonna be laying in the middle of the big trail like so much dust.

Okay, that's all for the John Wayne impersonation. I also do a mean Humphrey Bogart and the best Sidney Poitier in the world, outside of Sid himself.

Belly Laugh or The Joker's Trick or Treat

But now, I'm going to talk like the Joker. And pardners, the Joker's wild.

Wild as Dorothy's tornado. Madder than a liberal democrat with a budget cut.

And guess what, Bats? By the time you hear this, I won't be in Arkham Asylum anymore. In point of fact, I'm not there now. There's no wind and rain and lightning outside my window. That's just a bad memory, but one I wanted to share with you.

What I'm saying here, Cowl Head, is all the world's a stage and Heavens to Mergatroit, I've gone stage left on the Asylum. I'm in a new suit under a new spotlight. Crime's spotlight.

(long pause)

I'm calmer now. Shall we talk?

Good. Let us call this Joker Notes. Let us call this the first serial installment. Let us call it a brief history of my parentage. Let us call it a game. Let us call it entertainment and a clue.

(pause)

My. We're calling it lots of things, aren't we?

Okay. Here goes.

I was born in a small vat of chemicals. My mother and father was Batman. He's strict.

I'd like to talk about him. I'll keep it short and sour.

I hope to kill the sonofabitch.

But there are others that come first. I'm starting at the bottom of my hate list and working to the top. If you were a movie, Batman, you'd be five stars. And I'll save the best fun for last.

And Gordon, I give you four stars—make you fourth on the list. Don't be disappointed you didn't get top billing. You're an ache in my heart, but Batman, he's a pain in my soul.

Joe R. Lansdale

Right now I dream of Judge Hadley. You remember Hadley, don't you? He's the one said I was mad that last time and that I should never be released from Arkham Asylum, no matter what. He called me homicidal. Wrecked. Ruined. He made fun of my wardrobe. He's one on a list of five, and I think I've made it clear where you two are on that list. But for now, let me say I'm drawing a line through Hadley, and I'll add this:

Check his house, out by the nice, heated pool. And don't get him on your shoes.

(maniacal laughter and a series of coughs)

Excuse me. Almost choked.

Now I'll find a couch and lie down. Relax. Analyze my life. Next time, I'll shoot the works.

(click)

"The tape came in about three hours ago," Jim said. "No one knows how it was delivered, or who delivered it, but it was found at the front desk. We've theorized someone dressed as a cop brought it in during a shift change. The Joker or one of his thugs, probably.

"When I heard the tape, I got some blue coats and we went out to Hadley's, and it was quite a mess. It looked like an army had puked out there by the pool. All that was left besides the goop was his robe, swimming trunks, and house shoes. You see, Hadley always took a late-night swim before bed. Told me he started doing it when his wife died, because after that, he couldn't sleep unless he was worn out. Why, he has a heated pool, so he can do it year round."

"It's the sort of thing the Joker would know," I said. "Leave it to him to have all the right bad connections."

"Yeah," Jim said. "He's probably had a better crime

business and information center going from the asylum than some crooks got on the street. He's got enough money stashed away to pay for the contacts and to get things done. Anyway, one of the boys spotted something in the bottom of the pool, a gold coin about the size of a half dollar. We fished it out with a pole and a scoop. It had the Joker's face on it. Lab boys say it has pin-size holes in it, and when it hit the water, it released a colorless, odorless chemical that mixed with the water and turned it into an acid. It won't do a thing to cloth, plastic, metal, any of that. Just works on flesh and bones. It's major bad business. Stuff in that coin—and it was just a few drops— could have dissolved a killer whale and had enough left over to mush-out an aquarium full of fat guppies. That's it. You've got the low down and you've heard the tapes. Any thoughts?"

"Just one," I said. "Wish that tape had been three minutes of music."

Fifteen minutes later, I'm in the so-called Batmobile, roaring along past fine downtown skyscrapers with copper-colored glass reflecting sunlight bright as a promise from God; buildings with show windows full of orange and black crepe paper and ceramic pumpkins and holiday floral arrangements and mannequins decked out in masks and costumes that make them witches, Casper the Ghost, the Werewolf, the Frankenstein Monster, Dracula . . . or, Batman; darting through thick traffic, past gooseneck pedestrians trying to catch a view of me, as if they thought by will alone their eyes could cut through the smoke-colored windshield of the Batmobile and the sight of me were truly worth something.

Then I'm roaring out, into the older sections of Gotham

where trash blows across the streets like urban tumble-weeds and sad eyes look out of dirt-colored apartment doorways and dust-filmed windows; apartments whose tenants are not only people, but cat-sized rats and thumb-sized roaches and enough despair to put on pants and take a fast walk; sections where in one sense it is Halloween everyday, minus the festive.

I drive down streets I have no need to travel. Drive down them because they put me in touch with what I do and who I am; drive past the wreck of the once majestic Gotham Theater, formerly at the center of downtown, now part of the urban dead, and I turn my head to look . . . and review my past in an instant, as if it is all inside my head on a very short reel of black-and-white film.

My mental projector rolls and the film is fast and silent with dialogue cards. There is a SERIES OF SHOTS where I, Bruce Wayne, am young again, and inside the Gotham Theater with my parents, sitting in a middle row between them, sharing a bag of popcorn, watching the rereleased classic, *The Mark of Zorro.*

Scene OVERLAPS AND DISSOLVES to me and my parents taking a shortcut home, foolishly walking down the alley out back of the theater.

There is one streetlight in the alley. Its light is dirty amber and is currently the only true color introduced into this otherwise black-and-white scenario.

OVERHEAD VIEW. The three Waynes look like ants crawling through filthy maple syrup.

CAMERA SWOOPS DOWN, goes CLOSE on a MAN coming out of the shadows. He's carrying a revolver, wearing a slouch hat, oversized coat, and too-long pants. He walks like a man with a monkey on his back.

He points his revolver at the three of us, opens his

mouth, and a DIALOGUE CARD fills the screen. It reads: GIVE ME YOUR GOODS OR I'LL SHOOT.

Card goes away. My dad steps protectively in front of my mom. Man panics, FIRES. (Gun Burst is BRIGHT ORANGE.) Dad goes down.

Man FIRES again. (Another burst of ORANGE.) Mom's pearls take the shot before her throat does. The necklace snaps. The pearls pop away, hit the alley, and bounce in all directions.

Mom falls.

CAMERA FOLLOWS as Man flees into the darkness and the darkness closes like a mouth and we DISSOLVE TO CLOSE UP of me on my knees between my dead parents, my fists bunched into little white knots, my face lifted to the streetlight as if it is some god I can appeal to.

The COLOR of the streetlight becomes more distinct, more GOLDEN. It highlights the tears on my cheeks, makes them look like cold, wet gems.

Hold a beat.

Streetlight DIMS gradually, and—

—FADE TO BAT-WING BLACK

My mental projector clicks off and the reel automatically resets for another time, and I'm alone in my skull with gray space aplenty. I turn my head back to the street and drive on between worn-out, soulless buildings as if they are ancient mountain ranges and the car is a dark cloud full of thunder, rain, and lightning, going get-up-and-get-it toward the graying horizon of a bad October day. And inside that cloud is me, a single drop of captured rain, on a course I can't control, ready to spill at nature's decree.

(Entry, October 29th)

Today, I come to you to write that I'm a failure and a fool.

Here's the news, straight from the October twenty-

Joe R. Lansdale

seventh edition of the *Gotham Gazette*. I'll paste it on the page.

FAMED PSYCHIATRIST AND
POODLE DISSOLVED

Marilyn Chute, famed doctor of psychiatry, noted for her work with such infamous psychopaths as the Joker, was victim to a bizarre and unexplained murder yesterday morning. She was found partially dissolved along with her poodle, FiFi.

The body was discovered at approximately ten o'clock by her day maid, Tuppence Calhoun. Mrs. Calhoun said she let herself in with her key, and when she didn't see Dr. Chute, assumed she had gone shopping or out to answer a call from her office.

In preparing to clean the tub, Mrs. Calhoun discovered the shower was on and that the tub was full of a gelatinous mess containing a rhinestone dog collar, a shower cap, a mass of blond hair, white fur, pink dog toenails, and a purple party hat with a clown's face on it. Mrs. Calhoun is recorded as saying, "It was a damn silly way to die, wasn't it? Whatever happened to stabbing and shooting people?"

Police have refused to release details of this peculiar case, but Police Commissioner Gordon is calling Dr. Chute's death murder, and the Joker, who recently escaped from Arkham Asylum, is suspected. He was under the psychiatric care of Dr. Chute.

Critics of Commissioner Gordon and Batman, claim Dr. Chute was an obvious target, but was overlooked by both the police and Batman, who many criminologists claim, has been much overrated as a detective.

Dr. Chute is survived by a sister, Carolyn Holt of New Jersey, and a brother . . .

Belly Laugh or The Joker's Trick or Treat

The Joker told me what he was going to do, and who he was going to do it to, and I failed to see it. Now Dr. Chute is dead and something of a joke, even to her housekeeper, and, of course, that is the Joker's way.

He once said he got a belly laugh out of his crimes, and especially out of baffling me, and that's why he did them, and I'm sure his belly is rolling now.

He said he was going to get even with five people, and though there are literally hundreds of people the Joker might hold responsible for real or imagined ills, I should have considered his psychiatrist to be tops on his list. But I was too close to the matter. I was looking for people who had actually done something to him. Jim and I put him behind bars, Judge Hadley convicted him. Seemed logical that he would next go after the prosecutor. Possibly the cops who took him to the asylum. Attendants at the asylum. And thinking that, Jim and I decided to put twenty-four-hour surveillance on those people, others like them. The obvious choices.

But the doctor who was trying to cure him? The one person who thought there was a seed of humanity in him somewhere? The one who thought he could be rehabilitated? It isn't logical he would want to do her harm.

But the logic of a madman is a sane man's confusion.

I should have suspected. No, I should have known.

He said next time "I'll shoot the works." And it was a clue. Shoot for Chute, and by the works, he meant his chemicals. And he said he was going to lie down on a couch—as in a psychiatrist's couch—and he said he was going to analyze his life, as in analysis. . . . It was all there.

He must have known she showered with her poodle. She probably told him during one of their sessions. Some-

Joe R. Lansdale

thing to humanize herself and make the Joker comfortable, draw out his humanity.

But the Joker has no humanity. He filed it away. Found out where she lived, put the coin in the showerhead when she was out, or had it put there, and when she turned on the water for her morning shower, it activated the chemical, and . . .

The Joker merely had to wait and read about it in the papers.

When he said the tape was a clue, he didn't mean for Hadley, since he spelled that out. He meant it was a clue who his next victim was going to be, and I missed it. I thought it was merely chatter. A general warning that four others would die.

Now I have to ask myself the question: Who's next?

(Entry late October 29th)

Earlier tonight the Bat Signal struck bright against the night sky; a gold and black invitation to go downtown.

Alfred brought in my costume and I dressed and drove over to Jim's office.

When we were alone, I said, "Putting in a twenty-four-hour day, Jim?"

"Twenty-eight," he said. "The tape arrived an hour ago. They called me down to hear it. Thought you might like to hear it, too. Besides, if I can't get any rest, I want someone else to suffer with me."

"No rest for the wicked, and the good don't need any," I said.

(click)

Sung by the Joker: I'm an ole cowhand, from the Rio Grande . . .

Belly Laugh or The Joker's Trick or Treat

Enough music culture. Let's talk. Ah, here we are again with yet another clue. I suppose that now, after the fact, of course, you have figured out the clues in the last tape. Shoot, Batman, you should have got that. I really thought this would be tougher.

Now, here's my report, and I'm your reporter. If you can find where I'm holding court with a handful of stooges, then come and get me. In the meantime, I have to eat my lunch. Quite good actually, legumes and rice.

But, hey, you guys didn't turn this tape on to hear me discuss my lunch, now did you? You want to know who's next? Well, I've told you. Complicated, I assure you, but seems to me a smart detective like yourself, Batman, and you, Commissioner Gordon, his erstwhile companion, should be able to tap it all out. If you do decipher my little code, it best be before tomorrow, fiveish. If you don't have it by then. Too late!

Hey, my food's getting cold. I'm outta here.

(click)

(Entry, October 30th)

I listened to the two tapes repeatedly, came up with nothing. The minutes were ticking away for some poor soul and I had no idea who.

I took out the list Jim and I had made of possible victims. Jim had arranged for everyone on it to be given police protection, but we couldn't be sure the Joker's next victim was on the list. And even if we hit on who he planned to kill, it didn't mean police protection would help. The Joker is wily.

"Your lunch, sir."

I looked up. It was Alfred carrying a covered silver tray. "I didn't hear you come in."

Joe R. Lansdale

"No, sir, you were quite involved. . . . Excuse me, perhaps it's not my place, but don't you feel just the wee bit silly sitting here wearing your . . . Batsuit?"

"You wear a butler's uniform."

"It doesn't have a cape and ears, sir. This bat stuff, it's a little ridiculous, don't you think?"

"Truthfully, yes. But, it's my job to wear this suit. I'm a crime fighter. I don't want my identity known."

"I quite understand that, sir. Criminals are a cowardly lot and all that. A disguise to strike fear into their hearts, etc., etc. But, sir, around the house, here in the cave? It's like when you were a youngster and wouldn't take off your Zorro outfit. You slept in it. And then that dog you made wear a mask. I have to say, Master Bruce, this outfit stuff, it makes me nervous. A grown man and all. Wearing it out in the dark while beating up on people, that I can understand, but at home . . . quite disconcerting."

I pushed back my cowl. "Feel better?"

"Somewhat better, sir. I much prefer seeing your smiling face."

"Put the tray down, Alfred."

He set it on my desk, removed the lid. On the tray was a glass of milk and a sandwich.

"Jelly on this?" I asked.

"Of course, sir, isn't there always? I've made enough of those miserable peanut butter and jelly sandwiches to remember the jelly."

"Well, there was that one time . . ."

"I didn't feel well. I forgot. Please have me shot for that one failure. . . . Would you like me to eat it for you, sir? Not that I'm particularly fond of the mess, but you do seem a bit helpless at times."

"I can manage. Hey, this chitchat is great, Alfred, but I'm really kind of pressed here. We're talking about peanut butter and jelly sandwiches, and I'm trying to solve a riddle that could mean life or death. And I tell you, I haven't got the mind for it these days. What should be obvious isn't. I need a vacation in the worst way."

I began to eat. He had remembered the jelly.

"The Joker, sir?"

"Yes."

"What's this list?"

"It's too complicated to explain. . . . You wouldn't understand."

"Of course not, sir. . . . But what is it?"

"It's a list I've made from the two tapes the Joker sent me. Words from them that struck me as possible code words. That sort of thing. I'm trying to deduce from it who his next victim will be."

"Of course, sir. Might I see it?"

"If it will make you happy, Alfred. I'm going to eat."

Alfred looked at the list.

"I can't tell a thing from this."

"Didn't I tell you?"

"It's your penmanship, sir. Very messy. Might I listen to the tapes?"

I set up the tapes, turned them on, sipped the milk. Alfred picked up a pen, wrote in the margins of my list.

"Don't mess that up, Alfred."

"Hush, Master Bruce. I'm trying to listen."

When the tapes ran their course, I said, "Happy?"

"Well, sir, I don't have the mind for these things. Not like you. But seems to me the use of legumes is a bit out of place. Rather formal. Isn't that a bean or pea?"

"Yes, it is, Alfred. You're up on your agriculture. You'll note I've dissected the word and tried to spell numerous words with it, without success. Nothing that strikes a chord, anyway."

"Of course, sir, I'm quite sure you're the expert here. But isn't this Joker one to take offense at odd things? My understanding of him, sir, is that he doesn't have both his oars in the water. Correct?"

"Correct."

"He makes a point of saying he's giving you a report, says he's your reporter. He talks about holding court. About you and Commissioner Gordon tapping it all out, and that's what a court reporter does, taps keys. So, it seems to me he's talking about the court reporter. Perhaps he dislikes the idea of his madness being recorded. The Judge sent him up, as you like to say, and his psychiatrist stated in court he was mad, in much nicer and more conservative terms, of course, and the reporter made a record of that to be permanently placed on file. If we knew the court reporter's name . . . ?"

I put down my sandwich, punched up the trial transcripts and the court reporter's name.

"Bean," I said. "Jack Bean."

"Your legume, Master Bruce?"

I was uncertain if I should be happy or embarrassed. It wasn't the first time he'd done that to me. "Alfred, would you like to wear this suit and let me wear yours?"

"What? And look as ridiculous as you? I think not, sir."

I pulled on my cowl and got out of there.

So I went to stop a murder, tried to find Jack Bean. I told Jim my suspicions (though I felt guilty that I couldn't mention Alfred gave them to me), and he got the police in on it, of course.

Zip.

No Jack Bean. He wasn't doing any court reporting that

afternoon. The trial he was working had been closed for the day. Lawyer recesses, something like that.

We had officers combing all over for Bean. Had people calling around. He didn't answer the phone at his apartment, so we went over there, afraid of what we might find. Me and Jim in the Batmobile, followed by a pack of uniforms and detectives. That wasn't my idea or Jim's, but the city council has been big on police involvement in my cases lately. They want to be sure their officers are on the scene of anything big that goes down. So I had to play mama duck, let all the little ducks follow.

Jim showed the building superintendent his search warrant, and he opened up Bean's apartment. We went in and looked around.

No Bean, dissolved or otherwise.

I went next door and talked to a neighbor. A Mr. Monteleone. He was old and gray and wore knee-length shorts that revealed calves with varicose veins like hoses. He said he had lived in the apartment long enough to know Bean, and, "We have a drink together now and then, because you got to drink with someone so you don't drink with just yourself, know what I mean?"

He said he was confident enough about Bean's schedule to say he'd be in at four o'clock. He was always in at four o'clock.

"Think the Bean drinks a little too much," he said. "Know what I'm saying? They mostly give him the little stuff these days. Traffic violation trials, that kind of thing. See, the Bean does everything around the drinking. Likes to get home at four so he can have a little snort before the TV dinner is ready, then he watches the news and throws another one down his neck. After that, he watches some of the sitcoms, ones with the young girls on them, know what I'm saying here? Drinks while he watches. Whole

Joe R. Lansdale

bottle of Scotch, nightly. I been over there some. Had a few snorts myself. He don't hardly go out after he gets home. Lonely kind of guy. Know what I'm saying?''

I thanked him and he asked me if my cape got caught on stuff when I was running and jumping, and I said, "Sometimes."

I went back to Bean's apartment and Jim got all the cops to stand out of the way, and I started going through the place. The cops had already done that, but they hadn't found much. I didn't either. Some empty Scotch bottles in the kitchen trash. A few girlie magazines under his mattress. A nightstand with an alarm clock, a computer dating magazine, and coffee cup rings.

The bathroom was a nightmare. Greasy mirror, stained toilet. Tub with a crust instead of a ring, and a drain strainer full of lint and scum. If the Joker didn't get him, whatever was growing in that strainer might.

I kept looking.

Four o'clock, Bean came through the door.

He was short and stout with a few tufts of brown hair on the sides of his head. His dome was slick as the bottom of a china bowl. His nose was drinker's ruin.

To say that he was a little surprised to find us there, puts it mildly. He almost dropped the sack of groceries he was carrying.

We explained he was on the Joker's hit list, and that his apartment was being searched in case the Joker had rigged it with his dissolving chemical.

When he heard that, he went limp, sat down in a soft living room chair, and stayed there. His face oozed sweat. His blue shirt got so wet with it, it looked black. His eyes bulged. He leaned forward, looked like a toad ready to flex his legs and spring to the center of the room. He chattered like a squirrel: "You got something yet? Why me, huh? I got nothing personal against this Joker fella. I'm a court reporter, not a judge. I write down what's said by everybody. You check in the light fixture there? Might have hid something in the light? If I was going to hide something, I might put it there. What about it, huh?"

Jim leaned against the wall with his arms crossed. He looked at me, said, "Well? Find anything in the light fixture?"

"One more look about," I said, and I started with the bedroom again. As I searched, I took a nervous glance at the alarm clock on Bean's dresser, watched as the time crawled toward five.

We could get him out of the apartment, but I wasn't sure that would help. The Joker might expect that. He could be waiting somewhere with a high-powered rifle loaded with a pellet full of the chemical. Then again, he might not know we'd figured out who the next victim was. No matter how you went, with the Joker it was a crapshoot.

I checked the clock again. . . . Then it hit me.

The clock. Bean was the kind of guy whose schedule would be easy to learn. You could time him like the sunrise.

The Joker had made us aware of the time. The clock was in plain sight. . . . It added up.

I went over and picked up the alarm clock and pulled the miniature tools out of my utility belt and worked the back off.

There was a small explosive device attached to one of the Joker's coins and that was attached to the alarm. Pretty simple. I easily disarmed it. The alarm had been set to go off at five. It was now 4:45.

But what about the water? There had to be water to

Joe R. Lansdale

mix with the chemical. It had to be planned in such a way that Bean would get both the chemical and the water.

I went back to the bathroom. Looked in the tub, under the sink, in the commode. I lifted the back off the commode, looked in there. Attached to the float was a plastic explosive and a miniature clock. It was set to go off at five. It was a small amount, but it was powerful stuff. If it blew, the entire wall would come out, on both sides, and the water pipes would shatter and the apartment would be flooded with water. The water would mix with the chemical.

Bean would get wet, then dissolved.

I disarmed the explosive.

I called Jim in and showed him what I'd found. "It's harmless now," I said, "long as we treat the explosive with a little respect."

"It's got my respect," Jim said. "I'd give it a wedding vow if it wanted it."

Jim and I shook hands.

Five o'clock came and went.

Then the phone rang.

"Do I answer that, or what?" Bean called to us.

We walked into the living room. The phone rang again. Jim said, "Yeah, go on. You're in the clear. We found what we were looking for."

The phone rang a third time.

Bean let out a sigh. "Thank God. Hey, I owe you guys, big time. I was afraid things were all over for me, you know?"

The phone rang a fourth time.

He answered it and a stream of water sprayed out of the receiver and hit him full in the face, making his flesh steam like fresh dog dung on a cold morning.

Bean screamed and went down.

Belly Laugh or The Joker's Trick or Treat

Jim dove for him, but I grabbed him, pulled him back, yelled for the cops to stay away.

Bean's head wobbled like a fat lady's thigh, spread wide, went soft. His ears eased down his face as if they were flags being slowly lowered. He collapsed to the floor, squirmed. His head went from soft to liquidy. His eyes floated on the mess like grapes on vomit. His teeth sank into it like seeds. His head flowed slowly under the couch. The rest of his body was solid. It flopped once, went still.

The Joker's chemical, of course. The coin in the clock, the explosive in the commode. I was supposed to find those. The Joker had replaced the phone with one of his own. A coin in the receiver. Water pressurized inside. When Bean answered, all the Joker had to do was activate the device electronically, and Bean got a faceful of the chemical.

There was nothing we could do. It was over in instants. We stood there like idiots. A roomful of cops and the great Batman, the Fool Detective.

Then there was a snap and the base of the phone exploded sharply and something popped to the ceiling and drifted down.

A purple party hat with the Joker's face on it, floating to the floor with the help of a green paper parachute. It came to rest near the goop that was Bean.

Jim slammed his fists against his legs. "I thought we had him beat this time. It was after five."

"He said fiveish, and it's fiveish."

"I think we both need a long rest," Jim said. "Maybe retirement."

I didn't argue with that. There was something else to consider now. Jim and I were next.

I could almost hear the Joker laugh.

Joe R. Lansdale

(Entry, October 31st, Halloween Night)

I had to stop the Joker before it was Jim's turn. Since we knew he was four, there might not be a tape, and though he had good men, I didn't believe they could protect him.

And for the moment, neither could I. I was too exhausted. So much, in fact, that if anything were to happen, I would have been useless. My muscles trembled. Spots swam before my eyes. The contents of the Joker's tapes reeled through my brain and blended into mental white noise.

It was better that I chance some rest, then refreshed, go and stay by Jim's side. And once I made that decision, laid myself down, my mind let go.

First I thought of the Joker; thought of when he was part of the Red Hood Gang and I had accidently caused him to fall over a railing and into a vat of toxic waste that transformed him physically into what he was today.

Had it been an accident? Or had part of me wanted to do him in even then, before I knew what he was capable of? Do we sometimes sense our greatest adversaries? Taste the bitterness of past life experiences? Or is it something else? Something even more primitive, like a sense of smell that tells us that here is a predator. Beware!

All I know is that, in a sense, I had created him and was indirectly responsible for every murder he ever committed. Perhaps, without my interference, he would have become nothing more than a petty thief.

But I was too tired for guilt. I began to sink down, down, away from it all, and . . .

The dream is technicolor and I'm wearing my 3-D glasses and holding my Scratch and Sniff card. I am the camera eye and the CAMERA goes CLOSE ON the JOKER sitting in a huge chair as if it is a throne. The chair is upholstered in regal purple and there is a series of great, green gems screwed into the top of the chair's backrest. They glow as if filled with phosphorescent puss.

He's wearing a green, ruffled shirt trimmed in bright yellow, a deep-purple dress coat and pants, highly polished green shoes with purple laces, and socks with purple and green clocks on them.

He looks as he always looks. Skin white as flour, hair heaped high, the texture of seaweed, the color of fresh lettuce. His lips are blood-red and he's smiling, as he is always smiling: a wide, ugly smile showing plenty of nice, white teeth.

He laughs suddenly. Wildly. Quits.

He's a happy kind of guy.

Behind him, a heap of corpses percolate with rats and maggots and decay. I recognize many of the bodies as his victims.

One of them appears to be a huge bat.

The Joker JERKS FORWARD SUDDENLY, and the 3-D glasses make it seem as if he's coming out of the screen. He merely pokes his head into my space and says softly, "Boo."

SLOWLY, he resumes his restful position, continues to smile.

FLASHING LOGO at the bottom of the screen says for viewer to SCRATCH CARD. I do. I sniff, and am overwhelmed with nausea. The card lets forth ODORS of DEATH and ROT and CORRUPTION.

CLOSE ON THE JOKER. CAMERA FILLS with his smile.

HOLD THAT FRAME

(beat)

Joe R. Lansdale

Edges of frame start a SLOW BLEED of BRIGHT RED
BLOOD, and gradually it flows toward the center of the
dream screen until the screen is FILLED and the dream
darkens and—

FADE TO THE DEEP DARK PURPLE OF THE JOK-
ER'S COAT.

I awoke knowing I had discerned a truth, even if I was
unclear what that truth was. Exhaustion had allowed me
to rest for an hour, and I felt better. An hour's sleep to me
is like eight for some.

I sat on the edge of the bed and put my head between
my hands and went over everything I could remember
about the dream. It had been presented as a film, and I felt
that that presentation was my subconscious trying to tell
me something. Trying to alert me that I had been looking
around the answer to all this, instead of right at it.

I pulled on my robe and went down to the Batcave and
played his tapes again. They were riddled with film and
stage references. I had noticed them immediately upon
hearing the tapes, but deduced they were there for the
purpose of surrounding the nonfilm references so that
they would stand out and provide clues. For those of us
(Alfred) who had the savvy to perceive clues, that is.

I was thinking of waking Alfred up, putting him on the
case, when I decided to run it all through my head again:
the John Wayne routine, the cowboy movie talk about six-
guns and hoosegows and ponies and Stetsons and jail
breaks. Titles like *High Noon* and the *Big Trail* slipped in.
Humphrey Bogart, Sidney Poitier, Dorothy's tornado, "All
the world's a stage," a handful of stooges, four and five
star ratings, serial installment, spotlight, call it entertainment, a cowboy song . . .

Belly Laugh or The Joker's Trick or Treat

"Heaven's to Mergatroit," as that cartoon mountain lion Snagglepuss says, it hit me.

Obvious.

My subconscious had known the answer from the very first tape, but it had somehow been hidden behind a wall of hate for the Joker. I was trying too hard. I knew now why I had seen my last moments as a child in the form of a film when I drove by the Gotham Theater. The hind brain was trying to tell me something. It was giving me yet another film reference, telling me that all these things the Joker mentioned had one thing in common (and the second tape should have made this even clearer). A place where once upon a time they were all represented.

A place that had played revival films like *Birth of A Nation* and *Gone with the Wind*. Cowboy movies had shown there by the hundreds and cowboy stars had visited the stage and popped blanks into the air and twirled ropes. Some like Rex Allen, Gene Autry, and Roy Rogers had sung songs. Horses had even been on that stage. The screen had shown the Three Stooges, cartoons, and feature movies. Even *The Mark of Zorro*.

A strange and horrible warmness came over me.

I knew where the Joker was hiding.

Outside the Gotham Theater a shadow stepped out of the darkness, and the shadow was me. The October wind rose up as if surprised and blew a clutch of papers and leaves down the street. A soft-drink can rolled and clattered.

I soaked up the night and remembered when the theater was still brightly painted and brightly lit and there were gaudy posters behind the poster glass; posters like *The Mark of Zorro* with a man in black wearing a mask, cutting down the bad guys with a long, sharp sword. I

Joe R. Lansdale

remembered my dad's hand on my shoulder, my mom's hand holding mine. I remembered Zorro. I remembered gunshots that echoed in the alley out back.

I eased up to the door and tried it. It wasn't locked. I opened it and went in.

The lobby was surprisingly clean and there was a dim light and a mannequin in a clown suit standing behind the concession counter. The clown's hand was outstretched. It held a playing card. Above and behind the clown on the wall was a long orange banner with TRICK OR TREAT, BATMAN written in black.

Cautiously, I went over and took the card and turned it over.

It was a Joker. Written in the margins was: Happy Halloween. You are expected. Compliments of the Joker.

I went straight for the doors that led into the theater proper, pushed them open boldly, walked on in.

It was dark in there except for the light of the projector shining on the screen, showing it to be yellow and stained from age, tossed food, and drinks. The huge stage where performers and stars had strutted their stuff had gone gray. The crimson curtains on either side of it had turned the color of rust. There were shadows at the ends of the aisles and they hung like black crepe paper and wove their way between the rows and rows of seats. Due to water damage, the ceiling drooped like an old woman's bosom and cobwebs dangled from it like rotting gauze. The aisle carpets, once red, were blackened in the centers by years and years of spilled soft drinks and tracking feet. The blackness fled to the edges in little dark forks that looked like a sewage leak. The smell of mildew, rot, rat dung, and history hung in the air.

A film flickered to life on the screen. A section from *The Man Who Laughs*.

Belly Laugh or The Joker's Trick or Treat

I sensed movement, glanced over my shoulder at the sagging balcony. A skeleton was gliding down from it, catercorner, floating through the darkness toward me, squeaking as it came.

It was the sort of gimmick William Castle might have used to sell *House on Haunted Hill*. But this gimmick was holding revolvers and the revolvers were lifted and even as they spat fire, I dove between a row of seats.

The skeleton continued to squeak down the wire, snapping off gunfire. Slugs slammed into the aisle carpet, followed me, smacked the backs and seat cushions of the chairs. One bullet tore through the heel of my boot, clean as a hot needle through a blister; I could feel the heat through the sole, but it didn't touch me.

I sprang up from between the seats, put a boot on the armrest of a chair to get leverage, and leaped back toward the wire that held Two-Gun Bones.

As he touched the carpet, I grabbed the supporting wire with my gloves and used it to swing myself around and whip both legs into his face. He took it with a grunt and a discharge of teeth, dropped the revolvers and went loose.

It was, of course, one of the Joker's goons dressed in a hood and black outfit with a glowing skeleton painted on it. The wire and the harness he was wearing continued to support him, even though he was unconscious.

I kicked the revolvers into the dark between the seats, turned back to the screen.

The film had changed. Excerpts from the 1930 *The Bat Whispers* stuttered across the screen. I guess the film segments were the Joker's way of showing how he envisioned himself (*The Man Who Laughs*) and how he envisioned me (*The Bat Whispers*). Maybe he saw life as a movie. That might be an easier way to take it. As some-

Joe R. Lansdale

thing without real substance. Flickering light and sound, nothing more.

The wall to my right was rigged. A portion flopped open and two men rushed out. They were wearing masks, ghoulish glow-in-the-dark things. When I was a kid some of the movies had ushers dressed like that as a gimmick. When you're eleven or twelve, it's pretty spooky.

These days I was the one who played dressed up, and I was a lot spookier.

I moved, fast, incredibly fast. No brag, just fact, and met them halfway.

They were quicker and better than the Joker's usual muscle. For all his intelligence and stashed, stolen money, he has a hard time recruiting the right guys. No one wants to work for a homicidal clown.

But these two . . . better than normal.

But not that much better.

I slid to the left as the closest one threw a short, snappy punch at my head, and the punch slid over my right shoulder and I slammed him with a forearm in the solar plexus so hard, blood spurted through the mouth slit in his mask.

I kicked him in the face with the top of my foot, changed the looks of his nose. He went down.

Two seconds gone. Maybe three.

The other guy saw this, of course, and even though he had an automatic, he didn't look too confident.

Which was smart.

I dropped low and used my hands to support myself, twisted around and swung my legs at his knees and knocked his feet out from under him. His gun popped once and off-aim, then I was on top of him. I snatched the automatic from him as easy as taking a rattle from a baby,

Belly Laugh or The Joker's Trick or Treat

tossed it away, popped two sharp punches into his face, and he took a siesta.

I estimate it took about five seconds for all that. I must be getting old.

On the movie screen was the Joker. He was sitting in a replica of the time-traveling device from the movie *The Time Machine*. It was little more than a Victorian chair with a wheel at the back, decorated with colored lights. The wheel was spinning, the lights were blinking. In front of him was a control panel and a lever. He was wearing a purple suit and a shirt of canary yellow with a scarlet scarf tied loosely in a bow around his neck. His smile was wide and white.

His voice came through the speakers cold and high and crazy:

"You were a bit slow this time, Bat Sap. Getting too old to cut the mustard? I assumed you'd work out my little riddles eventually and I've been ready for you all along. Kept a constant welcoming committee on alert, and laid my little plans. I had hoped to go through my victims in order, however. Gordon will have to be number five. It's bothersome. But hey, I'm a flexible kind of guy."

I started moving cautiously down the aisle, ready for whatever.

"This time, Bats, my theme is the movies, and right now Kung Fu movies."

More of his men appeared. They came from the front of the theater, from the back, from the balcony on ropes. They wore black Ninja outfits with swathes of black cloth across their faces. They carried poles and swords and knives and chains. There were ten of them. They surrounded me.

That made it almost even. I was warmed up and not in a good mood and needed the exercise.

Joe R. Lansdale

I dodged a whirling blade, swept my attacker's feet from under him, and side-kicked him out of the aisle and through a chair. He didn't get up.

Good. I was a little busy.

I left-jabbed another, took his chain, hit him with it and he was out of the picture. I tossed the chain away, avoided the thrust of a *bojitsu* pole, then the pole was mine and I showed its former owner how to use it. A couple of times. He didn't enjoy the demonstration. He went down and I broke the pole on the side of another thug's head.

Things blurred after that. I stunned some nerves, broke some bones, and when the dust cleared, the Ninjas had all taken a trip to the Land of Nod.

I turned toward the stage and saw the Joker's image frozen on the screen. A spot in the stage floor opened up and the Time Machine replica rose out of it and locked into place. The Joker was seated in the chair. His teeth flashed like neon.

"Did you ever see the film *Mr. Sardonicus?*" said the Joker.

I paused, wary. He wouldn't show himself like that unless he felt protected.

"Near the end of it, William Castle paused the show and appeared on screen to let the audience choose the fate of the ghoul, Mr. Sardonicus, who, by the way, was a man with a very nice smile. Not too unlike my own. But alas, a sense of humor is not always appreciated. The audience was asked to show a card with a thumb on it—you got this when you got your ticket—and to turn it up for Sardonicus's survival, or down for his extermination. Those plebes voted he should be eliminated. I was quite crushed. I thought he was the hero of the piece."

Belly Laugh or The Joker's Trick or Treat

I had to make my play sometime. Had to get him to show his hand. I started to ease forward.

"Ah," said the Joker, "not so fast. You see, I lied. Your friend Commissioner Gordon is here with us, and you might say he's a little wired."

A light attached to the ceiling came on, shined brightly on a seat in the front row. I could see the back of Gordon's broad shoulders and silver-haired head. He was slumped forward, but I could tell he was wearing one of the Joker's party hats.

"He's unconscious at the moment, Batsy, but quite all right. But soon, the lights in Gotham will dim, and Commishy Gordon's skull will light up like a jack-o'-lantern with a big candle inside. Ah, not another step, or I throw the switch."

I froze, tried to come up with a plan while the Joker talked. It was his biggest weakness, talking.

"Ever see the movie *The Tingler*? That's where I got the idea. It's the one about this thing that latches onto a person's spine and stings them to death, or perhaps it would be better to say, tingles them to death, and . . . no, haven't seen it? Oh, and now you never shall. Too bad.

"But, as I was saying, when the movie came out, one of the promotional gimmicks was the seats in the theaters were rigged with a mild electrical charge and a voice on the screen would announce—the Tingler's in the theater, and bam, all the chairs in the place got a harmless dose of Ready Kilowatt. Nice idea, don't you think? Scared the piss out of me when I was a boy.

"Commishy, however, will not only get a dose of Ready, he'll get the old boy's lifeblood. I flick this switch all the way, and bam, you get to see Gordon's head fly off smoking.

"Isn't this something? I enjoy our chats so much, I

stray. Movie history is such a fascinating thing. However, the thing for me to decide now is the fate of our Commissioner Gordon. And this brings us back to Mr. Sardonicus and the Thumbs Up, or Thumbs Down cards. What shall it be?"

"Joker," I yelled. "Don't do it. Let Gordon go and I'll let you strap me in the chair."

"I'm going to get you anyway, Bats. Now, about Gordon's fate. I'm afraid there's no audience to do it. You've beat them all up. And since Commishy is out for the count, and you have a definite bias, and I so much prefer my own bias, I'm afraid that the burden is left to me. Or rather, my image on the screen will decide."

The screen Joker came unfrozen and lifted up a large card with a fist and extended thumb on it. The Joker smiled and turned the card so the thumb pointed down. The screen froze again.

"There you have it," said the Joker. "Say good-bye to the Commissioner.

I knew then he was going to do it and there was no reason to try and stall. I started running, and he hit the switch. There was a crackling sound and Gordon's head jerked and smoked and a lick of flame flashed off the side of his head and his hair and party hat caught fire.

I yelled, "Bastard," made the front row of seats, put a boot on the back of a chair, and sprang for the Joker, just as he pulled back the switch and threw it again.

Kilowatts sizzled and more flames jumped from Jim's body. He *was* dead. No one could take that kind of voltage. I could still feel the electricity crackling in the air, and could smell . . . plastic?

Even as my hands grabbed at the Joker's coat and I jerked him from the Time Machine, felt how light he was,

I realized, too late, the Joker had once again made me a fool.

He had used my rage against me.

The plastic replica of the Joker with the mechanical mouth and switch-pulling hand, exploded. It was filled with assorted Halloween candy and a nerve gas.

The explosion blew me off the stage.

An armrest struck me in the back, knocked what air I had left out of me. I lay crumpled on the floor between the stage and the front row, amidst Halloween candy and the burned replica of Jim. The electric shock had melted the plastic Commissioner and burned its clothes and hair off. The head had melted off at the neck and lay under a seat near my hand.

I was weak as a second-night bridegroom, but the explosion hadn't done any real damage, and I hadn't gotten as much gas in my lungs as I feared. I could feel its numbing effects, but it made me feel more slow than incapacitated.

But that was bad enough. It looked as if the Batman, who was born out back of the Gotham Theater, was going to die inside it. The real Joker appeared at the edge of the stage and looked down. He was dressed the same as his replica had been. He held a large, air-compressed gun in his hand.

"Trick or Treat, Bat Sap. I knew you couldn't resist getting your hands on me," he said. "Especially if you thought I had done Gordon in. And I will. Out of order, unfortunately. But, that's life."

I tried to breathe slowly, deeply, regain some strength. I eased my hand farther under the seat and touched the plastic Gordon head.

"I could have filled that model of me with my dissolving liquid, you know. But I wouldn't have had time to

gloat, and I gloat so well. . . . See, I've already turned
thumbs down on you. This pressurized gun holds one
large pellet of my dissolvent and water, and all I have to
do now is squeeze the trigger, and splat, you're bat guano.
So, before my gas wears off and you climb up here and
knock knots on my attractive green-haired head, I will, for
all the unhappy years you've given me, bid you *adieu*."

He laughed that insane laugh, and it went up my spine
and kicked around inside my head, and just before he
pulled the trigger, I grabbed the plastic head, twisted and
tossed it. It hit the gun on the tip of the barrel just as the
Joker pulled the trigger. The plastic head took the blast I
would have gotten, and the chemical splashed on either
side of it and on the Joker.

He yelped, jumped back, and dropped the gun. The
mess had splattered on his coat and pants, but hadn't
touched his flesh.

I was still weak, but I managed to pull myself over the
edge of the stage. It seemed to take hours.

The Joker was screaming with rage. He ran at me as I
came up on my knees, and he kicked, and as he did, a
thin blade sprang from the bottom of his shoe.

Normally, I could have blocked it with time to spare,
but I was still weak from the gas, so I only managed to
twist partially out of the way. The blade tore into my side
like a nuclear missile.

I grunted, slammed his shin with my forearm, and the
Joker went stumbling back.

I was on my feet now, and the Joker slapped at me
with his right palm. Again, too slow. His hand hit my
shoulder, and he had one of his souped-up joy buzzers
strapped to his palm, and when it hit me, a shock like a
lightning bolt went through me.

For a moment, I thought I'd go down.

Belly Laugh or The Joker's Trick or Treat

So did the Joker, and he got in too close.

I snapped out a lazy left jab and grazed his cheek and he went back a foot and his hand went inside his coat and came out with a deck of cards. He threw them at me. They were metal cards with razor-edged sides. I tried to dodge them, but it was like trying to move out of the flight of a flock of geese. A number of them hit me and stuck, the worst being one that tore through my cowl and cut deeply into my forehead.

I yanked it free and shook like a dog and the others flew out and away from me like panicked pigeons.

I smiled at the Joker.

He, of course, was smiling back. But there was nothing mirthful about his grin.

The effects of the gas had worn off, and I charged him with a yell.

He knew the bloodlust was on me and he tried to run for it.

I caught him by the shoulder and spun him around and hit him with a left hook in the midsection, and he blew out his breath and went skidding across the stage. He got up, wobbled toward the screen, put his hands on it, touched the bottom of his image, tried to get his breath back.

I calmly strolled over and took him by the shoulder and turned him around. I smiled at him. A nice, big smile.

He could hardly find his voice. "I give."

"Okay," I said, and hit him with a hard right cross that connected with the side of his jaw and knocked him through the screen and onto the floor of the room beyond.

The rip in the screen went from top to bottom, splitting the Joker's film image as if it had been halved by a giant cleaver.

I went through the split into the darkness and the light

Joe R. Lansdale

from the projector followed me in. I took hold of the Joker's lapels and pulled him to my height and let him dangle in my hands. He was unconscious. A bruise the color of my cloak was forming on his paper-white cheek. He looked like nothing more than a pathetic clown puppet. I thought of all the people he had murdered, all the lives he had shattered and haunted, including mine, and I thought how easy it would be to snap his neck, to make certain it all ended here.

Then I remembered where I was. The Gotham Theater. The place I had last been a child and my parents had sat on either side of me and I had felt loved. And moments later I had felt dark and empty because that love had been taken away from me.

I was a crime fighter, not a murderer like the Joker, and I hoped that's how I would always be. Still, I hoped Arkham Asylum held him this time, because next time around I couldn't be sure of the color of my soul.

I dragged him through the split in the screen and onto the stage, over to the Time Machine. I set him in the seat, unfastened the air hose from the gun and the compresser behind the curtains, and used it to bind him to the chair.

I stared at the projector light, watched dust ride down its beam. That beam had held all kinds of dreams and that night so long ago. I had shared a dream with my parents. A dream where a man in black fought the bad guys and always won and got the girl in the end.

I took in a deep breath, climbed off the stage, and checked on the Joker's men. A few of them were moving. I unfastened my cloak and used the pen knife in my utility belt to cut it into strips. I used the strips to tie the hands and feet of the thugs.

I used the rest of it to bind my wounds, then I went

Belly Laugh or The Joker's Trick or Treat

out of the theater and out to the Batmobile, used the phone inside to call Jim.

I put a hand to my injured side, walked down the alley and out back of the theater, stopped where my parents had fallen.

I glanced up at that one lonesome streetlight. Certainly it was not the same light of long ago, but it was in the same place. I looked at it the way I had that night when my parents lay on either side of me.

It occurred to me that maybe I, too, had been shot that night, only wounded, and that I lay in some hospital somewhere in a coma, dreaming all I thought I had lived. Living in a permanent dark world where a man can dress like a bat and fight a criminal who looks like a psychotic clown.

Sirens wailed in the distance.

—For Kasey Lansdale

Idol

ED GORMAN

1984

Knock.

"Hi, hon. Just wanted to tell you that—"

His mother peeks around the edge of his bedroom door and says, "Gosh, hon. You're kind of old for that, aren't you?"

Her voice and eyes say she wishes she had not seen her seventeen-year-old son doing what he's doing.

Pause, then: "Are you OK, hon?"

"Why wouldn't I be OK?"

"Well—"

"I'm fine. Now get the hell out of here."

"Hon, I've asked you not to talk to me that way. I'm your own mother. I'm—"

"You heard me."

She knows this tone. Is afraid of it. Has been afraid of it ever since he was seven or eight years old.

He is not like other boys. Never has been.

"Yes, hon," she says, already starting to cry useless tears. "Yes, hon."

they don't know my loneliness. they see only my strength. they don't know my loneliness.

1986

Open window. Autumn. Smell of leaves burning. In the distance a marching band practicing on the edge of campus. Smell of leaves rich as marijuana smoke.

He lies in his white undershorts on bed in this tiny off-campus apartment. Next to him girl sits stroking his chest. She is naked except for pink bikini panties.

"It's all right. Really."

"Sure," he says.

"It's happened to me a lot. You're probably just tired."

"Just shut up."

"Please," she says. "I really like you. Isn't that all that really matters?"

He slaps her, startling her as much as hurting her. Startling her.

i am beginning to understand my problem. i don't cause the headaches. he does. the impostor.

the impostor

1987

"So how do you feel about this man?"

"You know how I feel, doctor."

"Angry? Resentful?"

"Of course. Wouldn't you?"

Pause. "Tell me about the headaches."

"What time is it?"

"Pardon me?"

"The time, doctor. The time. I forgot my watch."

Sigh. "Two-ten. Why?"

"I'm in sort of a hurry today."

Ed Gorman

"We're not through till three."

"You, maybe. I'm in a hurry."

"You know your mother wants you to stay here for the entire session."

"Screw my mother."

"Please. Tell me about the headaches."

"What about them?"

"Do you know what triggers them?"

"No."

"Think about it a moment. Please."

Sigh. "Him."

"Him?"

"The impostor."

"Ah."

"Whenever I see him on tv or in the paper, the head-aches start."

Writes quickly in his notebook. "What do you feel when you see him?"

"Nothing."

"Nothing?"

"Literally, nothing. People think he's me. It's as if I don't exist."

He thinks: how seriously can you take a shrink who has three big warts on his face and who wears falling-down socks with battered old Hush-Puppies?

Anyway, he is beginning to suspect that the shrink may well be a friend of the impostor's.

Yes. Of course.

My God, why didn't he think of that before?

He stands up.

"It's only two-fifteen. It's only—"

But he's already going out the door. "Goodbye, doctor."

Idol

1988

He sits in his room with the white kitten his mother bought him to cheer him up after he quit college a few months ago. He lazes warm and drifting in the soft May sunlight the same way the white kitten with the damp black nose and the quick pink tongue lazes.

"Kitty," he says, stroking her, You're my only friend. My only friend."

He starts crying then—sobbing really. He doesn't know why.

i saw him on TV last night. waving. accepting their applause. he's convinced them now. everybody. they really think he's me. they really believe it.

1989

"I'd like to talk to you."

"I'm in a hurry."

"I'm serious about this."

He's never seen his mother like this. No "hon." No backing down. Almost angry.

"All right."

"Upstairs."

"Why?"

"Your room, come on."

What is going on here? She seems almost...crazed.

So up the stairs.

So past where the white kitty with the damp black nose and quick pink tongue lies on the landing in the sunlight.

Into his room.

Throwing open the closet door.

Pointing.

Voice half-hysterical.

Ed Gorman

"I thought you told me you were getting rid of all this stuff."

Feeling himself flush. "This is none of your business. You have no right—"

"I have every right. I've put up with this since you were eight years old and I can't handle it any more. You're a man now, or supposed to be. Get rid of this silly junk and get rid of it now!"

Instead of becoming angry, he just stands there, allowing himself to understand the truth of this moment. The *real* truth.

So the impostor has gotten to her, too.

His own mother.

Sensing this shift in his mood, she seems less certain of herself. Backs away from the closet.

"What's wrong with you?" she says.

"Did you let him touch you?"

"Who? What are you *talking* about?"

"You know, mother. You know very well what I'm talking about." Pause. Stares at her. For a forty-two-year old woman she is quite attractive. All those aerobic shows on daytime tv. All that eating of fruit and lean meat and almost never any bread. Certainly no desserts. "You did let him touch you, didn't you?"

"My God, are you—"

But then she stops herself, obviously realizing that would be the wrong thing to say. The very wrongest thing to say. (Are...you...crazy?)

He grabs her, then.

By the throat.

Choking her before she has time to scream and alert the neighbors.

It is so easy.

His thumbs press down on her trachea.

Her eyes roll white.

Spittle silver and useless runs down the sides of her mouth as she tries to form useless words.

He watches the way her breasts move so gracefully inside the cotton of her housedress.

Harder harder.

"Please," she manages to say.

Then drops to the floor.

He has no doubt she is dead.

the impostor has taken over every aspect of my life. i have no friends (sometimes i even suspect that it was really he who put the white kitty here) i have no prospects for a career because nobody believes me when i tell them who i am i have no—
he leaves me no choice
no choice whatsoever

Same Day (Afternoon)

He has never flown before. He is frightened at takeoff, having heard that the two most dangerous times aboard a plane are takeoff and landing.

Once in the air—except for those brief terrifying moments of turbulence, anyway—he starts to enjoy himself.

He had never realized before what a burden she'd been, his mother.

His thinks of her back there in his room, crumpled and dead in a corner. He wonders how many days it will be before they find her. Will she be black? Will maggots be crawling all over her? He hopes so. That will teach the impostor to mess with him.

He spends the rest of the flight watching a dark-haired stewardess open a very red and exciting mouth as she smiles at various passengers.

Ed Gorman

Very red.
Very exciting.

Same Day (Evening)

The city terrifies him. He has checked into a good
hotel. Thirty-sixth floor. People below so many ants.
Stench and darkness of city.
All those people in the thrall of the impostor.
Terrifying.
He has come here without an exact plan, but as he lies
on the firm hotel bed eating donuts and drinking milk the
late news comes on and the very first story gives him a
beautiful plan. A wonderful plan.
Tomorrow the impostor will receive an award from the
mayor.
So easy to—
so easy

tomorrow the world will know. my long struggle will
be over and i will be able to assume my rightful place.
tomorrow.

Next Day (Morning)

Warm spring day. The rear of the city jail where the
impostor often brings the criminals he apprehends.
Smell of city—gasoline and smoke and filth and loneliness—sight of city: the helpless, the arrogant, the
predatory.
His room, he wants to be back in his room...(the gun
sweatily in his hand as he hides behind a parked car)
but suddenly now the impostor is here—
—leading a prisoner into the rear metal door—
—the impostor; so confident-looking—
—in full costume—

—going into the door as —
—the gunfire starts
Two quick cracks on the soft still air
Two quick cracks
(you bastard—father-of-mine—you've been fooling
people too long; I exist now and you do not)
crack of pistol...
(and you do not...)

Same Day (Afternoon)

Around noon the story was on all the news media, bul-
letins on the networks, even.

And the would-be assassin (shot to death by police)
was identified.

So a neighbor came over to see how his mother was
doing after hearing such horrible news
and knocked and knocked
and went and called police
and
They find the body with no problem. Good-looking for-
tyish woman strangled to death, stuffed into a corner of
the bedroom.

One cop, the mournful sort, shakes his head.

What a waste.

He sees the closet door partially open and, being a cop,
curious and all, edges it open with a pencil (you've got to
be extra careful at a crime scene; evidence can be
destroyed so easily).

He looks inside.

"What the hell," he says.

His partner, who has been directing the lab man and
the man from the coroner's office and the ambulance
attendants, walks over next to him. "What?"

"Look inside."

Ed Gorman

So the second cop looks inside. And whistles. "All these costumes. They're just like—"

"Just like the guy he tried to kill."

"But if he had all these costumes you'd think he would have respected the guy, not wanted to kill him."

The first cop shakes his head. "It's a strange old world. A strange old world."

Same Afternoon (Later)

"Hey. Look at this," the first cop says.

"What?"

"Some kind of diary."

"Let's see."

They flip through pages. Open at a spot and read.

"it is no longer tolerable. the impostor must be killed because there can't be two of us. one is real, one is false. and after today, the real one will assume the throne of power."

"Now what the hell could he have meant by that?"

The second cop shrugs. "You got me, partner. You sure got me."

Dying Is Easy, *Comedy* Is Hard

EDWARD BRYANT and DAN SIMMONS

S eeing Johnny Carson rip off his own face, just like one of those effects in an early David Cronenberg movie, was bad enough. But what came next was truly grotesque.

I gotta admit, I stared. But then we all had to be an appreciative audience—the goons with Uzis and MAC-10s, and H&K miniguns made sure of that. If you're wondering how I know so much about all that cool ordnance, it's not 'cause I spend a lot of time on the street—it's because I see a lot of B-movies.

I really hope I live to go to a lot more. . . .

The Aladdin Theater is named after the dude that rubbed a lamp and got a genie. Right now I wish I had the three wishes that guy received. All of us here on the stage do. No genie coming out tonight. Nope, just pain, blood, and a whole lot of grief.

Frankly, it's enough to make me rethink my career. . . .

I admit it, I come alive—*truly alive*—only at night. Then I descend on the concrete canyons and brick catacombs of

Dying Is Easy, *Comedy* Is Hard

Gotham City, take the train into its decaying downtown between Art Deco skyscrapers from some earlier age, walk its rainswept streets and ratty back alleys smelling of garbage and the homeless, seek out its basement improv clubs and East Side nightclubs sandwiched in between the porno palaces and hotsheet hotels—the clubs smelling of cigars and cheap perfume and urine and something much worse: *flop sweat*—and then, only then, in the dark belly of this dying city, performing for the drunks and adulterers and lost souls and lonely insomniacs, *then* I come alive. Then—in the dark, with the bile of fear burning at my insides and the stench of failure and humiliation just a short arc of silence away—then my *true* life begins.

I know now that I'm not alone. There are others who come alive at night, in the back alleys of Gotham City. Others who wait through the mundane turning of days for the violent whirl of night's greatest realities. Others who shed their daylight skins and become *other people*. I know that now.

The creature that calls himself the Joker is one. The Batman—that human puzzle wrapped in a cowl and enigma—is another. I know that now.

And I almost understand.

This isn't going well. Where to start?

My name is Pete Tulley. I'm twenty-nine years old, black—or African-American as the self-appointed spokespersons of our race now say, not married, not living with anyone right now, and during the day I'm a manager of the Burger Biggie franchise on the corner of Sprang and Robinson. It's not really that bad of a job. The hardest part is keeping a steady flow of kids trained and working behind the counter, getting them to understand that Burger Biggie is a *job*, a responsibility, and not just a place to hang out and laugh with their friends while the customer stands and waits for his Biggie and fries. I'm a graduate of Burger Biggie Hamburger College—the franchise's four-week training school in Peoria, Illinois—and as stupid as that sounds, as easy as it is to sneer at the idea of a Hamburger College, the chain actually stands for something (even if that "something" is only good fast food, prepared promptly to nationwide standards of taste and quality of ingredients, in clean surroundings), and I try to communicate those standards to the people I train and manage. I must be at least partially successful at that since my Biggie at Sprang and Robinson has won the Gotham City metro area B. B. Excellence and Cleanliness Award two years running.

And despite the obvious temptation—since stand-ups are like fiction writers in that they use everything around them—I've never done hamburger franchise jokes in my routines. It seems like too cheap a shot. Plus, I owe *something* to the people who keep me employed in the daytime so I can come alive at night.

But I'll use the gags someday. In the long run, nothing is sacred.

I've been a stand-up comic for three years. Three years this March. Like most would-be comics, I started by getting a laugh from my family when I was a little kid. (I remember the first time—it was unintentional—I was six and watching a Dolly Parton special on TV and said, "I bet she can swim real good with those inflated things on her chest." If we'd been alone that evening, my mother probably would have frowned and my dad would have swatted me on the side of the head, but we had Uncle

Dying Is Easy, *Comedy* Is Hard

Louis and Aunt Nell and Cousin Sook and a bunch of other folks over—they'd been drinking beer since the picnic that afternoon—and the room just howled with laughter. It became a sort of family joke—Uncle Louis used to mention it about everytime we got together—and it was really the first time I'd been noticed by everyone. Or at least the first time they'd all noticed me and *liked* me.)

Anyway, it taught me that sex gets laughs, and if you can throw in some popular culture or a public figure, so much the better.

I went to Charity Hills High School—although there were no hills in our old Southside suburb of Gotham and by the midseventies there was damned little charity either—and I became a comic there just to survive. Charity Hills had inherited most of the Gotham City gangs by then, sort of gang franchises, I guess you might say, and to stay an independent you had to be incredibly smart or damn tough. I was neither. So I made myself funny.

The caption under my high school yearbook photo says "Always good for a laugh" and that was my armor and chameleon cloak. I figured that the jocks and street goons and dopeheads and musclebound dipshits who ordinarily showed their superiority by beating up wimpy types like me would think twice if I had a reputation as a clown. I figured that it might be easier for them to laugh at me—make me perform for their peers in the hallways and gyms and cloakrooms of dear old CHHS rather than stomp the crap out of me. And it worked. Most of the time.

Anyway, I started taking comedy seriously a couple of years ago, after I realized that nothing else in my life was going to give me a life worth living. I started out in the suburban improv clubs, getting in on amateur nights where people came to laugh *at* us rather than *with* us. That was okay. I was used to it. I always threw up before

a performance, but I soon began to judge audience response by whether I threw up *after* the show.

I spent a long, hungry summer out in the Los Angeles
area, getting booked for very few performances of my own,
but getting to see a lot of the greats in the field at their old
comedy club stomping grounds. The field of amateurs was
too rich for me to compete out there, so I came back to
Gotham City—where at least I knew a few of the club
owners, had done them favors and could get a few in
return. And besides, Burger Biggie doesn't have any franchises west of the Mississippi.

And so I came alive at night for two years and then
some, taking the 10:38 P.M. train in from Finger Park to
Gotham Center, performing for money when I could—
usually at one of the East Side back-alley basement clubs,
a place for the slum dwellers to come in out of the
cold and for the yuppies and dinner-jacket types to go
slumming—but usually I had to settle for another amateur
night, another contest, or another free-drinks and dinner-
if-you-get-here-early-enough performance.

I got to know most of the other comedy club circuit
people. A few went on to the ranks of the serious professional. One got rich and famous and died snorting bad
coke in Las Vegas last fall. Most got discouraged, dropped
out, and have been replaced by younger would-be some-
bodies. A few, like me, having hung in there and taken
what they could get—honing their material, slowly im-
proving their performances and on-stage personalities,
trying to make up in experience and sheer persistence
what they lack in talent. A few of these other survivors of
the Long March have become friends. Some of the rest are
real assholes. All of them, friends and assholes alike,
are competitors.

But in a strange way we are like some medieval guild:

Dying Is Easy, *Comedy* Is Hard

aging apprentices hoping to become journeymen and praying to be elevated to Master. We're sort of a family of misfit hopefuls, sharing nothing but our common dream and the fact that we come alive only at night, in front of the audience.

And then the Joker started killing us.

It was last November in that gray, dead-branch period between the childlike nonsense of Halloween and the all-too-adult loneliness of Thanksgiving. The Carob Comedy Club on Alameda and Franklin had been staging a three-week Comedy Countdown—shows every Tuesday and Saturday—with a bunch of us eliminating each other via applause-o-meter showdown for a five-hundred-dollar first prize. That sounds like a decent amount until you realize that Al Jacobs, manager of the Carob, had over a dozen amateur comics firing off their best material twice a night, two times a week for three weeks, and only the winner would end up getting anything.

Anyway, it was the final Saturday night and the original mob of stand-ups had been winnowed down to seven—me, my cracker friend Boonie Sandhill, a tired old ex-borscht-belt comic named Dandy John Diamond, a Roseanne Barr imitation called Tiffany Strbynsky, a gifted black teenager named Fast Eddie Teck, a beautiful but not very funny medical student named Diana Mulhollen, and George Marlin. I'd drawn the first slot for the late show and the audience wasn't just cold, it was frigid. I gave it my best shot—using my Cola Wars stuff where every major world event of the past three decades was explained as an incidental by-product of the global sales war between Coke and Pepsi—but either the material was too cerebral for this crowd or it just wasn't my night. I knew I was out of the running even before I took my bows, reset the mike on the stand, and backed out of the spotlight. At least Tiffany waddled onstage to a warmer crowd.

Al Jacobs lets us early casualties sit at the bar and down a few comped drinks while we watch the others work. Tiffany was hot this night, but she still was only a good imitation of the real thing and even though the applause-o-meter swung almost half again as far to the right as it had for me, I knew that the race would be between Fast Eddie and George Marlin.

Marlin was next and he hit the audience hard and fast. New Jersey was overweight but he never did fat jokes; his dialect was so Brooklynesque that it made Boone Sandhill's drawl sound normal, but Marlin didn't rely on dialect or borough in-jokes. He rarely did the off-color stuff that makes up ninety percent of club routines these days. George was just *funny* and he generally just schmoozed along with tales from his childhood and early adolescence that had the sense of *this-really-happened,* which every comedy bit needs and so few have.

So George was telling about his days as a lonely teen-ager and how he was convinced he was a superhero—the Dung Beetle, armored nemesis of evil-doers everywhere—and the audience was roaring and I was on my third vodka rocks and the applause-o-meter was pinning itself and I was wondering idly whether Fast Eddie's street-smart vulgar strut'n'jive routine could top this stuff, when suddenly George stopped in midroutine and stared at the microphone in his hand.

The head of the mike was growing, inflating like a balloon. George stepped back, still holding the thing and watching it expand, and because Al Jacobs was too cheap to install cordless traveling mikes, George got tangled in the wire and glanced back to see what was stopping him.

Dying Is Easy, *Comedy* Is Hard

Meanwhile, the audience was still roaring, thinking—as I did for a second—that the expanding mike was part of the routine, some phallic gag.

In those final seconds, George knew it wasn't part of the night's entertainment; the head of the mike was a metal sphere and it had grown to the size of a soccer ball. Still tangled in the cord, George started to drop the microphone as if it were the business end of a snake.

The audience roared. The mike exploded in some sort of shaped charge, taking off most of George's head and smearing the maroon curtains behind him with hair, blood, and brain matter.

Laughter is like an avalanche—slow to get started, but once its moving it has an inertia of its own. Even with the gasps and screams of shock, it took ten or fifteen seconds for the last waves of laughter to die out. Then, for a moment, there was silence except for a few sobs from a woman near the front.

George's pear-shaped body had stood there for a second or two, headless, his fingers still curved around the mike he was in the process of dropping. Then the corpse fell forward and hit the boards with a sound I will never forget, arterial blood sprayed the closest tables, and the room was filled with chaos as everyone—myself included—stood, shouted, cried for help, or merely screamed. I remember that Diane Mulholland rushed from backstage and knelt next to George—the knees of her pantyhose wicked red from the blood. She looked offstage as if seeking help. Al Jacobs rushed onstage, froze as if he were physically incapable of coming closer to the corpse, and stood there, wringing his hands and grimacing.

I set down my drink and stood on the lowest rung of

Edward Bryant and Dan Simmons

the barstool, just trying to see over the heads of the mindlessly surging crowd.

And then, a moment after the laughter ended and the shouts and sobs and cries of confusion began to ebb toward a more sinister silence, then the *laughter* began.

It was not quite laughter. It was more like the frenzied barking of a jackal or the amplified cough of a hyena than any sound of mirth I'd ever heard come from a human throat. And then the face appeared.

Ten feet tall, white-skinned and green-haired, teeth yellowed within the terrible rictus that passed for a grin, the giant head materialized and floated in midair above George's body. If George's corpse had remained standing, this bloated visage would have replaced his missing head like someone poking his face through a cardboard cutout at a boardwalk photo booth.

It took me a second to realize that I was looking at the Joker. Living in Gotham City most of my life, I'd seen news photographs and the rare snippets of videotape, but they had seemed unreal, cartoonlike, and this nightmare face floating above George's corpse was all too real.

Diane screamed and flinched away from the apparition. Al Jacobs backed to the edge of the stage, teetered, and crouched, holding one arm above his bald head as if ready to ward off a blow.

The Joker laughed. The image seemed solid. I saw the pores in the white flesh, noticed the pink gums above yellow teeth, and watched as the wide eyes blinked in merriment and pure insanity. The laughter echoed off walls and curtains as patrons fled, shoving over tables in their haste to reach the fire exits. Diane Mulholland slumped unconscious in a pool of George's blood.

The image of the Joker glanced down at her as if the projection could actually *see*, smiled, and lifted its long

Dying Is Easy, *Comedy* Is Hard

chin. It . . . *he* . . . was looking across the heads of the crowd directly at me.

"TUT, TUT, TUT," came the amplified voice. I remember seeing Charles Manson interviewed once on *Sixty Minutes*. Manson's voice sounded like Dan Rather's compared to the black-ice tones I heard now. "I GUESS THIS FELLOW HAS NO HEAD FOR COMEDY!"

The crazy laughter rose in volume. Behind me I heard shouts at the front entrance, knew the cops had arrived, but I wasn't able to turn away from that wild-eyed gaze.

"WELL, HE WON'T BE THE LAST TO GIVE HIS ALL TO LADY COMEDY," echoed the mad voice. The image giggled, and then a strange transformation came over the face. It was as if rats were scurrying under the white cheesecloth of the Joker's flesh. At first, I thought it might be a malfunction of the projector or whatever it was, but then I realized that it was the Joker's actual features that were shifting, sliding into different patterns, jerking like the expression of a doll in a clumsily made claymation cartoon.

The Joker was no longer smiling. His green hair seemed to wave like seaweed in a strong current as he glared down at the last fleeing patrons, flicked a glance at the corpse, and then returned his gaze to me. "THERE IS ONLY ONE JOKER IN GOTHAM CITY."

He was gone. The cops burst in, ran around, swung their revolvers in that self-conscious two-armed pose we see on TV every night, and shouted at each other over the din. Some stood around Gotham's corpse and looked as helpless as Al Jacobs had, while others rushed backstage, guns still drawn.

I knew they wouldn't find the Joker. I lifted my glass and finished my drink. My hands were shaking so hard

Edward Bryant and Dan Simmons

that I had to use both of them to get the glass to my mouth without spilling the last of my vodka.

They kept us until almost four in the morning. I'd never been interrogated before and it wasn't much like the movies. They didn't grill me, they didn't use the good-cop, bad-cop routine, and nobody shone a bright light in my face. In fact, they interviewed us one at a time in the long, narrow storeroom in the back of Al's club, and there was hardly enough light to see the two homicide detectives asking the questions. They sounded more tired than I was. One of them had a serious smoker's cough and sucked on lozenges between cigarettes.

Mostly, it was boring. They went over everything twice, then a third time. Then they started again.

"Are you sure Mr. Marlin said nothing to you in the green room?" the cop with the cough asked.

I sighed and began to give the same answer I'd given them thrice before. Then a shadow in the corner behind them moved, detached itself from the darkness there, and glided toward us.

"Holy shit," I whispered.

It was the Batman. I heard his cape rustle, caught a glimpse of the peaked points on the dark cowl, but mostly he blended into the darkness in that little room. Only his face and that weird emblem on his chest seemed to reflect light.

He glided forward until he loomed over me, wrinkles in that cape glinting like black silk where they glinted at all. The cops made room for him but said nothing. I *couldn't* say anything at that moment.

I know, you live in Gotham City most of your life, you're supposed to see the Batman all the time. Well, you

Dying Is Easy, *Comedy* Is Hard

don't, any more than you chat with Dustin Hoffman a lot
if you live in L.A. or lunch with Donald Trump if you
hang around New York. Oh, you see photos in the paper
every once in a while and I *almost* saw Batman at a
dedication of a new community center in Charity Hills
once when I was twelve . . . but my dad and I got stuck in
traffic and when we got there he was gone. You live in
Gotham, you take a sort of pride in being identified with
the Bat Guy . . . sort of like San Francisco residents are
proud of the Golden Gate Bridge . . . but you don't *see*
him. To tell the truth, it'd been so long since I'd even read
about him, that I'd sort of forgotten he was real.

He was real enough now.

I sat back, tried to look cool, tried not to gulp visibly
as this cowled face leaned forward, neck muscles all
corded under black silk, tried to listen coolly rather than
scream when that gloved hand touched my shoulder. I'm
thin, average height, but no wimp. Still, I had the definite
impression that his hand could pulverize my collarbone
and shoulder just by giving a squeeze.

He didn't squeeze.

"Mr. Tulley," he said. His voice sounded soft, almost
preoccupied. But I sure as hell wouldn't want to get the
owner of that voice angry. "Mr. Tulley, do you know any
reason why someone . . . even the Joker . . . would want to
kill George Marlin?"

"Uh-uh," I said, always a snappy one with repartee.

I could see his eyes through slits in that midnight cowl.
I'm pretty observant—stand-up comics have to be—but I
have no idea what color they were.

"Mr. Tulley, is there *anything* that you haven't mentioned which you think might help us with this investigation?"

"Uh-uh." This time I managed to punctuate it by shaking my head.

The Batman nodded—more toward the two cops than at me—and then he took a step back and seemed to blend back into the shadows like black ink spilled on a dark velvet cloth.

The cop with the smoker's cough led me to the door while I strained to keep from peering over my shoulder at the corner.

"Thanks, Mr. Tulley," said the detective. I could smell the lozenge he was chewing on. "Go home and get some rest. We'll call you if we need you, but I think this'll be all."

"Uh-huh," I said, grateful to be leaving, grateful to be getting out of that little room.

But it wasn't all. Not by a long shot.

Bruce appeared one day after the second murder.

It was three nights later, some of us were working the old Aladdin Dinner Theater, figuring that whoever was taking notes on comics for the joke-off would probably hit Aladdin's traditional Tuesday Night Laugh Riot.

Somebody hit it all right.

The Aladdin is one of the great old movie palaces built during the early days of the Depression. It's part Taj Mahal, part Pharaoh's tomb, a bit of Baghdad, and a whole lot of old-movie fantasy. The place is gigantic, with two levels of balconies, box seats, red carpets, murals, and corridors like caverns out of an Indiana Jones movie: rococo ornamentation everywhere, bronze hands holding torches for lighting fixtures, dusty chandeliers—the whole bit. Aladdin's had decayed to the point of being a downtown porno theater in the sixties, was converted to a disco

Dying Is Easy, *Comedy* Is Hard

during the seventies, was abandoned for a while, and then became a dinner theater cum nightclub during the mid-eighties.

The place was too big for comedy: the night Tiffany was murdered, there were almost as many of us waiting to go onstage as there were people in the audience. The rows of theater seats behind the tables were empty, the balconies were dark, and the private boxes were sealed off. The small lamps on the dozen tables near the stage shed little light. The place smelled of mildewed carpets, old cigars, and rot.

And *flop sweat.*

There was a plainclothes detective in the audience. Max Weber, Aladdin's manager, had pointed him out. He didn't need to. Anybody could have spotted the shiny black suit, paunch, clip-on holster, and white socks and made the old guy as a cop.

People weren't laughing when Tiffany died. She was having a bad night; the Roseanne Barr material wasn't working, there was a heckler down front whom she couldn't out-nasty, and she was sweating heavily . . . obviously just trying to get through to the end of the routine. I was on last, still at least forty-five minutes to go after Fast Eddie and a couple of others, so I was having a drink at an empty table and feeling sorry for Tiffany.

Suddenly, in midpunchline, a glass box came sliding down on wires from the dark catwalks above and slammed onto the stage, enclosing Tiffany as surely as an entymologist's plastic jar would trap a bug.

There was a click, the mike cord was severed, and Tiffany stumbled as some sort of bottom slid under her, sealing the glass box. It couldn't be glass of course—I realized even then that it had to be some sort of plastic or Plexiglas—but it *looked* like a glass phone booth.

Tiffany screamed, but her shouts were made almost inaudible by the cage. The plainclothes cop stared a moment and then jumped to his feet, groping for the gun on his belt.

The Joker walked onstage, aimed his cane, and shot the cop. Actually, the head of the cane flew through the air, trailing a thin wire, and slammed into the cop's chest. The fat detective spasmed and collapsed. We learned later that the cane had fired something called a taser . . . a sort of high-voltage stun weapon. It wasn't designed to kill. The Joker couldn't have known that the detective had been fitted for a pacemaker . . . or maybe he did.

Anyway, the cop spasmed and died, Tiffany's mouth moved as she pounded the Plexiglas, and the Joker bowed. He was wearing an old-style tuxedo, the formal effect spoiled only slightly by a bright green cravat he wore in lieu of a bow tie, purple spats, and purple gloves. He completed his bow and looked at Tiffany in her box as if he had just noticed her. "*God*, how sad!" He pouted almost effeminately. "*Poor girl* . . . trying *so* hard, and your only reward is *flop sweat!*"

The Joker snapped his fingers. Water began pouring from invisible ducts in the box, pooling around Tiffany's ankles. She screamed more loudly; it was just audible through the plastic. Fast Eddie Teck charged onstage, a switchblade knife in his hand. The Joker tasered him unconscious with a flick of his cane.

"For those of you who don't *know* theater talk," lisped the Joker, showing us flashes of his yellow teeth all the way back to the molars, "*flop sweat* is the ultimate pan notice . . . the sheen of ultimate failure, the glow of abject panic . . . the *perspiration of expiration!*"

The liquid rose to Tiffany's shoulders, then to her chins. Her orange silk caftan floated around her. She

Dying Is Easy, *Comedy* Is Hard

jumped, pounded at the walls, clawed at plastic. The fluid rose until only her mouth and nose were clear of it as she strained against the roof of the box.

I rushed toward the stage and stopped as the Joker tasered two would-be rescuers in front of me. He snapped his fingers and a second cane appeared in his other hand.

"Tut, tut." The Joker grinned. "Never interrupt an *artist* at work." He glanced over his shoulder at Tiffany. The box had filled with clear liquid; she was no longer struggling. A few final bubbles of air rose from her nose and open mouth and tangled in her swaying hair.

The Joker walked over to the box and patted the side of it almost affectionately. "You don't sweat much," he said to Tiffany's corpse. "For a *fat* lady."

A dozen of us had come out of the shock and horror sufficiently to prepare to rush the Joker *en masse*. He twirled his cane. "Oh, I wouldn't recommend giving fatso mouth-to-mouth," he said, showing an expression of revulsion. "You see, this *flop sweat* isn't *water*, it's hydrochloric *acid!*" He grinned at us, waggled gloved fingers, and said, "Ta ta! See you all—or at least the survivors—at the joke-off!"

He laughed insanely. A bunch of us climbed onstage, rushed him. The Joker calmly bowed, caught one of the wires above the box, and rose out of sight into the darkness.

It took us almost five minutes to find a fire ax to crack the plastic box.

It *was* acid.

The guy named Bruce appeared and performed the next night at the Carob Club. He was awful. He did a routine that wouldn't have gotten a laugh in 1952, much less

Edward Bryant and Dan Simmons

during the beginning of the hip, raunchy nineties. The jokes were flat, his timing was nonexistent, he didn't seem to care whether the audience was there or not, and his body language was *bad*. I mean, I saw the guy move before and after the show, and although he dressed like a cartoon of a pimp—zoot-suit-shouldered polyester gold jacket, baggy green pants, a matching monkey-puke-green open-collar shirt with layers of gold chains showing, even a greasy little Wayne Newton moustache that looked like an anemic caterpillar had crawled onto his upper lip to die—despite all that, this guy *moved* like an athlete. No, better than that, he was as unselfconsciously graceful as a big cat on the veldt.

But on stage . . . klutzville. He moved like Pee Wee Herman doing an imitation of Richard Nixon.

The audience didn't boo him, they just sat and stared as if a traffic accident was occurring on stage. There was even a splattering of applause when he got off—probably from pure relief. I mean, the man was *bad*.

That's why it was all the more confusing that night when I was hiking the six blocks to catch the subway up to Gotham Center where I'd catch the el out to Finger Park station, and who do I see down an alley but Bruce. I mean, I wouldn't have been surprised to see this guy heading down an alley in search of a flophouse . . . he wore one weird suit and had that handsome but driven look, sort of like some out-of-work actors I've known . . . but there he is, 2:00 A.M. in an alley, in the rain, and he's getting into a *limousine*. The chauffeur is some old guy, and it's some stretched European *übermenschen* limousine! It's hard for most of us to take the tension and abuse and *we're* all hoping for a break, the big time, money we can't make any other way . . . or at least any other *legal* way. So why the hell would this poor schmuck take all the abuse and

Dying Is Easy, *Comedy* Is Hard

embarrassment if he didn't have to? A guy who could afford a European limousine like that could buy an audience.

The next night at the Pit Stop, a strip joint that does comedy every Wednesday, Bruce was there again. Same routine. Same floppo, although this crowd was boozed up enough to start booing early. They were on the verge of throwing things when Bruce wrapped it up, bowed into that wall of boos, and walked calmly offstage.

Fast Eddie was ready to go on after him. Eddie leaned over to me and whispered, "Anybody'd look good after this jerk."

Later, Boonie Sandhill and I went up to this Bruce guy in the green room.

"Howdy, y'all," said Boonie, showing off the prognathous underbite that passed for a grin with him. "Caught your monologue, man. It's . . . uh . . . original. Real different. Makes the rest of us look the same as stripes on a coon's tail."

Bruce raised an eyebrow and nodded, obviously not sure if Boonie was pulling his chain or not. I wasn't either. We made introductions, shook hands. The guy's handshake was easygoing enough, but I had the idea he could crush my fingers like breadsticks if he wanted to.

"Bruce," said Boonie. "Is that your first name or last?"

The guy twitched a smile. "It's my stage name. My . . . stand-up-comic pseudonym."

Boonie rolled his eyes at the vocabulary. I said, "Any reason you chose the name Bruce?"

Bruce hesitated. "Homage to Lenny Bruce, I guess. He was sort of my hero."

Boonie and I glanced at each other. This guy's style and content bore about as much resemblance to Lenny Bruce's stuff as did Mr. Rogers.

Edward Bryant and Dan Simmons

"Hero, huh?" said Boonie. "Too bad Lenny O.D.'d on speed."

"Yes," said Bruce. He was watching the closed-circuit monitor the Pit Stop had to let the green-room folks watch the action on stage. It was a crude picture—stationary camera, black-and-white fuzzy picture with poor sound— but Bruce seemed rapt. "It is too bad," he said. "Lenny Bruce would have had a great future."

Boonie and I looked at each other again. This guy was as miserable a liar as he was a comic; anybody who knew anything about Lenny Bruce knew that he died of an overdose of heroin.

"How come you joined the cavalcade of stars?" asked Boonie.

Bruce rubbed his chin. The guy was older than I was, but I have no idea how much older. He had the sort of rugged but understated good looks that lets a man ignore birthdays between his early thirties and late fifties. "I wanted a crack at the Gotham City Laughs of Tomorrow competition," he said.

"You mean the big jerk-off?" said Boonie.

"Joke-off," I said. "We call it the joke-off."

Bruce nodded, eyes roving back to the closed-circuit TV. I had the idea that nothing made this man laugh; the idea of him making others laugh seemed . . . well . . . laughable.

"Don't you worry about getting killed?" asked Boonie. There was no banter in his voice now and very little southern accent.

Bruce raised an eyebrow. "Oh, you mean that Joker fellow. . . ."

"Yeah, that *Joker fellow*," mimicked Boonie. "He sorta caught some of our attention."

Bruce nodded as if mulling this over. "Sure, it worries

me. But I figure it's a chance I have to take to get a shot at the bigtime for the Gotham Comedy . . . ah . . . the joke-off. The odds seem decent."

Boonie started to make some smart-ass reply, but I surprised him and myself by elbowing him to shut up and saying, "Right, man. That's the way most of us feel. Say, Boonie and I are going out for coffee after the last show. Want to come?"

Bruce seemed to weigh the invitation with the same seriousness as he did everything else. "Yes," he said. "I would."

For the next week or so, Boonie and I spent a lot of time with Bruce after the show—in those thin, cold hours between the closing of the nightclubs and the rising of the sun through Gotham's smog banks. Usually we hit an all-night café, mainlined strong coffee, and talked about comedy. *Boonie and I* talked about comedy. Bruce listened a lot. To tell the truth, he was a nice-enough guy. Just way too serious to be funny. He was even serious about comedy. Actually, he seemed to want to talk about the Joker most of the time: What did we think made the Joker do what he did? Why would the Joker be killing stand-up comics? What did we think of the Joker's sense of humor?

"That ain't a sense of humor, man," Boonie answered more than once. "This Joker pissant is *nuts*. His idea of a punchline is pain." And then Boonie would say, "Y'all want to analyze everything, Bruce. Petey and me, we just want to get *laughs*."

"But just what, precisely, makes people laugh?" Bruce asked late one night, early one morning. Outside the diner, cold rain was turning to snow in front of the street-sweeping machines.

Boonie snorted. "Shit-fire, boy. If we knew that, old Pete and me'd be livin' in Bel Aire an' sittin' on Johnny Carson's couch twice a week."

"But there must be *some* formula," persisted Bruce. "Some secret."

Boonie shook his head. "If there is, nobody knows it. Good comedy's like . . . like good sex. . . ."

"Good sex?" repeated Bruce. Any other comic would have snapped back, "Is there such a thing as *bad* sex, lint brain?" but Bruce was listening again. Seriously.

"Uh-uh," I interrupted. "Not sex. Surfing."

Both of them looked at me.

"I mean it," I said. I'd had a good night. The laughs had been strong and constant and sincere. "When I was out in California last summer, watching them surf at Malibu, I realized that a good stand-up routine's like that. You gotta catch the wave just right . . . it's like judging the audience . . . then get a good start, stay right on the break or curl or pipeline or whatever they call that sweet point just under the crest . . . and then ride it for all its worth, but still know when to end it." I stopped, embarrassed, and slurped cold coffee.

Boonie stared at me. Bruce said, "And what's the secret of riding the wave?"

For once my gaze was just as serious as Bruce's. "The secret is using material that *means* something," I said, surprised to hear me talking this way. "To go at the thing that's most serious to you, most . . . well, most sacred . . . and to *make it funny*."

Bruce pondered his own coffee cup.

I pushed ahead. "I mean, look at your material, man. It's stuff you bought from a street-corner gag writer. Am I right?"

He nodded. I *think* he nodded.

Dying Is Easy, *Comedy* Is Hard

"It's not *you*, man," I said. "It has nothing to do with you. It's not what scares you, what hurts you, what bugs you . . . you got to go for the stuff that's hiding in the deepest closets, then get it out. Share it with others who're hiding the same thing. Make it *funny*. Take some of the sting out of it."

I had Bruce's attention. "Do you do that, Pete?"

"Yeah," I said and sipped coffee. I was lying. I never dealt with the core of *me*—the guilt and fear and pride and terror I'd felt since I was four years old and realized that I was black: middle-class, reasonably well-educated, not street smart, not cool, but *black*. I realized why and who I'd really been lecturing there: I'd never had the guts to do a routine about my childhood in Charity Hills, or what it means to be the only kid on your block who didn't belong to a gang. "Yeah," I lied again, looking at my watch. "Hell, it's almost four-thirty. I don't have to be at Burger Biggie until ten, but it's a little late." I threw some change on the table. "See you losers tomorrow."

Boonie gave me his hillbilly grin. "Yeah, y'all can see me hang out my dirty linen then. *I* ain't got no hangups about talkin' about my miserable upbringin' and poor but honest family."

"Yeah," I said, pausing at the door. "Tell us again about how you slept on bare mattresses with burlap for a cover . . . too poor to buy sheets or blankets."

Boonie grinned more broadly. "Shee-it. We had sheets. But they was cut full a holes 'cause of all the Klan meetin's we had to go to."

I shook my head. "See you tomorrow, Bruce. I'll watch *you* bomb, my cracker friend."

Instead, I watched Boonie die.

We were uptown, at the ritzy *Chez Harpo*, and the

place was crawling with cops. We were only a day away from the selection deadline for the joke-off, and there must have been forty comics competing for mike time that night. Bruce didn't survive the auditions for *Chez*, but he was there that night. So were about fifty cops: on the roof, backstage, in the audience, in uniform out front, and monitoring things from a trailer command center out back.

The mayor and the commissioner of police . . . what's-his-name . . . Gordon, had decided that the Joker comedy killings were making Gotham look bad. Whatever the reason for the security, I didn't see any way the Joker could get through it.

He did.

Boonie had them laughing. He was riding the wave real well, letting the laughter build and then punching it up higher, pausing at just the right spots, using the silences, when suddenly one of the silences stretched too far. The audience paused to breathe, waiting for the next funny bit.

Boonie started smiling as if he had just thought of something funnier than the story he'd planned to tell. The audience tittered in anticipation. Boonie's smile grew wider. His lips stretched back over his rear teeth. Some of the audience's laughter fell away, turned to gasps.

Boonie's color drained until his sunburned Georgia look gave way to a deathly pallor, grew paler still—by the time people started screaming, Boonie's complexion was the kind of white a corpse might show after a week in the water. His lips were stretched from ear to ear as if someone had pulled his cheeks back with meat hooks.

Boonie dropped the mike, gurgled something, and collapsed.

The cops went nuts. Bruce was the first one to Boonie,

but I was there a second later. My friend was dead, already cooling to the touch.

Bruce pounded his fist on his knee. "Damn, damn, damn . . ."

"What?" I said. "How?"

Bruce touched Boonie's neck where the tiniest dart was visible, barely larger than a mosquito. "Joker Venom. He's used it for years. Keeps altering the formula so no antidote works. Hardly elegant, but very effective. A message."

The cops were sealing all exits, searching the premises, frisking patrons, shouting orders.

Bruce shook his head. "The Joker's gone by now. Probably disguised as a police officer."

I was crying. I couldn't help it. "But why Boonie? Why him?" I spread my jacket over my friend's face to hide the terrible rictus. "I mean, he wasn't the best comic tonight. Certainly not the worst. Why'd that bastard choose *him*?"

Bruce seemed elsewhere—not in shock like the rest of us, merely—elsewhere. "I thought the Joker might be eliminating competitors," he said, almost speaking to himself, "but now I know it's something else."

I wiped away tears with the back of my hand. "What, dammit? Is he trying to sabotage the joke-off?"

"No. Definitely not."

Paramedics and cops had shoved through and pushed Bruce and me away from Boonie. They worked fast, tossing IVs, syringe cases, and technical terms around . . . but Boonie stayed dead.

I stood up and looked out over the heads of the crowd. "It doesn't matter," I said. "I'm going to enter that damn contest and win. Win for Boonie and for me. No way that this homicidal asshole is going to scare us away."

Edward Bryant and Dan Simmons

"You're right," said Bruce. "We do have to be in it. Both of us. And we will."

The word came just like a summons from the Almighty. Uncle Louis would have loved it. He always wanted me to be someone genuinely significant—like an African Methodist preacher-man. Becoming a fast-track management clone at Burger Biggie was sort of okay—but a no-account stand-up comic didn't cut it.

Anyhow, the message from God arrived via Gotham Bonded Messenger. No bicycle delivery here—nosirree. I was just heading out of my apartment to cover the night shift for an asshole buddy whose plane had gotten stranded in Cleveland when he'd gone home to see his father. Dad had started that long day's journey into kidney cancer. . . . Anyhow, I saw the sparkling silver BMW pull up to the curb. I figured it had to be a crack dealer, so I ignored it.

Naturally I was surprised when a hunched-over guy in a blue uniform got out and said directly to me, "You would be Mr. Tulley?"

I resisted the impulse to say something like, "Why yes, Mr. Stanley?" and just nodded my head.

The old guy crabbed up to me and handed over an envelope. Then he produced a smoky-gray Lucite clipboard and said, "Sign here." No "please."

What the heck. I signed. Could be there was an inheritance, though far as I knew, nobody in the family had died. Maybe it was a desperate creditor. I checked the return address. Just a box number in Clovertide, up on the north side.

I shrugged and ran my right index fingernail under the flap. The folded letter felt like vellum. I straightened it, smoothed the creases, and read the calligraphy. Classy stuff. At first I didn't register what it was I was seeing on that page. Then I let out a whoop that probably triggered all the car alarms on the block and raised at least a half-dozen of my more gris-gris–conscious dead kinfolk.

I was in. Damn. How about that. But I was supposed to report to some address up on the north side for an orientation. Tonight.

Faulkner said that when it came to sacrifice for writers, a good novel was worth any number of little old ladies. I figured I could extend that to artists of all kinds, so I kept it in mind when I called my understaffed B.B. and told the woman who answered that I was going to be a no-show tonight.

"What's wrong?" she said. "You sick?"

"Nope," I said. "I just got a formal notice saying I'm going to be competing in the big joke-off, the Gotham City Laughs of Tomorrow contest, the golden path to the Johnny Carson Show. There's a heavy-duty meeting tonight."

"Right," she said, clearly sounding as if she didn't believe the tone of my voice, much less a word I was saying. "Get in when you can, Pete. We really need you. Listen, take something, get better fast." She clicked off the line.

Yeah, right. I'd *better* get better fast. The joke-off was only three days away. And me, I was going to be there. Son of a bitch. I started humming along with the tune on the oldies station I'd left on as a burglar deterrent: "Laugh, laugh, I thought I'd die . . ."

I took the train north and got off at a station just a little different than my usual stop. This one had spotless

Edward Bryant and Dan Simmons

tile—and no graffiti—with tasteful turquoise accent
stripes. Maybe the stations downtown did, too, but you
would never notice for the krylon street art. When I got on
the T-local at the Sprang Street station, I'd seen a jagged
scream painted on the wall in Day-Glo purple: JOKER
LIVES. Someone else had sprayed an X over the second
word and added LAUGHS in bright scarlet.

The address on the invite was two blocks west. This
was a business neighborhood, lots of low office blocks in
brick and glass. It was getting dark now. I hardly saw
anybody who looked like me—hell, there was hardly
anybody at all on the street. They'd probably all headed
home at five to the 'burbs.

My destination was a nondescript office tower that
disappeared somewhere up there in the darkness. There
weren't any lit windows. When I walked past the alley
that bordered one side, I caught a glimpse of a familiar
vehicle—A European stretch limo parked in the back.

Bruce was here, too? I realized I was phrasing it in my
head as a question. I hadn't seen him perform since
Boonie bought the farm, but I couldn't imagine his im-
proving sufficiently to make any kind of final cut for
anything. I mean, he was a nice guy and he had heart, but
Jesus what a stiff.

"I think I owe this to you, Pete." The deep baritone
came from the darkness behind my left shoulder. I
jumped. A reassuring hand came down, the steel fingers
wrapping around my scapula. I wasn't reassured. "You
taught me some first-rate lessons."

"Holy shit!" I said. I knew who was there. "You scared
the crap out of me."

"I don't recall you being so scatological in your delivery," said Bruce. I could hear the trace of a smile in his
voice. I turned and looked at him. He was dressed som-

Dying Is Easy, *Comedy* Is Hard

berly in dark wool trousers and a black turtleneck. More like his namesake, it suddenly occurred to me. Good for him. Anything beat that Bozo zoot-suit he'd boasted the first time I'd seen him bomb. "Congratulations on jumping the final hurdle to the joke-off."

"You, too," I said. He put out his hand and I took it. Again, I felt like I was sticking my fingers in a walnut crusher. "Do you know what we're getting tonight?"

Bruce shook his head and motioned toward the dark building with the folded letter in his left hand. "I know only as much as you do."

Both of us started walking toward the front door. I realized there was a light inside, the dim glow from a gang of security monitors behind a lobby desk. The glass door opened as we approached. There were two big guys in rent-a-cop uniforms waiting for us. Both had mean eyes, though they each smiled. "Mr. Tulley? Mr., ah, Bruce?" said the bigger of the pair. At our nods, the other guy checked his clipboard and made marks. Obviously they'd been well-briefed. "Please take the elevator on the left and go up to the thirtieth floor. You both want room one-oh-one."

Bruce cocked his head. "Why is room one-oh-one on the thirtieth floor?"

The first guard shrugged. "I didn't set up the numbering system. I just know which place you're supposed to go."

"I was just wondering."

"You two are the last," said the second guard. "You better hurry. Mr. Carson's waiting."

We got in the elevator and punched thirty. As the doors slid shut, I said to Bruce, "Something significant about room one-oh-one?"

"Aside from the fact one wouldn't expect it to be on

the thirtieth floor, it's also the designation of the room in 1984 where prisoners encounter the thing they fear most.''

"Swell," I said. The elevator car suddenly seemed smaller, more claustrophobic.

Actually, room 101 turned out to be a respectably sized suite that didn't seem sinister at all. Nearly a dozen and a half comics were there, all ones I knew and a few I was friends with. Then there was Johnny. It was kind of weird seeing him without Ed or Doc. He was surrounded with four or five harried-looking aides. He was taller than I expected, but what can you expect when you've only seen someone on a nineteen-inch tube? I guess maybe I was expecting him to be nattily dressed in an Armani. Nope. He was wearing a perfectly tailored suit that I was pretty sure was from his own line. I couldn't be positive because I wasn't in that shopping bracket, but I figured Johnny wouldn't be disloyal to his own label.

One of his assistants raised his voice and said, "If you'll all find a seat, Mr. Carson would like to have a few words with you.''

I sat on a leather-upholstered couch with Bruce on one side of me, Diana Mulhollen on the other. She's such a sweet kid. I was glad she'd made the final cut. As long as I still won.

Johnny got up in front of us and said, "Ladies and Gentlemen, I'll keep this short. You're all here because you've been selected from among all of Gotham City's considerable ranks of the comically gifted." He grinned. "You're all among that select group of folks who end up going to parties that have been primed by some friend who told everybody else there, 'Hey, you've got to talk to so-and-so, he's the funniest guy you'll ever meet.' So what happens? You get there and everyone's looking at you expectantly, waiting for you to knock 'em dead." We

Dying Is Easy, *Comedy* Is Hard

smiled. Some of us snickered. Johnny smiled back and continued, "It's a tough life, being funny. It's our hope that the Gotham City Laughs of Tomorrow competition will make that life easier for some of you."

He went on to talk about the charities that would benefit, and about the live national TV hookup that would carry the proceedings across all America. Then he got to what I suspected most of us really wanted to hear about.

"The winner will be on the show the following week. We'll fly you out to Burbank and put you up like a king—or queen. And if that works out . . ." Johnny grinned and spread his hands beneficently. "There's no telling where you'll go. This will be the break of a lifetime."

I sensed eighteen indrawn breaths being held. Well, maybe seventeen, including mine. I'd glanced aside at Bruce. He didn't seem quite as mesmerized as the rest of us.

"My associates," said Johnny, "will give you full details about your time leading up to the competition. There will be," he added, "no formal rehearsals as such. The director will want to block out times with you, but you won't deliver your material." Diane and I exchanged glances. "The idea is to keep your humor as fresh as you can, as topical as you wish. Besides, most of you are already familiar with your fellow comics' routines."

Someone laughed appreciatively. There were smiles.

The rest was pretty much pro forma, with the exception of a revelation that stirred some enthusiasm. Robin Williams would make a special appearance at the beginning of the show. Very brief, but very funny, Johnny said. That was great. I couldn't think of anyone living I would rather have as a comedy role model.

Johnny asked for questions. There weren't many. Then he excused himself and turned us over to his aides,

Edward Bryant and Dan Simmons

who passed out laminated photo passes and rehearsal schedules. It turned out the telecast was originating from the Aladdin Theater, the very same place where Tiffany was drowned in *flop sweat*.

That didn't make anybody happy. Fast Eddie Teck brought it up. Johnny suggested we all just consider the competition a dedicatory memorial to Tiffany, George Marlin, Boonie, and the others in our little community who had died as the butts of the Joker's sadistic jokes.

Then the meeting was over. With a smile—I realized that Johnny had never displayed a straight face for the entirety of the evening—our host thanked us for our time and wished us well on Saturday night. People started to shuffle, shrugging on jackets and coats.

"Come on, Pete," said Bruce. "I need to be down at street level before the crowd."

I had no reason to stick around, so I beat him to the elevator and punched the button. There was something about Johnny's smile that weirded me out.

"One to a customer, gents and gentlettes," I said, "get'em while they're cold." Within five minutes I'd found myself in a situation that reminded me of doing volunteer labor (or not-so-volunteer if a guy were directed by the court to do a community service gig) in a downtown mission bread line.

When Bruce and I had exited the office building and walked to the head of the alley where his car had been parked, I found that the old codger who drove for him had turned that great gleaming barge around and popped the trunk lid. The luggage compartment was full of wrapped packages.

I looked down at them. "Bond market down, Bruce?

Dying Is Easy, *Comedy* Is Hard

You selling tailgate bargains now? Watches and Walkmen that fell off a truck, maybe?"

"I'm afraid not," said Bruce. "But I would appreciate it if you would walk over by the door and steer everyone here to me. *Everyone.*" The tone in his voice was all business. I wasn't about to say no.

Getting sixteen comics to congregate in the dark by an alley mouth where one of their colleagues was handing out butcher-paper-wrapped parcels was not the easiest job I've ever done.

"Listen," I said to them. "Humor him. Maybe he's the Joker. Just take a package."

"What *is* this shit, man?" said Fast Eddie, bouncing his packet on his palm a couple times. He tugged at the twine wrapping it, ripped some of the paper loose. "Old *clothes?*"

He was the last one to accept a package.

"All right," said Bruce. "Please, just a minute of your time. Then you can go."

They quieted. They crowded around the rear of the limo. They were still pumped up with the afterglow of having rubbed shoulders with the guy who could make the rest of their lives work like Swiss clockwork.

Bruce looked seriously at us all. "This might well save all our lives." His tone was convincing as all hell. "And if you think it's too weird, please, just trust me. It might save you from ending up like poor Tiffany or the rest."

Any grumbling or snickers ended at that.

"And if it is not something that's needed," Bruce continued, "then perhaps we still can provide a finale for the joke-off that no one in the audience will *ever* forget."

That was the hook. Having sunk it, Bruce went on. What he suggested to us was a hell of a lot funnier than any of his onstage jokes had been.

I like to think I own a healthy amount of self-confidence, but let me tell you—for three days I woke up soaked in, wore under my sodden clothes, and tried to wash off at night, more anticipatory *flop sweat* than had devoured poor Tiffany's whole body. I must have lost twenty percent of my bodyweight from evaporation, and didn't even have any spare pounds to lose.

I kept thinking about what I was going to spring on Johnny and Robin and sixty million viewers Saturday night. None of my usual material seemed funny anymore. Maybe it was time for fast-food jokes. Probably not.

Damn.

Maybe I could find a way to use the package Bruce had handed me out of the cavernous trunk of his limo as a prop. Maybe not. I wondered whether I was going to get ulcers out of this. Herpes lesions. Colitis. Pellagra. Pellagra?

I kept on sweating.

Saturday came and with it, the sort of feeling I hadn't had since I was five years old. I can remember wondering whether my folks would remember my fifth birthday. I wondered whether my dad would come back from a business trip down south. His trips on the road had been getting longer and longer. The feeling was anticipatory and scary, and a little sick with apprehension. When Dad showed and the cake started to smoke in the kitchen and the party started, it was almost an anticlimax.

I woke up at six, then dozed and rocked and tossed until about noon, when I finally rolled out of bed. My dad called ten minutes later to wish me luck and to inform me

Dying Is Easy, *Comedy* Is Hard

that the whole family would be home watching the show on TV. I'd gotten eight comp tickets for good seats at the Aladdin, but there were just too many in the family who wanted to go. So no one was. Dad had given the tickets to our church pastor and he was going to find worthy recipients. Shoot. I didn't say anything, but I was willing to bet I could have scalped those suckers for enough to keep me at least a month if I didn't win the joke-off.

Then Mom came on, and then Cousin Sook, and everybody else who was over at the house, and they all said they loved me and hoped I'd do 'em proud. I promised I would.

Then I went into the bathroom and threw up.

The Aladdin seemed a lot different than it had the evening of the fatal Tuesday Night Laugh Riot. The few handfuls of human beings, both performers and audience, who had been in attendance then had been dwarfed by this old Arabian nights deco barn. Tonight the two thousand seats were full. It was obvious that there had been a quick sprucing up. The sheets of paint, which had threatened to peel all the way off the ceiling and skate down into the crowd, had all been scraped and replaced. The gigantic stage curtains had been dusted—the maintenance crew must have beat them with telephone poles. But the place still smelled of mildew and outright rot.

The plan was simple. All us contestants were to be seated right at the front in the orchestra section. No hiding back in the green room. We would be in plain sight so the cameras could zoom in and catch our sick expressions as other performers outclassed us. Johnny was slated for the opening monologue; then he'd introduce Robin Williams, and Robin would hand the show back to Johnny. Then it

Edward Bryant and Dan Simmons

would be our turn. Five minutes max. Not even the fifteen Warhol had promised us all.

I amused myself for a while looking back for friendly faces in the rapidly filling auditorium. I didn't see any, at least no one who was familiar.

"Hello, Pete," I stopped craning my neck. Bruce settled himself in the theater seat beside mine. No mutant zoot tonight. He wore a perfectly cut tux. Very formal-looking. Class act. I started to rethink my policy of wearing exactly the sort of bright street clothes I had worn to the comedy clubs. At least my shirt was clean. I'd remembered to select one off a hanger in the clean end of the closet just as I was ready to go out and treat myself to a cab over to the theater.

"Hey, Bruce." I wished I felt as light as my voice. "How's it going?"

"I'm hoping for the best—and wishing you well." Those dark eyes stabbed toward mine. "You remembered to bring the package?"

I nodded. Yeah, I'd remembered after almost spacing it out. I'd been out the door with the key in the deadbolt before I remembered the parcel. Almost didn't go back. Then said the hell with it and unlocked the door again.

"Actually," said Bruce, surveying out colleagues, our friends, our competition, "I wish us *all* a great amount of good fortune tonight."

There was an undertone I couldn't quite interpret. "What's that supposed to mean?"

He smiled slightly—"Nothing important."—and hesitated even more slightly, but I still caught it. "Perhaps I'm a bit concerned about *flop-sweat*."

I laughed. "Don't worry. I've cornered the market right here in my armpits."

He touched my wrist reassuringly and sat back in his

Dying Is Easy, *Comedy* Is Hard

seat. The floor director signaled that it was one minute until airtime. The lights were already uncomfortably warm. Then the manic theme music—sort of a strange mixture of "March of the Marionettes" and the main theme from *Bubo the Clown's Afterschool Fun Club*—swelled up from the house PA system, and we were off.

God, the Gotham City Laughs of the Future competition started. The joke-off was on the air. I was simultaneously terrified and ecstatic.

And then, thirty seconds later, I was only terrified.

It happened almost as soon as the offstage announcer introduced Johnny and he virtually skipped onto the stage. The follow-spot found him and he waited patiently for the wild applause to die down.

"Good evening, ladies and germs," he said, grinning with all those sparkling teeth. "Or maybe just good evening, germs."

At that, I don't know what we all expected. Asian flu jokes, maybe.

That's not what we got. From the contestants' section, I had an especially good view of what happened next. Johnny cupped his hands into claws and reached up toward his own face. He sank his nails into his rosy cheeks and started moving his fingers as though kneading dough.

Then he ripped off his own face. He pulled away what seemed to be strips of pink flesh as the audience stared. As my little sister would say, it was totally gross. Another set of features emerged. I admit it—I was expecting Freddy Kruger.

It wasn't. It was Robin Williams.

Ripples of applause started with us in the front, then spread back into the loge and the balconies. On the stage,

Robin Williams grinned and it seemed like he was looking straight down at me. He held up his palms, acknowledging the delighted cheers.

I hadn't realized he was so tall.

Then Robin Williams ripped off his face, too. Just like Johnny. What the hell was this going to be, an endless series of Chinese boxes in the form of latex full-face masks?

I stared at the new persona of the man on stage. He yanked off his toupee and fluffed out his scraggly hair. Green hair.

Oh shit, I thought, along with, I'm sure, most of the rest of the audience all at the same time. It's the Joker.

The guy on the stage grinned from ear to ear, but he didn't look like a happy camper. "Ladies and gentlemen," he said, "a funny thing happened on the way to the theater." There was a great deal of consternation behind me in the audience. The Joker held up his hands for silence. There was a rapid-fire crackle of automatic weapons' fire and a few screams. The audience quieted down.

"That's better," said our lanky host. He slipped off his tux jacket and slipped the sleeves inside out. When he donned the garment again, I saw it was a tasteful metallic purple. This guy was for real, I thought. This wasn't another gag. I suddenly flashed on George Marlin and Tiffany and Boonie, all their faces, twisted and pained and dying.

I'll cop to panicking. I started to bolt out of my seat, but I felt a hand firm as wrought iron holding me down. "Hang in there," said Bruce. "You'll never get past his men."

That brought me back. I looked around. All the rent-a-cop security types were clustered around the auditorium doors. Funny, I'd never seen rent-a-cops carrying assault scatterguns and automatic weapons before.

The Joker cleared his throat with a sound like scraping snot off sandpaper with a putty knife. "As I was saying, a funny thing occurred. I happened by a nearby warehouse where your favorites, Mr. Carson and Mr. Williams, are presently safe but confined." He paused. "They said to say they were sorry they couldn't make it here in person tonight, but that they were tied up." The Joker laughed. He was the only one.

He stalked across the stage to the right, then back to the left. The spot followed. I noticed that the lighting tech had slipped in a purple gel. I had a feeling the Joker had covered every detail.

"If you're thinking that the outside world will see all this on television and collectively alert the National Guard and the marines, be advised I've addressed that possibility. Even as I speak, some sixty million of your fellows are watching an advisory crawl across their screens apologizing for technical difficulties. By way of substitution, a rerun of *Wild Kingdom* is playing." The Joker giggled.

"Now." The Joker stopped centerstage and leered down at us in the first few rows. "Let us cut right to the heart of the matter, figuratively now, later perhaps literally. I have reason to believe that among you is my old nemesis, the Batman." I could hear murmurs in the audience. "Do I speak plainly enough?"

I think the question was rhetorical. I leaned closer to Bruce. "The comics he killed . . ."

"Bait." Bruce's voice was quiet. I looked sidewise at him. He stared at the Joker like a tomcat stares at another tom who's invaded his territory. That fixedness frightened me.

"Don't worry," said the Joker. "You'll still get to see

Edward Bryant and Dan Simmons

the show you bought expensive tickets for, but you'll get a real bonus in addition. The comics who competed for the Laughs of Tomorrow finals are hoping for a new life. Now they can expect an additional treat—the possibility of death as well."

"He's gonna kill us all?" I said.

Bruce answered, "I don't think so. His plan will be mad, but it will still be a plan."

"Anyone who pays close attention to that caped clod who hounds me," said the Joker, "knows he possesses all the granite-jawed wit of Mount Rushmore. We are about to discover just how minuscule a sense of humor the man owns." He gestured toward us in the orchestra. "All of you up here. All eighteen. *Now!*"

I guess none of us saw any room for argument. Not with the Joker. Not with the two guys with Uzis who escorted us onto the stage.

When we were assembled like a herd—a gaggle—a flock—I don't know what they say out in the sticks—of sheep guarded by gun-toting goons, the Joker surveyed us cheerily. "You're all going to do your routines," he said. "I'm the judge for this. But guess what? I'm not looking for the funniest one anymore. I am searching for the worst, dumbest, least-funny among you. *That* one, I'm guessing, will be the Batman." He chortled. "*Then* we'll see just how a bad comedian dies on stage."

We all looked at each other. At least Diana Mulhollen and a woman named Winnie Morales had nothing to worry about. The thought must have occurred simultaneously to Winnie. She held up her hand like a schoolgirl.

"A question?" said the Joker, "or do you have to go to the little girls' room?"

"Do I gotta go through my routine, too?" said Winnie.

"Everyone does," came the answer. "My dark foe is a

devilishly clever master of disguise, even as I am. Each one of you is suspect.''

"But—'' said Winnie. I halfway expected her to drop her trousers and give the Joker some physiological proof of her not being Batman.

"No exceptions, unless you'd like to forfeit your participation in the competition. . . .'' The Joker's tone was ominous. Winnie seemed to pick that up. She said nothing and lowered her gaze to the stage at her feet.

"All right, then,'' said the Joker, his tone lightening. "Let's get to it. Time for our first contestant. Remember, friends, you get points for delivery and timing. For being funny, you get your life.''

This was absolutely crazy, I thought. Batman working incognito as an aspiring stand-up comic? Bat guano. I remembered the man I'd met in the police interrogation after George Marlin's death. That aura of brooding power wasn't anywhere among my colleagues.

I glanced over at Bruce as we both got up from our seats. That poor sucker might as well have a signed death warrant. He was as funny as—I tried to stop the thought. Too late.—a grave.

"Don't worry, Pete,'' he said. "We'll all do our best. We'll all pull through this together.''

Sure, I thought. Together—in a mass grave. One big pine box. Piano crate. God, was I getting hysterical? I took a deep breath. I figured I'd better start thinking about how to buff up my material to a higher sheen.

But as the Joker consulted his list, picking the first contestant, in my head I kept seeing a field of bleached skulls. Eighteen of them.

". . . so the chief says, 'Fine, then. I decree death by mongo . . .' '' And that wrapped up five minutes of pretty decent material by Goombah Dozois, the Cajun comic. The audience exploded into deafening applause. Goombah wasn't *that* good, but I'd gotten the feeling as we'd gone down the list of contestants that the crowd both needed a catharsis and wanted to do whatever they could to help us all survive. So they cheered everyone, good, bad, or indifferent. And even under the circumstances of being forced to be funny at gunpoint, or maybe *because* of it, some of us weren't even as hilarious as we would have been at, say, the Carob Club Comedy Countdown.

Goombah staggered out of the spotlight and rejoined us. The Joker scanned the list and said, "All right, my friends, we only have a few contestants to go." That included me. "So keep your pants on." Everytime he used one of those damned catch-phrases, we all cringed, not knowing if he was about to tie it to some crude wordplay-made-flesh. This time, he didn't.

"Our next competitor is . . . Mr. Bruce!" The crowd clapped. Bruce and I exchanged looks. His was enigmatic. He touched my arm with those iron fingers and then stepped into the spotlight. He blinked a couple times, I guess adjusting to the glare. He glanced at the Joker, then turned fully to the crowd.

"If any of you have heard me in the clubs, you know what kind of material I use. 'Hey, being a filthy rich kid isn't all it's cracked up to be . . . I remember how other kids brought their lunch boxes to school. I had caterers from Maxim's come to the cafeteria every day.' Not too funny, right?"

Right, I thought. Not too funny. Not then and not now.

Bruce paused a moment. A long moment. "I've been thinking a lot," he said, "about something my friend, Pete Tulley, told me." He shrugged. "I started thinking about some things I'd vowed never to think of again." I heard something in his voice. As little as I knew Bruce, I could still hear the keen of pain. "Let me tell you about someone I used to know."

I sneaked a look at the Joker. He was frowning, angular chin propped on one startlingly white palm, fingers curled up around his mouth like spider legs.

"This was when I was a student in the fourth grade," said Bruce. Huh? I thought. Richie Rich's childhood anecdotes? "A new school-year had just started and I was in my homeroom class for the first time. It was right after lunch and I was logy. You know, feeling about like an anaconda that's just eaten a goat. I could tell the teacher was, too."

Good delivery, I thought. He's picking up steam. The crowd could sense it. I saw some of the folks in the front starting to sit back in their seats instead of leaning forward anxiously.

"We looked like a perfectly good class, maybe thirty kids, all pink and scrubbed and full of enthusiasm. But as I said, we were all ready for an afternoon nap, and I think the new teacher was, too. Here he was, facing us all, and I think that for a moment, all he could do was to stare at us." Bruce shook his head and smiled. "I think he decided to try something new. He figured he'd stall us for a bit, make conversation while he was picking which way he wanted to take the class."

Hey, I tried to warn him telepathically, you're starting to wander, just a little. Get back on track.

"Finally—it was only a few seconds, but it seemed like an hour in my mind—he started with the first student at the near end of the far left row, a boy. 'Son,' he said, 'I'd like to find out a little bit about each of you. I want to ask about your families. Tell me something now, tell me what your father does.'

Edward Bryant and Dan Simmons

"So then the first boy said, 'My dad's a fire fighter.' And he told him about what his father did. I guess that worked out so well, the teacher went on to the next student, a girl. 'And what's your father do?' he asked. 'He's in the Army,' came the answer. 'He fights people.' And so it went," said Bruce. "On down the ranks of students, row by row, until he got to a young boy sitting right in back, in the very center."

I was trying to think, did I know this joke? It was new to me. I wondered where Bruce had dug up some new material. Or maybe he was spinning the truth, maybe this really was something that had happened to him back—I still couldn't quite believe it—when he was a fourth-grader.

"This little boy was short and dark—dark hair, dark eyes. He was quiet and very, very serious," said Bruce. "You could tell just by looking at him that he was lonely." There was the touch of something I couldn't immediately identify in Bruce's voice. Then it came to me—it was the sound of someone who wanted to cry, but couldn't. Just that tiniest of cracks.

"I was that little boy."

There was an odd tone in the way Bruce said it. I felt like I should hold my breath and stay very, very still.

"So then the teacher looked at the little boy and asked, 'Son, what does your father do?' I didn't answer, but just stared back at him. I think he suddenly knew that he ought to drop it then and there, but he didn't."

Bruce coughed and offered the crowd an apologetic half-smile. "But then it was for him about like it is for me now. He just kept on going, bulled right on ahead. He tried to get through what he thought was my shyness and said, 'It's okay, son, you can talk to me. Tell me what your dad does.'

Dying Is Easy, *Comedy* Is Hard

"I finally looked him straight in the eye and said in a low voice, 'Sorry, sir, he doesn't do anything. My father's dead.'"

Somebody in the audience gasped. I swallowed. This was weird. There was *something* about Bruce's delivery.

"He knew right then," said Bruce, "that he ought to get out of this any way he could. He should go on to the next student. He was entering some kind of Vietnam of primary education." He shook his head sadly. "He couldn't. God knows why, but he looked back at the little dark-haired boy—me—and said, 'It's all right, son, go ahead and tell me . . . what did your daddy do before he died?'"

Bruce paused so momentarily that I thought I was maybe the only person catching him swallowing.

"I looked back at him, still straight in the eye, and said, 'Well, he went *cckcckccckkkccckkk!*'" Bruce grabbed his own throat and mugged the visual image to go with the strangling sounds.

The crowd was stone silent.

It was like they didn't know what to do, didn't know how to react.

Then it began. A laugh somewhere in the balcony. A titter to stage-left in the loge. People giggled, groaned, started to guffaw. The laughter spread like the Philippine flu. So far as I could see, about the only people not absolutely breaking up were the thugs with machine guns.

Then the applause began to overwhelm the laughter. As best I could see Bruce's features from the side, he looked overwhelmed, too. He bowed slightly.

Above the roar of the audience rose a cackling from the stage. I turned my head and saw the Joker on the floor. Literally. He was holding his sides and roaring with

Edward Bryant and Dan Simmons

laughter, that terrible hyena bray I first heard at the Carob the night George Marlin blew his top.

I looked back at Bruce as he stared out over that ocean of reacting human beings. In his eyes I saw the shine of tears. What did this mean? I wondered. What had it cost?

The next one up was Winnie Morales. It was pretty obvi-ous she didn't relish having a turn in the barrel right after Bruce's bravura performance. She stared out over the crowd, obviously swallowed, then said, "Okay, so there were these three clergy-guys walking down the street. There was a Jewish rabbi, a Baptist preacher-fella, and an Irish bishop. They were on their way to play golf, when suddenly Saint Peter . . ."

And the next one up was me.

Well, I figured I could beat Winnie Morales. Maybe.

I knew I couldn't beat Bruce, but hey, I didn't want to. I just wanted to save my own hide. At least that's what I thought until I actually stood out there, bathed in a bloody red gel-light from the follow spots. I know it's a cliché, but time slowed for me.

Bruce's routine replayed in my head. Something came to me with all the subtlety of getting whupped up along-side the head with a flying mallet. I felt the shock of the brilliant white light, you know?

That tired old poor-little-rich-kid routine of Bruce's had somehow evolved to what he'd performed tonight. I was pretty sure it hadn't come easily. I still couldn't quite see all the cross-connections—it really was hard to see Bruce as a little boy in the fourth grade. But somehow he knew something about parents and death and had formed it into an awful-yet-effective story that had destroyed an entire theater.

It came to me. Yeah, he'd learned from me, all right. He'd listened to what I'd said back when he and Boonie and I'd been talking. Then he did the things I'd never done. He'd faced up. He'd gone *real.*

Just like I claimed to do, but didn't.

Hey, nothing like making myself feel like shit just when I was supposed to spend the most important five minutes of my life making people laugh.

The voice grated into my consciousness. "Oh, Mr. Tulley, are you going to perform or not? Has the cat got your tongue?"

Shit. I focused and saw the Joker smiling easily just a few yards away. Things snapped together inside. I hoped.

I nodded and took a deep breath. "Hey, how many of you out there realize I'm not really black?" That got a few titters. "Nope, truly I'm not. I'm black Irish."

"Oh, yeah?" That was maybe the first heckler of the night. Good, I thought. Then I squinted and realized I'd been needled by one of the Joker's goon squad.

So "Yeah," I said. "The name on my driver's license is O'Rio." The thug looked bewildered. Nobody out beyond the lights laughed, so I used exaggerated cheerleading gestures to spell out the name I said. This time there was a ripple of laughter.

"Good, you got it. Am I going too fast for you? Hey, let's go. You think it's *easy* being an Oreo in the inner city, man? I mean, you should have heard me playing the dozens with tough dudes on the corner. I mean, they got to serve first—

" 'Hey, man, yo mama wears combat boots when she gives it away in the alley.'

"So I snap back with, 'She ain't givin' it away, man.

Edward Bryant and Dan Simmons

She's in the alley pickin' aluminum cans outta the Dumpster to pay for my Harvard education, man.' "

More laughter. Thank God.

"No, I mean it—the other dudes from the block were like Fast Eddie Teck, you know? Carried switchblades. Me . . ." I slipped my hand into my hip pocket and pretended to snap something out. "One time this homeboy from the Night Vultures jumps me, and so I go for my calculator . . ."

A little more laughter. And so it goes.

When all of us were done, the Joker had the house lights brought up. The eighteen of us pretty much looked like the condemned, about to be shot as examples by some military junta in a soccer stadium.

"Well—" said the Joker. "That was quite a round of performances. I'm impressed that many of you, if you should survive this evening, might actually have a future in comedy—especially now that you'll have a great new experience to draw upon. Think of me as your agent of change; but remember, if you use any material pertaining to yours truly, to give me due acknowledgment. Otherwise I'll have to track you down and extract my fifteen percent." He giggled. "And I'll wager that, for most of you, fifteen percent is a great deal more than a mere pound of flesh." He looked contemplative, as though imagining harvesting his fee.

Then his voice changed mercurially. "Ah, yes, the matter of the incognito Bat-comic. I rather unwisely predicted I would have to make final disposition of the least funny of you." He ambled toward us. "Unfortunately that reflects badly on *you*." The Joker raised his cane and lightly touched it to Winnie Morales's chest. "Don't worry,

Dying Is Easy, *Comedy* Is Hard

my dear, you seem too much the mammal to be mistaken for my nemesis in a clever plastic disguise. Still—" he mused. There was fear in Winnie's expression. "—I really ought to be consistent in my declarations." Then he shook his head. "No, Ms. Morales, I won't slaughter you where you stand. The memory of your performance is punishment enough."

He stalked away, spun on his heel, walked back. "I have an idea. It had occurred to me that if the least funny of you *weren't* the Batman, what I might do is to follow the maxim of my old mercenary friends and simply kill you all and let God sort you out." I knew I was looking death in the distorted, grinning face.

"No," said the Joker. "One more chance. I must be mellowing." He chuckled, a horrible sound like a gerbil being pulled under the water and gargling as it drowned. "Yes, a chance. I'm going to extinguish the lights. When I bring them up again, I expect to see a clear sign that one of you is the Batman. I realize there is no phone booth—" He smirked. "Oh, yes, that's our *other* good friend. But you get the point." The Joker raised his hand. "All right, are you ready?" All of us sort of looked at each other. "If anyone tries anything funny, so to speak, my men will rake both the stage and the theater auditorium with automatic fire." I wondered if we'd all remembered our twine-bound, butcher paper-wrapped parcels.

"Now," said the Joker.

The lights went out.

Did you ever see *Spartacus*? There's that great scene where the Romans order the rebellious slave army to give up their leader and then first one, then another, and eventually every slave there proclaims, "*I am Spartacus.*"

Edward Bryant and Dan Simmons

I thought of that when the lights came up.

You see, we were all—all eighteen of us—the Batman.

I'd worn the costume from the package Bruce had given us under my clothing, as I guessed the rest had, too. In the sudden darkness, I'd struggled out of my street clothes, unfurled the thin cape from under my collar, and pulled the cowl over my head. I had donned the rest of the gear.

So here we were in the glare of the house lights. Eighteen Batpersons: white, black, brown, yellow, male, female, fit, paunchy, young, middle-aged. We were a sight.

The Joker stared at us. With some satisfaction, I saw there was genuine surprise on his face. Then he began to laugh.

I don't think it was wholly because we were all dressed in Bat-attire. It may have had something to do with the fact that all of us wore Groucho glasses, the heavy black-rimmed kind with the attached big rubber noses and bushy moustaches.

While we stood there waiting for summary execution, the Joker giggled, then chortled, finally whooped with merriment. Tears, or at least something viscous, dripped from his eyes. I thought the ends of his grin would meet around the back of his head.

When he finally could speak, he said, "Perfect. Absolutely perfect. Better than I'd ever hoped." He burst into laughter again.

And then he let us go.

It was that abrupt. The Joker made some hand motions. Smoke rolled across the stage. Blinding lights flashed. Choking, we fell to our knees. But then the fumes cleared. They weren't toxic.

The Joker was gone, along with his men.

Dying Is Easy, *Comedy* Is Hard

I felt a strong arm help me to my feet. Bruce. He set his
hand on my shoulder and steadied me.

It has been one hell of a show. You might say we'd
knocked the audience dead.

Just kidding.

I've had a lot of time to think about that night. I'm in
law school now—no more Burger Biggie, and no more
suggestions of seminary from Uncle Louis.

I still do some stand-up comedy, but there isn't a hell
of a lot of time. In such clubs as I still play, I've never
again seen Bruce.

About that night . . . I remember how I always used to
think I only came truly alive at night, when I could change
into somebody different from who I was in the sunlight,
somebody more powerful, someone who could move people to react.

I mean, I'm no dummy. I can put two and two together.
After what I've been through, there ain't nothing that
seems unlikely now.

The newspapers really did a number on what happened at the Aladdin Theater and the joke-off. The writers
speculated about why the Joker hadn't simply triggered a
massacre. The consensus seemed to be that the big *J* must
be entering some new phase of his "humor," something
seriously weird, maybe absurdist or the surreal.

Me, I've got a different idea. Maybe somebody just got
a little bored. No, check that. *Seriously* bored. And maybe
somebody decided that the lack in his life was his opponent.

He decided his antagonist had one crucial shortcom-
ing—no sense of humor. Or at least one so rudimentary it
needed a little jarring loose to set it in gear.

A worthy villain *needs* an equally worthy antagonist.
Just speculation, folks.

I keep my theories to myself. See, I figure that one day
I'll return to the night—and when I do, I might just need
a friend.

On the Wire

ANDREW HELFER

In his dream, he could hear his beautiful wife humming to herself as she worked in the kitchen. Through his window, he could see his two children playing in the backyard. As he lounged in his Lay-Z-Boy easy chair reading the afternoon paper, a handsome Labrador retriever slept quietly at his feet.

The late afternoon sun shone through the window, bathing him and his surroundings in its golden warmth. He looked up from the paper a moment, his eyes scanning across the wood-paneled walls of the den. He sighed with satisfaction. This was his kingdom. His domain. Life was good. He was happy.

The soothing tones of his wife's voice wafted in from the kitchen, barely outdistancing the tantalizing scent of meat loaf. "Supper's ready, dear," she sang, and in response, he rose from the chair's plush embrace to join the rest of his family in the dining room.

As he walked through the foyer connecting the two rooms he passed by a mirror hanging on the wall. Absently, he glanced at his reflection—and stopped. Something was wrong. Moving closer, he studied the face in the mirror—a face that could only belong to him. Brilliant blue eyes. An aquiline nose. A head of thick blond hair, sweeping back over his forehead. A hard, square jaw; thin masculine lips, a tan; healthy complexion . . .

This was not his face.

His eyes widened. "This is not me," he murmured in disbelief. A finger tentatively poked at the freshly shaven cheek, while another pushed down on his lower lip, pulling it back to reveal an even row of pearly white teeth.

"Dear?" his wife called from the next room. "I said that supper was ready . . . Is everything okay in there?"

"Is everything okay?" he muttered to himself incredulously. "Is everything OKAY?" Someone had done something to his FACE, for god's sake! Someone had entered his kingdom and performed massive plastic surgery on him when he wasn't looking! Someone has stolen his very identity out from under him! Who was this freak in the mirror? Certainly not HIM!

He could feel his stomach begin to turn. A tightening sensation, down in the pit of his stomach. A rhythmic pulsating, an invisible hand squeezing at the bottom of his stomach, urging up the partially digested remains of his lunch. Despite it all, his eyes remained riveted to the horror that faced him in the mirror. Unable to turn away, he felt the hot acid rising up toward his throat. Nothing could stop it—

"Honey?" the voice behind him said, startled. On the cusp of release, his lips pursed tight to contain himself, he spun around. His wife . . . his beautiful wife stood before him, a five pound meat loaf laid atop the serving platter in her hands. She had a quizzical look on her face. "Are you all right—"

Something inside him clicked, and his world went green. He could feel his mouth open wide, feel his jaws unhinge, his face split, his body crack apart . . . and explode in a torrent of brilliant emerald bile. . . .

He awoke with a scream, his frail body jolting upright from the nightmare-soaked sheets. Beads of sweat dripped from his forehead, sliding down over his impossibly disfigured jawline. His lips trembled with fear. He felt his heartbeat thundering through his temples, and fearing his brain might suddenly explode from the pressure, gripped the sides of his head tightly. The strawlike texture of the hair there reassured him somewhat . . . but still, he had to be sure.

Weakly, he rose from the bed, and wavered through the darkness of the flophouse room toward a sliver of light in the distance. Recently, he'd taken to leaving the bathroom light on during the night. It was a beacon of something . . . something he couldn't quite pinpoint, but its presence had proved comforting to him of late.

A moment, and he pushed open the door. The bathroom mirror was first to greet him. He sighed a sigh of relief. His complexion was chalk-white again. His hair was green again. His lips were a familiar blood-red hue. His teeth . . . oh, his teeth. How beautifully yellowed and rotting they were. He smiled. And the smile grew wider, and wider, his lips pulling taut against his teeth, his jaw, until what was once a smile was now a sneer of monstrous proportions, a gaping half-moon shaped wound.

On the Wire

He turned the faucet on, splashed some cold water on his face to wash away the last lingering effects of his dream and turned back toward the bed outside.

Refreshed, he lay down on his back, eyes open in the darkness. Soon—in a week or two, when the heat had died down, he'd get out of this fleabag hotel, reconsider his alternatives, and, inevitably, begin plotting the next round in his ongoing war with the Dark Knight and humanity itself. But until then, he was stuck here, with nothing to amuse himself but a deck of cards, a primitive black-and-white television set . . . and his dreams.

God, it was depressing.

An hour passed. At 3:00 A.M., he gave up on the idea of sleep and turned on the television. His fingers tapped on the remote-control changer buttons with increasing frequency as the moments wore on, the pictures becoming a montage, then a blur of rapidly evaporating images— snippets of commercials, videos, reruns, and ancient movies. In the midst of it all, though, something had caught his eye—something that spurred his imagination. . . . He switched back and forth along the dial, searching for it. In a moment, he'd found it.

"Lonely?" A woman's voice said seductively. The screen showed a picture of a sinewy male yuppie sitting on a leather couch, his brow furrowed, eyes cast heavenward as he considered her question. "Meet interesting people just like you—right now!" The image was replaced by one of the same men dialing a telephone number. "Dial the Pleasure Line! Talk to me and women who want to talk to you! It's a great way to make friends, meet new and interesting people . . . and it's only one dollar a call! Don't miss out on any of the fun! Call now!" A number flashed on the screen. He committed the number to memory and, after turning off the television, reached for the phone.

Seven digits later, a tape-recorded female voice—one he recognized as the same as the voice on the television—came on the line. "Welcome to the Pleasure Line," it said. "Prepare to let it all hang out. Nothing's sacred, everything goes . . . for only twenty cents a minute."

The tape recording abruptly came to an end, and he found himself floating in an electronic void. There was no one else there . . . at least, no one else he could hear.

"Hello?" he said, rather meekly. No answer. He cleared his throat and said the word again, and again, but was greeted only by silence. Another bad idea, he thought to himself. Another buck down the drain. He made a mental note to find and blow up the company that ran this particular phone service, and was about to hang up when he heard the woman speak.

"Hi," she said, her slightly nasal voice full of hope and smiles. And that was all he needed. From the tone of that single word, his mind instantly assembled a full psychological and physical profile of the woman. He knew how she looked, how she walked, how she dressed. He knew about her dreams, her hopes, her fantasies—and knew she would tell them all to him soon enough. He would listen patiently to the fantasy, and then mercilessly squeeze the ugly reality out of her. He'd make her beg for him to stop. And he wouldn't.

She was perfect . . . the perfect toy. The perfect mouse. Soon, he would pounce upon his prey. But until then, he reminded himself, to prolong his pleasure he had to be on his best behavior.

"Why hello, young lady," he answered coolly, not

betraying an iota of his secret knowledge. "What's your name?"

"Uh . . . Cathy. What's yours?"

"Call me . . . Jerome."

"Jerome . . . Jerome . . . you don't sound like a Jerome. Is that your real name?"

"No. Should that matter?"

"I dunno . . ." she said, thoughtfully. "But why not use your real name? It's only a name, after all. Lots of people have the same first name."

"Not the same as mine, my dear," he said, dropping in an element of mystery.

"Oh," she said, taking the hint. "Are you . . . famous? Are you not using your real name because I might recognize it?"

"Recognize . . . ?" he answered, feigning surprise. "Why . . . yes. But it's not you I'm worried about, dear Cathy. It's the others. The silent ones—the ones who listen in on the conversation of others and never say a word. They're out there, Cathy. I can feel them. What if I gave my real name and said some . . . personal things about myself. What if someone took down all those very personal facts of my life! It might very well ruin my career! Surely you can see the difficulty of my position here—"

"I didn't really think of it," she said, almost apologetically. "I didn't mean to force—"

"Someday, perhaps, I'll tell you who I really am. Perhaps. But until then, let's keep this on a pseudo basis, shall we?"

"Sure," she said, with obvious disappointment. "Whatever you want."

"But enough about me. Tell me about yourself, Cathy.

Andrew Helfer

Tell me everything—and start with what you look like. . . ."

"Well, I'd rather talk about—"

"Yes, yes . . . we'll get to me. But you first. Please. I need to form a picture. Just to get a sense of who I'm talking to."

"Well . . . I guess I'm pretty. Most people tell me I am, anyway. I'm five foot six, weigh one hundred and fifteen pounds, I've got blonde hair and blue eyes . . . and a pretty nice figure, I guess . . ." She paused, looking for something to cinch the visual impression. "There was this woman on the cover of last month's *Cosmo*," she said finally. "I guess I look like her . . . a little."

He took it all in for a long moment, savoring her mundane fantasy before beginning again. "Hmmm . . ." he said. "You sound very attractive. Almost too good to be true, eh?"

She tittered nervously, confirming that it was. "Now it's your turn," she said. "Tell me about yourself."

He cleared his throat and began, recalling the nightmare image in the mirror. "I'm six foot one. One hundred and eighty pounds. Blond hair. Blue eyes. I've got a good solid build. I work out."

For a moment there was silence. "Really?" she said breathlessly, anxious to believe him.

"And . . . I wear glasses." he said. Throw in an imperfection or two, just to keep it honest. "I'm a little nearsighted."

"Oh, wow," she said. "I wear glasses, too! Isn't that neat?" She waited for his reply, but there was none forthcoming, so she pressed on. "What do you do for a living? I bet you're a doctor or a lawyer or something like that. You sound so smart."

On the Wire

"I'm a criminal, Cathy. A very smart criminal," he said. "So smart," he continued, "that you might say I've gotten away with murder." He felt a gleeful snicker coming on, and bit his lip hard to keep it down.

She began to laugh. "You're so funny! I love it!" The laughter subsided. "Come on. Really. What do you do?"

"Actually, I'm an entertainer," he responded. "A comedian. Of sorts. One of the highest earning funnymen in the business, I'd guess."

"Really?" she said. He could hear the awe in her voice. "That sounds sooo exciting!"

"It pays the bills," he said nonchalantly. "After a while, it becomes a job like any other—though I must admit the element of danger continually refreshes the experience."

"Danger?" she said. "What kind of danger? Like people booing? Or throwing tomatoes? How dangerous can being a comedian be?"

"It has its moments," he answered. "I cater to a very unusual crowd. Even though I know they enjoy my act, down deep they'd like to see me dead."

"I don't understand," she said, clearly mystified.

"It doesn't matter. Nothing matters right now—except you and me," he said, adding a little French twang to the last bit. God, he could be charming. He heard her giggle. She was flattered. "Now you tell me, Cathy—what do you do for a living?"

"Well," she said. "Nothing as exciting as all that. I work down in the financial district. I'm a receptionist at a stock brokerage company. Maybe you know it—Butz Brothers?"

He did know it. He remembered robbing that particular company about five years before. A pretty good haul. He'd

Andrew Helfer

selected it because he thought the name was funny. Any company named Butz deserved to be cleaned out. "I think I've heard of it," he said.

"It's pretty boring, and the pay isn't great. But I'm going to steno school at night, because I'd like to become a court reporter. . . ."

"Ah . . . we all have our dreams. . . ." he said wistfully. "Are those your dreams, Cathy? To become a stenographer?"

"No, silly," she answered, tittering. "What I'd really like to do is be a TV star. On the soaps. To have people know my face when they see me in the street. To have them ask for my autograph. To go to those parties you see on *Entertainment Tonight*. That would be cool." She paused, sensing she might have revealed too much, not realizing he already knew it all. "I bet you get to go to those parties, huh?"

It was time. He ignored the question. Instead, he posed another:

"Are you lonely, Cathy?"

"Me? No . . . of course not," she said, a hint of nervousness in her voice. "I've got lots of friends. And I'm dating three different guys right now. Nothing serious yet, but . . ."

"Cathy, why did you call this number?"

"Because I'm bored," she answered defensively. "Just for now. I couldn't sleep."

"If you couldn't sleep, why not call one of your friends? I'm sure THEY would understand your problem."

"But—"

Time to lunge. "No, Cathy," he said. "The simple truth of the matter is, you're lying. About everything. Well, maybe not about the job—that seems mundane enough—

but everything else is a lie. The boyfriends. The description. It's all a load of crap . . . isn't it?"

Silence. "Isn't it?" he roared. He could almost feel her jump on the other end of the line.

"Yes," she said. He could feel all her energy, all her enthusiasm, drain out of her with that single word. She was beaten.

"You're fat, aren't you, Cathy?"

"Yes." Her voice was small. Almost inaudible.

"You're ugly, aren't you?"

"Yes."

"You have no boyfriends. No one pays any attention to you at all. You go to work everyday, ride the subways, walk the streets, take the elevator up to your office . . . but you're invisible. No one notices you. No one sees."

"Yes."

"And afterwards, you go home to watch game shows and soap operas and eat chocolate and junk food and get deeper and deeper into the lonely pit you call a life."

"Yes." She was whimpering now. Making soft snuffling noises as the despair took hold of her. He had her where he wanted her. Now it was time for the masterstroke.

"And you ask yourself—is this life worth living? And you think about the knife in the kitchen. About the pilot light on the stove. About the gas in the oven. About the pills in the medicine cabinet."

The line was silent. He continued.

"Go to the medicine cabinet. Get the pills and bring them back here. I'll wait for you. And along the way, stop in the kitchen. Turn on the gas."

Silence.

"It's the only way, Cathy. You know it. I know it. At

least you'll have some company on the way down. Isn't that what you want?"

She cleared her throat. She was almost there. He clenched his fist in divine anticipation. One more insinuation—one more bit of gentle prodding—would send her toppling over the edge. Then she would be his. Then she would—

"Yo', dude!" a new voice suddenly interrupted. "Is this the party line or what?" It was a young voice—he couldn't have been over eighteen years old. But it was enough. In the midst of this, the most delicate of psychological surgeries, some cretinous, addled-brained punk had knocked over his instrument tray, and scattered his scalpels all over the operating theater. He might still complete the surgery—but he had to be quick about it.

"Get off the line, punk," he growled.

"You talkin' to me, dude?" the kid said defiantly. "What're you, king of the phone company, or what?"

"Don't push your luck, punk," he answered. "Don't make me angry. We're in the middle of a conversation here. We don't want to be interrupted."

"Oh, yeah," the kid said. He could almost see him smirk. "A conversation. Right. Sure. That ain't no conversation, man. You're just playin' with the babe's head. Tryin' to screw her up. Make her cry. Why 'n't you leave her alone, dude. Why 'n't you just kill yourself."

"I can trace this line, punk," he said. He was bluffing and he prayed the punk wouldn't know it. What else could he do? "I can find out where you live. I can kill you. And your parents. Burn your house to the ground. Don't push me."

"You're full of it, dude," the kid answered. "Go ahead and trace it, if you can. I'm at a party right now, man—and I don't even know who's throwin' it! You killing anyone,

On the Wire

it's gonna be the dudes who threw this bash!'' The kid began to laugh, a slightly drunken hiccuping laugh. He was taunting him. It was infuriating.

"Final warning," he said, knowing that he'd already thrown down his last card. "Get off the line, or I'll—"

"I ain't talkin' to you anymore, creep," the kid said, dismissing him. "Where's the babe? She still there?" He paused, waiting for her to respond. "Yo', babe! You still out there? Come on—I wanna talk to you."

From somewhere far off, he heard her again, emerging from the despair-filled corner he had backed her into. Her white knight had arrived to save her, and she was rushing up to meet him. "Hi," she said. Her voice was hoarse. She'd been crying.

"Hi, babe," the kid said. "My name's Ronnie. What's yours?"

"Cathy. Nice to meet you, Ronnie."

"Likewise," he said. "I just wanted to tell you that this dude is a psycho. A nut job. Any dude plays with someone's head like that, they gotta be a freak. Know what I mean?"

"I guess . . ." she said. She was coming back. It was over. He'd lost.

"You don't wanna even talk to a guy like him," the kid said. "Scary dude. He's probably sitting in some hotel somewhere, all by himself, like, gettin' off on all this."

"You think?" she said. He could feel his anger reach a new level. He wanted to break in on the conversation, wanted to tear the both of them up into tiny pieces—but he knew his power was gone—and that, for tonight at least, he was totally, utterly impotent.

"I know," the kid said. "Guys like that—they're losers."

"I guess you're right," she said.

"Lissen. I'm at a party over on Northside right now. It's pretty cool. Lots of beers, good music. We'll probably go till dawn. Why'n't you come on over? It'll be fun."

"Really? You think it'd be okay?"

"Sure. Got a pencil?" He was about to give her the address when she stopped him short.

"Wait," she said. "What about . . . *him*. I mean, he's probably still listening—if he hears the address, he could come over and—"

"Don't worry about it. He tries anything, me 'n' my buddies, we'll kick his butt. Might even do this party some good—it could use a little excitement. Matter of fact," he continued, "if the psycho dude is still out there, I'd like to extend a personal invitation to him. You come on over, we'll give you a dose of some righteous hell." After the kid gave the address to her, he prepared to sign off. "You're sure you're coming?" he said. She sensed he really wanted her to.

"Absolutely," she reassured him.

"Cool," he answered. "See you then." There was a click, and the kid was gone.

The line fell silent. Still, he hadn't heard a second click, one that would have signaled Cathy's departure. Was it possible? Was she still there? Would he have yet one more chance to turn the game around and pick up where he'd left off? He pressed his ear hard against the receiver, as though that might improve his hearing.

He heard her take a deep breath. "You're a bastard . . . a sadistic bastard," she said in a measured, somehow confident voice. "What did I ever do to you? I called this line to have some fun! Because I wanted to be something I'm not! I look at myself in the mirror everyday. I can see what I am! I don't need a jerk like you to tell me. But what the hell's wrong with playing some other part once in a while?"

He was about to answer her, but the question turned out to be a rhetorical one. A click, and she, too, was gone. He was alone.

It was hopeless. He hung up the phone. He'd lost the game. The goddamned surfer punk had done it. It was all his fault. He wished he could shove his fist down the punk's throat and tear out his beer-bloated teenaged belly. He knew where they were. He had the address. He wanted to go to that party so badly he could taste it. Wanted to enter the house with his trusty Uzi in hand and mow them all down. Let God sort out which one was Cathy and which one was that damned punk.

But he knew he couldn't. He couldn't afford to be seen on the streets. Not now. Not yet. They all thought he was dead. If someone—a cab driver, a pedestrian, anyone—should identify him, the hunt would start all over again. And he wasn't prepared for that. All he could do was stay here. Sit in this hotel room, while the woman whose life he'd come so close to destroying discovered the meaning of life all over again.

God, it was depressing.

Nothing had gone as planned. Not even the slightest thrill was afforded him by that humorless God upstairs. He couldn't do anything right. He closed his eyes tight in the darkness, feeling tears welling up inside him. His life was a waste. There was only one cure for it.

He reached under his bed and groped around between mattress and boxspring until he felt the cool polished wood handle in his hand. He pulled it out and held the gun gingerly.

He snapped off the safety. Pulled back the trigger.

Andrew Helfer

Heard it click into place. Pressed the barrel against his temple. Squeezed the trigger.

He heard the *pop!* sound as the rolled-up flag with the word "Bang!" on it unfurled and bounced against his head. It smarted. But it felt good.

He laughed himself to sleep.

Fat Tuesday

NANCY A. COLLINS

It's a jungle out there.

That particular statement holds true for most major metropolitan areas in the United States. But when it comes to Gotham City, you're talking Amazon rain forest.

There's something about Gotham that seems to attract the more lethal—and strange—of the two-legged predators. Over the years, it has played host to the likes of the Joker, Two-Face, Catwoman, and, more recently, the Penguin. If ever there is a city haunted by its own bad dreams, it is Gotham.

Yes, it's a jungle out there.

But even as every jungle has its predators and prey, it also has its hunters.

And Gotham City's greatest hunter is very skilled, indeed, at finding and bagging the biggest, and most dangerous game to be found on its mean steets.

Fat Tuesday

"Hurry it up, Smitty! I'm freezin' here waitin' on you!"

"Haze, keep your voice down! You're gonna have every cop in Gotham down our shorts, you keep yackin' like that!"

Atkin "Haze" Haskill blew into his cupped hands and snorted derisively. "You know Fat paid off the local cops to make sure they'd be turnin' a blind eye tonight! You're scared of crossing the Batman!"

"You bet I'm scared!" Salvadore "the Locksmith" Martinez muttered as he finished picking the warehouse office's lock. Everyone called Martinez "Smitty," including two-bit punks like Haze.

"I don't see what the big deal's all about. He's just some jerk in a stupid Halloween costume!"

"You ain't from here, man. You don't know from squat! That dude took down *the Joker*! That ain't nothing to be laughin' at, get me?" He pocketed his set of twirls and hurriedly pushed open the door. "C'mon, let's get in, do the deed, and go, awright?"

"What does the boss want with just some stupid files from a stinkin' warehouse, anyways?"

"Beats me. But if Fat tells you frog, you say, 'how high?' if you get my drift?"

Haze grunted, shouldering past the older man.

Smitty cursed Joey the Nose for sending him out with this know-nothing kid. He'd have been better off pulling the job alone. But Joey the Nose was Fat's *capo*, and Martinez had been in the business long enough to know that you don't mess around with the chain of command.

The kid had a point, though. And it wasn't all under his hat. What was so important about a lousy shipping firm's records? If the office was anything to go by, the place was hardly rolling in dough—legit or otherwise.

Still, what Fat Tuesday wanted, he got. Or you better have a good reason for *why* he didn't get it. Like you being shot through the head.

Haze yanked on the top drawer of a nearby filing cabinet. "This looks like it."

"Whoa, Haze! Set off a flare while you're at it!"

"Look, why don't you worry for me, Smitty? If anything happens, *I'll* deal with it, okay?" Haze sneered, patting his shoulder holster.

Smitty shook his head and began searching the files. There was no point in talking to hotshots like Haze. The fool would sooner or later macho his way into the morgue. Probably sooner rather than later.

"Found it yet?"

"I think so."

Haze frowned over Smitty's shoulder. "Antarctica Exports, Inc.? What do they export? Ice cubes?"

"C'mon, let's just get out of here."

"You really *do* have a problem with this bat jerk, don't you?"

Smitty groaned and headed toward the door. Joey the Nose owed him one. Big time.

Haze hurried after his partner as he made his way across the darkened warehouse floor. Light from outside spilled through the skylights, providing patches of illumination.

"C'mon, Smitty! I was just jokin' with you about— what the heck was that? Sounded like a bird or something up in the rafters."

Smitty saw the silhouette of a monstrous bat, its wings spread wide, spill across the floorboards at his feet. He didn't bother to find out what would cast such a shadow. Martinez tightened his grip on the file folder and ran as fast as he could. He heard Haze yell something, but he kept running. Let the dumb punk find out the *hard* way.

The moment Haze saw the shadow, every joke and wisecrack he'd ever made about the Batman seemed to jam in his throat, choking him.

He made a cawing noise and spun around, clawing at his shoulder holster, just in time to see something sailing out from the shadows, and—it had wings! Wings as black as hell!

His finger tightened on the trigger and the gun barked, kicking in his hand. He knew he'd hit it— there was no way on earth he could have missed it at this range—but the demon-bat didn't stop coming, striking him full in the chest and knocking him onto the floor.

Haze screamed as steel-hard fingers dug into his wrist, forcing him to let go of the gun. He struggled to free himself from the weight pinning him to the ground, only to receive a right to the jaw that rocked his head back and brought blood to his mouth.

Haze moaned as the Batman dragged him to his feet by his suit lapels, thrusting his face so close to his own their noses all but touched.

"What are you doing here?"

Haze's eyes goggled as he got his first good look at his captor. Dressed in a dark cowl with peaked ears and vaned cape, the Batman looked more demon than man.

"I—I—"

Nancy A. Collins

"I *said*, what are you doing here? I won't repeat my-self again."

Haze had been in the business long enough to know how to hold his mud. Gotham's Finest had yet to get him to admit to anything besides being born, even when they had used their batons for choir practice. But *this* wasn't some doughnut-munching no-neck vice slob.

"We were just boosting some files, man! Honest! We're weren't out to steal anything but the files!"

"Who do you work for?"

"Fat Tuesday."

The Batman smiled, making Haze even more nerv-ous. "Ah, yes. Alcide 'Fat' Tuesday. Imported swamp-scum from Louisiana. What does he want with these files?"

"I swear I don't know, man! I swear!"

"The man who was with you—that was Salvadore 'the Locksmith' Martinez, wasn't it?"

"Huh?"

The Batman tightened his grip on Haze's suit front, lifting him onto his tiptoes.

"Yeah, that was Smitty, awright! Just put me down, okay?"

The Batman shrugged and let go of Haze's lapels. White-hot stars went off behind his eyelids as his butt struck the floorboards.

"If I tell you everything I know, will you let me go?"

"I'm handing you over to the police after you tell me where I can find Fat Tuesday."

"Are you crazy? He'll have my guts for garters if he finds out I even told you the time of day!"

The Batman reached down and pulled Haze back onto his feet, this time using his expensive Italian silk tie for leverage.

Fat Tuesday

"You don't understand; I'm not *asking* you."

"I—ack—think I—remember—ack . . . ack—where you can find him!"

"I thought you guys is supposed t'serve and protect?" The waitress yawned behind the counter at Zippee Do-Nuts. "You been here three hours an' the only servin' going on's been me refilling your coffee. Ain't there no crime on the streets t'night, or is it a holiday or something I don't know about?"

McIlhenny shrugged and bit into another Bavarian creme-puff. "What y'don't know don't hurt ya, Gertie. Ain't that right, Stoner?"

"You got it!" replied his partner. Just then, a sqawk of static burst from the portable radio resting on the countertop.

"...Investigate reports of gunfire at Antarctica Warehouse...seven-eighty-nine Meredith...repeat..."

McIlhenny reached over and thumbed down the volume on the radio and resumed chewing his pastry. Neither police officer moved from their stools.

"Say, ain't Meredith near here? Like a couple blocks over?" asked Gertie as she slopped coffee into their mugs. "Shouldn't you guys check that out?"

Stoner shot his partner a sideways glance before dunking his cruller. "It's nothing to get worried about. Am I right, Mac?"

"You got it. Any more of them eclairs, Gertie? Gertie? Wassamatta, cat got your tongue?"

Gertie stood, slack-jawed, behind the counter, staring in the direction of the shop's parking lot. The coffeepot slid from her fingers, splashing tepid brew onto her Supp-Hose and white loafers.

McIlhenny and Stoner turned on their stools, craning their necks in the direction of Gertie's stare. Stoner automatically reached for his service revolver, then froze.

There was something parked beside their patrol car. It was black and shiny, its armor gleaming under the lot's sodium lights like the carapace of an insect. Stoner had seen low-riders before, but nothing as chopped and lean and lethal-looking as the machine crouched on the other side of the plate-glass window. Even with its engine idling, he could feel the countertop vibrate.

As they watched, part of the armored vehicle's carapace retracted and a man—at least it *looked* like a man—emerged from the driver's side. He stood well over six feet in height and wore a dark, skintight costume, his face hidden by a close-fitting mask with peaked ears attached to a long, flowing cape.

McIlhenny felt the evening's coffee and pastries turn into sludge in his guts. "Oh, God. It's *him!*"

"Shut up, you jerk!" hissed Stoner.

The masked man removed what looked like a bundle of wadded-up clothes from the passenger side of his vehicle and strode forward, kicking open the door of the doughnut stand with one booted foot.

"Relax, gentlemen. I don't want to cut your coffee break short." With that the Batman deposited his night's catch, hogtied like a calf ready for branding, at their feet and left.

McIlhenny, Stoner, and Gertie were still staring in astonishment at the trussed-up Haze, his mouth gagged with an expensive silk tie when the Batmobile left the parking lot as quickly and silently as when it had first arrived.

"Who's Daddy's little precious? Who's my sweetie-lumps, hmmm?"

The baby alligator cradled in the crook of Alcide Tuesday's well-padded right arm grunted as its owner chucked it under its chin.

"Look what Daddy-waddy has for his little snookums!" Tuesday dangled a piece of raw chicken above the reptile's head. Something resembling interest appeared in the gator's eyes. With a quick snap of its jaws, it snatched away the proffered flesh.

"What a good boy!" That's Daddy's little Snapper!"

One of Tuesday's soldiers stuck his head into the office. "Boss, Smitty's back. He don't look so good, and Haze ain't with him."

Tuesday frowned, sending ripples through his chins. "Did he bring back the files?"

"Looks like it."

"Very well." Tuesday carefully replaced his pet alligator in its aqurium next to his antique rolltop desk. "Send him in."

Smitty pushed his way into the room before the goon had time to clear the threshold. The lockpick's swarthy skin was the color of cream cheese and his eyes all but bugged out of their sockets. "Boss! Boss, we're in deep this time!"

Tuesday pursed his rosebud lips and stroked the fluff of a goatee that decorated the first of his several chins. "Smitty, you look as if the devil hisself was on your tail!"

Nancy A. Collins

"It's the Batman, Fat! He ambushed us as we were leaving the warehouse!"

Tuesday's eyes turned hard, resembling twin pieces of black glass set in dough. "The Batman? Did he follow you?"

"No, but he collared Haze. And I'm bettin' that stupid punk spills his guts first chance he gets!"

"We'll see about that. What about the files? Did you get them?"

Smitty produced the manilla folder from the inside of his jacket. "Here they are, Boss. What's so important about Antarctica Exports that the Batman would be casin' the joint?"

Tuesday smirked as he thumbed through the papers inside the files. "Nothing—except that it's a front company for the Penguin."

Smitty swallowed and wiped the back of his hand across his lips. "P-Penguin?" Gotham City had a rep for freakish crime lords and the Penguin, after the Joker, was considered one of the nastier specimens.

"I'll teach that funny-lookin' weirdo to mess with my rackets!" snarled Fat Tuesday, waving the file folder like it was on fire. "I've been collectin' information about that slimy bird's business dealings for months now!" Let's see how he likes it when *I* start cuttin' in on *his* action, hmmm? I might not be able to get a man in close enough to take him out, but I sure can hit him where he lives—in his rackets!"

"But, what about the Batman?"

"You have a point there, Smitty. That vigilante is as much a thorn in my side as the Penguin! Perhaps a few weeks spend visiting my native environs are in order. After all, it *is* carnival time. . . ."

Fat Tuesday

"What about me? I'm sure the Batman made me . . . I need a place I can lie low for a while—until he gives up."

Tuesday scratched his first chin and looked thoughtful. "That might prove difficult, Smitty. The Batman isn't one to give up."

"Boss, I'm *beggin'* you! If they catch me again, they'll throw away the key!"

"Okay! Okay! I'll see to it that you won't be found."

"Thanks, Fat! I knew I could count on you to help a guy out!"

Tuesday waved a pudgy hand in dismissal. "It's nothing. Don't mention it, Smitty. After all, it's well known what a prince of a fellow I am. You better be going. But don't go out the front, okay? Take my private exit."

Smitty smiled nervously, bobbing his head like a puppet on a string. "Yeah. Right." He moved toward the backdoor that led to the alley behind the building.

"Oh, and Smitty?"

"What is it, Fat?"

"Be sure to give Snapper's mama my love."

Tuesday pushed the hidden button under the top of his desk and a trapdoor suddenly appeared beneath Smitty's feet. One minute the lockpick was standing with one hand on the doorknob, the next there was only thin air. There was a scream as Smitty fell into the water below, then the sound of something very large and very hungry hissing. If Smitty screamed more than once, the trapdoor sliding back into place muffled it.

Nancy A. Collins

Police Commissioner James Gordon frowned at the report lying on his desk, rubbed the bridge of his nose, and wondered—not for the first time—how he was expected to run the Gotham City Police Department *and* keep the city safe at the same time. One thing was for sure: he couldn't do it alone.

He glanced out the window of his office at the signal, a silhouette of a bat, cast against the clouds that hung over the city. He'd taken a lot of grief about relying so heavily on the Batman's help. Some of his detractors within the department had even gone so far as to suggest the Caped Crusader was a crutch, helping to shore up an impotent administration in the eyes of the public.

He opened his desk drawer and took out a cigar, still banded and wrapped in its shiny cellophane wrapper. He rolled the cigar between his fingers thoughtfully.

"You're not going to smoke that, are you?"

Gordon turned in his swivel chair in time to see the Batman enter through the window of his tenth-floor office. "I know that's against my doctor's orders. But there's nothing that says I can't still *appreciate* a fine cigar. And haven't you ever heard of coming in the front door?"

The crimefighter shrugged. "You never know who might be watching the door."

"You sound like a paranoid," growled Gordon as he returned his cigar to its resting place in his desk.

"I prefer to think of myself as being cautious. Is that being paranoid?"

"I still say it's antisocial, sneaking up on a man that way. . . . "

"*You're* the one who activated the signal." Batman

drifted over to Gordon's desk and perched on its corner, arms folded and a faint smile on his lips. They had this conversation, or a version of it, every time he appeared.

"That I did. That I did." Gordon sighed. "You remember a punk named Atkin 'Haze' Haskill?"

"Works for Fat Tuesday? I handed him over to some of your boys last night after I caught him burgling a warehouse I had staked out. I was casting for bigger fish, but he somehow ended up in the net. I managed to get Fat Tuesday's location out of him, but by the time I reached the address he'd given me it was deserted. What about him?"

"He's dead."

It was impossible to read his friend's face, but Gordon saw the other man's shoulders tense. "Dead? How?"

"Sharpened toothbrush through the left eye. Nasty way to go. He wasn't in the general population more than fifteen minutes before the hit went down."

"Fat Tuesday?"

"Who else? The fat guy's mighty vindictive."

"I want him, Jim. I feel responsible for Haze's death. If I hadn't forced him into telling me where I could find Tuesday—"

"It's not your fault—Haze knew the risk he was taking."

"It still doesn't make it right."

"How are you going to find him? It's like he dropped off the face of the earth."

"I have a good idea of where he might be located."

"Outside my jurisdiction, no doubt."

"Let's just say I've always wanted to go to the Mardi Gras."

Nancy A. Collins

Herb Horton has always wanted to go to the Mardi Gras. Ever since he'd first heard of the greatest free show on earth back in high school, twenty years ago, he'd fantasized about taking time off and wandering New Orleans's ancient cobbled streets, a tropical drink in one hand and a scantily clad harlequin on his arm.

Now, after years of toiling at the accounting firm in Gotham, he was finally on his way to the City That Care Forgot, for several days of hardcore partying. He fidgeted with his carry-on luggage as he waited for general boarding.

The flight attendant spoke into her P.A. system, smiling blithely at the various travelers assembled in the flight lounge.

"This is Gotham Air Flight Four-Ten, nonstop to New Orleans. First Class and Platinum Pass passengers may board at this time."

The tourist class passengers shifted and mumbled amongst themselves, checking their boarding passes and watches as the handful of First Class passengers moved toward the embarkation tunnel. The woman behind Herb nudged him and pointed to a tall, well-built man in his early thirties, dressed in an expensive camel blazer, a suitbag slung over one wide shoulder.

"Say! Isn't that Bruce Wayne?"

"The millionaire?" Herb lifted an eyebrow in mild interest.

The woman nodded eagerly. "I wonder what he's doing on a regular plane? You'd think someone like him would have his very own private jet."

Herb shrugged. He was hardly the type to dwell over the activities of society page jet-setters. His taste in public figures ran more to star athletes and other men of action, such as Gotham's own mysterious Batman. "Maybe he owns the airline."

"Yeah, I bet that's it," agreed the woman, apparently satisfied by this explanation for such otherwise unglamorous behavior.

Before Herb could be pulled into further discussion of the traveling habits of the rich and famous, general boarding was called and he shuffled his way down the gangway, all thoughts of playboy millionaires wiped from his mind.

"Welcome to New Orleans, Mr. Wayne. We hope you enjoy your stay at the Fleur de Lis." The concierge smiled, all but tugging his forelock.

"I'm sure I will."

"Is there anything you'd like sent to your room, Mr. Wayne? We have an excellent, four-star in-house restaurant. . . . "

"No, thank you. I'll be taking all my meals out and I expect I'll be coming in at odd hours. After all, this *is* Carnival."

"Of course."

After the concierge had left the room, Wayne expelled a lungful of air and shuddered. He hated how people acted around him in his civilian identity. If he had to choose between the fear and anxiety generated by the Batman and the obsequious toadying that accompanied Bruce Wayne, he'd take the fear. At least that emotion was genuine.

Checking to make sure the room was secure, he unzipped his suitbag and removed his costume. Good thing it was Mardi Gras. He could move openly among the citizenry without calling attention to himself,

Nancy A. Collins

something that could never happen in Gotham. He removed a compact stage makeup case, scanning the carefully arranged selection of realistic-looking fake noses, scars, bits of facial hair, and tinted contact lenses.

Now that millionaire playboy Bruce Wayne had made his appearance in New Orleans, it was time for another—less well-known—aspect of his personality to check in as well.

"It ain't much, but it's fifteen a night. Take it or leave it." The Honeydipper Hotel's desk clerk was dressed in a pair of baggy khaki pants and a soiled undershirt, a few days' growth of beard coating his chin. He scratched his protruding belly indifferently as the tall, broad-shouldered man in the merchant sailor's coat and cap eyed the room's cracked plaster, bare light-bulb, and arthritic furniture.

The merchant sailor grunted and handed the desk clerk six folded ten-dollar bills, who pocketed the money with the ease of a conjurer.

"What name should I put on the register?"

"Call me Ishmael."

"The desk clerk rolled his eyes. "Mardi Gras!"

Herb Horton studied the costume sprawled across his bed like an empty snakeskin. Although he was close to forty years old, he still felt a surge of boyish delight every time he looked at it.

It has cost him an arm and a leg, almost as much as a decent silk suit, but it was worth it. Since his divorce, he no longer had to justify such purchases to anyone

Fat Tuesday

but himself. And being an accountant, he'd long ago
learned how to manage his finances so he could afford
to occasional impulse-buy.

He skinned himself free of his street clothes and
began suiting himself up, luxuriating in the feel of
leather and spandex on his naked flesh. The costumer
he'd hired had gone all out on this one. It was an au-
thentic reproduction, right down to the canisters on the
utility belt and the insignia on the chest. There were
even foam-rubber muscles worked into the chest and
abdomen to mask Herb's less-than-heroic physique.

As he pulled the mask over his face, Herb experienced a thrill of anticipation for the night to come and
the mysteries that it held. He wondered if this was how
the *real* Batman felt before he ventured forth to battle
crime in Gotham's mean streets.

Mardi Gras. Time to put on a mask and let your true
face show itself.

The narrow streets of the French Quarter were alive
with hundreds, if not thousands, of revelers by the time
he made the scene. Bourbon Street was a solid wall of
people, some dressed in costume, others in street
clothes, all of them clutching plastic containers of beer
in their hands. Barkers worked the doors of the various
strip joints, promising forbidden pleasures and nameless delights to the drunken tourists that wandered
past, while street entertainers strummed guitars and
kept time on washboards. The crowd pulsed up and
down the Quarter like blood through a vein. There
were tourists and locals, dreamers and fools, predators
and prey, all so thoroughly mixed together one could
not be readily told from the other.

Nancy A. Collins

While there was a definite edge of danger to the evening's festivities, the Quarter did not exude the undercurrent of menace he found to be such a part of Gotham city's identity. While the city's oldest and best-known sector was alive with pickpockets, purse-snatchers, whores, pimps, hustlers, con men, and drug dealers, New Orleans's underworld lacked the more colorful— and dangerous—brand of criminal he was familiar with. Perhaps New Orleans didn't attract costumed sociopaths like the Joker and the Penguin because it didn't *need* them. Or costumed vigilantes, for that matter.

Before he could finish that thought, he glimpsed an all-too-familiar rictus grin and a flash of green hair. His heart sped up, flooding his system with adrenaline.

The Joker? Here? No! That's impossible! He's still in Arkham Asylum, trussed up in that special purple pinstripe straightjacket of his!

Still, he *had* been out of contact with Commissioner Gordon for a couple of days, and the Joker had managed to escape his keepers before. . . . He dropped back and followed the gaunt figure in the purple pinstripe cutaway jacket with the clown-white complexion from a safe distance. It would suit the Joker's twisted sense of humor to seek sanctuary at the Mardi Gras, hiding himself in plain sight.

The Joker turned a corner, disappearing down one of the lesser-traveled side streets. He hurried after his quarry, trying not to call attention to himself while at the same time not lose track of his prey. The Joker had halted in front of the doorway of a jazz club and he was talking to the doorman. The doorman laughed and leaned forward, kissing the Joker full on the mouth, smearing lipstick and clown-white onto his own face.

Fat Tuesday

Appearances can be deceiving during Carnival.

Herbert Horton couldn't have been happier if he'd died and gone to heaven. Here he was, dressed in a cool Batman suit, strutting his stuff in the French Quarter. He'd already had several people stop him so they could take his photograph. A couple of cute chicks had even waved at him from a wrought-iron balcony.

"Awright! It's the Batman!" crowed a youth in a heavy metal T-shirt, pumping the air with a balled fist. Herb returned the salute.

Yes, this was definitely a better idea than dressing up like a cowboy or a clown. It had been expensive, but well worth every penny. With his receding hairline and accountant's spread hidden by the suit, he could almost pass for the real thing.

"Help! Stop that man! Stop him!"

Herb saw the purse-snatcher the second before they collided head-on. The foam-rubber padding in the suit cushioned most of the impact, leaving him on his feet while the thief landed on the pavement with an audible thud. The purse-snatcher looked up into Herb's face and immediately turned pale.

"Don't hurt me! Don't hurt me!" the thief pleaded, lifting his hands in supplication.

For a moment he wondered what the hell the other man was going on about—then he realized that he wasn't seeing Herbert Horton, Certified Public Accountant, but the Batman, the dreaded Dark Knight Detective, whose appearance struck fear into the hearts of criminals everywhere.

A crowd was starting to gather around the two. Excited voices buzzed among themselves.

Nancy A. Collins

"What's going on?"

"It's the Batman! He caught the guy that snatched that lady's purse!"

"The Batman? For real?"

"Yeah! He knocked the creep down like he was nothin'!"

"Cool!"

"Way to go, Batman! Kick the dude for me, willya?"

"Yeah! Show 'im what-for!"

"Hey, Batman! Can I get your autograph?"

"Me, too!"

Herb's face began to sweat beneath the cowl he was wearing. This was starting to get weird. It was one thing to have tourists want to pose with him for their holiday snapshots, it was another to be mobbed.

"Leave me alone!" he snapped, shouldering through the knot of onlookers. Someone reached out and tugged on his cape, but he succeeded in snatching it free.

"Wow! It really *is* the Batman!"

Herb did not notice the two men who watched him from a nearby doorway.

"You see that? The Batman's in town."

"Fat's gonna wanna hear about this."

Herb shook his head, still unable to believe what had gone down on Bourbon Street.

I was mistaken for the Batman! Me! Herb Horton, mild-mannered certified public accountant!

The look in the purse-snatcher's eyes when he stared up into his masked face had been genuine fear. Imagine; someone actually *afraid* of Herb Horton! He'd have to land a position with the IRS to ever see that kind of raw terror again. To a certain extent, it had

Fat Tuesday

been exhilarating. But what if the guy had pulled a gun? His costume's foam-rubber padding provided enough protection to absorb a strong punch, possibly even deflect a knife blade, but a bullet fired at close to point-blank range? Forget it.

It was one thing to strut around and bask in the reflected glory and glamour of his hero, it was another having the responsibilities and dangers that came with the suit thrust on him. Still, for a brief, exhilarating second, he'd known what it must be like to *be* the Batman.

Wow. Whatta rush.

He turned down a narrow, partially deserted alleyway that ran between the St. Louis Cathedral and the Cabildo. He wrinkled his nose as the pungent odor of urine and beer assaulted his nostrils. A drunk teetered uncertainly as he relieved himself against the wall. Herb grimaced. That was certainly a sight he'd never see in Gotham City. At least not in *his* neighborhood.

"Shay, buddy—" The drunkard swung to block Herb's path. "Spare change?"

"I'm sorry, I—" Before Herb could finish his sentence, the sap came down on the back of his head.

The drunk, now miraculously sober, stuck a clove cigarette between his lips and lit it with a platinum lighter.

"So this is the infamous Batman, eh? Funny, I didn't think it'd be *this* easy."

At first the ringing in his ears was so bad it felt as if Jimi Hendrix were trapped in his skull with a wah-wah

Nancy A. Collins

pedal. Herb groaned and shook his head, decreasing the volume if not the pain at the back of his head.

He stared blearily at his surroundings; he seemed to be in a warehouse of some kind. And definitely not one of the trendier converted rental spaces, either.

"Ah! I see our guest is awake!"

Herb lifted his throbbing head and found himself staring at a grotesquely fat little man dressed in a rumpled seersucker suit. The fat man's buttocks were wedged snugly into a leather easy chair, his legs crossed at the ankles. He held a baby alligator in one chubby hand, chucking it under the chin like a post-menopausal housewife doting on her toy Chihuahua.

"Wh-where? . . . " Herb tried to lift a hand to massage his aching brow, only to discover he was securely tied to his chair.

"What's the matter, Batman? The southern climate too much for you? The humidity making you sluggish?"

Herb's eyes widened in alarm. "Wait a minute—you think *I'm* Batman? *Me?*"

"Come now, Batman! You don't think I'm going to fall for that 'you've got the wrong man' bull, do you? Word on the street up in Gotham is that you're hot to bring me down for that lousy punk Haze buying it in the slam. I know you've been on my tail."

"Look, I dont't know what you're going on about! I don't know anything about anyone named Haze! I don't even know who *you* are!"

"Please, Batman—let's drop this charade. It's really unbecoming of you . . . "

"I'm not playing charades!" Herb winced at the sound of his own voice echoing inside his head. "I'm *not* who you think I am! I'm not the Batman! I'm Herbert

Horton! I'm a certified public accountant, for cryin' out loud!"

"Really, Batman—I expected something more original from you!"

"If you don't believe me, then look at my driver's license!"

Herb nodded at one of the pouches on his costume's utility belt. "My wallet's in here—see for yourself!"

Fat Tuesday motioned for a hulking goon in a dark suit to search his captive. "Check it out, Momus. Be on your toes, though. He might have smoke bombs or sleeping gas pellets in there. . . . "

"Here it is, Boss." Momus handed his employer a man's brown leather wallet. Fat Tuesday flipped it open and studied Herb's bland face staring out from behind the protective plastic shield.

"See? What did I tell you?"

"This still doesn't mean you're not the Batman."

"What?"

"*No one* knows who the Batman is or what he looks like. And it says here you're from Gotham City."

"*So?*"

"So isn't it strange that you happen to show up in New Orleans dressed like the Batman?"

"It's *Mardi Gras*, for Pete's sake! It's just a stupid costume! If I was from Washington, D.C. and dressed up like George Bush, that wouldn't make me the President!"

"I'm afraid I simply can't take that kind of chance, Mr. Horton—or whoever you may be. . . . "

"This is ridiculous! I'm *not* the Batman!"

Fat Tuesday shrugged. "Either way, it doesn't matter. If you *are* the Batman you must die. And if you *aren't* the Batman . . . well, I can't have you wandering

Nancy A. Collins

off and complaining to the local authorities about being kidnapped, can I?"

"You're making a terrible mistake! I'm not the Batman! I promise! What do I have to do to prove it to you? Do your income tax returns for you?"

"Comus? Momus? Would you be so kind as to remove our guest from my presence?"

Herb struggled futilely against his bonds, cursing under his breath, as Fat Tuesday's henchmen descended on him. He recognized the slighter man smoking the foul-smelling clove cigarette as the supposed drunk who'd waylaid him in the alley.

"Don't wiggle so much," chastised Comus, dropping ashes onto Herb's cape as he spoke. "You're only gonna make it harder on yourself."

"What do you mean?"

Comus reached into his suit jacket and produced the biggest gun Herb had ever seen outside of a movie theater. He thumbed off the safety and jammed the muzzle against Herb's right temple.

"Guess."

It was amazing how the close proximity of a loaded gun to his head made everything leap into sharp, crisp focus. Suddenly Herb was acutely aware that every hair on his body was standing completely erect.

Fat Tuesday shook his head in dismay. "Hard to believe this bozo took down the Joker, ain't it, boys? You made a big mistake, Batman, coming down South. You shoulda stayed home."

Momus untied Herb and yanked him to his feet. Herb winced as the circulation returned to his arms.

"Where do you want us to waste him, Fats?"

"I don't care where you snuff him, long as it ain't in front of me. I want him shot throught the head, though.

And bring me back his mask! I wanna send it special-dee to our friend the Penguin, just to show him Fat Tuesday isn't the kind of man a pencil-nosed geek ought to mess with!"

"Right, Boss. One order of Swiss head-cheese comin' right up!"

Herb was too stunned to even protest. Somewhere along the line his dream vacation had turned into a nightmare, and he was unable to wake up. All he'd wanted to do was to go to the Mardi Gras and dress up as one of his heros, that's all. Now he was about to become the victim of a gangland-style execution, all because of a stupid case of mistaken identity. This was what he got for playing the tourist.

"C'mon, *Caped Crusader*, let's get the show on the road. I promised my kids I'd take 'em to a parade tonight," grumbled Comus.

"But—But—"

"I know; 'You're making a terrible mistake.' That's what they all say!"

Suddenly there was the sound of crashing glass from above. The four men looked upward and saw, suspended for a heartbeat, a caped figure costumed in black hurtling through the skylight, forearms shielding his face. The dark intruder hit the floor and rolled with the practiced ease of a trained gymnast. As Comus and Momus gaped, slack-jawed, the stranger leaped to his feat, tossing back his cape, revealing himself to be none other than . . .

Zorro?

Comus and Momus exchanged confused looks.

What th—"

Zorro jumped forward before either man had a

chance to react, knocking the gun from Comus's hand with a swipe of his saber. Comus shrieked and clamped his bleeding right hand under his left armpit.

"He cut me! He *cut* me!"

Momus let go of Herb and reached into his suit for his own gun, but it was too late. Zorro moved with the precision of a champion kick-boxer, planting his boot heel squarely on the bigger man's chin. Momus's eyes rolled back in his head and he sank to the floor without a single grunt.

"Shoot him! Shoot him!" Fat Tuesday squealed as Comus stumbled after his gun.

Zorro produced *bolo balls* from his belt and hurled them at Comus with a practiced flick of his wrist, bringing the goon down as easily as a *gaucho* roping cattle.

Zorro reached out and steadied Herb's shoulder. "Are you all right, Mr. Horton?"

Fat Tuesday pushed himself out of his chair, his face crimson from the exertion. "A trick! It was nothing but a dirty, low-down trick! I should have *known*! The Batman would never whine like that!"

Zorro turned to face the crime lord, pointing his saber at the other man like an accusing finger. "Fat Tuesday, I'm bringing you back to Gotham City to stand trial for the murder of Atkin 'Haze' Haskill and to answer questions concerning the disappearance of Salvadore 'Smitty' Martinez."

"You know, Masked Man; I'd really like to oblige you on that—but I'm afraid I'm going to have to ask you to—*drop dead!*"

Fat Tuesday produced something that looked like a TV remote control and pressed a button. Suddenly the

Fat Tuesday

floor beneath Zorro and Herb's feet gave way. Herb, who'd been standing near the edge of the trapdoor, managed to jump free but Zorro wasn't as lucky.

Herb looked into the yawning pit beneath the warehouse. The shaft was a good two-stories deep, and something big and reptilian could be heard hissing and thrashing around in the scummy water below. He expected to see Zorro clamped between the gator's powerful jaws, but instead found his rescuer clinging to the lip of the trapdoor by the tips of his fingers. Just as Zorro's grip began to slip, Herb reached out and grabbed the other man, hauling him free of the pitfall.

Zorro looked up into Herb's masked face and smiled crookedly. "Thanks."

Fat Tuesday's breath wheezed like a faulty steam-fed radiator as he hurried through the darkened warehouse to his waiting Rolls Royce parked in the alley. Sweat stains blossomed damply from under his arms and across his shoulders. He should have known better to come to New Orleans with only Comus and Momus as bodyguards! Those bumbling incompetents!

"Fools. I'm surrounded by nothing but fools! Isn't that right, precious?" he gasped to the pet gator he still held in one hand. "Ingrates and imbeciles, that's all they are! And what thanks to I get? Me? A prince of a fellow!" As he contemplated the injustice of it all, his grip tightened on the reptile until Snapper's eyes bulged from their sockets like water balloons. "It's not fair! Not fair at all! I—"

Fat Tuesday emitted a high-pitched shriek as Snapper's jaws clamped down on his pinkie. The gangster danced around, displaying an odd grace for a man of

Nancy A. Collins

his size, while waving his hand in a desperate attempt to free himself.

"AHH! Let go!"

Snapper dropped to the floor with a meaty thud. For a second it looked as though the reptile had one of those pink bubblegum cigars clamped between its rows of needle-sharp teeth.

"My finger! You bit off my finger! I'll *kill* you for that!" Fat Tuesday raised one of his massive, tree trunk legs in preparation of reducing his erstwhile pet to pâté. Before he could deliver the crushing blow, he clutched at his chest with his remaining stubby fingers, his face losing all color.

"No. Not now. Not. Now."

Fat Tuesday hit the ground like a four-hundred-pound sack of suet. The pain in his chest made his vision fade in and out like the picture of an old black-and-white television set. He emitted a cry of strangled terror as what looked like the Angel of Death loomed over him and looked down into his face.

"He's having a heart attack."

A demon's head swam into view. "So? Good enough for him."

"Go find a phone and call nine-one-one. I'll stay behind and administer CPR."

"*What*? You're actually going to try and save this sleazebucket's *life*? After what he did?"

"Mr. Horton, *he's* the cold-blooded killer, not *me*. I'm not going to stand by and watch another human die, even if he *is* a murderer. I may work outside the law, but I don't fool myself in thinking I'm *above* it."

Herb hesitated for a second then hurried off in search of a pay phone.

Fat Tuesday clawed at his dark savior's arm. Some-

Fat Tuesday

how he managed to find the breath to speak. "I—I can give you—P—Penguin—if you just—let me—go—please—Deal?"

The Angel of Death shook his head. "No deal. I can get the Penguin any time I like, Fat. What I *want* is *you*."

Herb sipped coffee from one of the patrolmen's Thermos as he watched the paramedics load Fat Tuesday's considerable bulk into the back of their ambulance.

"Yeah, soon as he stabilizes, they'll be shipping him back up to Gotham," the policeman explained. "Seems there's a warrant out for his arrest on a couple of murder charges—not to mention racketeering. Funny how you found him lying in the alley and all. . . . "

Herb grunted and shruggd. "Am I free to go now, officer?"

"Sure, Mr. Horton. If we have any more questions, we'll leave a message with your hotel. Thanks for your help."

"Just being a good citizen."

"You need a ride back to where you're staying, sir? We'd be happy to have a patrol car drop you off."

"No, thanks. I think I'll walk."

The policeman frowned. "Are you sure about that, sir? You don't know this neighborhood."

Herb grinned, pulling his cowl back over his face. "I'll chance it."

"Have it your way. Oh, nice costume."

Zorro was waiting for him in the shadows outside the police cordon. Dressed in the tight-fitting flared pants and loose silk shirt, it was obvious he didn't need foam-rubber muscles to give him a heroic physique.

Nancy A. Collins

"Thanks for not mentioning me to the authorities."

"You're him, aren't you?"

Zorro smiled and nodded.

"Can I ask you a question?"

"I guess so."

"You could have walked around New Orleans dressed as you normally do. So why did you decide to dress up like Zorro?"

The other man laughed and shook his head. "Mr. Horton, you of all people should know the reason behind my choice of costume! It's Mardi Gras! A time when you drop the mask you normally wear in favor of what, in your heart of hearts, you secretly wish to be!"

"But—you're the *Batman!*"

Zorro laughed and moved to rejoin the darkness, pausing long enough to deliver a salute with his sword before being swallowed by the waiting shadows. "Remember, Mr. Horton! We *all* must have our heroes!"

Creatures of Habit

PAUL KUPPERBERG

The cat padded across the alleyway, shrouded in the protective darkness of night, picking her way over the city's debris. From beyond the alley came the sounds of the city, the drone of car engines and the swish of their tires on the damp pavement, the murmur of a million voices, the muffled rumble of the subways filtering up from the tunnels below. The alley stank of the rotting discard overflowing the trash cans and Dumpsters over which she stepped. Car exhaust, the mingled odor of exotic foods from street vendors, vapors from the sewers that flowed beneath the streets all assailed her sensitive nostrils.

Gotham City was all sounds and smells around her. She purred, content with the comfort derived from their presence.

Gotham was where she lived and where she

Creatures of Habit

prowled, the place that provided her with everything she needed to sustain her.

She leaped up onto the top of an open Dumpster, balancing delicately on the edge. What she sought was nearby, would soon be hers. All she needed was a few moments alone to ferret it out. But she was accustomed to the solitude of her activities. She needed no one. She . . .

Froze.

A footstep scraped across the pavement behind her. Perched on the Dumpster's edge, fur bristling, ears straining, nose twitching to catch scent of the source of the intruder.

"No, no, no," came the soft-spoken response to her alarm. "You've no need to be afraid, little pretty."

The brown, matted cat turned her head to the sound of the voice and blinked large, glowing green eyes. There, at the mouth of the alley, stood a tall, slender figure. A human. The cat had been born of the streets, in a corner of an alley not unlike this one, and had never lived among these beings, had seldom experienced anything but torment and abuse from them. She had rightly learned to fear them.

"I'll be out of your way in just a moment," the human whispered in reassurance, advancing slowly into the alley. "You have your work to do and I have mine."

The cat sat, fur settling. She watched the human and purred. Humanity was the enemy, but this one . . . this one posed no threat. This one was a friend, indeed a kindred spirit. This one possessed the spirit and soul of the cat.

The woman paused before the watchful feline and extended a hand to be sniffed before gently scratching the creature's head with a claw-tipped leather glove. She was tall, lean, and graceful, her sensuous form

Paul Kupperberg

encased in a matte-black leather bodysuit, its lines broken only by the small leather pouch hanging at the gentle swell of her hip, capped by a sleek mask that hid the upper half of her face, except for the startling, catlike green eyes that peered out the mask's eye slits below a pair of cat ears. A full, red-lipped mouth set in a strong jaw turned up in a secret smile she shared briefly with the cat.

"This has been lovely, my dear," Catwoman purred, withdrawing her hand. "But I really must be going." She pointed into the air and the cat followed her hand with its wide-eyed, glowing gaze. "Up there."

The cat blinked as if in understanding and stood, stretching its thin little body as Catwoman leaped nimbly to the edge of the Dumpster beside her. She settled on her haunches to watch her newfound friend.

Several feet over her head was the extension ladder of a fire escape. Catwoman's eyes narrowed as she briefly judged the distance, then crouched and sprang up, her gloved hands grasping the ladder's lowest rung. She effortlessly swung her lower body up like a practiced gymnast on the parallel bars, landing with only the slightest rasp of shoe leather on rusted metal slats on the fire escape's lower landing.

The cat peered up at her for a brief instant, and with a remorseful meow in farewell to the only human ever to treat her with kindness, she turned back to the contents of the Dumpster to continue her search for the evening's meal.

Above her, Catwoman was on a quest of her own. On the balls of her feet, she ascended the fire-escape steps, her matte-black leather outfit rendering her nearly invisible in the night against the brick of the building darkened by years of grimy Gotham air.

Creatures of Habit

She stopped on the third landing, poised, listening
to the sounds from the city below. Car horns blared.
Voices rose and fell as citizens passed by the mouth of
the alley. Somewhere in the distance, a police siren
wailed mournfully on its mission of intervention in
someone else's misery. She didn't care where it was
headed as long as her work was uninterrupted.

Reaching into the pouch at her hip, Catwoman
smiled her secret smile once again. How accommodat-
ing that the treasure she sought was held by one who
made its acquisition by her so simple. Certainly the
window opening onto the fire escape where she stood
was protected by an alarm. This she knew merely by
looking at the grimy glass on which she could see
etched the fine line of wire that was there to prevent
its being broken by the crude method of entry commonly referred to as the "smash-and-grab."

But Catwoman was far too subtle a professional to
engage in so brutal and crass a practice. She pulled
from her pouch a small plastic box with a single toggle
switch on its face and, attached to its other side, a
suction cup. The box was quickly affixed to the windowpane, directly over the wire strip glued to the inside of the glass. The toggle switch was flicked on by
a clawed fingertip, and within seconds the box let out
a single, gentle tone.

The alarm was deactivated. The wonders of modern
electronics, she marveled, available to those who
knew the correct *wrong* people. Catwoman knew them
all.

Now her work was simple. From the pouch she produced a slender tool, the tip of which she applied to
the glass. With a barely audible hiss, she traced a circle in the windowpane with the glass cutter. A tap of
her knuckle at the center of the circle sent the etched

out glass to the floor inside the room with a crystalline tinkle. She reached through the hole left there, flicking open the simple latch holding the window closed.

Catwoman purred with delight as she slid open the window and stepped delicately inside. She closed the window behind her, disappearing into the dark office beyond the night.

A visit to this place the previous day in civilian garb and the guise of an interested customer had given Catwoman the layout of the office, so she had no need of a betraying light to guide her steps. She went straight for the wall on the far side of the office, snaking sensuously through the maze of office furniture and display showcases. Her goal was the large built-in, walk-in safe that dominated that wall. A Wm. Finger Deluxe Model M, Series A-194–. Installed here in the offices of the C. Paris Rare Book & Manuscript Co., her research told her, forty years ago. Security technology had, of course, grown by leaps and bounds in the forty years since the safe's installation, but the Model M was still regarded as a fine example of post–World War II safe building. A solid box consisting of three layers of one-inch-thick tempered steel plating, fireproof, bombproof, with inlaid door hinges and dead-bolt locks and four separate tumbler mechanisms that made cracking the locks next to impossible for all but the most experienced safecracker or someone equipped with a good supply of explosives.

All in all, a most formidable and impressive box. Except for someone in possession of the combination.

Someone, like Catwoman.

Once again, her acquaintance with the correct wrong people simplified Catwoman's task. In this instance, it was Buddy Wexler, a small, round-shouldered old man

Creatures of Habit

with a perpetual squint and a thorough knowledge of safes built in America during the last century. There was hardly a model he had not, at some point in his long career, gotten into before his retirement. And being a professional of the highest caliber, Wexler always sought the simplest way through the steel and locks confronting him. In the case of the product of the Wm. Finger Co. constructed over twenty years ago, that usually meant consulting the installation records copied late that same year from the company's offices. Most people, Wexler told her, amused, never bother changing the combination set at the time of a safe's installation, not even forty years later. It's too much trouble to memorize new combinations, he assured her as he handed her a slip of paper on which a series of numbers had been written in exchange for a sum of cash.

The dial spun beneath her fingers, first right, then left, then right again. Then, a metallic click and the safe's handle giving under a gentle push.

The safe door swung open and Catwoman laughed in delight.

Within the safe were shelves and on the shelves rested a wealth of paper rarities, the crème de la crème of the C. Paris Rare Book & Manuscript catalog: a first edition of Miguel de Cervantes's *El Ingenioso Hidalgo Don Quixote de la Mancha* from the sixteen hundreds; the original manuscript of *Alice's Adventures in Wonderland* in Lewis Carroll's own hand; a set of nine Shakespeare plays bound together, the first published collection of the Bard's work printed four years before the almost-as-rare and more-well-known First Folio; first editions of *Moby-Dick*, *Robinson Crusoe*, *Pilgrim's Progress*, and other rare volumes, many inscribed by the authors.

Paul Kupperberg

And the object of Catwoman's excursion into the night: the original, handwritten manuscript of T. S. Eliot's *Old Possum's Book of Practical Cats*.

There were far more valuable items housed in the safe, items that Catwoman would take with her for sale and profit in the world's extensive black market in rarities and antiquities. But the Eliot manuscript, she reflected with emotion approaching ecstasy as she lifted the leather folder containing the sheaf of papers, was for her own private collection. If she left here tonight with only this in her possession, she would consider the night's efforts an unqualified success. Little more than a bit of doggerel, this lesser of the poet's works was most famous for inspiring a long-running Broadway musical, but it had as its theme that which was close to Catwoman's heart.

Cats. Her life. Her pleasure and passion.

Her obsession!

"You've always been predictable, Selina," a deep voice rumbled behind her.

Catwoman knew, even as she turned with the manuscript clutched to her breast, whose voice it was.

He stood, framed in the doorway to the office, a tall, broad figure sheathed in shadowy gray and midnight blue. His face was hidden by a mask, pointed ears reminiscent of a bat's head rising from its crown. Shining on his broad chest was a brilliant yellow oval in which was emblazoned a jet-black emblem in the shape of a bat and, to complete the image, a billowing cape with a serrated edge hung from his imposing shoulders like batwings at rest.

"Hello, Batman," she said, her voice as casual as someone meeting a friend on an afternoon stroll through the park. "Fancy meeting you here, of all places."

Creatures of Habit

"Not so very fancy at all," he said, pointing a dark-gloved finger at the leather folder in her grasp. "The auction tomorrow of the Eliot manuscript has been in all the newspapers. I knew it was only a matter of time before you tried for it."

"But how could you have known I would try tonight?" she asked with a slow, sensuous shrug of her shoulders. Catwoman's tongue flicked out, briefly touching her suddenly dry lips. But there was no fear or apprehension attached to the gesture. This was something else, something that always seemed to grip her when she was in the presence of this man.

It was Batman's turn to shrug as he strode into the office, his hand held out as if to take the folder from her. "I've been keeping tabs on this place," he said. "It was still in the safe this evening at closing time. Tonight was your last chance at it before it was shipped to the auction house tomorrow morning.

"Now, hand it over, Selina."

Catwoman sighed. "You have no idea how you vex me, dear Batman. Don't you find it astonishing how our paths are always crossing!"

Batman stopped within a yard of her. "No. As I said, you're predictable."

"Oh, no," she cried in mock horror. "I'd hate to think that were so. But I do know what I can do to drive that silly notion out of your mind." Now Catwoman laughed, and her hand, which had been creeping toward the pouch at her hip as they spoke, came into plain view holding a Zippo cigarette lighter. She flicked it to life and the flame leaped up a full six inches to fill the dark office with flickering shadows.

"This"—she giggled with undisguised pleasure—"is something you *never* predicted!"

Batman started in surprise as Catwoman spun and

tossed the flaming lighter into the open safe. Into the midst of millions of dollars' worth of old, dry, and brittle paper.

Still laughing, Catwoman moved toward the window even as Batman sprung into the safe with a single leap. The lighter had bounced once on the floor inside the safe, the flame of the Zippo reaching for contents of the lowest shelf. The manufacturer of the lighter guaranteed its performance in even the stiffest wind, so its brief flight from Catwoman's hand to the safe didn't dim the flame.

A leather-bound book began to smolder. Batman grabbed for it, hearing as he did so the pounding of Catwoman's heels on the floor and the crash of glass as she dived through the window. As he swept the burning book and flickering lighter up in his hands, the sound of the rasp of her soles on the metal rungs of the fire escape reached him. He rolled out of the safe, holding both sources of fire away from the rest of its precious contents, snapping shut the lighter and slapping the small fire licking at the pages of the burning book out against his chest.

He was back on his feet in seconds, heading for the shattered window and the pursuit of Catwoman. But she was gone, swallowed by the night. Along with the Eliot manuscript.

A cat with matted brown fur sat on the fire escape among the shards of broken window glass, looking up at Batman expectantly. His lips set in a hard, grim line, the Dark Knight peered into the alley below. Catwoman had escaped him again because he had again underestimated her cunning.

He routinely faced and overcame foes who were both stronger and smarter than she. He survived the treacherous nights of encounters with danger and death with physical prowess and wits sharpened to the pinnacle of human perfection, yet this one woman all too frequently bested him with little more than a look from those startling green eyes.

What was the answer?

The cat's plaintive meow broke his train of thought and he sighed. Catwoman's time would come, he knew. It always did and always would, as long as she remained the creature of habit she had always been. Batman turned from the window to place a call to Commissioner Gordon to report Catwoman's success and his own failure.

The cat cocked her head to one side, waiting on the fire escape. She sensed this human might love cats almost as much as had the first one.

Selina Kyle was disturbed by the night's encounter. Oh, not by her failure to steal the wealth of books and manuscripts that had been within her grasp. She was happy just to have the Eliot manuscript, which she now set in a place of honor on a display stand in the bookcase in the den of her Gotham City penthouse apartment.

No, she thought as she walked over to curl into a large, cushioned chair facing the bookcase to admire her new prize. No, as far as she was concerned, she had fulfilled her mission. What was disturbing was Batman's observation about her behavior.

You've always been predictable, Selina.

As the Joker sought out novelties and chaos, as the Riddler persisted in taunting Batman with clues to his plans disguised as riddles, as Two-Face based his crimes on his strange obsession with duality, so was

Catwoman overly fond of items with cat-related motifs.

The only difference between them and her, of course, was that they were all quite insane.

So, yes, she allowed, in that way perhaps she *was* predictable. In some small measure. Lost in thought, Selina absently stroked the silky fur of Cassie, the Persian that hopped up on her lap. Why did she confine her activities to such *objets d'cat*? Could it be that like that ridiculous little Riddler, she had some sort of warped, subconscious ulterior motive?

"Nonsense," she hissed. The Persian perked up its ears and blinked at her. A tortoiseshell tabby and an orange tom leaped up to join the cat on her lap.

Criminals like Riddler and Two-Face acted as they did because they *wanted* Batman to catch them. They were psychotics and sociopaths whose obsessive behaviors were literal cries for capture and help. They were the ones who kept the padded cells of the Arkham Asylum for the Criminally Insane full and its psychiatric staff working overtime.

But Selina Kyle? She didn't fit that description. She had been arrested any number of times in the course of her criminal career. On those few occasions the authorities had been able to hold her, she had undergone psychiatric evaluations, each one resulting in her being judged sane.

And yet . . .

There was no denying that Batman had known exactly where to find her tonight. Nor was there any denying the feelings that gripped her when he was near. She had always tried telling herself that her feeling for the Dark Knight was that of respect for a worthy adversary. But she was being honest with herself now, thoroughly analytical. And if the absolute truth were to be known, even to herself, she had to admit there was more to her emotions than respect.

Selina Kyle took pride in needing no man to make her life complete. In her former existence, before there was Catwoman to sustain her and make her whole, she had lived an empty life, being used by any man who could pay the price for her services. But that was long ago, and now she would as soon kill a man before she allowed him to touch her.

So it was certainly not a matter of need.

But *want*. Now that was an entirely different matter.

Could Batman be the one to make her forget the dirty, unwholesome touches of the strange men of her past?

Selina became aware of the low, pleasured rumble of feline contentment. But the cats stretched out on and about her were all asleep, silent.

The purrs were her own.

For Batman?

Selina sprang to her feet, startling and scattering the cats, more deeply troubled now than when she began dissecting her emotional state. She couldn't believe what she was thinking. Since their very first encounter, Catwoman had always sought to triumph over Batman. To dominate him as she would dominate all men.

But now she was no longer sure. Now she didn't know if she wanted to win out over him ... or win him over.

This was going to require some very long, hard thought.

"Tell me, sir," Alfred Pennyworth said. "Might I spend another hour in the kitchen preparing some *other* dish you can allow to grow cold while you ponder the mysteries of the universe?"

Bruce Wayne sat staring out the dining-room window, chin resting on steepled fingertips, brow furrowed in deep ridges of thought. "No, Alfred," he replied absently, eyes fixed on something beyond the dark of night outside the glass. "No, thank you. This is just fine."

Alfred sighed softly to himself, his professional demeanor preventing him from too ostentatious a show of his displeasure. Mr. Wayne was, after all, the master of the house. And though Alfred had been hired long ago as the butler of the household by Wayne's parents, and in spite of the fact that he had literally raised young Bruce from the time of Dr. and Mrs. Wayne's deaths, the elderly British gentleman's gentleman always insisted on maintaining the proper level of decorum.

Which was not, he admitted with no small amount of pride (but only to himself), the easiest of tasks.

Because how many men in his position were servant, confidant, friend, and provider of first aid to the Batman?

Alfred stepped to the table and removed the plate of cold, untouched food. "Am I to assume, sir, that something is troubling you?"

Bruce Wayne made a sound deep in his throat, which Alfred interpreted as assent.

"Might I suggest speaking of it as a method of alleviating your concerns?"

Wayne looked at Alfred at last. "I'm sorry, Alfred. Did you say something?"

"Yes, sir," the manservant said patiently. "I was asking if you might like to talk out your problem vis-à-vis Catwoman."

Creatures of Habit

"Catwoman," Wayne repeated. "Selina. I suppose I should be grateful no one was killed tonight. Considering the murderous crime spree she's been on lately, that's some consolation."

"She is proving most vexing, yes, sir. But then, Miss Kyle is always a problem when she embarks on a rampage."

"The woman's insane, Alfred."

"Yes, sir," the butler replied dryly. "I accept the diagnosis from a man who wears leotards and a mask whilst leaping about the rooftops of the city in the dead of night."

Wayne suppressed a smile at Alfred's response. Sometimes, he thought, his old butler must have invented the fine art of sarcasm. "Point taken, friend, but you'll have to admit that there's a considerable difference between my motives and Selina's."

"Quite, sir. Flip sides of the same coin, as it were."

Wayne had come to expect this reaction from Alfred. The older man was as close to family as he had known since the murder of his parents by a mugger when he was a youngster. He had always been there for Bruce Wayne when he needed him, to talk or be comforted, when he limped home in the dark of night and the aftermath of his self-appointed crusade against evil. But Alfred Pennyworth would never approve of the way he spent his nights. He would support Bruce as best he could, he would mend his wounds when the crusade turned bloody, but how was he to approve of any activity that saw Wayne putting his life on the line night after night?

What was he to do but hate any activity that threatened the young man he loved as dearly as his own flesh and blood? Even if that was an admission Alfred would never vocalize, not even under the threat of the most heinous torture. Because that, of course, would be a breech of the decorum he so valued.

"Whatever my reasons, Catwoman's a criminal and a killer, and it's up to me to stop her."

"If you say so, sir. Although sometimes I must wonder . . ." But Alfred's voice trailed off and he shook his head as he started to turn with the dish in hand to leave the room.

"Wonder what?" Wayne asked.

Alfred stood with his back to Bruce Wayne for a long moment before turning back to his employer with a look of concern spread across his normally closed expression. "About Miss Kyle, sir. It would seem to me that she appears to prey on your mind far more than do other foes whenever you and she encounter one another."

"Meaning?"

"Meaning, sir, that you might wish to consider investigating your emotional state where Catwoman is concerned."

Wayne laughed, or at least made a sound as close to a laugh as he could muster in light of Alfred's words. "What are you saying, Alfred? That I've got feelings for the woman that are interfering with my work?"

"I merely think you have a tendency to . . . shall we say, obsess over Miss Kyle and her activities. Her crimes are terrible, to be sure, but no more, and certainly often less, than the acts of others, such as the Joker. Or Two-Face."

"Don't be ridiculous, Alfred. Naturally I'm going to think about her when she's active. But I think about every criminal I go up against."

Alfred nodded and his features settled back into their usual neutral repose. "If you say so, sir," he said,

Creatures of Habit

but he allowed a hint of skepticism to creep into his voice. He wasn't hiding anything from Bruce Wayne.

"I do," Wayne asserted. But he heard his old friend's doubt and it bothered him more than he was willing to admit. He was too tired to argue, though. And he had too much to think about.

Mostly about Catwoman.

"Will there be anything else, sir?" Alfred asked.

"No, thank you."

"Then I shall clean up in the kitchen and be retiring."

"Good night, Alfred," Bruce Wayne said softly, turning his gaze back to the black stare of the window. Alfred was almost out of the dining room when Wayne called out to him, "Before you turn in, Alfred, could you fix me something to eat?"

Alfred looked down at the plate of cold food in his hand and shook his head. "Certainly, sir," he replied. "How silly of me not to have thought of that myself."

The cat is largely nocturnal, a creature prowling the jungles and hunting in the night. Like her feline namesake, the Catwoman seldom hunted before the sun had set and darkness veiled her jungle, the Gotham streets. She was uncomfortable in the daylight, believing that sunshine revealed far too many flaws and imperfections in both body and soul.

But the night was part of her obsession. In the soft glow of the moon and the harsh glare of halogen street lamps lie her predictability.

This time she would walk abroad in the light of day!

Of course, the need to change required a number of concessions to form. The comforting bodysuit of black leather was unquestionably too conspicuous. So, too,

Paul Kupperberg

was she forced to abandon her trademark burglar's entrance to her goal. But, in the daytime, most targets she might strike would be open and accessible. All she need do was walk through open doors, welcomed like any patron or sightseer, and take what she wanted. Less challenging, to be sure.

But a definite departure from her established patterns. And oh, so infinitely dull in comparison.

Today Batman would not know where the Catwoman was to strike until after the deed were done. He couldn't possibly be waiting for her this time.

Selina Kyle slid smoothly from the rear of the taxi that came to a stop in front of the Gotham Gem Mart Building on Forty-seventh Street between Kane and Robinson avenues. The entire length of this one block was devoted to the buying and selling of precious gems, in storefronts, in stall-lined arcades, and in the hundreds of offices in the towering buildings along the street. Here, a hundred-thousand-dollar deal could be struck and consummated on the sidewalk, between two dealers in diamonds who were comfortable doing so on nothing more than a handshake. Forty-seventh Street, known in the gem trade simply as the Street, was perhaps the single most valuable stretch of real estate in Gotham City, its status having less to do with the property itself than with the commodity traded here.

The commodity that brought Selina Kyle here bright and early this sunny Thursday morning.

She paid the driver, treating him with a dazzling smile as reward for his services and sending him happily on his way as she entered the lobby of the Gem Mart.

Stylishly dressed in a black leather miniskirt, dark green silk blouse, and green pumps that accentuated her height and glorious stature, she moved past the security guard at the lobby desk, toward the elevators. She leveled her most dazzling smile at the uniformed guard, lifting her sunglasses to rest atop her short-cropped black hair, revealing dazzling emerald eyes that caused his breath to catch in his throat. He watched her, coming and going, his head swiveling as though on a pivot to keep his eyes glued to the long, slim figure until she boarded the next elevator and the doors closed on this green-eyed vision.

It was only after she was gone that he remembered it was his job to have her sign in and list her destination in the building.

What the hell, he thought. Prob'ly just some rich babe pickin' up a major rock she conned her poor schmuckuva husband into givin' up for her.

And she was probably worth every carat.

He hadn't been able to sleep.

Usually as the sun was rising he would be settling down for his few hours of daily sleep. He didn't need much to revitalize himself thoroughly, not if he did it right. Actually he didn't so much sleep as meditate, placing himself in a deep trance state where his mind and body refreshed themselves in the shortest possible time. A little bit of business he'd picked up in his study of a myriad of meditative disciplines over the years, one that came in handy since he didn't have eight hours a night to waste in unconsciousness. His days were spent immersed in business. His nights were occupied by the affairs of the night itself.

His natural element as the Batman.

But last night he lay there in his bed, eyes closed, breathing deep and regular, and totally unable to achieve anything approaching a trance as he replayed in his mind's eye, again and again, his encounter with Catwoman.

Something about it bothered him, something beyond her having escaped.

Something he had said.

You've always been predictable, Selina.

She hadn't liked that. She had tried to make light of it, but he could see the surprise in her eyes after he said it, he could tell that he had hit a nerve. Selina had never thought of herself as anything but a strong, capable foe whose actions were as clever as they were vicious. But now, by pointing out her greatest flaw, he made a big mistake. He had unwittingly challenged her and she was sure as hell to pick up the gauntlet.

To do that, Catwoman would have to act out of character.

That's what had been gnawing at the back of his mind as he tried to find a few hours of rest from his labors.

To accept his challenge, *she would have to act out of character!*

What would that mean? Fortunately her very predictability made her denial of it equally predictable. She would have to forsake the night. Give up her costume. Maybe even her burglary modus operandi. Guessing that much was easy.

Where it got difficult for Batman to call it was her obsession with cats.

Her theft of the Eliot *Old Possum's Book of Practical Cats* manuscript was the perfect example of her obsession. To throw him off truly, Catwoman would have to give up her signature crimes on top of everything else. But he didn't think she could go that far; she probably wouldn't think she needed to. Not Selina

Kyle, whose own identity was so closely tied up in her feline counterparts.

Then he remembered an article he had read in the latest issue of *Lapidary Weekly*.

Which was why the Batman was perched on the tenth-floor ledge of the building on Forty-seventh Street directly across from the Gem Mart.

Like a magpie, Catwoman had a fondness for bright, shiny objects, particularly those of great value. Especially if they had some sort of connection to cats. And while she would hate the analogy with the scavenger bird, she could no more help her attraction than could it.

Batman raised miniature binoculars to his eyes, looking down to the street far below and the taxicab disgorging a passenger before the Gem Mart.

He smiled grimly to himself, taking what satisfaction he could from being right about Catwoman's nature. A nature that drew her, like a bee to honey, to the tenth-floor office of Krinick Fine Gems, current owners of the Katz Canary Diamond.

"Yes, ma'am, twenty-five carats *is* most impressive," Lewis Krinick agreed with the tall woman in front of him at the display counter. She was absently sifting through a velvet-lined tray of diamond earrings, a customer eager to spend money, he was certain, but unsure as to what to spend it on. Most of his day was spent with women such as this one, women with far too much money and way too much time on their hands.

Though few, he had to admit, as breathtakingly gorgeous as she.

"I was quite intrigued when I read about it. In fact,

Paul Kupperberg

I was wondering." She started, hesitating, to lift a diamond-drop earring to one delicate lobe and admire the effect in the mirror on the countertop.

"Yes, ma'am?" Mr. Krinick inquired. But of course he knew what was coming. It had been the most frequent request since the acquisition, two weeks ago.

She turned her eyes from her own reflection to look into the face of elderly Mr. Krinick. "Well," she breathed, moving closer to him. He caught a faint whiff of milk on her breath. "I know this is probably an imposition, but I would so love to actually see the Katz Canary Diamond. That is, if it's available." She looked at him expectantly.

"I'm sure you'll understand that the Katz is a most valuable gemstone," he said. "Twenty-five carats, one of the most perfect canary diamonds in existence, and therefore one of the most valuable. I'm afraid insurance regulations require we keep it locked in our vault except when showing it for sale, Ms.—I'm sorry. I don't believe I caught your name, ma'am."

The woman waved her hand vaguely between them, smiling. "Well, no, I didn't give it. I usually avoid doing so on the Street. I find I get much fairer treatment if my identity isn't known during the negotiation process."

Krinick cocked his head to one side, intrigued now by something other than her beauty. "And, um, why might that be, ma'am?"

"Because of my husband, of course," she said. "Roger McDouglas."

Krinick's breath caught in his throat. Roger McDouglas was one of the richest men in the country, owner of the nation's largest privately held media conglomerate, and famous for his aversion to any media exposure of himself or his family. So while his name was famous, his face and the faces of his immediate family were virtually unknown. Krinick knew McDouglas was married to a woman much younger than himself, and that she was said to be quite the beauty.

And that, as some people collected stamps, she amused herself by amassing many of the world's most fabulous gemstones.

"Ah, Mrs. McDouglas," he said, almost stuttering out her name in the sudden rush of excitement that gripped him. He felt downright light-headed. Giddy. "I . . . of course, I would be honored to show you the Katz Canary. Please, if you'll just follow me."

Krinick snapped his fingers, signaling to his wife, who, engaged with a customer of her own on the far side of the showroom, looked his way. "Deborah," he said. "I'm going into the vault to show *Mrs. McDouglas* some items."

Mrs. Krinick raised an eyebrow at her husband and the stunned, stupid grin plastered across his face as he led the woman to the room at the rear of the offices where the vault was located.

Batman unclipped the compressed-air gun from his utility belt. Catwoman would be upstairs by now, working her way into the vault and the Katz Canary Diamond. He would be there when she emerged with it in her possession, catching her red-handed, with no room for doubt or trampling upon of her constitutional rights that might lead to acquittal in court.

He would have her this time. The *last* time she would ply her criminal trade on Gotham City.

From a pouch in his belt, Batman withdrew a small cylinder that he fitted into the barrel of the

Paul Kupperberg

compressed-air gun. To that was hooked the end of a slim, strong nylon rope. Then he took aim and squeezed the trigger. With a muffled cough, the cylinder exploded from the gun and flew across the width of Forty-seventh Street, striking the concrete over the window in the corridor outside the Krinick offices. The head of the cylinder shattered when it struck its target, driving the diamond-hard spike beneath it solidly into the wall itself.

Batman yanked sharply on the nylon rope and, satisfied that it was firmly embedded across the way, pulled it taut and secured his end to a flagpole support beside him. A small pair of handles with a grooved wheel between them produced from a clip at the rear of his belt under his cloak and fitted atop the rope completed his preparations.

Gripping the handles on either side of the rope in his gloved hands, the Dark Knight leaped from the ledge, launching himself into the air high above the street, gliding across the open space with his scalloped cape billowing out behind him like the wings of his namesake.

Selina gaped, eyes wide at the sparkling riches that lay before her on the crushed-black-velvet-lined tray in Krinick's hands.

They were just outside the closet-sized vault in the back room of the jeweler's office, an armed private security guard standing at attention not a dozen feet from where they stood. All around them were dozens of drawers containing thousands of precious gemstones, but there was nothing that could possibly equal the value or sheer overwhelming beauty of the Katz Canary.

Creatures of Habit

"It is amazing, isn't it, Mrs. McDouglas?" Lewis Krinick said softly, in reverential awe of the diamond.

"Yes," she said, her whispered reply almost a hiss. She could not take her eyes off the large oval-cut yellow stone.

"Yellow, so-called canary diamonds are quite rare, you know. Particularly of this size and quality," he said. "This one came from the Kimberly Mines in South Africa, dug up in 189–. It was purchased the following year by Marcus Katz, a London merchant, for his wife's birthday. He had it cut from its original form down to its current twenty-five-carat oval shape and presented it to Mrs. Katz on March thirtieth, 189–.

"The gem remained in the family until sixty years ago, when the Katz's daughter sold it. It's since passed through several hands until, naturally, it landed in my own just this past month."

"It's spectacular," Selina Kyle breathed. "I believe I read it's valued at over one and a quarter million dollars?"

Mr. Krinick smiled modestly. "On their own, yellow diamonds of this quality have sold at roughly fifty thousand dollars a carat. With its history and provenance, the Katz Canary is worth considerably more."

The woman reached toward the diamond and paused, her hand hovering over the large rock as she looked questioningly at the jeweler. "May I?"

"Of course, ma'am," he said smoothly. Behind them, the security guard narrowed his eyes, watching the tall, elegant woman carefully. While he didn't find her threatening, he was paid decent money to watch over the Krinicks' property. Besides, in this day and age, you could never be too sure about anyone, or too careful.

Paul Kupperberg

She picked up the diamond between two fingers, holding it as carefully as if it were an eggshell rather than a rock of the hardest substance in nature. She lifted it, slowly, to eye level, turning it so that its multifaceted surface caught the light of the overhead fixture. Sparkling like a chunk of solidified fire.

Beautiful!

"Yes," said Selina. "Yes. I'll take it, Mr. Krinick."

Krinick's heart began pounding like a trip-hammer in his chest. "Um, v-very good, Mrs. McDouglas. If you would care to step into my private office, we . . . we can discuss price and—"

Selina turned her eyes, alight with the reflective glitter of the diamond, on the old jeweler. "No, Mr. Krinick, I'm afraid you don't understand."

"I . . . don't?" he asked, confused.

"I said I'd *take* it and I meant *exactly* that!"

Her fist closed around the diamond and she laughed as her other hand snapped open the purse hanging from her shoulder. As she did so a thick cloud of gray gas exploded from inside, spreading rapidly through the small room. The guard gasped, reaching for his gun, but before he could do more than clear the holster, he tasted the gray gas in his mouth and felt it burning his nose, all putrid and greasy.

He heard a thud, the revolver falling from his numbed fingers.

Another noise, fuller and less solid than the hard steel of the gun. It was the sound of his own body hitting the floor. He was unconscious by the time Krinick's body hit and Selina's laughter filled the room.

"Thank you, Mr. Krinick," she said to the elderly man huddled in a lump at her feet. "I think that will be all for today."

Creatures of Habit

Still laughing, small filters in her nostrils rendering her impervious to the noxious gas swirling about her, Selina Kyle stepped over Krinick's still form and sauntered from the room with the Katz Canary Diamond growing warm in her clenched fist.

In the main showroom, she pulled the door to the back room closed as she called in, "Thank you, Mr. Krinick. I'll be in touch this afternoon about that. Good-bye now."

Mrs. Krinick looked curiously at the woman, who smiled and wiggled her fingers in a wave of farewell as she strode through the showroom. Her husband had seemed so excited about this Mrs. McDouglas's prospects. It was so unlike him to let so potentially a valuable customer leave unescorted. But she had to trust her husband's judgment on this, so she returned the woman's wave and wished her a good morning as the woman opened the door and left the office.

Into the corridor, where the Caped Crusader stood waiting for her.

"Going somewhere, Selina?" Batman asked.

Selina's surprise was genuine and, for a split second, paralyzing. "Batman!" she hissed. "How . . . ?"

"I think it would be obvious," he said. "I mean, really, Selina . . . the *Katz* diamond. Even changing ninety percent of your MO, you couldn't have been more predictable if you tried." As he spoke, before she could fully recover her wits, Batman's hand shot forward and grabbed her wrist, squeezing hard. The sharp, sudden pain caused her fist to open and the lump of yellow crystal to drop from her hand.

Selina Kyle screamed out in anger and pain.

The Catwoman leaped at Batman, her free hand curled into a claw, crimson-painted nails reaching for Batman's exposed cheek. Batman twisted back and to

Paul Kupperberg

the side, causing her clawed fingers to miss their target. He released her other hand suddenly, unexpectedly, causing her to stumble back as she tried to pull free of his grasp.

Catwoman's back hit the wall, but she used it as a springboard to hurtle herself, growling deep in her throat, back at Batman immediately. The Dark Knight was waiting for her, once more sidestepping her lunge and using her own momentum to send her continuing on her way, slamming into the opposite wall.

She was dazed, but she shook it off and spun, kicking off her high-heeled pumps as she moved. She was face-to-face with Batman as he came in at her, his blue-gauntleted hands reaching for her. She whipped up her arms, her forearms slapping into his wrists, one two, opening up his guard. She went in low, head down, like a battering ram into the muscular ridges of his stomach.

Catwoman felt his gut ripple as the impact doubled him over, heard his grunt of surprise and the rush of air escaping his lungs. She reached up, wrapping her hands around his forearm and elbow, and as she stepped out from under him, twisted and turned his arm, simultaneously sweeping her leg between his.

Batman grunted again, hearing the tearing of muscle even as he felt his left arm pop out of its socket, his leg buckling as Selina's leg smashed into the back of his knee.

He went down, landing heavily on his side on top of the diamond, unable to suppress a brief gasp of pain as the sharp facets dug into his ribs. He started to roll off it, to get back on his feet, but as he turned onto his back, the flat, hard surface of Catwoman's foot struck him on the chin, snapping his head back.

Creatures of Habit

Batman's eyes glazed over and he was barely aware of the sound of bare feet slapping against the linoleum floor, receding into the distance. The sound overpowered by the pounding pain of his dislocated shoulder in his ears. He decided, a little later, that he must have momentarily passed out from the pain, because by the time he was again aware of his surroundings, Catwoman was gone, except for the faint lingering floral scent of her perfume.

And the Katz Canary Diamond.

The damned diamond!

Selina paced her living room like a caged jungle beast, voicing her displeasure with a low, throaty growl. None of the cats who shared her apartment were in sight, hiding from her anger, having scattered when she first came home, hurtling her purse to the floor with a banshee wail of rage. She deserved to lose the diamond. That was the price she had to pay for vanity.

She had started off on the right path, the one leading to change and preventing Batman from anticipating her activities. But she hadn't gone far enough. Her ego had overwhelmed her good sense and she had wound up with Batman breathing down her neck for her misguided efforts.

Selina had abandoned virtually every aspect of her Catwoman persona. Except for the single, most telling detail.

Cats.

The *Katz* Canary Diamond, for God's sake. Cats . . . the cat eating the canary.

You couldn't have been more predictable if you tried, Batman had said, mocking her.

Paul Kupperberg

But he was right, damn him. Of all the prizes to be had in a city as large and filled with wealth as Gotham, she had picked one of the very few that would serve as a beacon to draw Batman to her. And she had done it *consciously*. She had thought all the other measures sufficient to throw Batman off her scent.

But even more disturbing was how well Batman was attuned to the way she thought. Hadn't she always before struck at night? Didn't she always operate in costume? Wasn't her method always to burglarize the premises?

And yet the first time she decided to change those things, he was right there!

She could understand his pinpointing the Katz Canary Diamond as something that would attract her larcenous attentions. She could not, for the life of her, see how he would know she would try for it *when* she did.

Had she somehow given herself away?

The only thing she could think of was her reaction to Batman's slap at her predictability. Selina had thought that she'd covered herself well enough, but she had obviously let something slip.

And Batman, dear Batman, knew her well enough to pick up on her slip and turn it to his advantage.

Correction.

Almost to his advantage. Even though she had not thought there was a chance he would show up, she had reacted well to his appearance. She had overcome both her surprise and Batman, escaping him easily.

Of course, she couldn't completely discount the idea that she had been able to take him out because she *had* been expecting him after all. Selina had to consider that the same subconscious motivation that made her so long adhere to her feline trademark also caused her to stay with it one more time. Because she wanted to attract Batman?

As much as she wanted to deny that, she wasn't able to dismiss it out of hand.

But there was a way she could *prove* she wasn't irreversibly and irrationally attracted to her greatest nemesis.

And that was to put behind her, once and for all, her cats.

"She's going to have to take it to the next step," Batman murmured, to apparently no one in particular in the dark cavern far below the cellar of Bruce Wayne's mansion on the outskirts of Gotham City.

Alfred, occupied with flicking a feather duster over a computer workstation several yards from where Batman sat, *sans* mask, revealing the brooding features of Bruce Wayne, turned in response to his mumbling. "Excuse me, sir? Is it your shoulder again?"

Wayne shook his head. "It's fine, Alfred. You did your usual excellent job setting it."

"Lord knows I've had enough experience." Alfred shrugged in resignation. "By my count, this is the twenty-third time I've been required to attend to that same shoulder. You might wish to seriously consider the surgical option to permanently remedying the problem that your doctor suggested, what was it, going on two years ago now?"

"One of these days, Alfred. When I can afford to take a month off for the surgery and recuperation."

"I see, sir," Alfred said with disapproval. "In other words, you'll have the surgery about the time pigs learn to fly."

"Something like that."

"Then am I to assume your sotto voce complaints were in reference to Ms. Kyle?"

Wayne scratched thoughtfully at his chin. "It occurs to me," he said slowly, "that if she's trying to throw me off her trail, she's going to realize now that she'll need to completely abandon her MO."

"Rather beyond the psychological capacity of your average costumed foe, I should think," the butler observed.

"Too far out of it. Selina's lived with her obsession so long, I don't think she *can* give it up. Considering what I know of her past, it's something she needs to maintain what passes for her sanity. She has to identify with the independent nature of cats in order to convince herself that she doesn't need anyone. Especially the men who abused her when she was younger. If ever there was a creature of habit, it's Selina Kyle."

"Hmm, yes. If you say so, sir. So where does that leave matters?"

Wayne stood and strode across the Batcave to the computer console Alfred had been dusting. "Slightly more complicated to anticipate."

"Ah, yes, I see." Alfred nodded as Wayne hit the switch to power up the computer. "Ms. Kyle will endeavor to break her habit by choosing a crime she feels to be unrelated to felines. But you believe her incapable of making so atypical a choice, regardless of her motivation for doing so."

"Exactly." Wayne began to tap at the computer keyboard. "Like I said, she's a creature of habit and it's going to be her habit that nails her."

Alfred watched as he accessed the computer bulletin boards. Within moments, Alfred knew, Master Bruce would be deeply engrossed in the flow of electronic information, seeking out some obscure little fact, some previously overlooked news item that would point the way to his final confrontation with Catwoman.

"Very well, sir. And while you're making Gotham City safe for honest citizens to walk its streets, I'll be upstairs making the manor safe from dust."

Wayne nodded without hearing, his attention rooted to the computer screen.

"It's a dirty job." Alfred sighed as he walked, feather duster in hand, to the elevator. "But someone must do it." He threw a last glance back at Bruce Wayne, oblivious to the world beyond the computer screen, as the elevator doors slid shut.

"Not that anyone would notice if it were not done . . ."

She had spent five days planning this one.

Five days, scouring the newspapers and criminal sources in the underworld. Five days looking at this job from every angle, exploring it down to the smallest, seemingly most insignificant detail. Because she had to be sure, one hundred percent certain, that nowhere in anything connected to this crime, in any way, shape, or form, was there anything to do with cats.

This was going to be the work not of Catwoman but of Selina Kyle.

This was going to be the job that broke for good her obsession with cats. And with Batman!

Wrapped in a tight, slinky white evening gown, her long, graceful neck accentuated by a delicate golden chain, more gold and diamonds in her earlobes and

about her wrist, Selina sat back comfortably in the
rear of the limousine as it wound its way up the drive
of the Whittington estate. This magnificent mansion
on the outskirts of Gotham City, set on fifty wooded
acres, was home to one of the city's oldest and wealthiest families. The Whittingtons had arrived in the New
World from England late in the seventeenth century
and, coming from old wealth, had amassed an additional fortune in manufacturing and, later, in the railroad industry.

Today, Ivo Whittington VII oversaw a vast financial
empire and, with his wife Alyce, was known the world
over for charitable works. And it was charity that
brought Selina Kyle, along with three hundred invited
guests, to the Whittington estate tonight. A fund-
raiser, to be exact, for the Gotham Museum of Modern
Art. The invited guests, the cream of Gotham society,
would be pledging money, upward of three million dollars it was estimated, for the construction of a new
wing to the museum.

But it wasn't cash that interested Selina Kyle. It
was the Whittingtons' own collection of modern art,
often separated and out on loan to numerous muse-
ums around the country, now reunited for display at
the fund-raiser before being transported to the
Gotham for exhibition.

And not a single picture of a cat in the bunch,
Selina thought, smiling in secret satisfaction.

Her target was a specific painting, recently acquired
by the Whittingtons and being displayed for the first
time tonight, a seventy-five-year-old piece by German
expressionist Franz Von Wolf entitled *Lying in the
Glade*, valued at $12.3 million. Von Wolf was consid-
ered one of the true geniuses of the German Expres-
sionistic school, but his anti-Nazi stance had led to

Creatures of Habit

the destruction of the majority of his works by the authorities and his own death in a Nazi concentration camp. Only three Von Wolfs had been known to exist until *Glade* was uncovered two years ago in the storage room of an Austrian collector.

The limousine braked to a halt before the brightly lit front entrance of the Whittington house. A butler in livery stepped forward, held the limo door open, and extended a hand to help Selina slide from the car.

"Your invitation, ma'am?" the servant inquired.

Selina produced an engraved invitation from her evening bag, a proof copy stolen just last night from the office of the printers who had produced them. Satisfied, the butler bowed at the waist and Selina passed by him, stepping into the mansion's elegant foyer. Stationed at either side of the door and in the foyer itself were large, attentive men in tuxedos, beneath which she could detect the bulge of guns.

Security guards, of course. With the wealth of jewelry on the necks and wrists of the guests, and the scores of millions of dollars' worth of art on the premises, security would be tight.

Selina wasn't worried.

She walked through the milling guests in the foyer, into the main salon, accepting a glass of champagne from a passing waiter as she went. She was in no hurry. She would take her time, double-check the layout of the house, make sure her escape route was feasible. If all went according to plan, she and *Lying in the Glade* would be long gone before the theft was discovered.

Selina wandered into the ballroom, her eyes scanning the crowd, determining the location of the stationary guards, guessing which of the men and women

circulating through the crowd were undercover opera-
tives.

"May I freshen that for you?"

Selina heard the words spoken behind her, but she
didn't bother turning to respond. Instead she drained
the champagne from the glass and held it up for the
waiter to take and replace with a full glass. "Thank
you," she said.

"You're welcome," he said, and a hand holding another glass reached around her to clink glasses in a
toast. "To your health."

Selina turned now. Either she was dealing with a
most impudent servant, or . . . a tall, dark-haired,
handsome-as-a-Greek-god, cleft-chinned stranger in a
tailored tuxedo that cost more than most people spend
for a car.

He smiled at her, dazzling white teeth flashing beneath a straight, chiseled nose. "I'm sorry," he said in
a deep, rumbling baritone. "I startled you."

Selina blinked. "Uh, no," she said. "Don't be silly."
She wasn't startled, that was true, but she did feel
suddenly . . . strange. Uncomfortably warm. She
couldn't remember the last time a man made her feel
this way.

"Good," he said. "So, are you a friend of the
Whittingtons or a patron of the arts?"

No, that wasn't exactly true. There was *one* man.

"Patron," she said, sipping at the champagne, regarding this man over the rim of her glass. "And yourself?"

"Oh," he said, flipping his hand vaguely between
them. "A little of both." He held out his free hand to
her. "I'm Bruce Wayne," he said.

Selina lifted an eyebrow at him as she took his hand

in hers. "*The* Bruce Wayne, of Wayne Industries and the Wayne Foundation?"

"Guilty. And you are . . . ?"

"Mitchell," she said. "Rena Mitchell."

"Pleased to meet you, Rena Mitchell," he said warmly, holding on to her hand.

"We . . ." Selina started, narrowing her gaze at him. "Have we met before, Mr. Wayne?"

Bruce Wayne sighed heavily. "Bruce, please. And if we had met, I'd have hoped you would remember. I know I would, which means this is a first encounter."

"Strange," Selina said. "You seem somehow . . . familiar."

"That's me," Bruce said with an elaborate shrug of mock resignation. "A dime a dozen."

Selina shook off the strange feeling that had gripped her and allowed herself a bright, genuine laugh. "Hardly a mere dime for a man of your status, Bruce."

"A dime, a dollar," he said, apparently growing bored with the topic. "It's all just money, Rena."

She looked into his eyes, searching. Something there, in the deep pools of black, something veiled, guarded. Something the tall, handsome millionaire kept hidden from the rest of the world. The something that reminded her of Batman.

"Oh, no, Mr. Bruce Wayne," she said playfully. "You aren't fooling me with that bored, playboy facade of yours."

"Facade?"

She nodded and sipped some more champagne. "A man as successful as you couldn't possibly be as shallow as you're trying to make me believe with your line of practiced cocktail-party chatter and that patina of ennui."

Paul Kupperberg

Wayne pretended to think that over and said, "Have you considered I might be some sort of idiot savant? A genius in business but useless in all other aspects of life?"

Selina laughed, almost charmed by his line, and then drained her glass. "No, Mr. Wayne. I most assuredly do not." Then, handing the surprised millionaire the empty glass, she turned and walked away from him, into the crowd.

Bruce Wayne held his smile until she was gone. He might not have fooled her.

But then, neither had Rena Mitchell, aka Selina Kyle, aka Catwoman, fooled him.

The Von Wolf was being held upstairs in a locked, windowless inner room. The only way into the room was through the door, with two uniformed and armed security guards in the corridor outside and a third inside the room with the painting itself. All three men, along with the undercover security personnel downstairs, would be on alert once the painting was brought downstairs for the unveiling in about one hour's time.

Selina checked her wristwatch as she walked up the winding staircase, yet another champagne glass in her hand. Plenty of time. The "chauffeur" who had dropped her off earlier would be waiting outside, hidden in the bushes below the window of one of the guest bedrooms at the rear of the house.

She paused on the upper landing and took a deep breath. Her plan was deceptively simple, the hardest part being some acting on her part. But the Catwoman was—

No!

Creatures of Habit

She wasn't the Catwoman. Not tonight, not for this job. She was Selina Kyle, plain and simple. She had to put Catwoman and all her trappings aside and think as Selina would think.

The plan, she reminded herself. Time to go into her act.

Selina splashed a bit of the champagne from her glass onto the front of her dress and quickly mussed her hair as she reached the top of the stairs. She let herself go loose, wobbling unsteadily on her high heels as she staggered down the carpeted second-floor hallway, thoroughly into her role as a drunken society woman by the time she rounded the corner of the hallway and the two guards at the door of the room containing the Von Wolf came into view. She was humming loudly, off-key, a stupid grin plastered across her face.

The guard closest to her, a tall, dull-faced blond man, stepped from his post beside the door as she came closer. "Excuse me, miss, but you're not supposed to be up here," he said.

"Tut, tut, tut," she said, a hint of a giggle in the slurred words. "I'm just a poor l'il lamb looking for th' poor l'il lambs' room."

"There're powder rooms for guests downstairs," the other guard said.

Selina stopped, swaying ever so slightly. "Occupadoed," she said solemnly. She giggled, pointing to the wet spot on her dress where she had spilled the champagne. "I gotta clean myself up." Then she turned serious, frowning. "D'ya know if cham . . . cham . . ." She stumbled over the word and laughed. "Champagne. D'ya know if champagne stains?"

"I wouldn't know, miss," said the blond.

Selina stopped in front of the door and the guards. She smiled at the two men. "Y'know," she said deliber-

Paul Kupperberg

ately, patting the blond's arm. "You're kinda . . . kinda cute."

And she belched. Which caused her to break into hysterical laughter. The two security guards exchanged looks, amused but trying to maintain a professional attitude. "Oh, God, I stink uv rumaki," she said, snapping open her purse. "You gotta think I'm some kinda pig."

"No, ma'am." The second guard grinned. "You've just had a bit too much to drink."

Selina pulled a tube of breath spray from her bag. She shoved the glass into the blond's hand. "Hold this," she mumbled, uncapping the tube. She raised it to face level and pressed the plunger.

The spray hissed out the other end of the tube, straight into the faces of the two amused security guards. They never knew what hit them, their eyes immediately rolling back into their heads as they slumped to the floor.

Slipping small filters into her nostrils, Selina knelt in front of the locked door and shoved the end of the tube into the crack at the bottom of the door. She pressed the plunger once again, emptying the dispenser of its contents. The gas would spread and fill the room in under thirty seconds. The guard locked inside with the painting would be unconscious in less time than that.

The empty tube went back into her handbag and she next took out a long, tapered wire with a hooked end. A lock pick. The door would no doubt be locked from inside, but considering this was an inside door, the lock would be more for privacy than security. Someone of Selina's skill could pick the lock faster than it would take to search the unconscious guards for the key.

Creatures of Habit

Fifteen seconds later there was a muffled click, which, a twist of the doorknob revealed, meant the lock was open. With a swift look around her as she pulled from her handbag a paper dust mask with an elastic band to hold it in place over her nose and mouth, Selina pushed open the door and slipped inside the room to claim her prize.

But found instead the Batman!

"Looking for something, Selina?" he asked, standing in the middle of the room, his voice muffled by the small oxygen mask over his mouth and nose.

Selina was speechless. She stood in the doorway, staring at him, her eyes wide with the questions racing through her mind.

"The painting's not here," Batman told her. "Once I figured out this was where you were going to strike, I had the police convince the Whittingtons to move all their art to a place of safekeeping."

"But . . . how?" Selina said, her voice a dry, thin croak. "I tried so hard . . . there was nothing . . . *nothing* that could have tipped you off."

She could see his smile through the transparent plastic of his protective mask. "I guess I know you better than you know yourself, Selina. I couldn't have missed this one with my eyes closed."

"No," she snapped angrily. "I checked this one from every angle. The Whittingtons don't even own a cat. The name of the artist is Von Wolf . . . *wolf*, a canine, not feline!"

"I knew you'd look for a target that had nothing to do with cats, but I also knew your subconscious would trip you up." Batman held up two fingers. "It did, in the name Whittington, right down to Mrs. Whittington's first name."

"Her first . . . Alyce?"

Paul Kupperberg

"Her *nickname*," Batman said. "It's well known in their social circle that her husband refers to her almost exclusively by her old sorority name . . . 'Kitten.'"

Selina blinked, surprised. "Kitten? I . . . I didn't know. . . ."

"And then there's the name Whittington itself. I'm sure you must have heard of the English legend of Dick Whittington's cat. Richard Whittington was—"

Selina finished his thought for him, her voice a dull monotone. "—a poor boy who came to London, where he made his fortune, supposedly when his cat was purchased for a vast sum by the King of Barbary to combat a plague of mice, and was three times made mayor of London in the early fourteen hundreds. Yes . . . yes, of course I know the story. I know everything . . . about cats . . . but I never connected the name—"

"You can run from your nature, Selina, but you can't hide from it," Batman said gently.

She looked at him with dead eyes. "I tried, though. I *really* thought I could. . . ."

Batman shrugged. "Even the name of the painting you were going to steal pointed in your direction."

"I don't . . . oh. Yes, I see. *Lying in the Glade.* 'Lying.' Say it fast, drop the 'g' . . . *lion* in the glade."

Selina Kyle, the Catwoman, began to laugh, hysterically, uproariously out of control, and jumped at Batman. She landed on top of him, swinging, nails raking across his cheek before he could throw her off. She was still laughing as she hit the floor, rolling, and regaining her footing in a single, lithe movement. Batman plunged after her as she ran out the door, back toward the stairs she had come up by.

Waiting at the bottom of the stairway, however,

Creatures of Habit

were several uniformed Gotham City police officers.

She hissed defiantly and, without pause, vaulted the railing midway down the stairs, landing in a crouch in the foyer. The partygoers had been cleared out of the area, so there was no one between her and the door.

Except for more cops.

She laughed, barreling into them, savagely smashing aside anyone who got in her way with slashing claws and pounding fists and feet. She knew Batman would be right behind her, and while she feared no police officer, she could not trust herself to take on Batman right now.

She couldn't trust herself with anything that had to do with the Caped Crusader. The man who knew her better, she was sure at that moment, than she knew herself. The man who could overwhelm her, if not physically, then emotionally. She had believed herself capable of overcoming the very thing that had sustained her all these years.

Batman knew differently.

He knew how her mind worked, even how her own efforts would work against her.

Without realizing how she got there, Selina Kyle found herself running into the edge of the woods that surrounded the Whittington mansion. Batman was far behind her now. She knew with certainty that she could lose him easily in the dark of these woods.

But not from inside her head. That was another matter altogether.

Selina Kyle had slept for almost twenty-four hours after making her way home from the Whittington estate. She had been physically and mentally exhausted by her efforts, and her earliest dreams were racked by visions of Batman, chasing her, catching her no matter where she turned, how she tried to hide.

And, later, of him overwhelming her. And of her willing acceptance of his mastery.

She had awakened from that last dream, drenched in sweat, her heart pounding. But not in fear. No, nothing like that. Because the events of the past week, coupled with her dream, finally convinced Selina of something she was sure she had known all along but had not admitted, until now.

Batman was inside her, for better or for worse. In her head, second-guessing her. But also in her heart, the two of them locked in some bizarre, love/hate relationship that provided her, at least, with a perverse and delicious thrill, with the heat between them when they met, the dreams that both haunted and sweetened her sleep.

She couldn't speak for Batman, of course, yet there he was, right behind her wherever she struck. How could he not be sharing her feelings when he was otherwise so close to her, so attuned to her actions? Oh, yes, even if he wasn't ready to admit it to himself, it was there. Because if their minds were so in tune, how far apart could their hearts be?

Selina sighed, feeling warm and curiously satisfied as she stretched luxuriously, sensuously on her sofa.

Her gaze fell on a page from the daily newspaper scattered about her. The Life-style section of the *Gotham Gazette* and its headline about a display of rare Oriental jade feline statues going on display at

Creatures of Habit

the Schwartz Galleries in downtown Gotham City caught her eye.

Batman couldn't help but pick up on that, she mused.

"It's *perfect*," she said to the Manx nestled contentedly in her lap. And Selina Kyle began to purr.

Gotham City Spring: a suite

MORT CASTLE

How to maintain the peace of society and the peace of the soul?

*—An Unasked Question of
Shakyamuni the Buddha*

*There are no coincidences.
Everything happens as it must. This is karma.
Freedom? Of course you have perfect freedom!*
—S. L. Yamashita Roshi

artist

Kyu Matsumoto is an artist: calligraphy, poetry, gardening, flower arranging, killing. Matsumoto himself, an enlightened man, one who has experienced satori, would never differentiate between these arts, set one apart from another. Each is "in the Tao," the Great Way, each is all, and all is all.

The morning light is good. Birds sing in his garden. Kyu Matsumoto sits in his robe at his kitchen table, the screen door leading onto the deck letting in a mild breeze that promises both warmth and humidity later.

He remembers an April day in 1949. Beautiful blond girl on the other side of the street. Peach-

Gotham City Spring: a suite

colored sleeveless dress. A fist-sized vaccination mark
on her upper arm. How sure of her loveliness and
place in the world!

Still he writes poems about her, even in his seventi-
eth year.

But now he wishes to paint and so he prepares, and
there, at the table, he begins.

A Zen painting is a wordless poem. It is an intuitive
capturing of an instant.

This spontaneity is achieved only after years of
practice with the traditional sharp-pointed brush set
in a bamboo stem.

The touch of the brush is light, fluid; it dances. You
might say that Mr. Matsumoto is a master, yet *he*
would not say this. The flat-stone ink dish, the brush,
the variations of the tones of the black ink, the ab-
sorbent paper, why should one seek to *master* these
things? How *might* one do so? One might as well declare, "I have mastered the night."

Mr. Matsumoto begins with the moon.

After all, he can look outside and not see it.

Thus he affirms the invisible.

Kyu Matsumoto paints—

—NOW!

> *The moon*
> *eccentric*
> *and out of shape*
> *the brush line*
> *twists*
> *how comic*
> *the roundness*
> *the moon*
> *unborn*
> *undying*

Mort Castle

how alive
how perfect

sister, sister, tiger

Your world and the cat's world are not the same.
                        —*Taisen Deshimaru*

The zoo opened at ten, and fifteen minutes after that
they met (where else?) by the felines. Eyes nearly
closed, the sole cat willing to show itself was a yawning tiger. Bored or quietly seething with rage or half
dreaming of the good, hot throat blood of a kill, you
could not say. Gotham City's zoo had not been modern-
ized, so its animals lived on concrete and behind bars.

"Tiger, tiger, burning bright . . ."

"No poetry, please," Selina Kyle said, "assuming
that is the start of a poem. I didn't ask you to meet me
so I could hear your rendition of 'I'm a Little Teapot.' "

So early and a workday, there were not many zoo
goers. Maggie the nun, Sister Magdalene, in her
habit, all social conscience and Christian compassion,
with a crucifix big enough to ward off King Kong Vampire.

Selina wore a white dress. Long sleeves. A white
hat. Too heavy on a day headed for a record high. In
an hour or so, she'd feel sweaty, and usually she *hated*
that because it reminded her of some of the . . . *things*
she'd been paid to do with men. And with women.
There was a lot Selina Kyle hated. She'd placed herself pretty high up on the list.

"What did you want, Selina?"

"Talk, I guess."

Gotham City Spring: a suite

The tiger yawned. It rose slowly, rippling movement, front to rear, retreating into shadow at the back
of its cage. Its eyes glowed at Selina. We know each
other, Selina thought. We *are* each other.

"Maggie, I . . . Look, this will sound stupid and it
probably is stupid."

"So only you and I and a tiger and God will hear."

"Maggie, are you . . ."

*Tiger eyes glow, burn bright. I ask Maggie a ques-
tion and the tiger asks me . . .*

"Are you *happy?*"

Maggie says, "Let's walk, can we?"

No lions to be seen. No panthers. *Cats hide in darkness.*

"You're asking because of my vocation, Selina,"
Maggie said.

"Nuns are *supposed* to be happy, right? Doesn't
Mother Teresa think it's a grand day when she Scotch-
tapes a leper's nose back on."

Maggie laughed.

"You can't laugh at that. It's a sin!" Selina said.

"Don't worry, I'll make sure I bring it up in confession." A pause. "Selina, you're not happy."

"Wrong, Sister Sis. I do an aerobic workout twice a
week, I've got cable television—"

"And you put on a cat suit and do whatever you can
to get yourself killed."

*I put on a cat suit—and become someone else . . .
something else!*

Ahead, under a flowering crab tree exploding with
new purple was a bench in need of paint. They sat.

Selina turned to look at Maggie. A discomforting
twinge as though she were looking at herself. No.
Maggie was softer. There were no hard edges. And
while her eyes were the exact same shade as Selina's,

Mort Castle

Maggie's held no bitterness in the infinite green depths. No rage.

"I am *not* 'always happy,'" Maggie said seriously. "I'm not the Flying Nun or the Singing Nun or the Lobotomized Nun. But I'll tell you, I have experienced happiness. Ecstatic happiness. Beyond that. Beyond words. I have known the profound and perfect peace of God that 'surpasseth all human understanding.' But it would mean nothing had I not also known the endless emptiness of despair."

Selina felt something hot and envious in her throat, a sudden flare on her face. She rose, glared at Maggie. "I don't need bumper-sticker religion, thanks."

"And I can't offer you any. I can only tell you what I have found."

"Let me guess. You've got—what's the name again?—*Jesus!* Do I win a Singer sewing machine?"

"There's a prayer, Selina. It's called the 'Jesus prayer.'"

"Catchy."

"'Jesus.' That's all you say. You don't say it aloud. You say His name in your heart and in your mind and in your soul. And you keep saying it and saying it. If you're washing the bathroom floor or cooking soup or arranging books on a shelf, you say His name, so that *everything* you do bears witness for Him, and then—"

"You wind up winning at bingo next Thursday."

Maggie looked at her sister. "Don't," she said. "Please."

Selina closed her mouth. Maggie said, "What happens is that Jesus is within you. The kingdom of heaven is within you, His kingdom. And yours. Selina, there doesn't have to be a gap between God and His children."

Gotham City Spring: a suite

Selina abruptly turned her back. *She's stronger than I am,* she thought.

Maggie got up, stood alongside her, touched her elbow. "Sister Selina, always feeling neglected. Always so mad and so full of hate."

"No," Selina said. "Not always."

"Tell me."

She couldn't help herself.

"It was one time Pop took us fishing. Maybe I was six. We went out in a rowboat. You remember?"

"No. I don't know."

"We didn't catch any fish. Pop let me light his cigarettes all afternoon."

"Pall Mall."

"Uh-huh, Pall Mall. Even though you wanted to light 'em, Pop made it *my* job. Remember his beat-up lucky Zippo? He told us these silly jokes, and he drank beer and blew smoke rings. . . ."

I can smell the oily-sting of lighter fluid and the smoke and the wood of the boat and it's almost like I can smell Pop, and then, suddenly, I don't know how, the Zippo is tumbling from my hand, and disappearing into the water, and I don't even think about it, I just toss myself after it, so what if I can't swim, and I see it, and it's going down, and down, and I'm going down after it, and then Pop's in the water and he's got me and he's tossing me in the boat, and he's all red in the face, yelling at me, "You little idiot! I love you! Baby, baby girl, you could have drowned because of a goddamned stupid lighter! You could have died."

And then Pop plopped her bottom side up over his knee and paddled her hard, yelling, "Don't you ever, ever, EVER . . ."

She wonders if she's ever again felt so fully loved in her whole life. . . .

"Selina?"

Clumsy in the dress, Selina ran—

—Away from memories. From family. From "could have beens" and lost possibilities.

—And from herself.

shadow in shadow

> *Even in warmest*
> *glow,*
> *how cold my shadow.*
> *—Issa*

It was 2:30 in the morning. It was warm, warmer and far more humid than you might expect or wish for spring. On the rooftop, in the unreal light of the half-moon, the Batman was a shadow within his own shadow.

In the alley below, the dumb drug deal he'd been tracking. Ultra-dumb, super-dumb, dumbhead in a drum dumb, the pilot for a TV series *Let's Make a Dumb Deal!* This transaction out of doors, perhaps so that if shooting were required, there would be no "surprises at the Holiday Inn."

Four on the seller team, four buyers. Clothing and mannerisms, unremarkable middle-class, living examples of the banality of evil. Among weapons visible, an economical and dependable Sten gun.

The Batman was about to explode. Just over seventy-six straight hours without sleep and he was hard *into* it, the zone beyond the zone. He watched, focused utterly, fully alive, almost amused that his gaze did not incinerate the lawbreakers.

Gotham City Spring: a suite

The Batman was silent, but there was no quietness within him. There was a heart perfectly synced to the pounding rhythm of Justice's stern drummer. There was the rush-roar of his blood in vital response to the blood of all the innocents that had been shed by Crime. There were the billion points of hyper-awareness, the tinglings, the nerve twitchings, and barely controlled anticipations. Vengeance was a *living* need within him; it defined the Batman.

Gotham is *mine*, the Batman thought. Whatever is wrong, *all* that is wrong, I will set right. I am the Caped Crusader. I *am* the Dark Knight.

His thinking was flamboyant, melodramatic, and he knew it. A psychiatrist might have had other evaluations, might have used the term "paranoid," "manic-depressive," "obsessive-compulsive," and "delusions of grandeur," and he knew that, too.

And . . . the Batman attacks!

Even as he threw himself from the roof that was his thought. He distanced himself from himself, regarding his self-created and fate-willed persona in the third person. More, he could *observe* the Batman, put himself outside himself to see the night city's guardian in awesome, cape-flapping descent as—

—There! His left hand shot out, *precisely* grasped the fire escape he'd planned to grasp, and the ladder smoothly tipped and slipped (WD-40ed), clatter-rang as it shot out and he rode it down, *down at them*—

From below: "Huh!"

"Damn!"

Confusion and shock. And terror. *Panicked* terror.

Exactly. Perfect.

"Get him!"

Get him? Not likely! Can't you understand? All the

Mort Castle

Dark Angels protect him and guide him! All the Dark
Angels swoop down with him as—
"He's . . ."
—The Batman's right hand snapped a batarang.
"Shoot him! Get . . ."
The batarang shattered a wrist. He heard the par-
ticular sound of breaking bone. The Sten rattled to the
pavement. Other weapons sought to lock in on him.
Futility. Stupidity! He was invulnerable.
He was the Batman!
He hurled himself from a height of just better than
nine feet above the drug dealers. He landed with his
boots on a man's shoulders, like in a circus spring-
board act.
A scream of astonishment and hurt!
Beautiful, that's what he thought as the Batman
felt-heard bones fracture and tissues rip. Using the
crumpling man as his launchpad, he propelled himself
into a forward midair roll, to land, precisely balanced.
He—
—Snapped a *savate* kick to the point of a jaw and
immediate unconsciousness to a brain.
—Cut off a curse with the edge of his hand across
an Adam's apple.
—Struck with an inverted forefist directly into a solar plexus. Felt the leaping spasm swirl back up his
arm from the man's traumatized body.
Ludicrous and surreal images. Bundles of silly-
looking green coming undone in a whirlwind explosion! Eyes cross, like a cartoon, attempting to focus on
the gauntleted fist that pulps a nose.
"Let's get serious, okay? We can deal, okay? Batman, let's deal, all right? Okay?" A quavering tone,
but it was meant to be the Ultimate American Voice of
Reason: *Talk* deal *when your butt is in the blender.* . . .

Gotham City Spring: a suite

—Blink of an eye and high-impact dentistry, courtesy of the Batman. Teeth spewing, white and jagged.

"Don't hit me! Don't hit me!" The Batman did not hit him. The brick wall the Batman slammed him into did the hitting.

Then he stood, hands on hips, surrounded by eight men out. He was posing—for himself. He took a breath, and another, and another. He understood Tarzan's victory cry after a kill.

There was blood on the alley walls. Blood on the cracked pavement. Blood looked rich and thick at night. This was the way he *expected* blood to look, the Batman realized, and it was a most matter-of-fact realization.

A groan from . . . *one* of them. He could not distinguish which one, which of the *scum*, perhaps stirring toward consciousness, had made the sound. They were all alike.

They were criminals.

The enemy.

This was war.

What he should do was just *kill* them. At the very least, society would be spared expense and annoyance. A single, simple blow per man. Dole out death like a third-grade teacher passing out identical valentines to the class so as not to favor one student over another. "Here's one for you, and one for you, and one for you," and that would be that. *Finis.*

And then—

—*The mark of . . . the Bat!*

On their foreheads, *his* seal, the bat sign, a warning to all who would dare prowl the nightmare roads of the dark side. . . .

He felt himself smile, and a genuine smile was so rare for him that he took notice and savored it.

No. Just . . . no.

Despite the temptation, he did not kill.

He was better than that.

He had been summoned to cowl and cape by destiny and the night and the ghosts of martyred mother and father, and whatever he was, whatever (and he was still determining that)—he was *not* a killer.

He was the Batman.

Police time now, the mop-up crew, and bring the big mop. Commissioner Jim Gordon, District Attorney Harvey Dent, he had allies in this war, men he could trust . . .

(*Allies? Trust?* Certainly, and Peter, make sure you deny Me *three* times, so they *really* get the message, and Judas, how's about you make arrangements for the Passover, okay? Put it on the Gold Card.)

Trust no one except yourself, said the Batman to the Batman. *Rely on no one.*

Carrying a briefcase in either hand, the Batman stepped from the alley.

He felt it. An instantaneous change in the air about him as he entered the sickish-yellow, humidity-steaming cone of light that radiated from the lamp-post at the entrance of the alleyway.

(Perhaps he felt an indefinable shift in the very *aura* about him, that aura that distinguished him as *more* than a man. . . .)

The attack came.

green eyes in the night

Longing cat, sad
how you must cry with

Gotham City Spring: a suite

your love—
or worse still,
without!

—*Yaha*

The Batman spun, dropped the briefcases. He ducked instinctively and moved in low, shifting from side to side, cautious, checking it all out, taking it all in. Focused.

Over him, the Catwoman's whip slashed the air. She made another try, whip cobra-striking out, but now he was in too close. He grabbed the lash. He rooted himself and yanked. No resistance. She let herself be reeled in—

—Then the Catwoman . . . *hissed*. He'd heard it before, and yet the sound disconcerted the Batman. It was not a woman imitating a cat. It was a cat's anger, and there was spit and fury in it. It was menacing, unnatural—and intriguing.

Slowly, slowly, the Catwoman, hips swinging, stepped toward him. There was something about her. There was something about her costume. Something that hid *and* revealed her.

The Catwoman purred. She licked her lips. Her eyes were a cat's green eyes and her eyes were a woman's eyes and there was no difference.

The Batman felt . . . confused. He thought of fingers stroking down a spine, grown-up sounds overheard (strange, so strange) when he was a child who should have been asleep, he thought of flesh on flesh, whispers in overheated rooms, he thought of earth smells and sweat, a half-heard laugh in the night that leads to murder or passion, a touch of roundness and softness unexpected, and then she came closer still, and there was that *tail* on her costume, moving as though it were *her* tail, and he tried to tell himself it made her ridiculous, but it did not.

The Batman felt an *unease* that was almost a fear, a fear of all he felt and did not understand.

The Catwoman purred.

She talked in a purr.

"I can make you happy, you know."

He could honestly say he did not understand happiness, but he did not say it. He desired her, feared her, but he could not say that.

What he said was, "What is it? What do you want?"

A shrug. A cat's loose and casual shrug. "Money," she said. "Money is good. Your playmates back in the alley had money, and I'd been planning to relieve them of it. Then you showed up."

"Yes," he said, surprised he didn't stammer. It was like being in third grade, giving an oral report on your dead bean-plant science-fair project.

As though it might lessen her ... *power* over him, he wanted to call her by her name, *Selina,* Selina Kyle. Her "secret identity" wasn't much of an enigma even if it hadn't yet been reported by CNN—but all he could say was, "I picked up on them—"

"And then I picked up on you," she interrupted. She *purred.*

She'd been following *him*, trailing him, he thought, and he hadn't known, and he wondered how long. . . .

She came at him.

No warning, no subtle body language, no tensing of shoulder, narrowing of eye. Nothing. She was all cat, split-second metamorphosis, repose to assault.

The Batman jerked back, rattled, letting go the whip, and her left cross missed his chin as she yanked the whip from his hold, and he snapped back again as

the Catwoman's straight-arm returning backhand
flew past—claws out!

And simultaneously the Catwoman kicked.

The Batman turned into it, moved closer, taking the
blow with his thigh and not his crotch.

He threw a left uppercut. There was little behind it.
But it was on the button, the chin, and she went back,
and rolled, and then—

On all fours.

Coming at him.

Smiling.

Smiling a cat's inscrutable smile.

And he wanted to make her *yowl*. He wanted to
claim her, to *tame* her, and make her *his*, and for an
inarticulate instant he understood age-old combat between men and women, understood John Wayne, understood misogyny and a half-dozen other issues that
are endlessly blathered about on talk programs hosted
by the drippingly sensitive.

She was the Woman Animal and he WANTED her
and she scared the HELL out of him!

This time her eyes *did* give her away. He moved
with cautious sidesteps. Kung-fu attack/defense "basic horse" stance. Waited.

She leaped.

Rolled.

The other way.

Grabbed a briefcase.

And ran.

He took a step.

Another.

Tired. He was tired.

I am the Batman, he thought. I am Guardian, I am
Justice, I am Victory, I am Righteousness . . .

I am . . . JERK!

Mort Castle

Sherlock Holmes, the world's greatest detective, had Irene Adler. For Holmes, as Watson put it, Irene Adler was *the* Woman.

And he had the Catwoman. . . .

Or she had him.

the cat's meow

> *i am an orphan*
> *at this party*
> *envious even*
> *of scolded children*
> *—Issa*

Happy? Want happy?

Then go the hell elsewhere, because I was happy—not! The green reasons lay spread on my saggy bed in my East End *el floppo grande*, a "studio apartment" with hot-and-cold-running roaches.

Sweaty and feeling like I'm sweating dirt. The dirty city itself. Welcome sweet springtime. I'm wearing panties and a T-top, sitting on the couch, pouring drink number three, *sans* ice. Styrofoam cup. House of Stuart. It was cheap and it burned and it suited one Selina Kyle. I felt cheap, and sure as God made ingrown toenails (try rapping your Jesus prayer at the podiatrist, Maggie!), I felt BURNED!

Damn it.

Damn him!

Gotham City's daring cat burglar. The Catwoman, Ms. *Live it hard and on the edge!* Breathe in the danger, roll around in its prickly vibrations, get into it.

"Oh, hell," I said.

Gotham City Spring: a suite

"Meow?" Otto said. He leaped up onto the middle sofa cushion. Otto was black, and as double ugly and raggedy as you'd expect pure alley cat to be. He was my only companion these days; he was also the only cat I ever encountered that actually went "meow," just as though he'd learned from a first-grade primer.

Otto put his head on my thigh. He snuffled. He sounded more like an adenoidal bulldog with a deviated septum than a cat.

"Otto," I said, "philosophy time. Why is it everything in my life is so incredibly *wrong*?"

Otto snorted.

"Stupid cat," I said.

I stood up. Otto meowed as I let him drop to the floor. I assumed it meant, "Stupid bitch."

And he wasn't wrong. I put the bottle of Scotch for the downwardly mobile and my Styrofoam crystalware on a tottering lamp table and went to examine . . . my loot. The take. The spoils . . .

Check the dictionary, chum, and you'll learn that what is spoiled usually *stinks*!

And the goddamned *counterfeit* money, the queer, the *snide*! STUNK, just as sure as God made stomach cramps. A scanner and a laser color printer, and voilà, hundred-dollar bills that looked slightly less genuine than what you get in your Monopoly set!

Oh, you can be sure Mr. Batman was laughing (oh, no, he's got heavier status than that—he is Mr. *THE* BATMAN!), laughing his bat-butt off right now. The joke's on guess who?

A flashback kicked in: Not so long ago (it seemed so long ago), when I was just discovering the—*power*— the Catwoman outfit bestowed on me—

—And the power it held over me—

Mort Castle

The Catwoman: The Batman. A rooftop encounter. Only fitting.

The Batman: So it's to be a war between us.

The Catwoman: It's always a war between the sexes.

The Batman: And who will draw first blood?

She *did! You bet she did! First round to the Catwoman. She cold-cocked him. Ka-Thwok! And she cut him, made him bleed. And she'd touched his blood. And smelled it.*

It's always a war. . . .

Time to escalate the war, Mr. *the* Batman! Time to *win* the war.

How do you win a war?

You destroy your adversary.

You *kill* him.

Zap! I had it all put together in my mind.

Take the Batman out and I would conquer my own weakness. I'd know it and the world would know it. Take him out and turn my own life around. Nothing would stop me, not ever again—

(—hurt me . . .

—again . . .)

Take him OUT! The cop, the vigilante, the Hey-hey A-OK Gotham Good Guy, and it would set everything right! Take him.

Hell. I couldn't even take out the garbage without the bag ripping and dumping coffee grounds, egg-shells, and an empty cat food can on my feet.

Selina Kyle—not even a wimp. Try wimpette.

I did not cry, even though my eyes sort of stung. You start crying when you're alone with just your damned cat, and maybe you'll never stop.

I am the Catwoman, I told myself, and I knew, I KNEW what I had to do.

Gotham City Spring: a suite

an old man

My old thighs—
how thin
by firelight.
—Shiseki

Matter of public record: Mr. Abraham Itzak Cohen, aka Abie the Patch, owned and operated the Chez What? which he opened in 1933. He presented the top jazz acts to what he persisted in calling "café society," even after there were no real cafés and damned little left of what he could consider society.

It was the rock-and-roll thing. It was the Vietnam thing. It was urban blight and shifting economics and nobody knowing how to tie a damned tie anymore, and so, in the early 1970s, Abie the Patch, no schmuck he, closed the Chez What? and retired from the life of a cabaret entrepreneur.

Not a matter of public record but decidedly a matter of not infrequent public suspicion and speculation: *Most* of Mr. A. I. Cohen's "other enterprises," from which he did not retire.

What Abie the Patch would tell you, plain *mamaloschen* (if he liked you) was he was a gangster. He'd been termed "Patch" because of his talent for "fixing up." Etymology: In the days of touring carnivals, you had to have a "Patch." The Patch handled community relations and PR. He made sure the local officials got properly bribed and, upon request, properly boffed by the kooch-show entertainers, and that no carny popped a biscuit into the oven of the mayor's daughter, etc. "Everyone's all right now, right? Right!" was the Patch's responsibility.

Mort Castle

For a long time Abraham Itzak Cohen made sure everything was all right now in Gotham City.

So that was why, this afternoon when he should have been listening to Miles or Monk or Montgomery, he was at a meeting at which he did not wish to be, a meeting at which virtually every other person present wanted him dead.

He felt like hammered dreck. He was too damned *old* for springtime, the crap in the air always making him cough, an embarrassing *eck-ick* cough.

Of course, maybe he didn't feel any too chipper because of the cancer. Liver, lung, and pancreas ... Thanks very much, we can stop the inventory right there. A secret. He knew he was soon going to be dead, and his doctor, who didn't want to soon be dead himself, was good at withholding information.

So Abie the Patch coughed, and behind him, Brian Roberts, his "bodyguard," patted him gently between his chicken-pointy shoulder blades. Brian the bodyguard was very big, very blond, and very bland, and had orders to kill Abie the Patch, Abie knew, "when the time was right."

The Right Time = When we figure out where the old bastard stashed the stuff he has on us. And Abie did have it—something *choice* on every one of them that would be an interesting piece of news for A) the cops; B) up-and-coming criminals; C) the *National Enquirer*; D) all of the preceding.

But for now the death under discussion and the reason for this conference was certainly *not* that of Mr. A. I. Cohen, Esq.

"The Batman has to be terminated. It's practical, eminently so," said Melville Chamberlain, who had become CEO of the Syndicate four years ago in one of the fairest elections ever held in the city.

Gotham City Spring: a suite

The Syndicate: At the top, gone the rough edges. Also gone the high drama and low comedy. An equal-opportunity organization, bachelors degree recommended, MBA preferred.

Melville Chamberlain (do you *believe* such a name? thought Abie the Patch) was sixty, but looked forty-five to fifty because of a tuck-around-eyes and unwattling-of-throat surgical combo. He sat at the far end of the high-gloss, utterly anonymous, boardroom table, and, let's tick them off (thought Abie the Patch): Mr. Y. P. Park, produce-shop protection, of Korean extraction, who can say an "l" or an "r" better than William F. Buckley; Ms. Rowena Bromley-Stigers, proprietor of a number of united "escort services" that could provide for any desire ranging from "the cringing ostrich trick" (only hinted at in the *Kama Sutra*) to . . . you fill in the blank; Mr. Jesus (Just call me "Hey!") Nuñez, volume refining and distribution of recreational chemicals, and Roland Kirby, Whiplash Lawyers "R" Us, and . . .

Gottenu, Abie the Patch thought. They all look alike! *These* are today's mobsters, wiseguys, heavy-hitting *goombahs* and *schtarker menschen*? No Blind Louie or Joey Splats or Thumbs Garrity or Tony Two-Stomp or Curly Moonglow . . . These jamokes got on an elevator to dig the music!

Include me out!

I am eighty years old and I weigh 101 pounds, and my insides are eating my insides, and I think maybe I have lived too long—

"Mr. Cohen?"

Melville Chamberlain. Obviously not the first time he'd asked . . . something.

"Yes, yes." Cohen nodded. He coughed. "I was thinking."

Mort Castle

"The Batman, Mr. Cohen," said Melville Chamberlain. "We cannot come to any sort of reasonable accommodation with him."

The Batman? Abie the Patch *liked* the Batman. The Batman had style. If the Batman played jazz, he would be Archie Shepp, the angry saxophone, tearing into it, trying to break it all down.

"He's a madman, Mr. Cohen. He cannot be reasoned with. No one is safe from him."

Everyone is a madman and no one is safe from anyone, Cohen thought, but we try to pretend otherwise.

"Last month, the Batman put the arm on one of our numbers runners. A few hours later he took down one of our affiliates active in the sports world who was attempting to, let us say, prearrange the outcome of a college basketball game. Both of our people tried to 'set it right' in a sensible manner, Mr. Cohen. The Batman told them both it would all be set right when every criminal was either in jail or in hell."

Style, thought Cohen, definite style.

"Mr. Cohen?"

Abie the Patch spread his hands. Such thin hands. Spiders at the end of willow branches. He said, "You'll pardon me, I'm old and I don't think as quickly as I used to. Why do you need me, Mr. Chamberlain? The Batman, he's a man. If he needs to be dead, then make him dead. You can find, I am certain, personnel with the . . . *requisite* talents to deal with this situation."

Melville Chamberlain rose. "Mr. Cohen, there's something about the Batman." You didn't hear it in the voice. That was as bland as yogurt. But it was there in Chamberlain's eyes. He was *scared* of the Batman.

They were *all* scared of the Batman!

Oy!

"Mr. Cohen, we think you can be of help with this.

You have a friend. He is known for his ability to . . . to *arrange* things."

"Yes."

"Double his usual fee."

"Triple," said Abie the Patch.

"Triple," Melville Chamberlain agreed. "With his standard guarantee."

"Of course," said Abie the Patch. He started to get up, but he didn't have quite enough strength to push back his chair, and he almost flopped back to the seat. But then Brian helped him ("Such a helper he is!"), and steady now, Abie the Patch gestured magnanimously, ostentatiously—just what he wanted it to be. "When have I *ever* refused to accommodate my friends and associates? Of course, I will talk to . . . my friend."

Abraham Itzak Cohen smiled.

The smile was for his own pleasure and not at all for them.

beneath the moon

> *what a moon*
> *if only she*
> *were here*
> *my bitter*
> *wife*
> *—Issa*

Kyu Matsumoto finishes his cigarette. He thinks. He has been thinking too much. He remembers a wife who used to love him and now hates him. Thinks of a son who lives in California and does something with computers and has had three wives and makes a great

Mort Castle

deal of money and is indifferent to his father—indeed, indifferent to the idea of having a father.

Enough. He will paint. This morning he will add to the painting begun yesterday.

Kyu Matsumoto's brush. It skims, glides, twirls over the paper. The paper and the brush. *No separation.* The brush and Matsumoto. No separation. No division.

Everything one. This is the natural way of things.

He is creating. He is arranging a painting. He is *growing* a painting. Memory? A glimpse of the future? The past is the past. The future is the future.

Matsumoto is alive NOW and keenly balanced on that hairline instant NOW between past and future and the ink and the paper and the vision are NOW!

The painting—

—A capturing of impermanence.

—Yet a master's art need never die.

No contradiction.

No contradictions.

There are no contradictions.

> *the cat*
> *all slinking curves*
> *beneath the moon*
> *beneath the emptiness*
> *beneath the moon*
> *how unhappy*
> *until*
> *the brush*
> *and the paper*
> *and Matsumoto*
> *and the moment*
> *give the cat*
> *a Buddha*
> *face*

Gotham City Spring: a suite

mirror, mirror

> *geese fly over the pond*
> *they do not*
> *seek to*
> *cast their reflection*
> *—from* The Zenzrin

He slept for twenty-four hours straight. He awoke, stretched when he got out of bed, feeling centered and rested, and went into the bathroom.

When he was ready to shave, he stood at the lavatory, the heavy, old-fashioned razor, double-edged blade, in his right hand, and for the first time this morning he looked into the mirror—*really* looked—and—

—Nothing.

—No reflection.

—*No one.*

He blinked. How about that. He smiled. He *thought* he smiled, anyway, because he felt the tugging at his mouth, but could see no smile in the mirror. No eyes. No one.

—No Bruce Wayne.

And he thought:

Once upon a time—

—There was a boy named Bruce Wayne and he was much like any other boy except that he was the only son of wealthy parents and then the mother and the father of that boy were killed they were mercilessly slaughtered they were shot *to* death *before the eyes of the boy who was Bruce Wayne and at that moment— NOW I understand—at that moment Bruce Wayne ceased to be there was an end to him and what came*

into being was an embryonic being the Batman the Batman THE BATMAN—

—*And that—he is—THE BATMAN!—is who I am.*

—*NOW!*

—Bruce Wayne does not exist. There is a lie called Bruce Wayne.

—Proof! He opens the razor, takes out the blade, runs it across the pad of his thumb of his left hand.

Nothing.

And then—

Flesh divided on an invisible line, angled through whorls and swirls (the marks of identity individuality), and then the blood line appeared and beaded up, and it hurt, a vicious, deep and *real* hurt, and he thanked God that it hurt, and he held his thumb over the basin, and watched Bruce Wayne's blood swirl onto porcelain and glanced up—fearfully—and saw a fearful and white and unshaven face in the mirror. He only glanced, afraid it would disappear, and then he cried out: "Alfred!"

Alfred was there, with raised eyebrows and "Sir?"

Then an arm around the shoulders of the sobbing Bruce Wayne. "All right, then. I have you. You're all right, Master Bruce. You are all right."

No, he wasn't all right, but better now ... better. For the moment. Screwed up? *Definitely*, but at least he knew it. The elevator did indeed go to the top—and kept on going.

Alfred put a Band-Aid on his thumb. He took him down to the Batcave. In uniform, locking himself into his true identity, his nature—he—*the Batman*—was in control. He could even push back the cowl to permit Alfred to shave him.

"Master Bruce," Alfred said, "do you want to tell me—"

Gotham City Spring: a suite

"No," he—*the Batman*—said. "I don't want to. But I have to. I think . . . I think I had a genuine psychotic episode, Alfred. Call it an existential identity crisis, like you're supposed to have when you're a teenager—"

"Forgive the interruption, sir," Alfred said, "but I don't think we can say you were *ever* a teenager."

The Batman shook his head. "I don't know. I . . . Alfred, I need help."

"I'm here, sir. You know Leslie Thompkins would—"

The Batman interrupted with his palm out. Social worker Leslie Thompkins had comforted him that hellish night Martha and Thomas Wayne were gunned down; she knew about the Batman, the Batcave, everything, she . . .

She loved him.

And Alfred loved him.

He had to turn away. It hit extremely hard.

"No, there's someone else I have to see, Alfred," the Batman said. "I suppose I should have a long time back. But the truth is, I was scared."

Then the Batman felt cold and neither the face of the faithful Alfred, nor the sign of the bat upon his chest, nor the familiar walls of the Batcave made a difference as he whispered, "He still scares me."

ducks on the water

> *There's a little white duck*
> *sittin' in the water,*
> *Little white duck*
> *doin' what he oughta!*
> —*American Folk Song*

Mort Castle

His friend Mr. Cohen has invited him for three o'clock, but Matsumoto has not gone walking in the city for a while, and so he leaves early—

—If one were speaking of philosophy, one might say Kyu Matsumoto walks in the Tao. He walks the Middle Path, the Great Way, with angels on one side and devils on the other, and he does not choose between them.

But Kyu Matsumoto seldom speaks of philosophy. Why talk of what cannot be understood with words? Better to save your breath—for breathing!

So, if you asked him (politely), "Where are you going?" and he knew you to be a student of Zen, he might (politely) say, "Quite!" But if you were not a Zen student, then Kyu Matsumoto might (politely) say, "Ducks."

With an easy stride that makes it seem as though he is going nowhere and certainly is in no hurry to arrive, Kyu Matsumoto heads toward the lagoon in Gotham Park. He smells water and the special seasonal scent that one must think of as "green."

Kyu Matsumoto is reflecting on death and poetry; one cannot think of poetry without thinking about death.

> *Let us go*
> *over the river,*
> *and sit*
> *in the shade*
> *of the trees.*

That is Thomas Stonewall Jackson's death song. Simple and elegant, but surpassing it, believes Kyu Matsumoto, is Goethe's exquisite:

Gotham City Spring: a suite

More light!

How *good* to think of these words on so splendid a
day! How good to be wearing his favorite clothes: An
unlined, beige, double-breasted suit, which was quite
the style twenty years ago when he purchased it. His
footwear: Nikes. They make you feel like gravity is
the illusion that it is! They are satori shoes, and he'd
gladly endorse them as such.

But it is his tie that is the *best*! It has a bold picture
of the square-headed dog and the little redheaded girl
from the comic strips. Because she has no eyes, you
sense she can see all that needs to be seen! Yes, the
orphan child is very Zen!

In the water, riding on their reflections, the ducks!
Mothers and their young! Matsumoto lights a cigarette. Ducks quack counterpoint. Ducks bob here and
there, a ballet. Tails up and wagging, they seek food
in the bed of the lagoon.

Kyu Matsumoto inhales, exhales.

The ducks look funny in their hunger.

He should have brought bread for the ducks. He finishes his cigarette. Grinds it out in the dirt, takes the
butt toward a wastebasket.

Perhaps he can find something.

Matsumoto has his head in the trash can by the
tree, has just spotted several potato chips, when they
come upon him. He will get the chips later.

There are six of them, high-tops, baggy pants, a tat-
too, some acne, some scars, and for all of them, hair-
cuts that make them look as though they've booked an
imminent trip to the electric chair.

Skinheads.

Emerging from the trash can, Matsumoto says,
"Hi." "Hi" is his favorite English word—because it

sounds like *hai*, Japanese for "yes," and thus your greeting is also an affirmation.

"Hi, your ass . . ."

Matsumoto sighs.

He knows they want a tangible reason to hate Japanese. Or Koreans. Or Cambodians. Or African Americans. Or Hispanics, Pakistanis, Jews, Laplanders, or Micronesians . . .

Very well, then. Very well.

Karma.

So, then. So. Quite. It must be done with as little commotion as possible. The ducks must be considered.

Matsumoto strikes. Without thought. Without hesitation. Spontaneous. *Mo chih ch'u.* Effortless effort.

—Ruptures a spleen.

—Breaks an arm in two places. White of bone wetly piercing the different-colored layers of meat of a forearm.

—Fractures a kneecap. A hundred lines of fissure radiate under the sole of his Nike.

—Breaks a nose.

—Dislocates a hip, shearing off the socket with the most grating "rasp" noise one could imagine.

—Walks a screaming skinhead into a tree and unconsciousness.

—Sees—happily so—one young man running off, leaving his former comrades sprawled about.

But the ducks have been frightened. They are far out in the lagoon.

When he comes to the park next time, he will not forget bread for the ducks.

And popcorn.

Ducks like popcorn.

So does he.

Gotham City Spring: a suite

old friends

So often the world in haze
thinking of past things
how far-off they are
—from The Zenzrin

The man took up too much space with his graceless-
ness; he had no idea how to breathe, Kyu Matsumoto
thought as Brian Roberts conducted him to the living
room. White-carpeted, the size of a municipal parking
lot in a major city that had a balanced budget.

Matsumoto smiled a greeting at Cohen. *How old he*
was! How old I am! He took the matching cushioned
chair on the other side of a small table on which stood
a cut-glass decanter and two shot glasses. Ceremo-
nies.

The chairs were angled so that people might look at
each other or not. Cohen was a gracious man,
Matsumoto thought.

"You pour, please," Abie the Patch said.

"Yes."

Matsumoto doled out shots. They sat and sipped.
Matsumoto thought it good to be with his friend.
There were no others. Not anymore.

And Chivas Regal. Excellent.

"Do you want to hear something funny?"

"Certainly," Abie the Patch said.

"Suntory," Kyu Matsumoto said.

"That is funny," Abie the Patch said. "Japanese
Scotch." He ran his tongue over his upper lip. "Mr.
Matsumoto, you're younger, more in touch than me.
What the hell kind of world do we have when people
don't drink real booze anymore? White wine. French

water with bubbles in it. *Gottenu,* you know what you do with water with bubbles? You make an egg cream, that's what you do. You spritz it on your plants."

"Or you sit and watch the bubbles," Matsumoto said. The Chivas inside his mouth, a hot, wet line descending to his middle, and then the warmth. Fine. *Very* fine.

Cohen had a remote control in his lap. He held it up. "Do you want to guess?"

"No."

"How many years and you *never* guess."

"So everything is a surprise."

"Even inevitability?"

"Yes."

"And destiny? And chance?"

"Yes."

Abie the Patch touched a button. Across the room, the obsolete reel-to-reel tape recorder ticked into play.

Almost lighter than the air it set in motion, the music came from the Jensen speakers. A bass, not keeping any set time, and drums, a steady hiss of cymbal, and the piano, individual notes. There were vast distances between the instruments, spaces and freedom between the singular notes of the piano. These were musicians who knew how to play silences, *Zen!*—and Matsumoto entered the music, the Scotch warmth easing the dissipation of any barriers, as this moment of NOW became (of course of course) the only moment, here with his friend. . . .

Then the music was done. *Nothing* gold *can stay. Nor can anything else. Buddha!*

"Bill Evans," said Abie the Patch.

"Thank you," Matsumoto said, deeply touched.

"You are welcome. Another drink?"

"No, thank you."

"Mr. Matsumoto?"

Business, and Matsumoto did not look at Cohen; it would have been impolite.

"The Batman," Abie the Patch said. "My—*associates*—want him terminated. These jamokes, they don't even know how to talk gangster. *Terminated*, not whacked, not hit, not rubbed out. If you told one of 'em you were taking him for a ride, he'd figure a test drive in a new Acura."

"I understand."

"Triple the usual. And of course your guarantee."

Kyu Matsumoto nodded, knowing that Cohen would sense it if not see it. When he consented to arrange a killing, he pledged his own life as bond. *Nothing at all—yet they considered it everything!*

"Of course," Matsumoto said, "you may tell them that should I not bring about the death of the Batman, then I will most certainly kill myself."

"Why don't you pour again," Cohen said. "Some things I want to . . ."

Matsumoto poured. The two old men drank and talked quietly. Mr. Cohen, Abie the Patch, very quietly, asked his friend for help, a favor that would fix up—everything.

dokusan: a meeting of master and pupil

*—cat leaps from the shade
into the moment, where we are*
    —Lucien Stryk

"Please come in," he says. "You are Miss Kyle."

It is the next afternoon. "Yes," she says. She wears

Mort Castle

jeans, a T-shirt proclaiming, DON'T SAVE THE WHALES—
THEY'RE ANNOYING, carries a duffel bag with her *gi* and
her whip—and her Catwoman costume.

Matsumoto's home is airy. There is something ethe-
real in the way the light enters, this afternoon. On the
wall over the sofa is a picture, not Japanese or European in manner. It is called *Cat Dreaming of a Fish*,
Kyu Matsumoto says, when he remarks her noticing
it. The cat, curled tight on a background the precise
shade of blue that you see in dreams, has above it a
fish—rather the *skeleton* of a fish. "You wonder if a
dream fish before it became a meal in a dream had
a dream of a worm, don't you?"

"I don't know," Selina said. "What will learning
from you cost me? Fighting skills. I didn't come here
for an art lesson."

"No," Matsumoto says. "You need a lesson in man-
ners." He grabs her nose. He twists. She drops the
duffel bag. Tries to strike back. Tries to yell.

Can't.

The pain corkscrews down inside her—filling her as
though she were hollow—and corkscrews up, all the
way up into her hair. Consuming and paralyzing. The
only movement she's capable of: lifting up on her toes.
The only sound she can make: a peeping "Ow-ow-
ow—led go ob my node."

"Certainly," says Matsumoto. He seizes the lobe of
her ear. He twists. She's on her knees. Previous pain
a mere prelude for ... PAIN! She's on the verge of
passing out.

Matsumoto calmly says, "The *Kyosaku* school of
Zen, just in case you have suddenly developed an interest in metaphysical considerations, uses a good-
sized stick to awaken a student to the Buddha nature.
I don't believe in that myself.

Gotham City Spring: a suite

"Let us speak together, if you please."

At the kitchen table, they sit. Talk. He lights a cigarette. He seems utterly at ease and, at the same time, utterly aware. His smoking is not something to do. He *smokes*.

When she talks, he hears.

Her *sensei*, she tells him, her teacher, Ted Grant, taught her his own style a mixture of gung fu, tae kwan do, and "down 'n dirty." Now Ted says there is nothing more he can show her, and so she has come here.

She must learn more.

—*Must*.

She has to kill someone.

She tells him who it is.

Karma, thinks Matsumoto.

"Come with me," Matsumoto says.

By the door to the basement, he opens the closet where he stores the cleaning supplies. He hands her a feather duster. He takes out a vacuum cleaner.

"This is a Eureka," he says. "Anything else you need, I'm sure you will find."

"I don't understand," Selina says.

"Quite," Matsumoto says.

"But . . ."

"Ah, this is *mondo*. You ask questions, I give answers. Very good."

"You mean like a koan," Selina says. "Kind of a riddle, like what's the sound of one hand clapping?"

Matsumoto slaps her. A good shot that instantly reddens her cheek and makes her blink. "That is the sound of one hand clapping. No, we are not playing mind games. There are other ways to satori, to achieve liberation.

"A Eureka is extremely spiritual. It's spiritually

spiritual. Cleanliness is next to godliness. Buddha, you know, was an atheist. The moment he was dead, his disciples made him a god."

"I'd rather pay money for you—"

"Again, one hand clapping?"

"No!"

"The dreaded Oriental nose-kneading technique . . ."

"No!"

". . . bend your ear . . ."

"NO!"

"You will clean the house. You will live here six days a week. I have a small room with a futon and a nice chest of drawers from the Goodwill. There's a nine-inch color television, too. My son sends me televisions. Either Saturday or Sunday is totally yours.

"I will pay you ten dollars a day. I will teach you what you can learn.

"Your training begins with the Eureka. In Japanese we refer to it as *if yu nu sushi*. That means Eureka-Zen. Traditional *and* technological. Quite progressive."

"I can't, Mr. Matsumoto," Selina says. "I have a cat."

"Nobody has a cat, Miss Kyle. But the cat is welcome here."

"I . . ." Selina swallows hard, thinks hard. She ought to get the hell out of this loony's house right now. Benny Hill meets Bruce Lee!

But somehow she doesn't really want to.

She thinks, He smokes Pall Malls.

mondo: questions and answers

*a three year
old child*

Gotham City Spring: a suite

> *sees the world*
> *as haiku*
> *a one year*
> *old child*
> *points at the moon*
> *what is*
> *is what is*
> *who needs*
> *more*
> —*from* The Zenzrin

It's ... Cleaning Woman! Uh, didn't she used to be, was it, uh, THE CATWOMAN! Yowl! Spit! Hiss!??? Were you starting to forget? Was she? Ten days of "domestic service," and starting to take pride in your ability, girl, to eliminate even *numero uno dust speck* on a venetian-blind slat or a water splotch on the kitchen-sink faucet.

It was crazy. That's what she thought when she thought about it, so she made herself not think about it.

She carefully wet-mopped the tile floor in the downstairs "family room." It was quite American. A twenty-seven-inch television console, a gift from Mr. Matsumoto's son on the top of the set, one of those hideously memorable "black jaguar ashtrays" from forty years ago. A Ping-Pong table. Ping-Pong was "very Zen," Mr. Matsumoto had told her, beating her three straight games last week.

Also very Zen (said the *roshi*, meaning "teacher"): Frisbee, especially if you played with a dog. Dogs were always "in the Tao," never bound by bad karma. Dogs did not bother with choice: "To Catch or Not to Catch the Frisbee"; no Airedale terrier felt compelled to be a canine Hamlet.

Zen ... Okay, she had questions—after first asking

Mort Castle

if it was all right to ask questions. (She had not
wanted to get her nose tied into a knot or her earlobe
snapped like a rubber band.)

Zen was one of the martial arts? Like judo or
hapkido or . . .

No. Certainly not. It was more like fresh-baked
goods, but not quite.

Was it a religion?

No, definitely not. Except for those who had made it
a religion.

What about an afterlife?

What about it?

But . . . But . . . But . . .

Try these home-grown koans, "teaching riddles,"
from right here in the old red, white, and blue USA,
land of Ohio-assembled-Hondas:

"Who's on first. What's on second."

"Who's on second?"

"Who's on first . . . ?"

*Zen is now. NOW. Zen is being alive in the NOW.
Unity with the NOW and the mind and body. No hesitation. NOW. Confidence. Attached to nothing.*

*We do not seize the day. The day does not seize itself.
Nor does it seize us.*

*We are all into it NOW and that is what is what
is. . . .*

That is all *there is and it is quite sufficient, purpose-
less and perfect. . . .*

She knew plenty of koans. Pop had taught her—

—Do you walk to school or take your lunch?

—Where is it colder: in the winter or in the country?

—My father and your father went to different
schools together.

—How high is "up"?

Oh, and by the way, Mr. Matsumoto, how do you kill

someone? How do you make him deader than hell for double-damned sure?

Simple. Hit him very hard where and when he is very weak.

Enough! Better to mop-mop-mop the floor. Funny, she felt almost as though the mop were mopping and the floor helped it along and she had her hands on the handle and there was no exertion, not the slightest, that was required. . . .

WHACK!

Her mouth flew open. She let go of the mop handle. She spun, left buttock burning. "Hey!"

"Tag," Mr. Matsumoto said. "You're it." He stood holding a Ping-Pong paddle.

"Where did you . . . what did I do?"

"You cleaned the floor. You mopped so well that you were lost in your mopping."

"Isn't that it? Isn't that *part* of it?"

"Part? All is all. Nothing is nothing. The air is all to a flying bird, the water is all to the swimming fish."

"And All is Nothing? Is that what comes next?"

Kyu Matsumoto smiled. "After his satori, Buddha was asked, 'Are you a god?' He said he was not. 'Then what are you?' he was asked. 'I am . . . awake,' he said.

"From now on, I will sneak up on you from time to time. Catch me if you can."

Several times she did.

words

i speak nonsense
and begin again
—Bill Wantling

Mort Castle

One night, I don't know why, I just start talking to him, you know? And what I tell him is just about everything. I mean, it's stuff I have never told anybody else. It's stuff I haven't even told myself.

And I guess I get pretty carried away, because, next thing I know, I'm blubbering, just going liquid. I think, if Mr. Matsumoto had touched me, tried to hug me, or even just patted me on the shoulder or like that, I never could have stood another minute with him.

But what he did was hand me his handkerchief.

Then he recited a poem of Shinkicki Takahashi:

> *I don't take your words*
> *Merely as words.*
> *Far from it.*
> *I listen*
> *To what makes you talk—*
> *Whatever that is—*
> *And me listen.*

I loved that old guy then.
And I knew it.

satori

Only when you have no thing in your mind and no mind in things are you vacant and spiritual, empty and marvelous.

—Te-shan

This is what happened to me.

One night we ordered a pizza and Mr. Matsumoto

Gotham City Spring: a suite

had had a few drinks (he drinks *good* Scotch—not the Liquid Plumber brands), and I did, too, and the Comedy Channel was showing Laurel and Hardy. We were both, I'd say, a little on the *faced* side. When Laurel is saying, "I can but he can," I'm laughing like hell, saying, "Ah, so! Very Zen!" And Mr. Matsumoto is laughing like hell at me and Stan and Ollie.

A commercial. I want popcorn, so I say, "I want popcorn."

"I want popcorn, too," Mr. Matsumoto says. "I have some in the cabinet. Orville's gourmet."

"Not microwave. That sucks."

"Certainly not. And don't say sucks. It's vulgar."

So I'm in the kitchen, shuffling the frying pan, sure that I did get the oil hot enough, and popcorn is starting to tick, just a tick here and then there, and the outside sounds of Mr. Matsumoto's garden, all the little living things I maybe have never even thought about, are making sounds like popcorn, and all the sounds are coming together, and everything that exists is the sound of popcorn EXPLODING, a perfect moment of CHANGE—

tick-tick-Pop-
ticktick-the-seeds-pop-
change-tick—
And outside, in the garden, I hear Otto's cry, just a statement and a longing, and it's a sound maybe that could have come from me, but it means he is looking for love but will happily settle for the chance to kill a bird or a field mouse and I understand and have no need to understand as all these possibilities rush at me rush at me rush at me

tick-tick-tick
tick tick
—which we are

tick TICK TICK

Butterflies!
   Fallen leaves
      LEAP back to the branch!
   Impossibilities!
   jesusjesusjesus
   jesusjesusjesus
   jesusjesusjesus
   jesusjesusjesus
   jesusjesusjesus
Effortlessly, wondering, I shifted the lid of the pan. A single kernel shot up. It burst at the height of its leap.

And it was me.

I was free.

Burst open. White, so very white.

And new.

And ready to begin.

—And later, Mr. Matsumoto showed me how to kill the Batman.

—Or anyone.

peace

the charm's
wound up
     —William Shakespeare

It was a Friday evening. In another two days, it would be summer. A half hour before sunset, Kyu Matsumoto called upon Abraham Itzak Cohen. On the end table between the old friends, a bottle of Chivas

Regal. Two shot glasses. And two candles in simple glass candlesticks.

Brian Roberts asked, "Mr. Cohen, is there anything else you need?"

"No," Abie the Patch said. He slipped his thin hand down under the cushion of his chair. He pulled out the .22-caliber snub-nosed Colt revolver he'd secreted. He shot Brian Roberts smack dab in the middle of the forehead, a third eye above a surprised look.

"Like riding a bicycle," Cohen said. "You don't lose the touch."

The old men drank Scotch. Cohen tapped his temple. "All in here. All of it. You know, the putz was supposed to take me out once he found out where I had it. Couldn't think for a minute that people can actually learn and remember things. Back in vaudeville, I knew a guy who'd memorized the entire Oxford English Dictionary. Died broke, the schmuck."

"Not just in your mind now, I'm sure," Matsumoto said.

"No."

"A death poem, Mr. Cohen?" said Matsumoto. "It is customary."

"Light the candles. I'll think a moment."

"Do you need to think?"

"Please, I'm Jewish," said Cohen. He thought. Then he said:

Mr. Monk
Mr. Coltrane
I join you
we share
our silences

"Good," said Kyu Matsumoto. He lit the candle for his friend, then one for himself.

Mort Castle

"Good *shabbos*," said Abraham Itzak Cohen. He smiled. "Peace be unto you."

"And unto you peace," Kyu Matsumoto said. Cohen put the barrel of the pistol to his own temple, elbow stuck out at an awkward angle, and pulled the trigger. The noise was not very loud, nor was there much blood.

Matsumoto blew out the candle closest to him. Satori, the blowing out, the extinguishing of all desire. His death poem came to him without thought:

> *laughter*
> *cats*
> *bats*
> *buddha*
> *no regret*

He reached for the pistol.

in a garden

> *Don't weep, insects—*
> *lovers, stars themselves,*
> *must part.*
> *—Issa*

Melville Chamberlain, Y. P. Park, Rowena Bromley-Stigers, Jesus Nuñez, etc., if you are looking for the Syndicate (Gotham City division), try jail. Slammersville.

For a while at least. Until the right lawyer and the right judge make the right arrangements so that this

Gotham City Spring: a suite

sector of the American economy can continue to function.

Who put them there?

Who listened to Cohen's tapes?

The Batman.

The Catwoman.

The students of Kyu Matsumoto—

—Who sit in shadows and remembrance and contemplation, in Matsumoto's garden.

"We are not so very different, are we?" she says.

Once he said, "We are on opposite sides," and she said, "Of the same coin?"

But coins have an edge. And coins can have no sides at all.

"I am not others and others are not me," he says.

"We are what we are," she says.

As is the moon.

As is . . . everything.

Thanks to—

Sheldon Castle, my father, for the home-grown koans.

John Kamplain, of the land of sturdy tents.

Lucien Stryk, for permission to use his poetry and the poetry of the Japanese masters that he and Takashi Ikemoto have translated.

Catacombs

ROBERT WEINBERG

The mind of a madman is like the Catacombs—a twisted maze of dark corridors leading ever downward.

—*Justin Geoffrey*

Police Commissioner James Gordon shook his head in disgust. In all of his years on the police force, he had seen more than his share of bizarre crimes, but tonight's matched any he could remember. It wasn't just the brutality of the murders. Death was never pretty. It was the sheer *ferocity* of the crimes that bothered him.

Riordan, one of the investigating crew, wandered over. He was a burly, redheaded Irishman, his eyes normally twinkled with good humor. Not tonight.

"Six dogs, Commissioner," he said, drawing in a deep breath as if trying to banish the stench of blood from his nostrils. "As best we can tell, there were six of them. We won't know for sure until we wake somebody at the kennel."

Gordon shivered. Six of them—Dobermans, the

fiercest, deadliest attack dogs known—dead. He shivered, mentally correcting himself. *Not merely dead.* They had been ripped to pieces, torn to bits, as if by some monstrous jungle beast. *Slaughtered.*

"The jewels?" he asked.

"Gone," answered Riordan. "Just like at the other stores. Case smashed, all the gems taken."

"No clues," said Gordon, stating the obvious. "The thief, whoever . . . or whatever, was too clever for that."

"Nothing so far. Fingerprint boys are dusting the counters. But we ain't had much luck up to now."

"Nor will we tonight," said Gordon. "This maniac doesn't make mistakes. At least not foolish ones."

Pulling a package of gum from his coat pocket, Gordon stuffed several pieces into his mouth. Chewing gum was a terrible habit. It looked foolish and was bad for his teeth. He planned to quit. Someday. But not tonight. Not as long as a homicidal jewel thief stalked Gotham City.

The crimes had begun two weeks ago. The first attracted little attention. In crime-plagued Gotham City, a midnight robbery at a downtown jewelry shop was nothing out of the ordinary. That the criminal had managed to circumvent the elaborate store alarm system raised a few eyebrows. Just a few. To the police, it merely suggested an inside job.

Not so the second theft. Like all of the thefts, it also took place in the downtown, high-rent district. Flashman's Jewelry showcased some of the finest diamonds in the metropolis. Along with a state-of-the-art technology, the owners employed two full-time night watchmen. Ex-cops, they were tough, reliable, totally dependable pros, able to handle any emergency. At least they managed fine until that night.

The thief struck sometime between midnight and

Robert Weinberg

dawn. Ghostlike, the burglar evaded all of the outer alarms and scanners with ease. The police found no sign of a forced entry or exit. The only evidence of the criminal's passing were the looted display cases. And the corpses of the two men set to guard them.

Gordon sucked in a deep breath, remembering those bodies. Both men had been horribly mutilated by their unknown assailant.

One guard had been savagely disemboweled, his ripped-out guts littering the floor of the showroom. The police discovered him facedown in the ruins of his own intestines. The dead man's horrified expression had shocked even the most hardened investigators.

The fate of the second watchman made it quite clear to the commissioner that they were dealing with a homicidal maniac. The coroner's report told a grisly tale.

Knocked unconscious by his attacker, the stunned guard presented no threat to the robber. The thief could have made off with the jewels without any further violence.

Instead the crook had ruthlessly slashed the man's neck and face to ribbons. There was hardly enough left of his features to make a positive identification. Worst of all, several huge gouges in the guard's body indicated that after killing him, his slayer had *devoured* parts of him.

More crimes followed. All involved jewels or rare gems. Another night watchman died, in as gruesome a manner as his predecessors. Tonight it had been six guard dogs, torn to pieces, their limbs scattered haphazardly throughout Beaumont's Department Store.

"You checked on the Joker?" asked Gordon, shaking his head to clear the cobwebs of memory.

"He's locked in tighter than a drum at Arkham Asylum," Riordan replied. "I made double sure of that as soon as the call came in. Just as you instructed me to, sir. No way that madman committed these crimes."

"I know, I know," said the commissioner, frowning in annoyance. "Besides, the Joker always kills for a reason, however twisted it might be. These murders are so . . . senseless."

"You pegged it, Commissioner," said Riordan, shuddering. "None of this stuff makes sense. You know what they're saying on the street?"

"That werewolf nonsense," said Gordon, snorting in annoyance. "Forget it, Riordan. No member of the animal kingdom other than man ever develops a taste for diamonds and rubies. A human mind is behind these crimes."

"Commissioner! Over here!"

It was Jacob, another member of the lab team. He was standing about twenty feet from the gem counter, excitedly pointing at something on the floor.

Gordon hurried over. Mutely he stared at what the officer had discovered. A pool of blood covered the floor. Outlined in the center of it was a paw print. A huge paw print—the paw print of a gigantic cat.

2.

THE KILLER IS A CAT! proclaimed the huge headline of the *Gotham Daily News*. Sipping a cup of black coffee, Bruce Wayne studied the story over breakfast. Features grim, he ate slowly, chewing his food mechanically. The gruesome details of the latest slayings were not designed for a hearty appetite.

When he finished, Wayne folded the newspaper

Robert Weinberg

neatly and placed it beside his plate. A cold, righteous
anger burned in his heart, but as always he kept his
feeling under tight control. Temper tantrums too often
led to mistakes in judgment. And in his continual war
against crime, the slightest mistake might be fatal.

Closing his eyes, the millionaire contemplated the
facts as presented by the newspaper. Little had
changed since the first robbery. The police were still
baffled. They had no idea how the thief broke into the
jewelry stores, or how he evaded the security systems.
It was as if the killer walked through walls. Even Gordon, the best of the bunch, expressed bewilderment
over the bloody paw print. It was definitely a case for
Batman.

Wayne sighed, feeling incredibly weary though the
day had barely begun. Sometimes, late at night, unable to sleep, he wondered at the unceasing parade of
madmen who plagued Gotham City. Many times it
seemed that his entire life was spent dealing with one
lunatic after another. Was the gigantic metropolis a
breeding ground for insanity? Or, more to the point,
was it his presence, the opportunity to challenge Batman, that attracted the fiends? The question gnawed
at his conscience, but he had no answer. Perhaps
there was none. All he knew was that without him
more innocents would die. And that he would not allow.

Banishing all thoughts of doom and gloom from his
head, Wayne pushed away from the table and rose to
his feet. A big, powerfully built man, muscles like
steel bands rippled in his arms and chest. Because he
was so perfectly proportioned, the millionaire's size often surprised people when they encountered him for
the first time.

That no one had ever linked him with the mysteri-

Catacombs

ous Dark Knight was mute tribute to his consummate skill as an actor. "Sloth personified" was how one newspaper columnist described him. Wayne had laughed for days after reading it.

Ten minutes after breakfast, he entered the hidden underground sanctum beneath Wayne Manor he called the Batcave. A vast complex of workshops and laboratories, it was here that he transformed himself from man into superhero—Bruce Wayne into Batman. And, he hoped, it was here that he would find the answer to the phantom thief.

Using a computer grid of downtown Gotham, Batman pinpointed the location of each robbery. He noted that all of the buildings were located in the older section of the city, an area that had remained the same for nearly a century. Following a hunch, he called up the plans for all of the structures. Studying them, he was disappointed to note that several different architects had designed the stores. It seemed highly unlikely that four different firms would have constructed similar buildings.

Then, struck by another thought, Batman ran a secondary scan on the locations. Exactly what did the buildings have in common, if anything? A minute later he knew he had found the right answer.

The police continued to draw a blank because they were asking the wrong questions. They kept trying to discover how the phantom thief broke into the buildings. They were stumped trying to solve a series of impossible crimes. Only Batman realized the truth. The burglar was not breaking in. He was already inside the stores when the alarms were set.

The facts flashed up on Batman's computer screen as he accessed the proper reference file. A hundred years earlier, a huge network of underground tunnels

Robert Weinberg

had been excavated nearly a hundred feet below the surface of downtown Gotham. These passages, nine feet high by six feet wide, had relieved street congestion during a time when wagon traffic was threatening to overwhelm the city's hub.

Connected directly to the railroad yards on the south side, the tunnel system offered direct access to numerous department and retail stores in the downtown area without contributing to urban gridlock. Small railroad handcars were used for deliveries. Over eighty buildings were linked to the network by offices in their subbasements. In the winter, even coal was transported through the passages.

The decline of railroad transportation and the rise of the trucking industry rendered the underground network obsolete. Trucks brought products directly from the manufacturer to the retailer, avoiding middlemen and costly handling charges. Fifty years ago, the tunnel system was officially closed, all of its stations sealed.

Now, Batman suspected, someone had reopened them for business. However, instead of using the tunnels for deliveries, the criminal mastermind was making withdrawals. The Dark Knight's eyes narrowed as he noted that the vast tunnel network had been dubbed the "Catacombs."

A movement in the corner of his eye caught Batman's attention. It was Alfred, his butler and confidant. His presence here in the Batcave meant he had something important to say. Alfred knew better than to disturb him while he was working.

"What?" asked Batman.

"The local cable-TV talk show just featured an interview with Inspector Lincoln," Alfred declared in

Catacombs

precise, clipped tones. "I thought you might be interested in what he had to say about this case."

That Alfred knew he was working on the jewelry murders did not surprise Batman in the least. His butler had a sixth sense about such things. That Lincoln, one of the thickest, most incompetent police officials in the city, had any thoughts about any crime was much more astonishing.

"And what pearls of wisdom did the good inspector offer the good citizens of Gotham?" asked Batman with a faint smile.

"He intimated that Catwoman was behind these crimes," Alfred said solemnly. "As to evidence, he offered none. Evidently he saw no reason to confuse the issue with facts."

The grin disappeared from Batman's face. Catwoman was one of his most mysterious and deadly foes. A cunning and resourceful jewel thief, she had battled him to a draw a number of times in the past year. Trained in the martial arts, she was as dangerous as she was beautiful. Catwoman was as ruthless an opponent as any Batman had ever fought. But she was no killer.

That Lincoln thought otherwise was no surprise. The inspector's head was so wooden it attracted termites. Still, his opinion was bound to cause trouble. Catwoman would regard Lincoln's remarks as a personal insult. And she was not one to take an offense lightly.

"Let's hope Catwoman missed that broadcast," said Batman, turning back to the computer monitor. "This case is trouble enough without her getting involved as well."

3.

Unfortunately Catwoman did see the interview. It was hard to miss it. Lincoln's remarks were prominently featured on the local news reports of all the major TV channels at both noon and 6:00 P.M. And repeated endlessly as sound bites on twenty different radio stations throughout the day.

That Catwoman found the inspector's accusations offensive was borne out by the gaping hole that currently appeared in her television screen. She had angrily tossed a handy vase at the set only seconds after the police officer finished speaking. Unlike her nemesis, Batman, Selina Kyle, aka Catwoman, did not believe in keeping her temper under control. Especially when she was accused of crimes not of her doing.

Though over an hour had passed, she was still furious. Her long slender fingers, capped by sharp, pointed nails, clenched and unclenched uncontrollably as she paced the floor of her apartment. The claws of the cat, Inspector, she thought darkly, are unforgiving. And I do not forget an insult.

However, most of her rage was not directed at the blowhard official. Selina Kyle was nobody's fool. That cat's footprint had been no accident. The real mastermind behind the jewel robberies had hung a perfect frame on her.

By now everyone in Gotham City believed that Catwoman was responsible for the thefts and killings. Unless she proved herself innocent, she would be haunted by the murder rap for the rest of her days.

Grand larceny was one thing. If the authorities managed to nab her for robbery, it would be a long sentence in the state pen. Selina felt quite confident that no jail could hold her. Three premeditated murders, however, were a sure guarantee of the electric chair. And Catwoman had no illusions of returning from that.

Equally important, the fortune in rare gems called her. As the master cat burglar of Gotham City, she considered the jewelry trade her private territory. Selina hated interlopers. According to her twisted brand of logic, those diamonds and rubies actually belonged to her. Silently she vowed to even the score with the phantom thief. And make the stolen booty her own.

Eyes narrowing with concentration, Selina reached for the telephone. Time to call in some favors, she decided, dialing a well-remembered number. Her lips curled into a cruel smile. Nobody squawks better than a frightened politician.

Before embarking on her career as Catwoman, Selina had earned her keep in an equally illegal fashion. For years she had sold her body to the highest bidder. Specializing in domination and perverse pleasures, she serviced a wide range of both male and female clients. Many of them numbered among the glitterati of Gotham City. Though they had tried to keep their identities secret, no one ever managed to deceive Selina Kyle.

Always an opportunist, and gifted with an exceptional memory, she had filed away detailed notes on their secret vices, along with an extensive photo scrapbook, for darker days. If nothing else, Catwoman believed in preparing for the worst. That was why she was the best at everything she tried.

Three phone calls and an hour later Selina leaned back on the sofa, a sly smile caressing her lips. Sleep might come hard to several politicians tonight. A little

fear was good for everyone, including the stuffed
shirts in city hall. After today, they might even consider celibacy. Though she strongly doubted that. Nor
did she care.

What mattered was that she was sure she knew the
phantom crook's secret. According to a very highly
placed source in the mayor's office, Commissioner
Gordon was convinced that the thief lurked in the old
freight tunnels beneath downtown Gotham.

Another unimpeachable source, this one in the police department, confirmed that story and added that
a full-scale manhunt in the notorious Catacombs was
scheduled for the day after tomorrow. The wheels of
justice spun slowly in the vast metropolis. Which
suited Catwoman fine. Tonight she planned to invade
the underground maze. And deal out her own brand of
justice.

4.

Far beneath the city streets, a solitary figure stirred
on a makeshift bed of huge pillows and expensive
throw rugs. Scattered about the huge chamber, a
thirty-foot square with the dark mouth of an old
freight tunnel embedded in each wall, sat stacks of
treasure from more than a dozen merchants of downtown Gotham. Not all the prizes were of equal value.
Rare gems filled antique goblets while only a foot
away rested half-finished boxes of potato chips. And
cans of Coca-Cola stood side by side with rare vintages of fine wine.

Yawning, the reclining man sat up, rubbing the last
remnants of sleep from his eyes. His skin, the color of

old ivory, gleamed in the light of two ornate candles that cast strange shadows on the far wall. Tall and lean, he wore a long flowing white robe that left only his head and hands uncovered.

His face resembled an ancient Egyptian death mask. Thin bloodless lips framed a gash of a mouth. Narrow ears pressed flat against his skull. Short black hair matted his head, emphasizing the deep yellow of his complexion. Gaunt cheeks and long, needle-like eyebrows that met over his beaklike nose combined to draw attention to eyes of unusual power.

Dark green, hypnotic in intensity, they glowed with a seemingly supernatural brilliance. Strange, catlike eyes, they perfectly matched in color the one piece of jewelry that he wore—a huge multifaceted emerald dangling on his chest, held in place by a thin chain of purest gold. With each breath the man took, the massive gem pulsed with unnatural life.

In one swift, fluid motion, the yellow man rose to his feet. All around him, as if in response, the floor rippled with life. Cats—cats everywhere—rose to greet their master. Black cats, gray cats, gold cats, striped cats, alley cats and Siamese cats, hundreds of cats stretched and arched their backs as the robed figure raised his arms above his head as if in prayer.

He smiled, a death's-head grin that held no humor. His gaze swept across the room, and he laughed cruelly at a joke only he understood. In seconds, reacting to the slightest change in their master's mood, the feline horde howled in delight. The dimly lit chamber exploded with sound.

Grimacing with annoyance, the yellow man flicked one hand in a sharp gesture. On his chest, the emerald flared green, reflecting his displeasure. As if cut by a knife, the noise ceased instantly. Here, truly, was

Robert Weinberg

the master of this immense pack. He was the Lord of Cats.

"Silence, my pets," he whispered, in a harsh voice that echoed from the concrete walls. "Your wailing disturbs my concentration."

For an instant he stood frozen in place, a faraway expression in his deep green eyes. A brief look of satisfaction crossed his face. "The Midnight Slayer returns," he declared, sounding pleased. "As I command."

From out of the nearest tunnel emerged a patch of darkness darker than the dark, blacker than the night. A killer beast, with glowing yellow eyes and a mouth full of flashing teeth. Nine feet long from head to tail, and weighing more than two hundred pounds, it killed with a casual grace and ferocity unmatched by any other member of the animal kingdom. A monster rarely captured and never tamed, the Midnight Slayer was a giant black panther.

Growling deep in its throat, the big cat padded its way across the concrete floor to the Lord of Cats. On the man's chest, the great green emerald pulsated with raw energy. Gradually the menacing rumbling in the beast's chest quieted, then stopped. Almost docile, it came to a stop less than a foot away from the robed figure.

Clenching the blazing jewel with one hand, the yellow man bent down and gently scratched the panther behind the ears. Incredibly the monster purred with satisfaction like a giant kitten. Slowly, ever so slowly, it sank peacefully to the ground.

With a sigh of relief, the Lord of Cats straightened. Even when he used the full power of the emerald, it was enormously difficult controlling the mind of the huge leopard. Most big-game hunters considered black

Catacombs

panthers the most dangerous of all predators. Savage beyond belief, they lived only to kill. Still, as long as the Lord of Cats held the Heart of Sekhmet, *he* was beast's master.

Originally captured in Central Africa, the Midnight Slayer had spent most of its life in a major California zoo. The Lord of Cats had "liberated" the monster soon after embarking on his unique quest. It had served him well with fang and claw ever since.

"Tonight I sense she will come," he whispered, kneeling beside the unmoving panther, as if telling the beast his deepest secrets. "The one I desire as my bride. Who more fitting a mate for the Lord of Cats than the Catwoman?"

Lazily the panther lifted its immense head and snarled, baring immense fangs. "No reason to be concerned," said the man, chuckling. "There will be others to slay—many others. Our work here is almost finished. I baited a trap for Catwoman with your paw print. She had no choice other than to investigate.

"Once Catwoman joins us, we shall abandon these tunnels. I grow tired of the darkness. There are other cities to plunder, other treasures to take, other deaths to savor."

The Lord of Cats raised the emerald to his forehead, placing the throbbing jewel on the bridge of his nose, directly between his eyes. An eerie green light filled the chamber. Instantly all of the cats were on their feet, their eyes fixed unwaveringly on the man holding the gem.

"Go now," he commanded. "Spread throughout the Catacombs. Serve as my eyes and ears. Let no human walk through these tunnels undetected. Obey me, for I am your lord." His hands pressed the emerald even tighter. "I am the Lord of Cats."

And, like the wind, they were gone, scattered throughout the maze of Catacombs, leaving the Lord of Cats alone with the Midnight Slayer. Patiently they awaited the arrival of Catwoman.

5.

Entering the Catacombs proved quite easy for Batman. He only hoped that leaving would pose no greater difficulties.

At six that evening, millionaire playboy Bruce Wayne arrived as scheduled at Lewiston's Gem Emporium, located in the heart of Gotham's exclusive jewelry district. Accompanying him was a small army of caterers, decorators, and unidentified craftsmen. While the tradesmen hurried about, transforming the store's main showroom into a lavish reception hall, Wayne cheerfully discussed his plans with William Lewiston, the tuxedo-clad, white-haired manager of the place.

"I'm having a small, intimate party for a few friends tonight," he confided, sipping a glass of white wine handed to him by his ever-present manservant. "Things get so boring at the mansion sometimes. I thought a little night on the town would be much more entertaining."

The wrinkled look of disapproval on Lewiston's face made it quite clear what he thought of Wayne's plans. However, the older man wisely kept his opinions to himself.

Unknown to the general public, Lewiston's had suffered a major cash-flow crisis a few months ago. Sluggish sales forced major cutbacks at all levels of the operation. Bankruptcy seemed only a matter of time.

Then, unexpectedly, a sudden influx of hard currency changed everything. The emporium carried on with no interruptions in sales or services. As the economy recovered, so did the jewelry business. The momentary crisis past, the store flourished.

Only a few members of the Lewiston family were aware of the source of those necessary funds. Control of the century-old family business had quietly shifted to Bruce Wayne Enterprises. Day-to-day operations of the firm were still handled by the regular employees. But financial operations were tightly controlled by a board of overseers responsible only to the flamboyant millionaire.

Tonight was the first time Wayne had indicated anything more than a passing interest in the jewelry store. Face white, his lips tightly pressed together as if to keep from screaming in outrage, William Lewiston escorted his new boss on a tour of the premises.

"Where does that lead to?" asked Wayne, waving his wineglass at a padlocked door at the far end of a dusty storeroom.

"Down to the subbasement," Lewiston replied. "Dreadful place actually and no longer used for anything. Long ago the furnace was located there. This building is one of the oldest in the city. Our establishment has been situated here for over a hundred years."

"How fascinating," said Wayne, his bored tone indicating his true feelings. Then, casually, he asked, "In the winter, coal was delivered . . . ?"

"Through the Catacombs," answered Lewiston. "You are aware of the tunnel system?"

"I own a number of properties in downtown Gotham," said Wayne. "Though none quite so close to the old central routing office of the passageways."

"We boarded up the entrance to the maze years ago," said Lewiston. "The city stopped using the tunnels back in the early forties." The older man chuckled. "Though there was some talk in the sixties, during the Cuban missile crisis, of using them for fallout shelters."

"Wasn't the Cold War wonderful," said Wayne. Grasping the store manager by the elbow, the millionaire steered him back into the main showroom.

"No reason to worry about your fancy displays," Wayne said soothingly, patting Lewiston on the shoulder. "I would never do anything to jeopardize an important investment. Trust me on this. When you arrive tomorrow, you'll swear that no one was ever here."

It took five minutes and several dozen more assurances before Lewiston could be convinced to depart. Another half hour passed before everyone else had cleared the showroom. Finally only Bruce Wayne and Alfred remained.

"Nine o'clock," said the millionaire, glancing down at his watch. "The phantom thief never strikes before midnight. That gives me three hours or more to locate his lair."

"You refuse to let the police handle this matter?" said Alfred, disapproval sharp upon his face. "There is still time to make an anonymous phone call to Commissioner Gordon."

"I suspect Gordon knows all about these tunnels," said Wayne, opening a large box brought in by the workmen but left untouched during the preparations. "But department procedures limit his capacity for fast action. By the time he sends men into the Catacombs, our murderer will be long gone. Besides," he concluded as he carefully checked the contents of the container, "a single man stands a much better chance of finding the killer than a squad of policemen."

"Especially if that man is Batman," said Alfred, with a heavy sigh.

"Correct," said Wayne, emptying the special apparatus onto the floor. "Give me a hand with this stuff, Alfred. It's time for me to visit the Catacombs."

Five minutes later Batman stood ready to enter the underground maze. Few people would have noted that somehow the Dark Knight appeared different than usual—bulkier, bigger, his muscles not as well defined beneath his costume. Only his long cape, dark and mysterious, seemed unchanged.

In one hand he held a small but powerful flashlight. Built to exacting specifications, it cast a pale white light that was visible for only a few feet. A second similar device was hooked to his belt. In dangerous situations where a normal light would betray his presence, Batman relied on such lanterns until he was extremely close to his quarry. Of extremely rugged construction, the lights were built to take a beating. In the absolute blackness of the underground maze, they were a necessity.

Gripped in his other hand the crime fighter held a small lightweight dart gun. It was loaded with the most powerful tranquilizer pellets available. Batman wasn't sure what beast lurked in the Catacombs, but he was taking every precaution. Three dead guards and a half-dozen dogs ripped to pieces demanded it. One scratch from these darts would knock an elephant off its feet.

"Don't forget to move the food around on the plates

a bit," he instructed Alfred as he pulled free the last of the boards blocking the entrance to the abandoned tunnel system. Like the gaping mouth of some ancient, gigantic dinosaur, it waited silently for him to enter. "After all, Bruce Wayne entertained his friends here for hours. Or so we told Mr. Lewiston. And our employees."

"I will make sure the evidence is properly faked before the workmen arrive tomorrow to carry it all away," said Alfred, gazing nervously into the darkness. "Shouldn't you be carrying some sort of map, sir?"

"Memorized," said Batman, tapping the side of his head. "Not that it matters much," he continued, taking his first step into the maze. "The Catacombs all head in one direction. Downward. *Ever downward.*"

6.

Batman was not exaggerating when he claimed to have memorized the map of the entire freight transportation system. Gifted with an exceptional memory, he had spent years perfecting it through rigorous mental training. One glance at most simple diagrams was all he needed to master them. A more complicated drawing, like the maze, required greater concentration but not much more time.

Nor had he misled Alfred when he stated that all of the tunnels led downward. The Catacombs converged in one huge shipping depot well over a hundred feet beneath the city streets.

The entire freight system had been designed to serve an area stretching from the railroad yards on the south side to downtown Gotham. Hundreds of shipments passed through the corridors every day. In order to keep operations simple, from the very beginning of the endeavor two sorting areas had been maintained.

One was centered at the train station, where goods from all over the country arrived and were separated for transportation downtown. The second, even larger distribution area, was located scores of feet beneath the buildings it serviced. From here, freight and coal were sent to smaller sorting centers where they were prepared for delivery. They were then shipped by handcar through tunnels to their proper destinations. Ruling out the main depot as too dark and dismal, Batman was convinced that the phantom thief was headquartered in one of the substations. The problem was finding the proper room without alerting the phantom killer to his presence.

Cautiously, he started down the tunnel leading from Lewiston's Jewelry Emporium. The passage was a concrete oval nine feet high by six feet wide, with a flattened floor and roof. Wide metal tracks were the only evidence that railway handcars once traveled in this same direction. The corridor walls were flat and unbroken, showing no signs of age. Every ten feet there was a small niche for a gas lamp, but none was in evidence. To Batman, it seemed as if he were walking through a gigantic tube thrust into the earth.

At first, the intensity of the darkness was not overwhelming. Especially since a sliver of light filtered down the tunnel from the open landing. However, forty yards into the passage, the tunnel angled thirty degrees to the right. Now Batman's flash provided the only illumination in what was otherwise a pool of absolute blackness. The effect was startling, almost frightening.

Batman paused, abruptly conscious of an unnatural tightness in his chest. His breathing came in short shallow gasps. And he could hear the blood pounding in his head. The Dark Knight was afraid.

Normally the darkness held no fear for him. For years he worked with it, capitalizing on superstitious criminals' fear of the night and its supposed terrors. However, this darkness was different.

It was not merely the inability to see outside the small circle of light the flashlight provided. More than once he had been blinded in battle or caught in lightless traps. Always he managed to fight on without the least problem. In a moment of epiphany, Batman realized it was his present location that frightened him.

A thousand tons of rock rested over his head. Only a thin wall of concrete, more than a century old, stood between him and being buried alive. This darkness was so complete, so absolute, because light could not reach a hundred feet beneath the street. Walking through these tunnels was like traveling in the domain of the dead. The passageways were aptly named the Catacombs.

The air was heavy and stagnant, breathable, but stale and lifeless, like the air in a tomb. And silence hung over the tunnel like a shroud. The comparisons, apt as they were, did nothing to relieve Batman's apprehensions.

Shaking his head in annoyance, the Dark Knight forced himself forward. The more time he wasted worrying here, the better chance he gave the phantom to escape.

Another fifty yards and the corridor branched left and right. After a second's thought Batman took the

right-hand passage. Downward, ever downward, the
tunnel continued.

He walked in silence, the only noise the soft scrape
of his boots on the old concrete. And the sound of his
breathing.

Nothing stirred, nothing moved. The passage walls
were remarkable in their sameness. Not a crack
showed in the concrete, even after ten decades.

A thin layer of dust coated the floor. It was unmarked by footprints of any type. If a phantom
haunted these corridors, he had never used this particular tunnel. Which suggested to Batman that there
was little chance of him being discovered. His hopes of
surprising the mysterious killer rose as he continued
descending.

Again the tunnel split, and this time Batman took
the left passage. Though supremely confident of his
memory, the Dark Knight was still pleased to note
that the tunnel sloped downward. And the dust covering the floor was still unmarked by human passage.

Ten feet ahead, at the fringe of the light, something
moved in the semidarkness. Instantly Batman froze,
instinctively raising the dart gun. Senses alert, he
waited for something to happen. Nothing did. After a
few seconds he took a tentative step forward, then another.

Two points of light glared at him from the blackness. Batman blinked in astonishment. A large tomcat
silently entered the sphere of light cast by his flashlight. Without a sound, the yellow-and-black-striped
cat circled him, as if checking out what he was doing
here. Finally, as if signaling its approval of his presence, the cat meowed once. Then, without another
sound, it bounded down the corridor and disappeared
in the darkness.

Robert Weinberg

Batman shook his head in bewilderment. He was positive that Catwoman was not involved in these crimes. Yet the presence of a cat in the tunnels seemed to indicate otherwise. Suddenly he realized that letting the animal escape might have been a major mistake. Hurriedly he set off after the beast.

7.

About the same time as Bruce Wayne first made his presence known at Lewiston's Jewelry Emporium, Catwoman entered the Catacombs. Selina found no special significance in the name given the tunnels. Nor was she the least bit afraid of what horrors might lurk underground. Though gifted with an exceptional mind, Selina Kyle possessed little imagination. She considered the darkness her friend and ally. The absolute blackness of the Catacombs held no fear for Catwoman.

An abandoned building on the far side of downtown Gotham offered her access to the tunnels. An old book she found in the library detailed the history of downtown and provided a map. Only whispered memories greeted her as she pulled back the few old rotten planks guarding the tunnels from the outside world.

As always when pursuing her lawless ways, she wore her cat costume. Originally designed for a rich man's party girl, the black cat suit had undergone a number of startling changes since falling into Selina's clutches. An underlayer of thin nylon mesh strengthened the garment so that it could not be easily ripped. Padding at her knees and elbows lessened her vulnerability, as did a layer of high-density foam packed in her face mask. While keeping the outfit's tail, she had reinforced it with a steel chain. In tight situations, it served as a dangerous surprise.

Her fingers ended in sharp, curved metal hooks almost an inch long. She thought of them as her cat's claws, and more than one man had felt their sting. Tucked through her belt, Selina carried a twelve-foot-long leather whip. She handled the deadly weapon with a skill born of many months of constant practice.

Her feet clad in soft, form-fitting boots, Selina jogged down the long concrete corridor. In one hand she held a tiny flashlight that emitted a pencil-thin beam of light. It was all the illumination Catwoman needed. She knew exactly where she was going. Like Batman, she was headed down.

Each time the tunnel branched into two, Selina pulled out her map. Always, she picked the passage leading deeper into the earth. She was convinced that the criminal mastermind behind the thefts and murders lurked in the lowest level of the Catacombs. Because that was the location she would have chosen if planning the crimes.

Twenty minutes and nearly a mile into the maze, Selina encountered her first cat. It sat peacefully licking its paws in the direct center of the tunnel, almost as if expecting a visitor. Catwoman rubbed her eyes in astonishment. The last thing she had expected to find in these tunnels was a stray animal.

She blinked, then rubbed her eyes again in annoyance. The cat was nowhere to be seen. It had calmly waited for her to appear, and then vanished. With a snarl of suspicion, Catwoman pulled the whip from her belt. Cats as sentries seemed unlikely, but so did killers who operated from Catacombs beneath

Robert Weinberg

Gotham City. She continued onward, her every sense alert.

Five hundred feet farther, the corridor branched again. This time a big black-and-white-striped cat sat in the right-hand branch. It meowed loudly when Selina approached, then bounded down the corridor out of sight.

"Damn it," swore Catwoman, a touch of awe in her voice. "If this isn't a scene right out of *Lassie*. With me playing little Timmy."

Shrugging her shoulders, Selina followed her feline guide. Another two hundred feet farther, the tunnel split a third time. Waiting there in the mouth of the left branch was the cat she was following. Sitting next to it was a pale gray Siamese that stared at her with unblinking eyes. As Selina drew close the two animals, as if possessing one mind, turned into the passage and scampered away.

Each time their party crossed another tunnel, it picked up another cat. Soon Selina trailed nearly a dozen animals, all descending farther and farther into the Catacombs.

In a rare moment of self-doubt she wondered if entering the tunnels had been a terrible mistake. Her reception indicated she was expected. Though her ability to control cats was remarkable, it seemed to be nothing compared with that demonstrated by her unseen quarry. There was something uncanny in the coordinated responses of the animals. Something terrifying.

A sliver of yellow light far ahead was Selina's first indication that she was about to meet the master of the maze. By then she estimated she had been traveling through the passages for over an hour and gone several miles into the system. The patch of illumination grew larger and larger, showcasing the diverse pack of cats now only a few yards ahead of her.

Emerging from the tunnel into a large concrete vault, square-shaped, ten yards on a side, Selina immediately noted that each wall of the room opened into a tunnel exactly matching the one she had followed. Though she remembered her exact route here, leaving by the wrong exit might cause her serious problems. But before she could safely anchor the proper location in her mind, her gaze fastened on the center of the chamber—and her eyes widened in astonishment.

A man lounged on a throne of pillows, surrounded by more cats than Selina had ever seen in one place. There were hundreds of them—big and small, young and old, male and female—all watching her with an unwavering stare that was almost hypnotic in intensity. Still, it was their master who commanded her attention.

Long and lean, he was dressed in a long white robe that revealed only his head and hands. His skin was the color of old ivory, contrasting sharply with hair as black as night. Thin bloodless lips twisted in a smile of recognition as dark green eyes stared deep into hers. On his chest an emerald of incredible size and beauty throbbed with unnatural life.

"Welcome to my lair," said her host, waving one hand about the chamber in a sweeping gesture. His voice, deep and powerful, filled the room. "Welcome to the kingdom of the cats."

"The kingdom of the cats," Catwoman repeated, carefully noting the piles of expensive jewelry haphazardly scattered on the floor. "How nice. Then who the hell does that make you?"

"Can't you guess?" asked the yellow man. Reaching

to one side, he gently ran his fingers across the top of a huge black pillow. Selina gulped in sudden shock as, without warning, a massive head rose off the ground and she found herself staring into the savage eyes of a gigantic black panther.

Her host chuckled. *"I am the Lord of Cats."*

8.

She was all he had imagined and much more. A quiet feeling of satisfaction engulfed the Lord of Cats. The Catwoman would make a perfect mate. Once he subdued her will to his.

"Sit," he commanded, gesturing to the cushions that littered the ground. "Please make yourself comfortable. Would you care for a glass of wine? I've been anticipating your arrival all evening."

"You have?" said Catwoman, lowering herself to the floor. He noticed with grim satisfaction that she carefully sat with her back to the exit, facing both him and the Midnight Slayer. She did not trust him at all. Which was exactly what he expected. Those who trusted too easily made easy prey.

"Wine?" he asked again, raising a bottle and two glasses. "A fine selection from the best Gotham City has to offer." He laughed. "With disappearing gems dominating the news, no one notices missing furnishings or a few bottles of excellent vintages."

"Sure, sure," said Catwoman, her eyes never leaving his as she took a filled goblet. "But let's get back to that remark about expecting me."

The Lord of Cats sipped his drink, as if assuring his guest that the wine was not drugged. He was much too wise to attempt anything so childish with a huntress like Catwoman. For her he needed a much more subtle trap.

"Come now," he said slyly. "After leaving not a clue at any of my earlier crimes, did you really think I was so inept as to miss a bloody footprint at my latest triumph? I instructed the Midnight Slayer"—the beast growled at the mention of its name—"to step in that pool of blood. It was my way of sending a message to you. Call it an invitation, if you like. An invitation to my lair."

He smiled again, very pleased with himself. "An invitation that obviously worked."

"I'm here," said Catwoman. "But on my terms, for my reasons. Understand?"

"Of course. You are my guest. I assure you no harm will come to you here."

"I appreciate your concern," she replied, a faint touch of mockery in her voice. "Considering the blood already on your hands."

"Bah." He snorted in annoyance. "Mere mortals. Their deaths mean nothing to ones like us."

"Like *us*?" she repeated.

"Exactly," said the Lord of Cats, sliding his right hand up across the Heart of Sekhmet. Like a jolt of electricity, the power of the sacred stone flowed through him, increasing the force of his mind tenfold. Catwoman's eyes flickered with emotion as his words battered her will with incredible mental force. "We are the Chosen of Sekhmet."

"Sekhmet?" she asked, puzzled. And eager to know more.

"The Mighty One," said the Lord of Cats. "The lion-headed goddess of Egypt known as the Eye of Ra. You

Robert Weinberg

and I, and those few others like us, are her disciples, her children. We are the people of the cat."

"I don't understand," said Catwoman, her eyes never wavering from his.

"Listen, then, and I will tell you the story of my life," he answered. "The story of my destiny. And yours."

Settling back on the cushions, he focused all of his attention on Catwoman. By the time he finished his tale, her mind would be under his control. Her will, what little remained, would exist only to serve him.

"My name is Landros Bey. I was born in Egypt, the most ancient of all lands, forty years ago, on a night sacred to the lion goddess, Sekhmet. My mother, a woman of unlimited wealth, owned a huge villa on the outskirts of Cairo and I was raised there. No mention was ever made of my father, and I learned through painful lessons never to raise that question. However, from time to time over the years my mother hinted of dark secrets best not revealed. It was soon quite clear to me that my birth was not the unexpected result of some casual liaison. My education reinforced that conclusion."

Bey paused, taking another sip of his wine. Catwoman remained motionless, mesmerized by his history and the power of the Heart of Sekhmet. "During the daylight hours, I was taught the arts and sciences by the most brilliant minds in Cairo. At night, my mother and I traveled to secret rendezvous in the oldest sections of the city, where I gained knowledge of a different sort."

His voice lowered, and the shadows in the room seemed to lengthen. "Ancient, wizened men instructed me in the ways of black magic. It was in Egypt that civilization first started. Modern history

began less than two millennia ago. At the time of the
birth of Christ, our culture dated back thirty centuries. The greatest sorcerers of the world practiced in
the shadow of the Sphinx. Their wisdom became my
heritage."

"Why you?" asked Catwoman, surprising him with
the question. She was not yet completely under his
psychic domination.

"I was the Chosen of Sekhmet," replied Landros
Bey. "As are you. And probably others who never realize their full powers. We are people of the cat.

"There is no logical explanation for this gift. Nor
were my teachers, wise in the ways of magic, able to
offer me any answers. Certain individuals are born
with a special *affinity* to cats. We are bound and
bonded to the cat kingdom. We are drawn to felines,
and they are drawn to us. We think like them, understand them. Our souls are in harmony. Perhaps, if
those who believe in reincarnation are to be believed,
we were cats in a previous existence."

The Egyptian raised the hand that held the giant
green emerald. "My mentors and my mother instructed me in the old ways, the dark ways, because
they feared me—they feared the power I possessed.
This one treasure my unknown sire left with my
mother, commanding her to present it to me on my
thirteenth birthday. She dared not disobey."

Bey caressed the jewel. It pulsed with an inner
light, the green glow reflecting off his green eyes. "In
the ancient scrolls it is known as the Heart of
Sekhmet. A living gem, it gives the owner the power
to communicate with beasts. To become Lord of Cats."

He saw no reason to mention that the jewel's aura
enabled the user to impose his will on lesser minds,
including those of his feline followers. And on any hu-

man unsuspecting enough to let him weave his spell. A few more minutes of conversation and Catwoman would be his, body and soul, forever.

"My mother and her friends planned a great future for me. Unfortunately I had no desire to be a pawn in their schemes. My mind was my own. As soon as I was able, I took my leave of them and their petty dreams. Master of my destiny, I came to America, eager to sample the pleasures of the flesh."

Bey smirked. "For two decades I reigned supreme as the greatest animal trainer in the world. Never before had anyone handled lions and tigers with such ease. My skills were constantly in demand by movie and television studios. I earned astronomical sums each time I toured with the circus. No one ever questioned the source of my expertise, and I knew better than to tell them.

"Women, power, and fame were all mine. For years I wallowed in the excesses such power brings in its wake." He paused. "Then, when normal pleasures no longer excited me, I turned once again to the darkness of my youth. More than one innocent perished in my quest for greater thrills, new sensations."

Face flushed red with blood, the Egyptian knew he was revealing too much. But he could not stop. "Yet it was not enough. I wanted more. I hungered for companionship—a mate. *You.*"

Catwoman's eyes bulged in surprise. Immediately Landros Bey realized he had made a mistake, but already it was too late. Even the Heart of Sekhmet could not overcome Catwoman's innate distrust of men.

Sluggishly she struggled to her feet. Her eyes never left his, but now suspicion filled her gaze. No longer passive, she raised her whip and pointed it at him.

"You're not playing with a full deck, Bey. If you think a few tricks with kitties and a roomful of diamonds are gonna persuade me to call you sweetie, then you're really crazy."

They were both on their feet now. But before the Egyptian could answer, a yellow-and-black-striped tomcat raced out of the right-hand tunnel. Meowing loudly, it skidded to a stop only a few feet from its lord. Frowning, Bey pressed the Heart to his forehead. In seconds his grimace turned into a cruel, cold smile.

"What a pleasant surprise. The famed Batman approaches."

The Egyptian waved a hand and the monstrous beast at his side rose off the floor. Bey nodded once and the huge gem between his eyes blazed. With a savage growl that shook the chamber, the black panther hurtled forward into the right-hand tunnel.

"No man," said Landros Bey, laughing harshly, "not even Batman, can survive the fury of the Midnight Slayer. Tonight the Dark Knight dies."

9.

Batman fired only one shot. And it missed. Out of the darkness charged the black panther, moving with the speed of an express locomotive. The merest whisper of its paws striking the concrete floor provided the Dark Knight with his only warning. There was no time to think, no time to aim. Reacting by instinct alone, Batman raised and fired the dart gun just as the huge jungle cat burst into the white light of his flash.

Sheer chance triumphed over human competence. The exact instant Batman pulled the trigger, the pan-

ther launched itself into the air at the crime fighter.
The tranquilizer dart passed harmlessly between the
monster's widespread paws and clattered harmlessly
to the concrete thirty feet away.

Batman got no second chance. The giant leopard
slammed into him like a cannonball, the force of its
impact knocking him to the floor. Huge jaws snapped
at his face while the killer's massive front paws ripped
and tore at his torso. An ordinary man would have
died then. But Batman was no ordinary man.

Acting with astonishing speed, the Dark Knight
shoved his left arm into the panther's gaping mouth.
Desperately he pushed his elbow deep into the monster's throat, forcing its jaws open wider and wider.
Angrily the beast responded, trying to rip the offend-
ing limb to shreds. But its gigantic fangs drew no
blood. Nor did its claws, tearing with mindless rage at
Batman's chest.

The night watchmen's deaths had made a strong
impression on the Dark Knight. He had recognized
the mark of a killer beast and acted accordingly before
entering the Catacombs. Beneath his uniform he wore
lightweight, fiberglass body armor, similar to a bullet-
proof vest. The panther's claws and teeth battered
him terribly but could not cut through the protective
gear or rip his mask.

Using his free hand, Batman grabbed the giant cat
by the throat. Squeezing with all his strength, he
pushed the leopard back. The monster's rear paws
desperately clawed the floor, but the concrete offered
it no purchase. Inch by inch, the black panther slid off
Batman's chest and onto the ground.

Adrenaline pumping, the Dark Knight forced himself up to his knees. His main concern was not to let
the panther bring up its rear legs so that it could rip

at him with all four claws. Armor or not, his body could only withstand so much punishment. After an eternity he made it to his feet.

His breath coming in short, sharp gasps, Batman clenched his strong fingers even tighter on the beast's throat. Mewling in pain, the panther relaxed its jaws for an instant. Immediately Batman wiggled his trapped arm a few inches forward.

Seconds ticked by as man and beast remained locked in deadly struggle. Each time Batman felt the panther loosen its grip, he pulled his limb forward another few inches. Finally only his hard fist remained in its mouth. Pulling it free, he knew, would offer the leopard a new opportunity to bite his unprotected face. Instead he jerked to the side, lunging with his whole body. Together, he and the cat crashed to the cement.

This time, however, Batman was on top. Powerful knees dug into the panther's rib cage. The crime fighter's elbows pressed into the leopard's upper front paws, holding its slashing front claws apart. And his mighty fingers continued to tighten on the beast's windpipe. And tighten.

Five minutes later Batman wearily rose to his feet. The gigantic beast on the floor remained inert. It was dead, strangled by the Dark Knight. Later, when the body was discovered and examined, the police found that along with a crushed windpipe most of its ribs were cracked. Man and beast had fought to the death. And man had triumphed.

Shakily Batman grabbed his dart gun and flashlight, dropped in the first instants of battle. The killer beast no longer threatened anyone. But the Dark Knight's mission still remained. It was time to confront the monster's master.

Robert Weinberg

10.

"Enough idle chitchat," said Landros Bey, turning to Catwoman. His voice rang with simmering passion. "You have heard my story. And my offer. Reign with me as Mistress of Cats. *Or die.*"

Selina forced herself to remain calm. The Egyptian's hypnotic spell broken, she now recognized Bey as a homicidal maniac. All of his promises meant nothing. Sooner or later he would grow tired of her or find himself attracted to another woman. His proposal amounted to nothing more than a death sentence.

"I've always been a loner," she said quietly, revealing none of her inner thoughts. "Adjusting to a mate, even one as desirable as you, might be difficult."

The Egyptian smiled, visibly relaxing. Which was exactly the response Selina expected. Megalomaniacs, especially male ones, were so easily fooled. Their monstrous egos made them willing victims. For all of his mystic powers, Bey was still governed by his lust. Catwoman intended to take full advantage of it.

"You mentioned astronomical sums?" said Selina, letting a trace of greed creep into her voice. The thought did excite her. But she was playing for much higher stakes—her life and liberty.

Bey nodded. "Wealth beyond your wildest dreams," he declared. "These jewels amount to nothing more than tawdry trinkets when compared to the treasures in my possession. As my queen, you will share in the finest collection of gems ever assembled."

"You make it sound quite inviting," said Selina. She was playing for time, waiting for the right moment to strike.

Unexpectedly the huge emerald on Bey's chest

flared brilliant green. The Egyptian staggered, almost losing his footing, as if punched in the head.

"Impossible!" he screamed, his face turning blood-red with rage. "It cannot be!"

"Bad news?" Selina asked, inching her way forward. She suspected that her necessary diversion was about to arrive. Landros Bey was guilty of a sin made by many, many others. He had underestimated Batman.

"*He* killed the Midnight Slayer," said Landros Bey, anguish rippling through his voice. The Egyptian's hands curled into fists. "But he shall not escape my wrath. I swear it!"

Selina's face betrayed no sign of emotion, but inwardly she exulted. Though she hated to admit it, Catwoman was relieved to hear that the Dark Knight had survived the panther's attack. Few men attracted her, least of all cops. But deep within her soul, Selina Kyle knew there was something special about Batman.

Cautiously she slid another step closer. This time Bey noticed the movement. His green eyes narrowed in anger. "Do you think to play me for the fool?" he said venomously. "Beware. I am Lord of Cats."

"And I," answered a deep, resonant voice from the mouth of the right-hand tunnel, "am Batman."

Landros Bey gasped in fear. Standing in the mouth of the black passageway, the Dark Knight presented a frightful, menacing figure. Tall and powerfully built, huge cape draped around his broad shoulders, he looked almost superhuman.

Ever alert, Catwoman noticed the numerous rips and tears in Batman's uniform. Though he appeared unharmed, the barest hint of a tremor indicated to Selina that the battle with the Midnight Slayer had seriously weakened the crime fighter. He was in no condition to fight Landros Bey. And the hundreds of cats the madman still controlled.

Evidently the Egyptian realized that, too. "This will be a great pleasure," he said, the Heart of Sekhmet throbbing with energy. His voice turned shrill with passion. "Kill—"

Catwoman acted. Like the tongue of a snake, her whip flicked out at Landros Bey's chest. The Egyptian, caught completely by surprise, shrieked in horror as the dark leather snapped against his skin—and cut through the gold chain holding the telepathic jewel.

The Egyptian grabbed for the emerald, but he was an instant too late. Like a streak of green fire, the Heart of Sekhmet plunged to the concrete floor. With a blinding flash, the gem exploded on contact, shattering into a thousand fragments of brilliant dust.

Kill, Landros Bey commanded before the destruction of the Heart of Sekhmet. But he never completed his order, never named his victim.

Kill, demanded the Lord of Cats. And his word, unchecked by any further wish, was law.

With one voice, five hundred cats howled madly. Landros Bey, his expression puzzled, waved his hands futilely in the air. "Stop, stop," he shouted. "I demand you to stop!"

Catwoman, immediately sensing the horror to follow, sprinted for the right-hand tunnel and Batman. Grabbing the Dark Knight by the arm, she pulled him into the black corridor. As she suspected, he had no strength to resist.

"Let me go," he protested feebly. "I can't let the Lord of Cats escape."

"Nothing to worry about," said Catwoman, dragging Batman farther into the passage. Behind them, a man's high-pitched voice bellowed in incredible pain.

The scream followed them for a long, long way up the tunnel. "Nothing at all."

11.

The next night the police staged a major search expedition through the Catacombs. Nearly a hundred men participated in the raid, hoping to discover the lair of the phantom thief. In the third vault they searched, they made a grisly discovery.

Dead cats filled the chamber. There were hundreds of them, terribly mauled and mangled; bitten, scratched, clawed to death. For some unknown reason, they had turned on each other in an insane orgy of destruction. Not one animal remained alive.

Buried beneath them was the horribly mutilated body of a man. No one had any idea of who he was, nor did positive identification seem possible considering the condition of the corpse. The body of a huge black panther, discovered in a tunnel leading off the chamber, only added to the mystery.

Even Bruce Wayne wasn't sure of the whole story. Once she was convinced he was not too seriously injured to ascend the Catacombs on his own, Catwoman had vanished into the darkness. Bruce was not terribly surprised that none of the reports about the police dragnet mentioned recovering the stolen jewels. Catwoman believed in taking advantage of every opportunity.

Somehow Batman knew he would encounter her again.

C&W

JON HAMMER and KAREN McBURNIE

Three info-mercials and an old episode of *Ponderosa*. Or was it *Bonanza*? What exactly is the difference between *Ponderosa* and *Bonanza*? He didn't know, but it was a question he asked himself on the graveyard shift on a moonless Tuesday, trying to stay awake at the front gate of exclusive Gotham Woods Estates. Guarding all that wealth, the cream of the Gotham society, and they couldn't even spring for cable in the kiosk? He just had to get off nights before the terminal boredom killed him. But what was that? It sounded like a cat at the door.

"Well, Hoss," he said to the flickering blue screen, "by the power vested in me as security guard, looks like I'll have to play nursemaid to a kitty now. I'd better. Knowing the crackpots I'm working for, that critter could probably buy and sell me ten times." He adjusted his uniform's cap, wondering if by any chance it had fit the last guy.

Another tentative mew came from just outside the booth. He got down on one knee, and slowly, so he wouldn't startle her, he slid the door open. But there wasn't any cat, just a slim, black leather boot. He jerked his head up and saw a black mask. "Meow," said the mask, and then all he saw was black.

"One squirt of my knockout spray and he went over like a blue serge redwood," Catwoman snickered as she hopped into the cab; her faithful hench-kitten Tura rolled the van through the gate.

"Rocky Dexter's estate is a mile up this road. It should be impossible to miss—his front gate is a replica of the one Elvis built at Graceland."

"Blochenstein must be one serious Hank Williams fanatic if he's willing to shell out a half million for these tapes."

"He's a collector, Tura, by definition he's crazy. And they aren't tapes, they're acetate recordings. Please don't ask me what an acetate looks like, all I want to see is that lovely cash at the end of this caper.

"Whoa! This is the joint. Time to go to work."

Catwoman slipped from the van into the cool stillness of the night. With feline grace she gained the top of the wall and paused, every nerve drinking in the scene. This is what the poet meant by the dead of night, she thought. Only the silhouette of the darkened mansion could be seen by the faint starlight, and in the profound silence the only evidence of life was in the air itself. She felt a little breeze on her face and drew in a lungful of the icy wet. It smelled green. Like the immaculate lawns of Gotham Woods Estates and like the piles of crisp legal tender it took to live here. Crouched on top of the wall, Catwoman felt the anticipation building in every muscle of her body, the suspense of a lioness who first glimpses her prey. Noiselessly she slid down into the shadows of the grounds.

This was going to be as easy as five hundred Gs ever gets, Catwoman purred to herself as she glided stealthily toward the mansion. Then suddenly she froze in her tracks, her satisfied smirk dissolved into a wary scowl. She heard a scrabbling noise from behind. Looking back, she saw the figure of a man struggling to the top of the wall with a strenuous grunt. He heaved himself up, clumsily caught a boot on the way over, and landed with a groan, butt-first on the lawn. Catwoman watched from behind a tree as he brushed the dirt off his rear end and loped on up to the side of the house, passing, in utter oblivion, within a few feet of her hiding place. When he was close enough, she could see he was tall, with light hair almost to his shoulders, and he wore suede western boots and dirty Levi's, a denim jacket, and a bandanna around his neck. Who the hell was this rodeo clown?

He didn't go to the door, but instead walked to the side of the house and began trying windows. Great leaping catfish! He was an amateur burglar gumming up her own beautiful plan! This was beyond bad luck. In another minute the jerk would trip an alarm and every doughnut shop in Gotham City would empty out. The cops don't dally when the call comes from this end of town.

She had to move fast. In an instant, as the slim prowler reached for a window sash, she flew at him with a flying kick that knocked his legs out from under him with startling violence. In the time it took

for him to hit the ground with a painful thud she had
the line off her utility belt and ready. In a flash he lay
expertly hog-tied beneath her, as shocked and immo-
bile as a calf at branding time. Angrily Catwoman
ripped the bandanna from his neck and shoved it in
his mouth, which by this time had begun to gulp
rhythmically like a beached carp.

"Next time you're going to have to be quicker on the
draw, cowboy," she hissed in his ear. She dragged him
awkwardly to his feet. He was easily six feet, but skin-
nier than she had thought, and she could manage him
with a fireman's carry. Cursing him silently with each
step, she lugged him back to the compound wall. With
Tura's help they got the lanky, writhing obstacle up
and over and into the back of the van.

"Tura, get rid of this hick *right now*." Catwoman
was seething with rage. "You take the van, leave me
the bike."

Tura could only nod and try not to look hurt that
she was so abruptly dismissed from the big score.

"I will not allow this bush leaguer to ruin my lovely
caper. I'll meet you back at the lair." And before Tura
could think of questioning the prudence of leaving
Catwoman half-blind with anger and on her own, she
was gone.

"Well, I don't know what I'd do to stop her. You
don't reason with Catwoman." Tura sighed to herself
as she reached around the supine figure on the van
floor and extracted his wallet. He was trying to look
as brave as he could, gift-wrapped and helpless. Pock-
eting the cash, she read his driver's license. "And
what do I do with you, Alvin Nash?"

Alvin gave her a wink and tried to grin around his
red bandanna.

Jon Hammer and Karen McBurnie

Catwoman's rages didn't last long when there was work to be done, and by the time she had made her way back to the mansion all her faculties were again concentrated on the job at hand. With characteristic speed and efficiency she disabled the alarm system and entered Rocky Dexter's home. The decor appeared to be late seventies rococo Presley. Blochenstein's information about the house proved very accurate.

She located the vault in the floor of Dexter's office and with the aid of this masked cat burglar's most divine new invention—a wafer-thin computer chip that transmitted the safe's combination number visibly onto a wristwatch screen—was soon holding a square metal box containing the lost Hank Williams acetates.

Tura had hidden Catwoman's bike behind the low stone wall to which was attached a sign warning of exclusive Gotham Woods Estates' strict security. Catwoman kicked the vintage jet-black Harley Sportster to life and sped into the night, purring happily with the pitch of the perfectly tuned fifty-five-cubic-inch motor between her knees, a half-million-dollar prize in her saddlebag.

It was thirty minutes' drive from Dexter's estate to the seedy waterfront district. The sky was just beginning to show a predawn blue glow, but the Gotham Fish Market was already a hive of activity as Catwoman rolled up to the warehouse across the street. To the casual observer this building seemed surely to have been abandoned for decades, yet as the Harley approached, the steel riot gate opened with well-oiled efficiency. She was home.

As she got out of the elevator to enter her living quarters, Catwoman could hear the sound of Tura's acoustic guitar. When did she learn that song? In a festive mood she called out, "Tura, have you been taking lessons?"

"Um, yes, Catwoman. You could say that," Tura answered sheepishly, rising to greet her. She let her dark, wavy hair shade her face. Behind her, Kit, another of her hench-kittens, stifled a laugh. Neither of them held a guitar.

Catwoman stopped. She carefully put the metal box on the table, pushing aside a couple of half-nibbled take-out orders of fish and chips. Her eyes narrowed as she strode into the loft. "Tura, you're not trying to tell me . . ." They were trying to tell her.

There on the leather couch with his dusty cowboy boots resting on *her* coffee table was Alvin Nash. Seeing his captor again, he hurriedly set aside the guitar and, country gentleman that he was, rose to his feet with a little bow of his head.

"Good morning to you, ma'am. I hope you won't be too angry with the ladies for showing me the courtesy they done." His hand reached up to his bare head as if to tip his hat.

Catwoman's eyes flashed at Tura. "What have I told you about bringing home strays?"

"But *really*, you don't have to worry," Tura nervously attempted to reassure. "Alvin has no idea where we are! He was blindfolded the whole trip. We just wanted to hear him sing a couple of his songs before we let him go."

Alvin's mother hadn't raised any fools. He'd better break the ice in a hurry or risk another beating. By the looks of it, he'd need every ounce of charm he could squeeze out. That ain't ice, it's a glacier, he thought.

"If you'll pardon me for saying so, ma'am, but you

Jon Hammer and Karen McBurnie

sure are one mean roper. Have you done much rodeoin'?" Alvin displayed his most winning grin.

She had to admit the boy had nerve. To avoid the impulse to laugh, Catwoman held Tura's paws to the fire a little longer. "A pair of long legs and a mouthful of compliments is just like catnip to you two, isn't it?" She glared at them convincingly. "I'm disappointed. Don't make me think you're too soft for our business."

She watched with satisfaction as Tura's face fell. Her anger gave way to amusement at her kittens' antics. It wasn't hard to see Alvin's appeal. Who wouldn't want a lanky, singing cowpoke for a toy. Only make sure he isn't any more than a plaything. "You can keep him for a while, but then he goes." Catwoman turned, took a few steps, then sharply shot back, "And be certain he can't find his way back."

The girls breathed relieved sighs, happy that they were off the hook. "Alvin has been singing us the most wonderful songs, Catwoman, he's really talented," Kit gushed. "He plays every week at the Wagon Wheel down on Edsel Avenue."

"Oh, really?" CW stretched herself onto the arm of an intricate and fussy-looking chair, the slippery sheen of her cat suit an enticing contrast to the plush splendor of the chair's brocade.

"So what dirty little deed were you up to at Rocky Dexter's tonight, then? I'd think if you were going to force your talents upon the man, you'd at least try it on a night you could crash one of his big showbiz parties."

Tura started to speak, but Kit beat her to it. "He already *has* a contract with Dexter!" she said with an irritated toss of her canary-yellow mop top.

"Oh? If you're such a success, what were you doing

skulking around your boss's estate at three o'clock in the morning?"

"That's a long story," Alvin Nash cut in as he settled back on the couch. "And if I'm to tell it, I'll need to start at the beginning." He took a long, thoughtful sip of his tallboy.

"I come to Gotham City five years ago, hitchhiked all the way from Kewanee, Illinois, with my guitar on my back and twenty dollars in my jeans. I got a room in that dump across from the bus depot—you know the one they call the Motor Lodge, even though they got no place to park your car? Every night I had to go to sleep with all the lights on and the radio blaring just to discourage the roaches from sharing the bed. For a time I was washing dishes and playing my guitar for tips in whatever dive would let me, just to keep body and soul together.

"Then one day this feller in my ho-tel—Lester's his name but we call him Spike 'cause his hair kinda pops up on top like a railroad spike, y'know? Anyhow, he gets a job filling in for the regular bartender over the Wagon Wheel. So one night, it's Spike's birthday and we're all drinkin' his health in the Wheel after hours. Spike gets me up on stage and Mr. Walters—he's the owner—he liked what I could do with a song, I guess, because the next thing you know, I got me my own showcase once a week at the Wagon Wheel! By and by, some girls from Dexter Music started showing up there to see me every Thursday. They kept bringin' their friends and then one night they ac'shly got Rocky Dexter himself down. Guess that was about a year later. Of course, to hear him tell it, he discovered me. I suppose Janine 'n Betsy got a raw deal, but they said it was nothin' new, happened all the time. They would go out and find acts, then Dexter'd take the credit.

"Well, the minute he 'discovered' me, Mr. Rocky Dexter starts barking at me through his paper clip—that's one of his 'eccentricities,' chewing paper clips. It 'pears you can't be a big man in the music biz without cutting up like you ought to be in Arkham Asylum. Anyway, through his paper clip he mutters that I'm a genius and so forth. He tells me to meet him in his office the next day, he's gonna make me a household name, just like Red Pop. Now, recording for a big outfit like Dexter Music has been my one dream since I was a nipper, but at that moment I was busy thinking what a crackpot ol' Rocky seemed to be, and I swear he knew I was thinking it, because just then his secretary, Valerie, she says something to him and he starts cussing at her like a madman. I couldn't tell you exactly why, but I was sure he had that temper tantrum just to impress *me*!

"Dexter's way of doing business spooked me plenty, but I still felt like I was going to strike it rich. I mean, I was more excited than an alley cat given the deed to Disneyland. Oh! No disrespect intended, ladies! I guess I reckoned someone that nuts wouldn't let nothing stop him if he took a mind to make me a big star.

"I signed the contract, recorded some demo tapes, and I—I mean everybody loved the tapes: the producer, the musicians in the studio, the A and R folks. They were convinced I was the next big thing! But Mr. Dexter was in an ornery mood the day he heard it, they tell me. Had a nutso fit and started screechin' that I was 'too country.' He give me the deep freeze, refuses to see me, won't take my calls. I sure didn't know *what* to do. My whole world caved in.

"Then a couple weeks later Spike dragged me into his room—the radio was on and he told me, listen to this song. I didn't see at first what he was driving at because it sounded like that kind of awful country pop that ain't *real* country and it ain't real popular with me, but then I realized it was my own song! Rocky had slicked it up so bad I didn't recognize it. After that my songs kept turning up on the radio butchered like hogs in a Tennessee smokehouse—all sung by Dexter's stable of Vegas-styled hillbillies. The kind of cats think the can of snuff in the back pocket of your three-thousand-dollar hand-embroidered jeans by Ralph Lauren makes you a good ol' boy. I was fit to spit. I couldn't understand why Dexter wouldn't give me a chance to do my music my way. By then I realized he had no interest in developing a new talent, he wanted me for another cog in his hit factory. He needed my songwriting to prop up his established acts, as tired a bunch of has-beens as you'll find clawin' at the backdoor of the Grand Ol' Opry. You can bet I kicked pretty hard when I saw the path Rocky Dexter was pushing me down, but it did no good. Once he makes up his mind about anything—an' it's always a snap decision—ain't no turning back.

"One day I got so fed up I had to give Mr. Dexter a piece of my mind. It's always like hunting snipe, getting in to see him, so I had Janine sneak me in to his office. He stammered a bit, caught unawares as he was, and then tells me that he was making me *some* money and I should be grateful, since my singing career 'flopped.' How he figured I was a wash before I even got a record out I do not know. He pulls my contract out from under his lunch and shows me where it says that ninety-eight percent of my song-publishing income was to go to Dexter Music, for promotion, publicity, and so on—well, I never had a thing to promote! I asked where the two percent was from all the hits other folks were making with my songs, and he laughed. He said that with big corporations payments naturally took a long time, given that it all had to funnel through channels: accounting, residuals, taxes, benefits, etce'tra. I told him I wanted my master tapes and my contract back. He looked me straight in the eye and said, 'What contract, my boy? I own you, kid, and the only way you make any money in this business is on my say-so. Get used to it.'

"By then security had arrived to show me the door."

"What about your lawyer, Nash?" Catwoman interrupted.

"Urhhhh." Alvin buried his face in his hands. "Man, I was greener 'n the Joker's hair back in those days. I didn't have a winter coat back then, I sure didn't have a lawyer. When I was about to sign, Dexter recommended this guy Artie Mopp—"

"Artie 'the Cleanup Man' Mopp?" snorted Catwoman.

Alvin shrugged, embarrassed. "Artie represented an arm load of talent, Mr. Dexter told me. 'Course later I realized I'd been had.

"I got the runaround by Artie Mopp's office, too. Then one night he came in the Wagon Wheel, I went right up to his table, and I told him right out, you're my lawyer, you're supposed to be working for *me!*

"He swallowed a mouthful of chicken-fried steak, and cool as January, shoots back, 'When you bring me as much green as Dexter Music, then I'll be playing ball on your team, kid.'

"I told him, why didn't he never give me a copy of my own contract? So then Mr. Mopp drops his fork on his plate, real loud, like to nearly bust it, then picks up the cloth on his lap and dabs his ugly pink lips, says, 'Dexter gave it to you months ago. It's not my fault if you've mislaid it.' Then he turns his back on me!

"Sittin' next to Mr. Mopp were a big, pumped-up goon and a puny mug—he's all dressed up in black silk and stuff."

"Not the Nightlight?" Catwoman growled.

"Mopp called him Louie."

"That was Louie 'the Nightlight' Minescule, Alvin," said Catwoman. "Dresses like a chorus boy in a cheap road-company *Guys and Dolls*, always in black with a white carnation. Always ready for a funeral. He's a common East Gotham racketeer. Even if Artie Mopp *is* a lawyer, I'm surprised he'd associate with the Nightlight."

"So this Louie has his thug throw me out of the Wagon Wheel! My second home! In front of everyone! Then Spike tells me they threatened the management, tellin' Mr. Walters to ban me from there!

"I mean, I ain't stupid, I got me set up with a free lawyer for the arts, Ms. Siobhan Blask, Esq. She worked darn hard and demanded to see my contract and have it declared illegal. That woman endured months of endless runaround with Dexter and eventually threats to her firm and her family. Finally the case took up her time, so she couldn't make a living, and she told me that she'd hafta bow out. Those guys at Dexter Music have a whole floor with nothing but lawyers. Forget till the cows come home, they could sit on my claim, petitioning and making motions till the whole herd up and died of old age. So I'm still singing for my supper in Gotham City.

"Today I just felt so nasty inside, I took to the crazy notion the only thing left for me to do was steal back my contract. Just the kind of dang-fool idea that comes over a fella who spends too much time brooding in an empty glass down at the honky-tonk. I been reduced to being a petty thief."

"That *is* sad. I detest *petty* thievery," cooed Catwoman, the professional condescending to the amateur. Still lying on the arm of the chair, she stretched out all of her muscles and wriggled her fingers in the air. It wasn't a bad bedtime story. But honestly she empathized little with the poor sap. Alvin's a good egg and Dexter's obviously a slimeball; white hat, black hat, the End, and so what? Though she *could* understand what the girls saw in the lanky cowpoke. *Hmm, just for fun . . .*

"Why don't you visit my room in half an hour?" hissed Catwoman, cool as a snake, to Alvin. *Ha!* That'll make the fur fly! She smirked at the steamed looks Tura and Kit traded, even as she knew she would toss him out on his shell-like ear if he dared. *Meow!*

"Myrna! I need cigavets!"

The puffy, silver-haired man barked into the intercom. His red-and-white suede Roy Rogers costume fit him like a sausage casing. Roy Blochenstein's office covered half the fortieth floor of the Gotham Securities Tower. The rest of the floor held thirty of his U.S. staff, a conference room, a gym, a kitchen, and a dining room. His office was decorated in what one newsweekly waggishly dubbed "Bunkhouse Moderne." The walls were covered with split logs salvaged from a Tennessee-hill-country cabin two centuries old. The furniture and western knickknacks were bought at auction from the estate of William S. Hart, the first movie cowboy star. Cowboy-and-Indians curtains one could expect to see in Beaver Cleaver's bedroom framed the huge plate-glass windows. Daniel Boone hats and Tom Mix capguns filled a large display case covering one wall.

Myrna, a sober-looking woman with a brightly colored pant suit glued to her generous curves, walked into the room with a don't-give-me-any-lip look on her face. "All out, Blochy. Sorry." She turned and headed for the door.

"Out! I have to have a cigavet *now*! Why can't you do anyting? You are supposed to have two cartons on hand at all times!"

"Are you going to give me the money for the cigarettes, Mr. Blochenstein?"

"I have no cash. I owe you the dough. *Get me cigavets!*"

"You owe me three hundred and sixty dollars and counting, Blochy. I don't got any money to lend to you today, anyways."

"Then you borrow it from somebody. Get going!"

That deadbeat. Myrna had been a working gal for fifteen years. She'd seen executive big shots of all stripes, and it never failed: the richer they got, the cheaper they became. Still, Blochy took the prize. She stuck her head in her desk drawer and rummaged for change. As she came up with a handful of fuzzy quarters, a black leather glove reached over her desk and buzzed the door to the inner sanctum.

"He's expecting me, doll." Catwoman smirked as she sailed into Blochenstein's office. Geez, Louise, the nuts that guy associates with.

Catwoman scanned the billionaire's digs, a tasteless blend of down-home bric-a-brac and state-of-the-art

Jon Hammer and Karen McBurnie

electronics equipment. "Here's the hotcakes you ordered, Blochenstein."

The startled businessman struggled to retain his
composure. Catwoman pulled the container from her
satchel and set it on the desk. Blochenstein quickly
lifted it off the wood and wiped the surface clean.

"Thank you, my dear." From a ceramic cookie jar
decorated with the image of a bucking bronco, he removed stacks of bills, fanned the bundles, and tapped
the pile on his desk first vertically then horizontally
to even it out.

Catwoman leisurely riffled each bundle of fifty one-
thousand-dollar bills. "Thanks, Blochy, but"—her
voice was icy—"there's a grand missing." Her eyes
drilled into his head.

"Really? I can't imagine how . . . I counted it . . . but
of course, if you say I'm short, I'll . . ." He began fumbling furiously for his wallet. "Here! Here it is!"

"Nickel-and-dime chiseling on a deal this size," said
Catwoman sadly as she carefully took from the wall a
coiled bullwhip. She could see it was a good twelve
feet long when she let it slither out on the floor in
front of her feet. A label on the handle told her it was
the same whip Karl Malden used on Brando in *One-
Eyed Jacks*. "Bad Blochy. Now Catwoman spank."

Sweat poured down the trembling billionaire's face.
The elegant masked predator before him coolly raised
her braided leather weapon, and with an expert
twitch of her wrist the cord seemed to spring with a
life of its own from the carpet to Blochenstein's thick
neck. His hands grabbed at the whip, the lash
wrapped tight around him. A wicked jerk of her arm
sent him down on his precious knotty-pine floorboards, where he thrashed about, his face first cherry
then an unhealthy blue.

"Nice toy, Blochy. I'll take it with me, if you don't object." She planted a black stiletto heel in his chest and loosened the bullwhip. "Next time you pull anything like that, fat boy, I won't be playing."

Blochenstein lay at her feet puffing like a locomotive. The fear in his face disappeared as he watched her laugh down at him. From his humiliated posture he actually managed a sickly leer. "I'll play any game you like, Catwoman."

Catwoman's grin evaporated. "You can sure take all the fun out of torture." She sighed. "Billionaires."

Stepping over the disabled mogul, she strode to the desk. She grabbed the cookie jar and removed the cash, deliberately dropping the ceramic container, which exploded into shards on the floor.

"Oops." She brought a gloved hand to her pouting lips, a mime of remorse as it shattered. Catwoman made for the elevators as Myrna stood at the door, doubled over in laughter.

Rusty Walters wasn't having *anyone* tell him what he could or couldn't do. He'd taken enough of that guff during his twenty years in the merchant marines. On the last day of his last voyage, his career before the mast had left him with two things: a bank account healthy enough to buy himself a tavern, and a deep loathing for all things nautical. He was so sick of the sea he couldn't look a glass of water in the eye anymore. So what if he'd never been inland more than ten miles in his life, he was going to run a cowboy joint. So he opened the Wagon Wheel, where the old salt's eyes need never be offended by the shiny binnacles and lobster traps and antique diving suits that had plagued him through the years in a hundred water-

Jon Hammer and Karen McBurnie

front gin mills the world over. There would be no ships built in bottles or superfluous rigging covering the ceiling; Rusty lived and breathed honky-tonk now. And he sure didn't take orders from anybody anymore, not in his own place.

Alvin Nash brought in a good, regular crowd; a good singer and a hit with the broads. The kid was decorative. Rocky Dexter and his goons could take a flying leap. Yes, sir, Nash was going to play this Thursday like any other week. Funny thing was, after Rusty had worked himself up into a state where he could tell Dexter's gang to go to the devil, they took the news of the kid's return with uninterested shrugs. That sure left Rusty puzzled. But he was wise enough not to be relieved.

"I'm mighty pleased you all could come to see the show tonight, ladies," Alvin drawled, holding open the stage door for Catwoman's two apprentices. Tura gave him a slow wink as they slunk past into the bar. "It's a shame Miss Catwoman couldn't come too—ugk!"

Alvin suddenly found himself sitting in the alley behind the Wagon Wheel with the wind knocked out of him, the direct result of a stiff-armed blow to his chest that had sent him flying through the door. Two primates wearing matching suits towered over him as he cautiously rose to his feet. Not only were they both in gray suits, they were wearing identically sized gray suits. Tweedledumb and Tweedledumber. Who was their tailor, Gorillas 'R' Us? One suit leaned on the door as Tura and Kit pounded on it from inside. The other jabbed a beefy finger into Alvin's solar plexus, sending waves of pain tearing through his rib cage.

"Hey." The suit poked him again. "The boss wants you."

Waiting in a darkened corner for Alvin was Rocky Dexter. The muscle tossed Alvin to him like he was playing beanbag.

"I know it was you pulled that job at the house last night," Rocky sputtered, spitting a paper clip on the blacktop. He was apoplectic with rage. "You little crud, you don't know what you're up against, bumpkin. No one does Rocky Dexter. I own this town. I own this street. Heh—I own *you*. I may terminate you—or *ex*terminate, if I get pushed.

"You want I fix it so you can't walk? How about never being able to use those string-picking, thieving little mitts of yours again? Don't be stupid, boy. I've already screwed your career. I've made a mint of your songs! Screwing you was child's play. I screw people for a *living*. It's a business. But you stealing from me, that's not playing the game, Nash. Think hard about it boy, tell me where the acetates are and I may let you live."

"Honest, Mr. Dexter, I—I don't know what you're talking about. I didn't steal anything from you."

Dexter shook his head sadly. "Cowboy, this is serious as cancer. You just don't get that yet. Okay, boys, do your thing. He'll talk, and I sincerely hope it's before he croaks." He turned away quickly and ducked into the waiting limo, which rocketed out of the alley and onto Edsel Avenue.

The car nearly knocked Kit down as she and Tura ran out the front of the club. They sprinted to the mouth of the alley in time to see one of the goons crushing Alvin in a bear hug. The other thug, humming to himself like a busy craftsman, twisted the singer's hand up in his face for a good look at his own finger bent back until it touched his wrist.

"This little piggy's hurting real bad, ain't it, soldier? In ten seconds it'll be busted, but don't worry. I got nine more to play with. Where's the stuff at?" Sweat and tears flooded Alvin's eyes, so he could barely see his tormentor's face. He was shaking so violently the other hood had to hold the singer's face still with one massive paw to keep the mangled hand in front of his eyes.

Running to Alvin's aid, Kit sent a distress signal to her boss via the microminiature radio attachment of the pink-rhinestone-encrusted cat collar that encircled her wrist.

Tura attacked, followed closely by her partner. When they were nearly upon them, the goon holding Alvin charged. He made a grab for Tura, getting a handful of her hair. With the split-second timing of a well-rehearsed acrobatic team, Kit slammed her Doc Marten boot down on his instep, forcing him to release Tura, who instantly aimed a roundhouse kick that split the thug's face open. He screamed and fell to his knees, pawing at his face. The other villain finished breaking Alvin's finger, then put the singer out of commission with a swift cross to his jaw. Alvin promptly crumpled. He began to get the feeling he might die then and there, beaten for something he hadn't even done. The one with the good nose ran headlong at Tura, but Kit, who had bounded to the top of a Dumpster, took a flying jump at him, landing both boots in his kidneys. By this time the other goon had found his legs and gotten a hold on Tura. Between trading blows with King Kong she was able to yell out, "Get out of here, Alvin. *Now!*"

He shook off the pain enough to stumble to the door of the club, yelling, "I'll call the cops!"

"*No!*" screamed the torpedoes *and* the cat gals in unison at the mention of Gotham's finest.

Tura and Kit knew working on the thugs separately was their only hope. The guy with the broken nose was on his feet now, but he was slightly dazed. The girls each grabbed an arm and smashed his head into the steel fire door of the club and he went down like the *Titanic*. Kit ran over the fallen thug and into the Wagon Wheel.

Tura tried to follow but the other man mountain snatched her arm, jerking her back into the alley. She heard the door slam behind her as she took a punch to the gut and fell in a heap.

"Now it's payback time for Miss Busybody." He giggled maniacally. The murderous creature pulled out a gleaming straight razor, ready to autograph her pretty face.

But as he lowered the blade to Tura's pale flesh, he was distracted by a high-pitched *whir-click, whir-click*. It was Catwoman throwing back handsprings down the alley, picking up speed and momentum with every flip. The gorilla turned to see a fifty-mph kick coming straight at his head. He went flying ten feet, all the way to the rear of the alley, the razor embedded in his own thigh. His scream was the stuff of nightmares.

"Thanks, boss," panted Tura, "that was a—"

"Yeah, a close shave!"

Amid floor-standing vases of fragrant flowers and silver trays of complicated Italian pastries, Catwoman's gang and Alvin recuperated in the safety of the hideout. Her spectacular ultramodern sound system was tuned to WGC, broadcasting vintage bebop jazz. But sweets and music weren't doing the job tonight; Catwoman was still in a rage. She ground her teeth. She wrung her hands and paced the floor, still seething over the beating her protégés had taken.

Kit, sipping coffee from a nineteenth-century porcelain cup, tried to lighten the mood by suggesting they roll Dexter in cornflake crumbs and fry him in oil. That got Catwoman howling with laughter, though Tura's laugh was halting and suppressed by the pain of two cracked ribs. She was sporting a nasty black eye. Alvin was looking mighty black and blue, too, plus half his right arm was in a cast and sling. The cast was decorated with cartoon cats bearing greetings from Kit and Tura. Kit was missing a patch of hair. They looked like what the proverbial cat dragged home.

"I know!" said Tura, intent on lifting their spirits, "We find an empty pool, right? And we kidnap Dexter, throw him in it, don't feed him for like a week, then we get real big hooks and bait 'em with cheeseburgers and . . ." Kit and Catwoman were passing champagne through their noses at this point. Alvin stared at these wild women, nearly incapacitated by laughter, and wondered if it was all talk.

"Darrrrling! Don't worry!" Catwoman tried to reassure him when she read his worried expression. "We'd never do something so ridiculously—*unprofitable!*"

Alvin joined in the think tank. "If you all are serious about getting revenge, you think about this; only one thing in the world Rocky cares a rat's behind about and that's Dexter Music. Why don't we start our own label and put Rocky Dexter out of business?"

"Because that would involve *working nine-to-five,*

dearest." Tura laughed as she licked cannoli cream from her fingers. "You couldn't see us all laboring like *that*, could you?"

Alvin shook his head in agreement.

The cunning grin that always signaled one of her more brilliant brainstorms lit up Catwoman's face. "You've given me a purrfect idea for a caper, *mon petit çhou*," she said, strolling over to Alvin to reward him with a little caress. "We want to ruin Rocky Dexter, and as Alvin suggests, the only place to really hurt him is in the wallet.

"You, my dear," she continued, stroking Tura lightly behind the ear, "must begin practicing your singing. Alvin will tutor you and write some music for you. Kid, I'm gonna make you a star! Ah, there is nothing so sweet as revenge, my kittens, and we're going to have a ball every step of the way."

Alvin was at no loss for inspiration. He dashed off some songs faster than he ever had in his life. Coaching the beautiful Tura from morning to night proved to be no chore either. When he wasn't working with Tura, Alvin met with Catwoman to tutor her on the ins, the outs, and the who's whos of the Gotham music game.

Finally Catwoman and Alvin developed their strategy in detail. Kit and Tura were briefed on the step-by-step plan. Studio time was reserved, and Tura cut her single with the help of Alvin and his band. To safeguard their anonymity Tura and Kit wore wigs and cat's-eye masks. Alvin and the other musicians tied bandannas over their faces, train-robber style.

They found a tiny independent company called Spare-Time to press and distribute the new single by

Jon Hammer and Karen McBurnie

Tura's new alter ego, Tabby Jo Jeter. As soon as the
record was pressed, a video was made.

Working in her new identity as Tabby's manager,
Simba Voleuse, Catwoman had already planted outra-
geous rumors in the gossip columns guaranteed to
keep her the talk of the town: a Kuwaiti prince tried
to pay cash and livestock for a date with her. Her record played backward gives her recipe for corn bread.
She was a famous child star who married at fifteen. . . .

Ms. Voleuse traded hundred-dollar bills for the
Gotham Intelligencer and *Globe* to run photos of
Tabby Jo Jeter in her signature costume: a deep red
jumpsuit with jewels and rhinestones, around her
hips a big Elvis-style utility belt with a glittering
cat's-head buckle. Tabby Jo T-shirts and buttons were
distributed free to concert-goers. Publicists were given
island vacations in return for arranging their clients'
cameo appearances in Tabby Jo's debut video.

One afternoon Kit and Tura were surprised by a
sleazy-looking stranger who had somehow gained entrance to the hideout. The guy's hair was trained into
a classic salesman comb-over. He was dressed in loud
mismatched plaids and sporting a gold chain around
his neck. Kit and Tura looked at each other, then
rushed to pin him to the wall, knocking the breath out
of him. "Whoa, Tura! Kit! It's me! Alvin!" The girls did
a double take and dissolved in a giggling heap.

"What happened to you, cowboy? Were you kidnapped by a band of used-car salesmen?" hooted Kit.

"These are my promotin' duds! I've been visiting the
radio stations, pushing the Tabby Jo song. Dig this."
He slapped Kit on the back and boomed in an FM dee-
jay voice, "Hey, how ya doin', pal? You the program director here?" He put out his hand for Kit to shake. She
gave him her hand, which he commenced to pump vig-

orously, and after he finally let her go, she found a folded bill pressed into her palm.

"I bring you the new release from Spare-Time Records, by superstar Tabby Jo Jeter. Sure hope you can give her a listen." The girls examined the portrait of Ben Franklin.

"It's real, if that's what's worrying you. And that's nothing but getting-in-the-door money. We're going to be spending thousands at every radio station in the country to get this thing played. It's without a doubt the biggest payoff ever. Your boss sure likes to spend her dough!" said Alvin, still unconsciously wearing his happy-huckster grin.

"But, Alvin," said Kit, "your songs are so sweet even Tura can't wreck 'em! We don't have to bribe 'em to play the record." The glamorous Tura stuck out her tongue at her sister-in-crime.

"Aw shoot, if it only worked that way." Alvin frowned. "The world ain't so honest as all that. These guys at the stations are bought. If you don't pay, they don't play! Geez, listen to the radio and you'll know that without a doubt. I honestly think they don't give a hoot about music no more. They're not in their jobs for *love*, they're in it for *dough*!"

As soon as "I Got a Two-Timing Hell-Raiser in a Civil Ceremony" hit the airwaves, the country was in love with Tabby Jo. Alvin's catchy tune and tight arrangement had romanced pop fans and solid country listeners alike. That and the most blatant payola radio has seen since the fifties. The song was a bona fide crossover hit, charting on the country, pop, and even, absurdly for a country tune, the urban contemporary charts!

Jon Hammer and Karen McBurnie

Naturally it didn't hurt the cause any when Simba Voleuse messengered *Musicday*, the top industry tipsheet, a little gift to show appreciation for the swell job they did. This little token of esteem was not cash this time, it was a squeaky cat toy filled with a fine white powder. Tabby Jo Jeter's debut single went to number one that week.

A modern, streamlined, shockingly vulgar, cream-colored limousine sped around one of the Gotham expressway's high curving overpasses. Cradled in the rich leather cocoon of the backseat, Rocky Dexter set the copy of *Billboard* down next to him. Tabby Jo Jeter on the front page *again*. This chick comes out of literally nowhere and now you can't pick up the paper or turn on the radio without she's on it. He felt a small g-force tugging at his sensitive stomach as they took another turn. He slapped the chauffeur's glass angrily. *Oi*. Where were the frigging Tums? His ulcer hadn't flared up this bad in years. When his stomach turned sour, it meant one thing: Rocky was yearning. He wanted, he lusted, he pined for, and his gut hurt like the devil. He *needed* to sign Tabby Jo Jeter!

"Artie," Rocky screamed into the cellular speaker phone, "tell me the word on this broad Tabby. And Spare-Time Records? Who the hell ever heard of Spare-Time Records? They're *nobody* and they're *killing* me!"

The distant voice of Artie Mopp rasped through the speaker. "Who knows? The last record Spare-Time put out was a home instruction, you know, like 'Stop Smoking While You Sleep' kind of thing. All of a sudden they have this Tabby kid and the crumbs are paying the deejays twice what you are, Dexy. Word is they've upped your notes all over town. And for them program directors who are arctic explorers? Spare-Time ain't tossin' 'em a gram, they're shellin' out like a half an ounce of the happy powder."

"Idiots!" screamed Dexter. "Do you know what I'll have to come across with to top their chart buys? Five figures! How can we spend that kind of loot every day? How do *they* spend it?"

The car whizzed by a towering Tabby Jo Jeter billboard. Tabby's teeth sparkled and Dexter's stomach writhed.

"I got to have that Tabby Jo character. I got to get her away from these nuts at this Spare-Time Records just to save my own hide! Who can compete with the money they're spending?" Rocky shrieked.

"Think you can?" Artie asked. "She's already hitting like a ton of bricks. You'll have to pony up plenty wampum to steal."

"Nobody romances talent like Rocky Dexter! I'll get the studio to pull some more of that jerk hillbilly yahoo's songs and cut one with Tabby Jo!"

"Sure, Rock, but there's a lot a bread behind this chick, maybe her manager's loaded."

"Yeah? Then I'll bet the skirt'll kill for *more* dough. Just who is this Simba Volulla anyway? A lucky rookie, that's who. A green manager with a nobody label and one fluke hit. Kid might never crack the charts again. Could be all washed up, forgotten. She knows if she links herself with Dexter, she's a player. She's in with us big spuds."

"Don't forget, Rock, she's already playing the game," stammered Artie Mopp. "You can bet she's no pushover."

"Hmm. Artie, my boy, in that case, double the reason to get Tabby Jo Jeter on Dexter Records."

Jon Hammer and Karen McBurnie

The biz had never seen as manic or as public a display of spending as Rocky Dexter laid on in the courting of Tabby Jo Jeter and Simba Voleuse. Monday, there was the videostrobe in the middle of downtown's entertainment district, glaring for all to see: a thirty-foot Rocky Dexter offering a rose, with the headline I LOVE YOU AND GOTHAM CITY LOVES YOU, TABBY JO! over and over for seventeen long hours. Tuesday's lunch at the Gotham Yacht Club brought the paparazzi out in full force, and they got a lensful. Dexter gave Tabby and Simba matching Mercedes convertibles. Catwoman traded hers in for cash on the way home. Wednesday, Dexter hosted a reception in Tabby's honor at the Czarina Room of the city's most over-the-top hotel and presented a diamond watch to Tabby and a ruby bracelet to her manager. By Friday the cash was in the envelopes. He'd purchased Tabby Jo's contract from Spare-Time Records. Tabby Jo signed her telephone-book-thick Dexter Music contract that same day. So confidential were the particulars of the deal—the hefty advance monies, shares of Dexter Music stock, and perks—that the company's file clerks were only permitted to store sealed copies of the document. One important clause in the agreement was that Alvin Nash would be released from his own contract.

Tabby Jo's single was to be immediately rereleased on Dexter Music's label. And Tabby was scheduled to go into the studio that night—with Alvin Nash and his band—to rush-record an album. *Musicday* snapped a picture of Rocky Dexter positively beaming. Yeah, he could buy anything, anyone, anytime.

The automatic eye of the wrought-iron gates opened smoothly to admit the sleek, midnight-blue automobile, then slowly closed behind. Darned if they don't always make me feel secluded, thought Bruce Wayne.

He was feeling rather lonely lately, anyway. And particularly after tonight's charity event, one more room full of hopeful ingenues who could stimulate his eyes but do little for his mind and soul. Finding stirring, intelligent people to converse with was always a difficult task. Thank goodness Commissioner Gordon was due for dinner tomorrow evening, Bruce thought as he pulled the car around the front of the house and stepped out onto the cobblestone drive. He walked up to the great arched doors of Wayne Manor and let himself in.

Alfred, polishing the silver coffee service to an immaculate shine, did not notice the heir's return. As he worked he busily performed a sort of bizarre shuffle to some lively music coming through the earphones of his Walkman. Bruce allowed an amused smile to brighten his dark features when he said, "Evening, Alfred."

"Oh! Good evening, Master Bruce! I regret to say I failed to hear your entrance."

"Yes, Alfred, apparently lost in a musical reverie. What were you listening to? Vivaldi? Or Tchaikovsky perhaps?"

"I blush to admit, sir, that it was a selection of a somewhat more plebeian kind, though, I hasten to add, no less moving for its humble origin," said the butler. "A new hillbilly chanteuse. Miss Tabby Jo Jeter is her name, I believe, sir."

"Alfred, you surprise me! Frankly I've never had any patience for that brand of twangy caterwauling. I confess country music has always left me cold."

Jon Hammer and Karen McBurnie

Bruce Wayne's ever-faithful manservant discreetly lowered his eyes and uttered with deference, "Perhaps, if you'll forgive me, sir, that is because you have never lost your woman nor taken to strong drink."

"Alfred, I believe there are depths to your soul that I shall never plumb!"

Entering his darkened study, Bruce Wayne glumly tugged on the black silk bow at his neck. What a colossal waste of his talent these charity dinners sometimes seemed. But that was selfishness. He knew the Wayne Foundation was as important a force for good as his alter ego, the Batman. Bored, that was his problem. He flicked on the television and bounced the remote on the taut, red leather couch, then wrestled his massive shoulders out of his dinner jacket. A tabloid entertainment news show materialized on the blue screen before him. He picked up the remote to zap it over to CNN, but paused when he saw it was a story about Tabby Jo Jeter, Alfred's new sensation. Amazingly erudite old bird that Alfred; Bruce Wayne chuckled to himself. Just imagine, Horatian odes *and* hillbilly love songs both buzzing about that wonderful brain! Let's see what all the fuss he was making is about.

"Dexter Music mogul Rocky Dexter has signed Ms. Jeter to a contract which sources say is *the* most generous deal in history. In addition to the splash she's made with her hit single, Tabby Jo is making waves in the music business establishment with her mysterious masked manager, Simba Voleuse. No one seems to know why Voleuse chooses to present such a bizarre public persona, but all agree her business savvy is unequaled. Industry insiders and fans alike will be watching Tabby Jo's fairy-tale success unfold, Mary."

"I know *I* will, John!"

Simba Voleuse. Something about that name made
the short, coarse black hairs on the back of his neck
bristle. He clicked off the set and stared unseeing at
the blank screen. The Batman knew his sensitive instincts were not to be ignored. His French was rusty
to say the least, but he was almost certain *voleuse*
meant "female thief."

"Alfred! Step in here a moment, please. How's your
Swahili, old fellow?"

"Not as comprehensive as it might be, I'm sure,
Master Bruce," the faithful retainer intoned as he
swept into the study.

"But you would say that 'simba' is a kind of a cat,
correct?"

"A rather large cat, sir. It's not my language expertise speaking, sir, but rather my knowledge of old adventure films. I believe the people use it to describe
the lion."

"I thought so. Simba Voleuse. Alfred, fantastic as it
sounds, I suspect your favorite singing sensation may
be managed by none other than Catwoman!"

"Yes, I see sir!" The canny old gent's eyes, like those
of his master, shone with excitement. "I agree that
this bears looking into."

"At once, my friend. Not a moment to spare when
'the game's afoot' as Holmes says."

If it was Catwoman, what could be her angle? Actually appearing to *work* was not her style at all. Entering a legitimate business venture was too out of
character. That worried him.

A week later, deep beneath Wayne Manor, the Batman
sat before the bat computer, hunched like some medieval scribe. He pored over the mass of information

ready at his fingertips through the world's largest anticrime data base. A polite "ahem," audible over the low hum of the powerful mainframe, interrupted his labors and the Batman turned from the terminal to find the trusty Alfred wheeling a tea cart off the elevator.

"Pardon the intrusion, sir, but as the hour is late, I took the liberty of preparing refreshment."

"You're a mind reader, Alfred," said the cowled crusader, taking a cup of steaming cocoa and a smoked mozzarella-and-tomato sandwich from the tray. "Fuel for the engines of justice, eh?"

"If I might ask, sir, how is your investigation of Catwoman's latest endeavor proceeding?"

"Interesting developments, Alfred. I've certainly uncovered a vast network of corruption in the record business. But even in an industry where tax fraud and conflicts of interest seem to be the norm, it's hard to fathom why Dexter Music hasn't been investigated before.

"To give you an idea of how much power this Rocky Dexter commands, in the past ten years over one hundred civil suits have been brought against him. None of them ever reached a judgment. Each was dropped. Now, maybe his lawyer is an expert at settling out of court, but looking at the company he's known to keep, I sincerely doubt any of the cases have been settled, period. I think intimidation is a more likely explanation."

"So it seems this captain of industry is a common hooligan, sir?" asked Alfred.

"All signs point to yes, my friend."

"But—" Alfred began.

"But why is he permitted to operate so blatantly on the fringes of legality?"

"Why, yes, sir."

Batman leans back on his chair. "Several factors contribute, I believe. First, in as flamboyant a business as his, Dexter's devilish ways are for some reason an emblem of his power. Because he acts like a gangster, he is treated with the highest degree of respect by his peers. Secondly, he's a very wealthy man. Finally, Dexter contributes generously to many political campaigns, which naturally wins him much influence. Photo opportunities with celebrities provide invaluable publicity for politicians. I've brought this to the commissioner's attention and his investigation is sure to bring those involved to justice."

"But what, sir, of Catwoman? What is her interest in this man's schemes?"

"That is what still puzzles me night and day, Alfred. Night and day."

"I'll leave the tray here, sir, should you desire additional nourishment. If there is nothing else you require, I shall retire now. Good evening, Master Bruce." Alfred glided from the room.

The Batman continued pondering. There would be no sleep until he found some answers. What would Catwoman want with such a sleazy but still fundamentally legitimate business? Well, if Gotham City's music industry was as profitable and as crooked as his findings indicated, perhaps she merely wanted a piece of the pie. Or perhaps she was hoping to beat Dexter at his own game, and so, to rid himself of competition, he approached her and made it worth her while to join forces. Perhaps the two crooks had planned more diabolical activities and the record company was merely a front for their association.

Or could she have been planning to *take over* the multimillion-dollar corporation that was Dexter Music? God knew, she was clever enough to obtain most anything she wanted.

There was another possibility. Bruce had no hard evidence that Catwoman was involved in this business at all. But that's the most pathetic brand of wishful thinking I've ever been guilty of, thought the Batman. No one but she could call herself Simba Voleuse. And yet he couldn't help but think maybe this one time she wasn't planning the crime of the century. Perhaps Catwoman *had* finally abandoned the life of crime! Now that she found herself a huge success in a colorful business, perhaps her appetite for fun and power and wealth was satisfied. It was too good to be true, though. As for me, Batman thought, I know I'm only human, the mind susceptible to the thoughts of my own pleasure. As much trouble as she's brought on herself, I can't deny I've enjoyed her company. . . .

My *God* it must be late, and I must be weary! How could I even *think* . . . In the end she's nothing but a thief! She uses her charms as just another weapon in her criminal mischief. What a colossal fool I am to forget that, even for an instant.

"Sid! All right already, Sid. If you'll just stop busting my chops for ten seconds!" Rocky Dexter howled hoarsely into the car phone. Phew! No rest for the wicked, Rock. In my own car people got to give me angina. "Look, Sid, in case you forgot, *I'm* the president of Dexter Music, *you* are a bean counter! What, I don't *know* the company's cash poor right now? Am I a dope? I sign the artists, I decide how much we spend on promotion, you jut cut the checks, pal. Understand me? Am I getting through to you? You're a pencil pusher, you can't know from talent."

"I'm sorry if you think I'm pushing, Rocky." Sid's voice sounded thin and metallic. "But it's my duty to tell you Dexter Music is tapped out. This Tabby Jo Jeter signing has drained us. At this point we have two assets: the catalog and the artists' contracts, and now I hear we may have to sell off some rights just to pay the bills."

"Yeah? Well, you didn't hear that from me. That back catalog is worth millions. Why, the Hank Williams stuff alone could bring in enough to cover the overhead for a year." Sure, if I knew where in Hades the acetates were. "I'm waiting for the optimum moment to release the package, that's all. Anyway, this Tabby Jo is worth every nickel. When her album hits the street, we'll be riding higher than my great-uncle Osgood's trousers."

"I hope you're right, Rocky. If this record isn't the biggest hit in our history, we are sunk."

"Okay, Sid, you keep the bill collectors away a couple more weeks, I guarantee we have the smash of the decade. In the meantime I have an idea that may save some money. So long!"

Rocky hung up and reached for a Cuban corona out of the limo humidor. He squinted at the streets of Gotham rushing by the window as he nipped off the end. Trimming a little fat around the office wasn't a bad idea. He picked up the receiver of the cellular.

"Hello, Hollander? I have an idea to cut down our overhead. Listen; when Sid Schulman goes out for lunch, I want you to put a wall over his office door. . . . Yeah, build a whole wall! You deaf, or what? Leave his stuff where it is, I want it to look like there never *was* an office there, get me? When he comes back, you let him look for the door awhile, then security tosses his can out of the building. Forever . . . I don't want to hear your bellyaching! Just do it."

The clock on the top of the Gotham Securities Tower read 4:17 A.M. as the Batmobile flashed by a lone garbage truck as it made its leisurely rounds. Bruce Wayne had just spent much of the wee hours outlining the results of his investigation of Dexter Music to Commissioner Gordon and his guests, two high-ranking officials of the FCC. The payola, the extortion, the tax evasion had all been laid before them in unimpeachable black and white. Now subpoenas were being issued. A grand jury would convene within a week to determine if there were grounds to indict Rocky Dexter. The feds were confident Dexter Music would be shut down in a matter of weeks, but there was something missing. There was still nothing to tie Catwoman to Rocky Dexter, save the large stock deal her protégée, Tabby Jo Jeter, received on signing with Dexter Music. The Batman couldn't shake the suspicion that he was letting Catwoman slip through his fingers. The Batmobile streaked soundlessly through empty midnight streets. He knew this case wasn't yet closed.

That afternoon, in the posh offices of the Katz, Mauser Brokerage House, mere blocks away from Gordon's office at Police Plaza, a svelte young woman in a crushed-velvet bodysuit was concluding an important transaction with Jeremy Katz.

"That's right, I want you to sell every last share. Simple as that."

"I apologize, Miss Jeter, if I seem a bit mystified." Jeremy glanced up at the portrait of his grandfather glaring at him from over Tabby Jo's shoulder. Old Man Katz looked none too happy, but what could Jeremy do? "As you say, it's your money, but all our projections show great potential for Dexter Music. It just doesn't seem prudent or, forgive me, even logical to divest at this stage of the game, especially since you own over a third of the shares offered by the corporation to date."

"Look, Jeremy, the bottom line is I wouldn't bet a dime on the future of Dexter Music. Gambling, that's all the market is, right? So we understand each other, I came to you because you have a reputation for discretion."

Tabby Jo gave him a wink. Oh, God, so that's it, thought Jeremy. She heard that I handle the Penguin's portfolio!

"I need efficiency in this matter. This is the number of a Swiss account. I want all the shares sold and the cash deposited by the end of the day," she said, rising.

"Yes, but . . ."

"No 'but.' Yes will do."

She flew from the room, leaving Jeremy alone to gaze at Old Man Katz. His dead grandfather's oily stare seemed more disapproving than ever.

The wind ripped through the Batman's cape as he peered through the violet night to the glowing sodium grid of the streets fifty floors below. At these sterile heights, the city spread out at his feet, surrounded by the cool, silent spires of midtown Gotham, he could almost forget the evil that prowled the streets. The im-

Jon Hammer and Karen McBurnie

passive architecture spoke nothing of the corruption he had spent his life fighting.

On another floor of this skyscraper Tabby Jo Jeter was making her television debut on a live late-night comedy/variety program. Batman had watched in secrecy as Tabby Jo and her guitar player arrived by limousine. Her manager, "Ms. Voleuse," had followed the car on a slick, early-model motorcycle. The Batman knew time was running out. It was the eve of both the release of Tabby Jo's album and the convening of the grand jury. If he was ever going to find out what Catwoman's angle on all this was, it had to be tonight.

When she and Alvin Nash left after the show, Tabby Jo Jeter found that hiding behind her movie-star shades didn't do anything but attract more attention. She found a dozen autograph hounds waiting at the stage entrance.

For the first time in her short career Tabby Jo was not accompanied by her manager. The fictitious Ms. Voleuse was nowhere to be seen, but Catwoman in full costume had preceded the two musicians out of the studio.

"You and Alvin better stay and satisfy your public," teased the feline mistress of crime. "I have to go drive the last rusty nail into Rocky's coffin."

While Tabby Jo signed autographs Catwoman mounted her Harley Sportster. Kicking over the motor, she called out, "Enjoy it while you can, Tura. This was your last appearance."

"I didn't forget," Tabby/Tura replied huffily.

A wide-eyed woman wearing something between a housedress and a muumuu in a pattern of fluorescent pink daisies the size of sunflowers, broke from the pack and ran over to Catwoman.

"Catlady! Catlady! Can I have your autograph there? You're my all-time favorite criminal."

"Very flattering, I'm sure," said Catwoman graciously. She signed the dog-eared book on the page after Eartha Kitt. As she sped off, a pair of dark eyes quietly marked her every move from a loading dock across the street.

He had to take every precaution not to alert his quarry. The Batman knew just how slippery she could be. Luckily Simba/Catwoman had been careless enough to park her motorcycle where he could easily find it. He had tagged it with a homing device that could be tracked by the Batmobile's computers from a distance of five miles away. He settled into the sculpted interior and watched the dot of green light on the screen. It was moving west on State Avenue. She was headed over the river.

He followed her for nearly an hour, hanging back a mile or two, through the vast industrial wastelands that lay across the water from the great metropolis. Past the mammoth storage tanks and oil refineries and fetid canals, mile after mile of crumbling nineteenth-century factory buildings bordered by lonely stretches of toxic marshland, she rode on through each circle of this industrial inferno until she came to a large warehouse adjoining a CD pressing plant.

By the time Batman crept stealthily up to her Harley, Catwoman had already cut her way through the wire fence and broken the lock on the door. Stepping out of the floodlit yard and into the shadow of the warehouse, the Dark Knight pulled his cape around his body. He would wait in ambush for her exit.

Jon Hammer and Karen McBurnie

The minutes ticked by, the buzz of the sodium lamps the only sound. Then a flurry of sharp footsteps and Catwoman burst through the door at a run. Suddenly the Batman pounced. From the near invisibility of his hiding place he came at her with the speed of a cobra. Startled, Catwoman aimed a kick at the crime fighter's head but failed to connect. Pivoting on her toe like a dancer, she spun at him again, this time dealing a blow with her knee that caught him in the stomach. He grabbed for her leg as she threw a third kick, this one to the chest. Though off balance, he was able to pull her off her feet. Catwoman landed on her back, but with a quick roll she was up again. This time the Caped Crusader launched himself at her before she could unleash another volley of blows. His superior size and strength easily overwhelmed her at close range. Catwoman found herself struggling in vain, crushed in the viselike grip of his iron arms.

"Simba Voleuse, I presume?" the Batman scolded into her ear. "I knew it was you the first time I heard that ridiculous alias."

"Like I care," she spat, squirming to regain the upper hand. She jerked an arm free and quickly sent a karate chop to his temple. In a flash he grabbed her wrist and with a painful squeeze forced it behind her back.

"Your foray into the music business is over, Catwoman. Rocky Dexter is going to be arrested in a matter of days and I doubt that his company will survive the payola investigation the government is beginning this week." The Batman's voice was low and even, despite the exertions of the battle.

As he spoke Catwoman's frantic writhing stopped abruptly and she looked up at him in amused surprise. Then she laughed, a cold vengeful laugh. His stomach sank a little at this strange reaction.

"Ruined Rocky Dexter, did you? Thanks, Bat-dope. But in the future, if I need your help, I'll ask for it." Catwoman smirked. Still held in his powerful grasp, she twisted her arm until she could just see her wristwatch. The mocking tone left her voice. She looked at him earnestly. "In the meantime, big boy, I strongly suggest we move away from this warehouse in a hurry. Unless you have nine lives."

Before he could consider where this trick might lead, Catwoman, applying every last ounce of her strength, spun the Batman around until his broad back faced the warehouse. In that instant an almost supersonic thud shook the ground. The doors of the building exploded outward in a wall of flame, the force of the blast knocking the cowled crime fighter flat on top of Catwoman. Shaken for a moment by the blast, the Batman took a savage right cross to the jaw from Catwoman, who made a dash for her bike.

The Batman stumbled to his feet and listened to the roar of the Sportster fade into the night. The street was littered with melting CDs and jewelbox cases. None of this made any sense to him. He would have thought Catwoman had more pride in her own abilities than to stoop to sabotaging her competitors' product. Absently he flipped a burning jewelbox over with his toe and watched, amazed, as the name Tabby Jo Jeter turned to ash. Why? Was Catwoman a Svengali destroying her own Trilby?

"Kit, darkling, bring us two bottles of champagne from the cooler. The ones from the Cannes heist last year."

Jon Hammer and Karen McBurnie

Candles warmed the huge parlor room, and perhaps, Catwoman hoped, their soothing glow would calm. Tura, still in heavy television makeup, readied the ice and silver bucket, never for a moment taking her eyes off the display of *Introducing Tabby Jo* CDs that decorated the mantel. "Wow," she said to herself.

Catwoman turned on the news. A fashion show was on the screen. ". . . don't think we'll be seeing these ensembles on the streets of Gotham this season or anytime soon. Eliza Press, Seventh Avenue."

"Thanks, Eliza. Now here's a late-breaking story sure to have deep repercussions in the business world and the music industry all the way down to the consumer in the record shop: in a press conference today, businessman Roy Blochenstein announced his takeover of the collapsed Dexter Music."

The squirrel face of Blochenstein appeared on the television screen. "It's a tremendous opportunity!" he sputtered.

The news reader continued, "The troubled Dexter Music corporation had fallen on hard times of late. First, rumors that huge cash and stock offers made in the wooing of overnight sensation Tabby Jo Jeter, compounded by declining profits for the second year in a row, crippled the company financially. Sources say Dexter was hoping to recoup their fortune with the releases of Jeter's album and a rare lost Hank Williams session. Now we learn Rocky Dexter has been named as the key figure in the largest payola scandal in over a decade."

"Ha! We really hit him where it hurts! Rocky won't have two dimes to rub together after the government is through with him. And now that twerp Blochenstein is buying his company out from under him, how about that?" Tura laughed as she turned to

Catwoman. The smile perished when she saw the ice in Catwoman's eyes.

"Yes, how about that," the mistress of crime said grimly. "We did a good job ruining Rocky for our own purposes, we did an even better job of driving down the price of his company so Blochenstein could buy it for a song. That dumpy little freak is no Hank Williams fan, he was after Dexter Music from the start. And like a sap I helped him do it for free." Catwoman flung the crystal goblet she was holding across the room, where it shattered into a million shimmering bits. Tura and Kit froze in fearful anticipation of the next violent expression of rage. "*Blochenstein.* He'll pay for thinking he can use Catwoman!" she bellowed.

Alvin Nash, out of bravery or stupidity, ventured a comment. "He'll pay, that's for sure. If not in this world, then in the next."

Catwoman shot him a withering glance.

"Well, what I mean is this," stammered the flustered cowpoke. "That ol' boy bought himself more than a record label. He bought perdition!"

"Thank you, Rod Serling," Tura snorted.

"No! Now, I'm serious. After what I seen of the music business, and I know Rocky Dexter ain't unique, I believe there must be a special circle of hell reserved just for record executives."

Alvin managed to get this out in his folksiest drawl wearing his winningest grin, and that was enough to break the spell. A purr began to emanate from Catwoman, which changed to a chuckle. Tura and Kit traded looks that told how relieved they were the mood had lifted. For now Alvin Nash has extinguished the Catwoman's fiery temper. His remark had helped level the delicate scales of Catwoman's strange justice. She no longer felt she had been bettered. For now.

Hide and Seek

KRISTINE KATHRYN RUSCH

Rain, dripping through the steps of the iron fire escape, felt like ice. Robbie shoved closer to the Dumpster and shivered. The air smelled of rotten meat, and the green metal Dumpster was cold, although not as cold as the rain. He pulled the soggy blanket around his thin shoulders, and scrunched under the thick cardboard he and his mother had been using as a tent.

He wished she would get back. He was hungry.

Sometimes, if he closed his eyes, he could imagine the living room of the apartment, with its threadbare couch, photographs, and small black-and-white TV. He could rerun, in his mind, the soap operas his mom used to watch, as well as his favorite cartoons. The scarred wooden coffee table served as dining table, and he would sit on the floor and eat peanut butter and jelly sandwiches while waiting for his dad to come home.

To think he used to hate it. He had thought the apartment stupid. He wouldn't invite his friends over so that they could see how he slept on that couch, while his parents used the only bedroom. He used to hate the smell of decades-old grease and wish that the place wouldn't be so warm.

Now he thought he would never be warm again.

The patter of rain on the garbage kept time with his pounding heart. Mom had told him to wait. She promised food. But she had been doing that a lot lately, and once she hadn't come back till the next day. He had spent the entire time pressed up against a Dumpster. When she finally came, she smelled of cheap booze, and was full of apologies.

Amazing how things could change so fast. His dad hadn't come home on Christmas Eve, and by New Year's it was clear he wasn't coming back. His mom started drinking worse than before, and wouldn't stop, even when Robbie asked her to find a job. The landlord threw them out in January—Robbie had to wake his mother to give her the news—and they went from shelter to shelter, trying to find a place to hole up at night.

Lately the shelters had been full, and Robbie's mom still wouldn't let him do anything. He was eight. He could get a job selling newspapers or something.

A ringing on the iron stairs above made him open his eyes. He thought he caught a glimpse of a black-clad foot disappearing up the escape. He held his breath—he had already learned the other people on the street could be mean—but he didn't hear anything else. Slowly he pushed the cardboard away from his body and stood up.

The rain had slowed to a sprinkle. His stomach growled, and his mother was nowhere in sight. He would eat anything, but he had already scrounged through the dumpster behind him. Maybe if he went

Kristine Kathryn Rusch

out into the street, he could beg a little money from people passing by.

He made his way into the alley, stepping over garbage, careful not to make any noise. As he stepped onto the rain-slicked concrete, he heard a squawk above him. He looked up in time to see something black and white hurtling down toward him. It landed in his arms before he had a chance to duck.

He was holding a small stuffed penguin. Its fake fur was soft and rich, and its button eyes seemed almost alive. Stuffed animals were baby toys, but this one was warm and reminded him of days when he could sleep where it was dry. He cuddled it to him, and sniffed the perfume of its fur. Something that wasn't wet and miserable and cold. Something that had a little bit of value. Something he could love.

He closed his eyes and squeezed the penguin. It squawked again. For a moment, he felt as if he were being lifted in loving arms, cradled against a warm chest, held as if he mattered.

And then he felt nothing at all.

The woman hadn't bathed for days. The smell of her skin lingered under the odor of cheap liquor that clung to her like perfume. Her clothes were ripped and ragged, her hair matted against her skull. Her eyes were dark circles in her dirty face.

She was maybe twenty-five.

Commissioner Gordon couldn't really tell. Not that it mattered. She had been screaming in the lobby, threatening officers, and calling for her kid. Rather than have someone jail her before hearing her story, he brought her into his office.

Now he wished he hadn't. The smell would last for days.

He pushed open a window and looked down on the Gotham skyline. Rain had cleared the smog from the air, and left the streets slick as ice. Neo-Gothic buildings towered over more conservative constructions. The blare of horns and sirens beat a counterpoint to the woman's breathing; the sounds the voice of the city itself.

Gordon made himself turn around and face her.

She looked small behind his polished oak desk. Her thin hands clasped in front of her. She was shaking.

"Tell me about it, ma'am," he said as gently as he could.

"Downstairs, they told me to get out."

"I know," Gordon said. "They were wrong. They thought you had come in to get warm." He would have to talk to the boys. Usually they showed more compassion.

"They wouldn't listen to me."

That's because you smell like you've been on a three-day drunk, Gordon wanted to say, but didn't. "I'm listening to you."

She nodded and took a deep breath. "My boy's gone."

"Your boy?"

"My son." The words came out in a rush. "I come back with some food, you know. I told him to stay put and he always does. He's a good boy. But he wasn't there, so I figured he got hungry and went to get something for himself. Only he never come back. Not all night. And Old Skeezer said someone else was in the alley yesterday."

Gordon clutched his leather chair. The smell was

Kristine Kathryn Rusch

making him dizzy. "Let me get this straight. You live in an alley—"

"No, sir. We stay at the shelters. Only the past week, they haven't had enough room. I found this spot out of the rain, and my boy's been staying there." Her voice rose with each sentence. "You've got to find him. He's only eight. He's never lived like this and he don't know . . ."

Her sentence trailed off, but Gordon understood the end of it. He doesn't know what dangers face him out there. Drug dealers, pimps, white slavery, casual violence. No matter how hard he and his force worked, they couldn't keep up with it. Every day something new happened.

He looked at her, saw the fear in her grime-streaked face. It had taken a lot of courage for her to come here, especially since many homeless people lived right at the edge of the law. The boy meant a lot to her, was probably all that she had left.

At twenty-five. Jesus.

He came around the desk and put a hand on her shoulder. A shudder ran through him, but he made himself offer as much comfort as he could. "I'm going to take you out front and have you give your boy's description to an officer. Then we'll give that description to every squad, tell them it's urgent to find him. In the meantime, we'll call the Rose Hill Shelter for you, get you a place to stay—"

"No!" She spoke the word with such force that spittle sprayed the air. "Don't make me go to no shelter. He'll never find me."

Gordon suppressed a sigh. "Okay," he said. "Then be sure you tell the officers which alley is yours, so that we can find you, too."

She nodded, and he put his arm around her shaking frame as he led her into the front office. This time, he didn't mind at all.

Lisbet buried her face in the remains of her dolly. Inside the house, her mommy screamed. Daddy's voice stopped after each slap. Lisbet wanted to crawl under the porch and die, like the puppy did after Daddy threw it against the wall.

First the puppy, now dolly. Lisbet took a deep shaky breath. She wouldn't cry. Three-year-olds are too big to cry—that's what Daddy said. He would hit her if she cried.

That's why he was hitting Mommy now. Because Lisbet cried. "Can't you keep that brat quiet?" Daddy yelled. And Mommy said, "Maybe you should have left her dolly alone," and then he hit Mommy, and Lisbet ran to the porch.

Where she leaned against the stairs, stroking what was left of her dolly. Every time she looked up the sun had gone farther down, sending little pink ribbons across the sky. Across the neighborhood, kids were outside, playing, shouting, and laughing. But Lisbet was too little to go out of the yard. Daddy said so. Lisbet didn't have any friends.

Daddy had stopped yelling inside. Mommy was crying, and the backdoor slammed. Lisbet pushed closer to the stairs. She didn't want Daddy to see her. She didn't want Daddy to tear her like he had torn her dolly. She pressed her eyes shut and waited. A car started. She hoped it was Daddy's, but it probably wasn't. Daddy was probably sneaking around to the front, to come get her. He was going to yell at her like he yelled at Mommy.

Something soft touched her arm and Lisbet screamed. She clapped both hands over her mouth, but the scream was already out and echoing in the neighborhood. She looked around, but didn't see anyone. Not her daddy, not anyone. Then she looked beside her. A stuffed penguin rested against her arm. It was black and white, and pretty, like dolly had been when dolly was new.

She reached out and touched it with a shaking finger. The penguin was real. Then she gathered it in her arms and pulled it close.

The penguin squawked. Lisbet smiled.

Bruce Wayne stood in the rain-slicked alley, under the amber glare of a fading streetlight. He clutched a rose to his chest, not feeling the thorns stab his palms. Although his eyes stared ahead, he didn't see the damp brick wall, the remains of the hotel, the litter covering the street.

He saw a man with a gun.

A man with a huge smile and eyes so cold they looked like ice. A man who spoke nonsense words. Nonsense words that circled in Bruce's head long after the police had removed his parents' bodies. Long after someone had scooped his mother's pearls from the mud-covered street. Long after Bruce had grown from little boy to man.

Even now, he couldn't put that nightmare behind him. Alfred had done the best he could, raising Bruce, but Bruce still felt he owed the night. He needed to stop bullets from shattering worlds, needed to provide little boys a safe place to grow up.

The anniversary came around, just like it did every year, and his parents still didn't return. They would never return.

Bruce knelt near the spot on the once-bloody pavement, the spot where his parents' lives had ended over a bit of money and a few jewels, the spot where Bruce's childhood had disappeared with a grin and a glance from ice-cold eyes.

He set the rose down, his own blood mixing in the raindrops.

"I miss you," he said.

She was asleep.

Stacy circled her mother, lying prone on the couch, one arm covering her eyes, the other trailing to the floor. The television blared a rerun, but Stacy didn't turn the set down nor did she change the channel.

Instead, she went into the kitchen and began to clean dinner off the wall.

Little good-for-nothing slut! her mother had yelled. *Can't cook nothing right. I work all day to provide you with a good home, and what do I get? Nothing. I like macaroni and cheese a little runny. You got the cheese stuck too hard to the noodles.*

And to the wall, Stacy thought. She took a sponge and scrubbed, trying not to leave stains or peel the paint. Her mother might forget the incident once she woke up, but it would be just Stacy's luck that her mother would inspect the walls, the floor, the entire kitchen.

When she was finished, she rinsed off the sponge in

the sink and washed her hands. Her arms ached, and she knew her back would ache in the morning. But she couldn't think about that now. She took a few slices of white bread, the kind that teacher said wasn't good for her, from the breadbox, balled them up in her fist, grabbed her comic book, and went outside.

The light had faded, leaving the street in darkness. Their house was one of the few remaining on a block now filled with convenience stores and boarded-up buildings. Mom had inherited the house from her parents and had taken it because she didn't have to pay for its upkeep. It was cheap, not nice, her mom said, as if she expected someone to argue with her.

Stacy hunched over the back stairs, flipping the pages in the book, and putting little pieces of bread in her mouth. She should have eaten while she cooked, but she was afraid that Mom would know. But how would Mom know a few bites of macaroni and cheese from an entire boxful? She could count bread slices. Stacy might have to pay for that in the morning, too.

Something squawked at her feet. Stacy started. She looked down and saw something small and furry staring up at her. Her throat went dry. The little furry thing didn't move. It was black and white like a skunk, but they lived too far inside the city for skunks. She inched down the stairs and stopped on the bottom one.

It was stuffed. Someone had left a little stuffed penguin on the sidewalk, and it looked brand-new. She was scared to pick it up, scared someone would yell at her, scared she would get blamed for touching something so new. But it was pretty, and it looked lonely, too. She reached down, and with one quick movement cradled the penguin against her chest.

It squawked as it moved, and the sound made Stacy

jump. She clutched the toy tightly and scanned the darkness. Something was out there, something big.

And it was coming toward her.

Sergeant Bill Gilroy yawned and climbed out of the squad. He both hated and loved nights like this. Hated them because he had nothing to do. He and Isaac, his partner, drove around like teenagers on a Friday night, circling the same old pattern over and over again. But he loved these nights because they meant that, for once, things were going right with the world. As he told his wife, he would love it if human relations improved enough so that he would be out of a job.

Isaac remained in the squad, hunched over a cold cup of coffee, monitoring the radio. Bill hated cold coffee. He wanted something hot, and maybe a little snack. Dinner had been an undercooked hot dog with ancient onions and even older relish. He wanted something to wash the taste from his mouth.

As he walked down the sidewalk, he listened to the quiet. Even the horns were silent. No sirens, few voices. A bum leaned against one of the boarded-up walls. Bill tossed him a quarter, even though he knew the Chief wouldn't approve. The Chief wanted every homeless bundled into a squad and taken to a shelter. But the shelters were closing all over the city—lack of funds—and every time Bill had followed procedure during the last week, he and his homeless find had been turned away. Being turned away from charity seemed to discourage these folks more, and Bill wasn't up to breaking hearts just to follow the rules.

If he had a million dollars, he would give everyone

a home, a job, and a bit of self-worth. But he didn't. He barely had enough money in his pocket for hot coffee and a small snack.

He heard a squawk behind him and whirled. A small boy stood alone on the street corner. The boy was no more than six, and wore ragged clothes and a too-small jacket. Bill hated seeing kids like that.

He walked toward the boy, but the boy didn't see him. The boy's gaze was fixed on something off to the side. Bill watched the boy bend over cautiously and pick up a small black-and-white object. The boy turned, and the object reflected the streetlight.

The boy held a penguin. A stuffed penguin.

Bill swallowed. A shudder ran down the back of his spine. He opened his mouth to yell, but nothing came out. The boy bent his head over the penguin, and the toy squawked.

The boy smiled.

Bill ran, wishing he could call for Isaac. The night had been too quiet. Dammit. Now this.

The boy closed his eyes, joy evident on all his features.

Bill glanced around for help, saw nothing. No one else. He was alone.

When he looked back, the boy was gone.

A mad crush of people, all made-up, dressed in formal suits, muted dresses. Gordon saw hands, mouths, microphones, paper, tape recorders, but none of them seemed attached to anything else. God, he hated this part of his job. He wished he could tell the driver to let him off on a different corner, but then the press reports would claim he was avoiding interviews (which he would be) because he had something to hide (which he didn't).

He shoved open the heavy sedan door into the teeming mass of bodies.

". . . the Penguin's back? . . ."

"Commissioner!"

". . . stealing children? . . ."

"Commissioner?"

". . . plan to do about it? . . ."

"Commissioner!"

". . . call Batman? . . ."

He put his head down and plowed through the reporters as if he were a tank and they merely foot soldiers. They grabbed his sleeves, his coat, his arms, demanding, always demanding. The stairs looked like a gauntlet, a neverending mountain of concrete, that he had to climb, toting these pariahs with him.

Halfway up he stopped. The crowd hushed. Camera lights blinded him, microphones got shoved into his face. "Look," he said. "I just got here. I don't know what we're going to do. This is a horrible turn of events, just horrible. We'll stop it. I can promise you that much. We'll stop it."

He turned and climbed three stairs before the reporters followed him, with their frustrated cries of "Commissioner! Commissioner!"

He made it to the glass doors, pulled them open, and hurried inside, leaving the voices to echo faintly behind him. *We'll stop it,* he had promised. But he didn't know how. What would the Penguin want with children? The greedy little man had only been interested in wealth before. Wealth and stopping Batman.

Kristine Kathryn Rusch

"Commissioner?" One of his aides stopped him by placing a hand on his arm. Gordon looked at him a moment before recognition set in. Gordon ran a hand over his face. Concentrating too hard. This job got to him sometimes.

"We have a briefing set up for you, sir, before you see the mayor."

A briefing. The phone call had been briefing enough, waking him from a sound sleep, invading the warmth of his bed. Children, for godsakes. What did the Penguin want with children?

Gordon sighed. He supposed he should go in. He just wanted the meeting with the mayor over with. The mayor's questions were often as impossible as the reporters'—only with the mayor, he was required to answer.

"All right," Gordon said, "but this meeting better be what you called it—brief."

He followed the aide into a conference room, ignoring the knot that felt like fear at the base of his stomach.

Bruce Wayne pushed a button on the remote and the picture on the wide-screen television disappeared. He leaned back in the leather armchair and inhaled the rich scent. His head was pounding.

No one had contacted him. He didn't know why.

"Frightening, isn't it, sir?" Alfred, trusty Alfred, giving voice to the feeling that gnawed at Bruce. He wondered what the children were doing, trapped in some hellhole under the city, without food, maybe, or water. The Penguin probably had some grand scheme planned, some way of getting ransom or a lot of money.

But from homeless kids? Children of the poor?
It made no sense.

"Why haven't the police contacted us, Alfred?"

"You know that they like to see what they can do
on their own first." Alfred hovered behind Bruce's
chair, the perfect gentleman's gentleman.

"They're good people, Alfred, but if they wait too
long, these kids could get hurt."

They could die. Bruce didn't speak the words aloud,
but he didn't have to. Alfred already knew that.

"Seems to me that you have a meeting to attend,
then, sir."

Bruce stood up. "Seems to me you're right.

His white gloves hid his whitened knuckles. He
gripped the gold-topped umbrella tightly, his diamond
cufflinks flashing in the room's bright lights. He adjusted the sleeves of his tuxedo, then leaned forward
on the umbrella, his attention on the television screen
behind the ornate black bar.

Everyone else in the room watched, too. Four men,
two women, assistants, also dressed in black and white.
They lacked the tension he felt in his own body.

The white carpet trailed down to the black chairs.
He adjusted the geometrically designed black-and-
white pillow behind him, never taking his eyes off the
screen.

The reporter was slim and pale. She wore a single
strand of pearls around her neck and a light peach
dress that accentuated her pallor. She stood on the
steps of city hall, the building rising like a tower behind her. Her voice, like liquid fire, oozed out of the set.

"... no word yet from the city or the police depart-

Kristine Kathryn Rusch

ment. Not even a confirmation of what we all suspect—
that the penguin-shaped toy is more than a clue to the
mastermind behind the scheme, that it is, in fact, a
confession. And as long as the police squanders its
time in meetings, more children will disappear. And
the Penguin will go free. For Channel Thirty-four
News, I'm—"

"Shut it off," he said, waving a gloved hand.

The picture winked out.

He resisted the urge to pace. He hadn't expected
them to discover him so soon. No one had cared about
those unfortunate children until they disappeared. He
smiled with a touch of bitterness. He would have to
remember that lesson—sometimes a worthless item
gained value when it was stolen. Because someone
else wanted it, the item suddenly had price.

Only this time he didn't care about price.

"What are we going to do, Boss?"

He looked up, unable to tell who had spoken. It didn't
matter. They all were capable of asking the same
asinine question.

"Do?" he replied, folding his gloved hands together,
and smiling with a confidence he didn't feel. "Why,
we're going to create a diversion."

As he scaled down the roof in the cover of growing
twilight, he felt the city's power pulsing around him.
He paused, looked it over, wished he could see the
children living in squalor—all of them, in one quick
second. He wondered how Penguin picked his victims,
how long he staked them out, how he found the exact
moment to approach them—and what he did with them
when he captured them.

Hide and Seek

Batman continued his progress down the side of city hall. He knew once he reached the right window, he would tap on it, and they would let him in. But he took his time going down, allowing himself to absorb the city, to absorb the blackness around him.

Funny, he never thought of himself as Bruce Wayne at these moments. Bruce Wayne was a little rich boy with an unfortunate past. Batman was strong, almost invincible, a man with no past who lived in the cover of darkness.

A light reflected out of a large set of windows. Batman stopped on the ledge outside, and rapped as if he were knocking on the mayor's front door.

They were all inside: the mayor, the aldermen, the police commissioner, and they were arguing by the look of them. Half a dozen used coffee cups sat on a nearby table, by an oversized coffee urn. Sandwich wrappers filled a garbage bin near the table. The men were standing, but office chairs were skewed in all directions.

A long day then. A day in which they could settle nothing. They would be tired, frustrated, and short-tempered. Batman rapped on the window again. Commissioner Gordon looked up and indicated to one of the uniformed officers to open the window.

The officer yanked the window across its track and stale cigarette-coated corporate air gushed out. Batman took a deep breath, stepped across the sill and inside the room.

"Thank God you're here, Batman," the Commissioner said.

"We were just trying to decide if we needed to send for you."

Kristine Kathryn Rusch

"I think this case is going to need all of us," Batman said. He closed the window, and his cape billowed around him. "What do we know so far? Any ransom demands?"

The Commissioner shook his head. "We have reports from all over the city. By our estimates, he's taken at least twenty-five children, and the wealthiest one comes from a family that earns ten thousand dollars per year."

"No demands to the city? No threats?"

The mayor shook his head. "Nothing."

Batman whirled, hands clasped behind his back. Odd that the question of motive should bother him more than anything else. And yet, he felt that was central to the entire affair.

"Tell me about the kids," he said.

"Most are homeless," the Commissioner replied. "Most of the ones who have moms also have files at child welfare or with the Gotham Hospital."

"Abused?"

The Commissioner nodded. "Even though the parents deny it. They all insist on getting their kids back. One man is threatening to sue the city for failing to protect its citizens."

"Charming," Batman said. He paced, his leather boots silent on the tile floor. "We have a mass kidnapping here, with no ransom demands."

"And as we've been in here, discussing plans, four more children have disappeared."

A shudder ran down Batman's back. As they stood there, children could be dying. The Penguin could be using them for some weird experiment, thinking that the children were unwanted.

Unwanted. Hmmm.

"Commissioner," Batman said. "Get your squads to round up as many homeless children as you can find, and give them twenty-four-hour guard. Mr. Mayor, sir, we need access to child welfare records and we need to match them with Gotham Hospital. Anything, any possible hint of abuse, and the kid is out of the house and in police protection until we get this thing solved."

"And where do you propose we put them?" the mayor asked. "We're losing federal funding for most of our shelters. We've had to close three in the past month."

"Reopen them, and staff them with volunteers if you have to. If you put announcements in the papers, I'm sure the good citizens of Gotham will help fund your efforts."

"I don't think even that will be enough," the Commissioner said.

"Then let them sleep here," Batman said. "I'm sure someone will come up with money for sleeping bags, cots, and food."

"Children in city hall?" The mayor shook his head.

"Have you a better plan, sir?" Batman asked.

"No." The mayor looked down at his hands.

"Once the squads have found the children, we'll start looking for clues, witnesses, anything that will lead us to those missing kids."

"And I'll be working on it, too," Batman said. He walked to the window and paused. "It looks, gentlemen, that once we solve this case, the issue of homeless children is one that Gotham is going to have to address."

Jack was sitting on the rubber mat outside the YMCA. The building was closed for the night, but hot air seeped out the space between the glass door and its frame, and warmed the sheltered entry. It was a good place to sleep on frigid nights when the shelters were packed.

He picked at a hole in his canvas running shoes and tried to ignore the rumbling of his stomach. He had managed to lift three candy bars that morning, but they hadn't gotten him through the day. Looked like tomorrow he would have to go rooting through garbage cans in order to get a good meal.

A cop car pulled into the Y's circular driveway. Jack leaned against the door, feeling the icy glass through his thin cotton shirt. The car stopped. Jack's heart was beating in his throat. Please don't let them see me, he thought. Please.

Footsteps crunched along the concrete sidewalk, heading toward him. At the last minute, Jack looked out and saw a young cop ambling up the way. Jack burst out of the entry, arms and legs pinwheeling, and ran across the lawn.

"Hey, you!" the cop yelled. "Hey!"

The car started and followed him across the driveway. Jack was running as fast as he could, but his legs were short and the cop was in good condition. He was keeping up. Jack scrambled for a grove of trees, only to have a red-and-blue light flash in his eyes. The next thing they would do is turn on the sirens.

He stopped running and stood panting at the edge of the grove. He didn't think they'd come after him like this for three small candy bars. His entire body shook. At least the cell would be warm—and if he was lucky, maybe they would feed him.

Hide and Seek

The cop eased his run into a jog. He stopped in front of Jack and crouched down. "Young man," the cop said, his voice soft, "you have a place to sleep tonight?"

"Why?" Jack asked.

"Because"—the cop glanced at the squad, but his partner stayed inside—"we have some creep who's going around picking on homeless people. He likes kids."

Jack's shivering grew worse.

"We're opening some of the shelters just for kids, and finding others a place to stay. What d'you say? You come with me?"

Jack ran his hands across his arms. The shivering wasn't stopping. "You got food?" he heard himself say.

The cop smiled. "Plenty."

Jack sighed and allowed himself to be taken away.

Ringing. Buzzing. Sirens. Abner Markowitz struggled out of a sound sleep and sat up. The noise clanged around him, making his ears ache. He pulled the satin sleep-mask off his face and blinked into the grayness.

The windows looked undisturbed. A thin light filtered in through the linen curtains. The armoire hadn't moved. Nor had the chairs. But he couldn't hear anything over the din.

Ringing . . . buzzers . . . sirens. His alarm system!

Abner threw back the satin comforter and winced as his bare feet hit the cold hardwood floor. The police would be on their way, and he should remain up here where it was safe, and quiet.

But he kept thinking of the Renoir, out on the table, waiting for Hans to fix the frame. Someone was downstairs, among his precious art, pawing through his

Kristine Kathryn Rusch

trinkets, his livelihood. Someone had invaded his private domain.

And he wouldn't stand for it. He pulled on his bathrobe and unlocked the glass gun-cabinet. His fingers hesitated for a moment, then he took the Colt .45 off the rack. He had no bullets for it—he had no bullets for any of them—they were all part of his collection. But it didn't matter. In the dark, the Colt would look impressive.

He walked across the floor, careful to avoid the obvious creaks. The thief probably couldn't hear anything with the alarm system blaring—if the thief had remained once the thing went off. Most likely, the culprit disappeared as soon as the first wail echoed in the neighborhood.

Abner walked down the circular staircase, shivering as he went. He'd have to keep the heat up at night. He was going to catch his death. He held the gun in front of him, pleased that at least his hand was steady. His throat had gone dry, and he had to breathe through his mouth in order to keep quiet.

He strained to listen beneath the alarm, but the ringing, buzzing, blaring covered everything. Someone could be smashing the Degas statues and he wouldn't hear a thing. He would have to change that.

He got to the bottom of the stairs and resisted the urge to turn on a light. He walked slowly, noting with a sinking feeling that the Degas were missing from their pedestals. The jewelry cases stood open, and the walls looked bare.

The sirens grew louder, mocking him. He lowered the gun. No one was here. The thief had tricked him. He had taken everything, and then triggered the alarm.

Hide and Seek

Red and blue lights circled outside. Abner sank to his knees, no longer caring about the police's arrival.

Ellen huddled on the cot in the far corner of the gymnasium. She pulled the rough woolen blanket over her shoulders. It smelled of mothballs and her grandma's attic. She stifled an urge to sneeze. She rolled over to face the wall and pretended to be asleep.

She was one of the lucky ones. She had a cot. A lot of the kids were lying on mats on the floor, sharing blankets. Some of the kids were laughing and giggling, pretending this was an excuse for a slumber party, but Ellen knew better. Her daddy had argued when the police pulled her out of the house, but her mom stood quiet and white-faced. Ellen wanted her daddy now. He would help her. If he could. The only person he couldn't stand up to was Mom.

Ellen buried her face deeper into the pillow. In the morning, if they let her go home, Mom would be there, holding a wooden spoon and yelling. *You told, didn't you?* Mom had hissed before the police took Ellen out the door. Ellen hadn't had a chance to answer. The policemen had firm grips on her arms. They said she was in danger and they had to protect her. She glanced over her shoulder at Mom as the policemen put her in the car. Mom's arms were crossed in front of her chest, her mouth set in a familiar thin line.

Mom would get her when she got back. Even though Ellen said nothing, not even the day the counselor had pulled her out of class and asked if anyone hurt her at home. Not even then. *No,* Ellen had replied. *I'm just clumsy.* The counselor hadn't believed her, and neither had the doctor on the third visit. *How many times can a little girl break her arm in the same place?* the doctor had asked quietly as she examined the wound above the elbow. *Does somebody grab you there too hard, honey?*

Ellen had told Daddy once, a long time ago, and he had laughed. *Your mama is a passionate one,* he said.

Ellen closed her eyes, trying to drown out the whispers and the giggles. Someone had told. Someone had seen and told. That was what Mom thought when those government people came. She had hit Ellen even harder after that, only she made sure the bruises didn't show. Ellen had to sit out of gym for a week because it hurt to breathe.

And she would go home to that. In the morning. Mom would be there with her spoon and her thin mouth and her angry words.

But that was the morning, and it wasn't here yet. And maybe, just maybe, someone would take pity on her, and she would get to stay.

She huddled deeper under the blankets. She might even be able to keep the cot.

Bruce stood and stretched. The Bat Cave was cold, except in the one small corner where he sat. The computers and equipment kept that corner running hot.

"Tea?" Alfred asked.

Bruce whirled. Alfred set a tray on the table behind him. Next to the teapot was a plateful of hero sandwiches, stuffed almost six inches high with meat and veggies. They smelled wonderful. He couldn't remember the last time he ate.

He took one of the sandwiches and poured tea into the mug, then nodded his thanks to Alfred.

"Any progress?"

Bruce sighed and ran his fingers through his hair. "I don't know what it means yet, Alfred. All the information falls into patterns, but the patterns make no sense."

"Perhaps if you talk about it . . ."

Bruce took a bite of his sandwich. Salami, cheese, pickles, and onions. The Penguin would be able to smell him a mile off.

"All right, here's what we have," he said. His voice echoed in the cave's vastness. Above him, the bats rustled. He took another bite of the sandwich, chewed and swallowed before going on. "All of the kids, at least those our witnesses saw, disappeared after receiving a stuffed penguin. The penguin would fall from a great height, or be placed somewhere obvious where the kid couldn't miss it. The kid would grab the toy, there would be a noise, the observer would look away, and then the kid would be gone. No trace, no note.

"The kids are all linked by their unhappy childhoods and their relative poverty. Rich kids have unhappy childhoods, too"—Bruce paused and stared at his sandwich for a moment, then took a savage bite from it—"but the Penguin doesn't seem concerned with that, even though the rich kids would be the obvious target.

"It doesn't follow any logic, Alfred, at least not any logic that would make him money."

Alfred handed Bruce a napkin. "It seems to me that a profit-motive may not be at stake here."

Bruce wiped his mouth, then set the sandwich down. "What are you saying, Alfred?"

"Have you ever read *Oliver Twist*?"

Bruce's stomach flopped. He had read *Oliver Twist*. He remembered quite vividly the scenes with the criminal Fagan, who taught the boys he cared for how to steal for him. "Are you saying he might be doing a Fagan?"

Alfred shrugged. "I simply think you must look at all the possibilities."

"That changes everything," Bruce said, turning back to the computer banks. "I'm going to have to look at the figures again."

Commissioner Gordon stood in the center of the gallery. All the lights blazed. Track lighting illuminated the places where framed art once hung—a small penguin sticker marking each picture that had been removed. The soft lighting over the statue pedestals revealed little penguin toys, and a penguin robot had its plastic hand blocking a motion detector.

The penguin robot had set off the alarm, after all the work was done.

Abner Markowitz still wore his bathrobe. His hair was tousled. He sat behind a glass desk, watching the police, with no hope in his eyes.

Markowitz had the best gallery in town. It included one-of-a-kind items, like a Rembrandt sketch appraised at $1.2 million. Gordon had checked out the security system himself and had pronounced it the best in the world.

And now this.

Whoever had done the work had been in the gallery for an hour, maybe more, to set everything with such precision. Plus managing to carry off the art without

anyone hearing. Markowitz stated he had been
awakened by the alarm, and his bedroom was in a loft
off a circular stairway. Sound would have carried easily into that loft. The thieves had to be very quiet.

Gordon poured a cup of coffee from the cut-glass
coffeepot standing over in the corner. He carried the
cup to Markowitz and sat across from him. "I'm sorry,
Abner," he said.

Markowitz waved his hand. "You did all you could,"
he said. "The system was the best money could buy."

"I think we'll be able to get it all back."

Markowitz smiled. "Save it for the other customers,
Commissioner. I appreciate the sentiment, but it
makes no difference to me whether or not the merchandise gets returned. The insurance will cover my expenses."

"We know who did this," Gordon said. "It's just a
matter of tracking him down."

"I'm still ruined." Markowitz's voice was soft. "In
my business, making the deal is the crucial thing. I
have hundreds of contacts, all of whom believe that
my world is safe—they can trust me with their precious
items. Well, my world is no longer safe, and with the
appearance of those little penguin stickers, gaudy as
they are, my contacts will disappear like—" he smiled
bitterly, "like a thief in the night."

Gordon patted Markowitz's hand and stood up. He
wished Batman were here. Something bothered him.
Something about the caper struck him as odd. He
wanted to discuss it with someone who saw beyond
the trails of evidence, who looked for patterns and
thought in a nonlinear fashion.

He sighed. It wasn't worth using the Bat-signal. Bat-

Kristine Kathryn Rusch

man was already tracking the Penguin. When they found the children, they would find the art. It had to work that way.

He threw back the tail of his tuxedo so that he wouldn't have to sit on it. Then he sat on the rolling stool and gazed at the Rembrandt sketch. It was nothing, really. One night's doodling for the master. A charcoal line here, another there, depicting a European street. The sketch wasn't even completed.

One point two million dollars. And now that he stole it, he would probably be able to sell it for more.

He gazed at the Degas sculpture, ran a gloved hand over the ballerina's well-carved head. Beautiful, but not as beautiful as the living children he'd been stealing for the past week.

"Well done," he said. He stood and the stool rolled away. An assistant caught it before it knocked over a statue at the end of the concrete floor. The warehouse was cold. He would have to get someone to check on the proper temperature for art storage.

Two other assistants stood by the warehouse doors. "Begin making a few inquiries about who might be interested in all of this," he said. "Subtle inquiries."

He grabbed the gold-handled umbrella and headed out of the warehouse. A year ago, he would have checked all of the merchandise, but now he had other things on his mind.

"And," he said as he stopped in front of his assistants, "I think the Gotham Night Depository might be a suitable next target."

Hide and Seek

Tyson sat under the overpass, listening to cars rumble on the concrete overhead. The river ran beneath him, its oily waters cold and uninviting. He sniffled and wiped his nose with his sleeve. He managed to smear the dirt, but it didn't matter. There was no one here to care.

He crouched over and hugged his knees to his chest. He hadn't eaten in almost twenty-four hours, and then he had had a box of stale crackers. Cops were everywhere, in every alley it seemed, near every Dumpster. He couldn't even go in a store and lift something. They all seemed to be looking for him.

That's what Mac had warned him about before they hitchhiked to Gotham. "At some point, the cops will know you, and then they'll want you to keep moving, to get out of their way. They'll dog you and pick you up, and make you leave their town. So you can't stay in one place too long. Got that, kid?"

Tyson had nodded. He understood, but he never thought it applied. He thought Mac was too obvious, too big and too slow. Tyson could slide in and out of places undetected. He could get into little cubbyholes that adult men couldn't even see. He had been on the street longer than Mac thought he had, and he knew tricks Mac hadn't even thought of yet.

But he had never seen cops comb the homeless community like this. It scared him. He didn't understand it. And he wasn't sure what, exactly, they were looking for.

A rustle beside him made him jump. He glanced over, careful not to make a sound. A stuffed animal rested in the joining between the overpass and the dirt. Some kid must have left it there.

Kristine Kathryn Rusch

He looked away again, disappointed that it wasn't food.

Then a shiver ran through him. The penguin hadn't been there before. He hadn't seen it, and it was too new to be left lying in the dirt. Someone had put it there.

He didn't want to go to it, but he did want to at the same time. He was afraid some cop had put it there to catch him and lead him out of town. But he didn't know why they would try such a ploy with him. He was too old for toys. They would have done better to leave him food.

He stared at it for a minute, and the toy stared back. It had cold glass eyes and a wide beak. Its fake fur was black and white, and it had wings instead of arms. A penguin.

Careful to remain quiet, he slithered across the dirt toward it. Then he grabbed it with his right hand, keeping balance with his left. The penguin squawked, and he dropped it, heart pounding.

No one came. Nothing happened. He was safe.

He reached for the penguin again.

He crouched on the roof, cape wrapped around him, hood protecting him from the world. The night was black, but the yellow glow of the streetlight illuminated the tight walkways between the warehouses.

The Gotham police were doing a good job finding the children and giving them shelter, but he wanted to find children that the police hadn't yet.

He had found one small boy, sleeping on a pile of newspapers between the deserted warehouses. He had watched the boy lie down shortly after nightfall, and had crouched in position, remaining motionless, pretending to be part of the building.

He was about to shift slightly to keep the blood flowing when he heard the whisper of footsteps on the roof across from him. Batman kept his breathing quiet and watched as two thin figures, dressed in black, approached the edge of the roof.

"Told you he'd be here," one of the figures said softly. "The cops haven't gotten this far out yet."

"We need to signal Clyde," said the other.

"You do it. I'll get the bait down there."

One of the figures pulled a walkie-talkie from his belt and spoke softly into it. The other pulled out a stuffed penguin and attached its collar to a thin wire. Then the figure laid out flat and slowly eased the penguin over the edge.

Batman watched the toy. He didn't care about the men. They couldn't help him—at least, not yet. The toy landed with a small squawk right next to the sleeping child.

The boy stirred and rubbed his eyes. Batman quietly attached the line to the edge of the roof, so that he could swoop down if he had to.

The boy stretched and was about to lie back down, when his hand brushed the toy. The penguin squawked again and the boy jumped back, startled. Then he reached a tentative hand forward and touched the toy.

When nothing happened, the boy grabbed the penguin like a drowning man would clutch a life preserver. The toy squawked, and then something fell near the entry to the walkway.

Batman resisted the urge to glance in the direction

of the new sound. He kept his gaze on the boy. The boy closed his eyes, and two figures stepped out of the shadows. They cradled the boy in their arms and carried him out to the street.

The figures on the other roof were gone. Batman stood and hurried down the side of the building, calling the Batmobile as he went. The 'mobile pulled up to the curb and he followed the car with the boy, careful to keep a good distance so that he wouldn't be seen.

The car weaved through backstreets until it reached the hills outside Gotham. It turned on a dirt road in a small copse of trees. Batman followed, his fingers tightly gripping the wheel. The road bumped and jostled along, the Batmobile's wheels balancing each thump. Leaves flew around him, and the road grew tougher to follow. Finally it disappeared altogether.

He stopped the 'mobile and got out. The evening air was crisp and cold, and smelled faintly of damp earth. Nothing except a thin stand of birches surrounded him, and his were the only tire tracks within sight.

There had to be an entrance somewhere. He had lost them in a place as hidden as the entrance to the Bat-cave.

He would find it.

Commissioner Gordon wiped the sleep from his eyes as he sped down the empty streets. The call had awakened him from restless sleep, one in which he was dreaming of Rembrandts and children's toys. He turned the corner and saw lights blazing at the Gotham Night Depository. Red and blue lights whirled against the building's whitewashed surface, and at least twenty officers milled under the orange glow of the streetlight.

The building itself poured light into the street. All the doors were open, illuminating the growing crowd.

Gordon suppressed a sigh. He hoped that someone had thought to secure the perimeter.

He got out of the car and pulled his jacket closer. Voices echoed in the night along with the rumble of car engines. He walked up to the officer in charge.

"How bad?" he asked.

The detective shook his head. "Empty."

Gordon ran a hand through his silver hair. "Who responded to the call?"

"Gilroy. Saw the perps."

Gordon pushed his way past the milling officers. They had put up a police line and two rookies were enforcing it with unusual care. Gilroy was sitting on a squad, a white cloth pressed to his forehead. Blood had run down his cheek and caked on his chin.

"Sergeant," Gordon said.

"Commissioner." Gilroy sounded tired.

"Have you had someone look at that?"

"It's a bump." Gilroy pulled the cloth down so Gordon could see. A bump was forming just under Gilroy's hairline, and a long ragged cut ran just above it. The skin was already turning purple from the force of the blow.

"When we're done talking, I want you to get to Gotham General. Is that clear?"

"Yes, sir." Gilroy put the cloth back against his skull. "It's bleeding a lot, but then head wounds always do."

Gordon sat down beside him. The car's hood was cold. "Tell me about it."

Gilroy didn't look at Gordon. "Issac and I—that's Sergeant Isaac Nelson, sir—we've had this beat for two years, and we usually go past the depository once an hour. The lot's well lit, as you can see, and we've never seen a car in it. The nightman takes the bus to and from work, and he's—he was—there for more than twenty years."

The nightman was dead, then, Gordon thought. It kept getting messier and messier.

"So, when we saw two black sedans in the parking lot, parked near the Dumpster so they'd be hard to see, we got nervous. Isacc stopped near the front door, and I buzzed so that the nightman would let us in."

Gilroy slouched a little more. The air smelled of blood and sweat.

"The next bit all happened so fast. It was like each second took an hour. I was looking through the double-doors and I saw him, sir, spread out on the floor, and blood oozing its way from under his desk. I yelled to Isaac that there was trouble and he should call for backup, when alarms started going off in the whole building. At first I thought I done it, you know? But then I saw these guys running for the door. I tried to back away, but I didn't get out of the way fast enough. They were as surprised to see me as I was to see them. One of them pulled a gun, but the other one said, no, not too much killing, and so the guy swung the butt at my head. I went down, pulling my own gun, but by the time I raised it, Isaac was bent over me, pushing my hand away. I guess I blacked out. The sirens were wailing and the alarms buzzing, and the nightman was dead on the floor. Isaac wanted me to sit, but I went upstairs, thinking maybe another guy was on

duty and he was alive—I wasn't thinking too clearly—
but I stopped moving when I got to the vaults. I thought
I was seeing stuff. You know, those penguins
everywhere. I thought I was flashing back to the kid—"

"What kid?" Gordon asked.

"A few nights ago, I saw one of them kids disappear.
I wrote a report—"

"What does that have to do with the vaults?"

"The stuffed penguins, everywhere. They're just like
the one that the kid grabbed before he disappeared."

A little frisson of excitement ran through Gordon.
Maybe things would turn around for them. Maybe the
stuffed penguins were actually a break. "Thanks,
Sergeant," Gordon said. "That helps. I'll get someone
to take you to Gotham General."

He spoke briefly to one of the detectives to get a ride
for Gilroy, then he headed into the building.

The depository still had the stifling hot feeling of
an enclosed building. The forensics teams were ex-
amining the corpses, the photographer getting ready to
take pictures. "I want to see the vaults," Gordon said
to a nearby detective.

"Sure thing, sir," the detective said. He led Gordon
up a flight of metal steps to the second floor. The large
elevator was being dusted for prints and so was out of
commission.

The doors to the vaults were wide open. Gordon
walked through them and his breath left his body. It
was like walking into an F.A.O. Schwarz display. Dozens of stuffed penguins sat on all of the shelves, as if
left in trade for the missing cash.

Gordon picked one up. It squawked. A small hole
appeared in its beak as it made the sound, and then
disappeared as the sound ceased. He handed the pen-

guin to the detective. "Let's analyze these," he said. "And see if they're the same as the ones at the gallery site. Then let's see if we can find out who makes them— and who ordered them in quantity."

"Yes, sir," the detective said in a tone that told Gorden they were already on that trail. Good. That meant he would get the answers quicker. And be just that much closer to putting that Penguin creature behind bars.

Scotty put his head on the arm of the couch, pulled his blanket beside him, and tucked his thumb in his mouth. The couch smelled like Daddy's coat, the one he said Scotty couldn't touch. The couch was soft like Daddy's coat. Leather, the policeman had said. The policeman covered Scotty wtih a quilt and then had asked another policeman if he thought Scotty would wet the couch.

"I don't pee the bed," Scotty said in his best grownup voice. Only babies did that. He closed his eyes, but all he could see was Daddy's hand yanking him from bed, the smell of pee in the air. Scotty remembered how much it hurt, the last time he had peed the bed, and so he tried to use the bathroom three and four times a night. It didn't always work, but he and Mommy had been able to hide the mess before Daddy found it.

"I hope not," the policeman said, "or the Commissioner will have my hide."

They had given Scotty a room to himself. The other kids were downstairs in the great big cold hallway. They tried to put Scotty down there, but he had acted like a baby, screaming and crying and having bad dreams. It was just that some of the kids were so big.

In the dark, he thought they were Daddy, and he didn't want them to touch him.

The policemen were wondering if they should take him to see a doctor. They had gasped when they took off his clothes. The "owies" hurt, but Scotty always hurt. Daddy said it made him tough.

The policeman ruffled Scotty's hair. "We're going to take good care of you, little guy," he said.

Scotty smiled at him, then snuggled deeper in the couch. The policeman said there was a bathroom through the side door, a private bathroom that Scotty could use whenever he wanted.

And, they said, Daddy would never hurt him again.

Daddy would be really mad.

But if the police protected him, it wouldn't matter. Would it?

Bruce Wayne felt a tightness in the pit of his stomach. He gripped the car's upholstered seat and forced himself to relax. He had a lot to do today, too much to let old memories overcome him.

But, in those few hours of sleep he got every night, he saw faces, children's faces, tear-streaked and alone, trapped with a man holding a gun. Once he woke up, hugging his pillow so tightly that it had burst. Feathers coated his sweat-covered body. He had cleaned up the room in silence, then had gone down to the Bat Cave to see what else he could find.

Nothing. Statistics and patterns were no longer the answer. He had to explore that section of woods and find out where the car had gone.

First, though, he had to expiate some guilt.

Kristine Kathryn Rusch

Alfred stopped the car in front of city hall, and Bruce let himself out. He ran up the stairs, his suede coat flapping behind him. A group of adults stood halfway up, holding signs. LET OUR CHILDREN GO, one read. CHILDREN = POLICE HOSTAGES, read another.

Bruce ignored them as he made his way to the wide double-doors.

A police officer stood in front of them, arms crossed.

"I would like to see the Commissioner," Bruce said.

"Have you business with him?" the officer asked.

"He's not expecting me," Bruce said, "but he'll be happy to see me."

"Give me your card," the officer said. "I'll see if he wants to speak with you."

Bruce handed the officer a business card. The officer opened the door and handed the card to another officer inside. Through the doors, Bruce could see cots spread out all over the marble floor.

"Isn't this supposed to be a public access building?" Bruce asked.

"We're making room for the homeless in it right now, sir. We've had a rash of kidnappings. We can't just let anyone in."

Bruce nodded, then rocked on the balls of his feet. So they had used his ideas after all. Good. He knew they were using the high school gymnasium, and the grade school, too. He had never expected that so many children needed protection. And these were only the children of the poor. He wondered how much space they would need if they added the children of the rich and the middle class.

The inner door opened. "He will see you, sir," the second officer said.

Hide and Seek

Bruce thanked him and went inside. The picketers
let out a scream of protest that he could hear through
the closing door. He walked across the mat to the other
set of doors and opened it to a cacophony of sound.

Kids laughing, crying, shouting. Balls bouncing. All
echoing across the marble floor, the marble staircase,
the huge marble dome above them. People in the offices
had to be going crazy.

A few kids were sitting on cots, playing jacks. Others
were playing with dolls. A few more had a card game
going in the middle of the floor. Most, however, were
curled away from each other, huddled over books or
comic books, or just staring at the wall.

All were too thin, and most sported bruises on their
arms and legs.

Bruce walked around them, and up the marble staircase to the Commissioner's office. The sound magnified
with each step he took, and the overheated air smelled
of child sweat and dirt.

When he reached the second-floor balcony, he noted
that all the glass office-doors were closed. People were
hunched over their desks as if they could block the
noise with their bodies. This, clearly, was a very temporary solution.

The door to Commissioner Gordon's office was open.
His secretary, a stout woman with a genial face, waved
him forward.

"He's expecting you, Mr. Wayne," she said.

As Bruce walked by her, he noted that she wore a
Walkman, and its volume switch was on maximum.

He knocked on the stout oak-door, then turned the
knob and went in. The Commissioner sat behind his
wide desk, a cup of coffee in his hand. When he saw

Kristine Kathryn Rusch

Bruce, he put a finger to his lips and nodded toward the couch.

A towheaded little boy slept there, thumb in his mouth, ragged blanket clutched in his small hands. Both the boy's eyes were black-and-blue, and his cheekbones shone prominently in his face.

Gordon stood and led Bruce back into the reception area.

"He's sleeping like the dead," Gordon said, "but I didn't want to wake him. Somehow I think it's been a long time since he's slept this deeply."

"When I heard all this on the news, I had no idea things were so bad," Bruce said.

Gordon shruged. "We know the statistics. One in four families have reported instances of abuse. But we didn't go by that. We went by guess and by golly, using hospital records, suspicions, and aborted police reports. Most of these kids will have to go back to their families when this is over. Unless they're willing to admit something has happened. We've got social workers talking to all of them, but it's a delicate balance. The worker can't put any suggestion of abuse in the kid's head or the court will throw out the case. But abused kids are trained not to talk about what goes on in the home. It breaks my heart."

The tightness had returned to Bruce's stomach. He had no idea either. He also had no idea how regulated the system was. He supposed it made sense. It was better to keep a kid in family than move the kid out— assuming that the family was loving. And who could prove that?

"I came to help with the efforts," he said. "There's not much I can do. I have very little time to volunteer.

But I have resources to share. I came here prepared to give the city fifty thousand dollars to help in the short-term crisis, but that's probably not enough. I'll double the amount, and you must promise me, Commissioner, that you'll get in touch with me if you need more."

"I—" The Commissioner glanced back at his office, as if looking at the kid for reassurance. "I—that's very generous of you, Mr. Wayne. Beyond generous. I'm sure that the fifty thousand dollars will be more than adequate."

"I don't think so. We'll start with one hundred thousand dollars," Bruce said. "The more I'm discovering about this problem, the more I realize that throwing money at it is only the beginning." He wandered back into the Commissioner's office and looked at the sleeping boy. How had he failed them? All of them? He had vowed to stop crime, to protect the city, and that had certainly meant the children as well.

"We can only do so much," the Commissioner said softly behind him. "Imagine the ramifications if we took a child out of a good home, just on suspicion. There the child was doing fine, and we would ruin his life."

Bruce shook his head, then turned and faced the Commissioner. The expression on the Commissioner's face reflected his own. Things were easier when criminals stole or killed or shot someone. When it got down to the complexities of family interactions, simple solutions didn't work.

"Let's go back out front," Bruce said. "I'll write you that check."

Kristine Kathryn Rusch

He tugged at his white gloves, then leaned on the gold birdhead on the handle of his umbrella. Stacks and stacks of money surrounded him, some piled almost to the ceiling of the warehouse. His associates stood at the door. He doubted he could trust them with this kind of money, but then there was so much here that it hardly mattered.

"Better," he said. "We can use this. Perhaps we should go for a few banks and armored cars next."

"Perhaps," one of the associates said in a very hesitant voice, "we should lie low for a while."

"No." He tugged at the sleeves of his tuxedo, then began to pace. "We need to continue the diversions, at least until we have what we want. They're still too focused on the children. We have to stop that."

The associates remained quiet while he walked back and forth. The money smelled green and oily. He loved that scent. Finally, he stopped walking.

"Let's hire a few thugs. Hand them a wadful of this stuff. Tell them nothing. Have them do some small jobs for us until they get caught."

"If we handle it, no one will get caught," as associate said.

He rapped the floor with the tip of his umbrella. Once. The sound echoed. "The point is," he said in as measured a tone as he could manage, "for them to get caught. We want the police to spend their time interrogating people who don't know a thing. We want the police off our backs. In fact, let's fill these hirelings with a few erroneous details, and let them lead our good friends at the Gotham police department on a wild—Penguin—chase."

He laughed, the distinctive sound making his associates wince. He turned to his nearest associate, a black woman who looked resplendent in black and white. "Make sure these thugs know nothing about us," he said. "Not this room, not the children, nothing. But do give them a few stuffed toys. The more we can mislead, the better. Understood?"

"Understood," she said.

He laughed again. The authorities weren't even close.

Batman stood in the copse of trees. It looked different in the daylight. The birches were evenly spaced, the leaves covering the ground with the precision of a Bateman painting. The dual tire-tracks had gone to this place. His continued on alone.

He had already explored the ground and found no obvious opening. Yet something had to be here, something big enough to swallow a car—and quickly. Most likely something that could be activated by remote control.

He kicked the leaves aside and finally found what he was looking for.

The loose dirt became solid across a thin, almost invisible, line. He bent down and rubbed his hand across the line. The loose dirt rolled beneath his fingertips, but the solid stuff scratched his palm. It felt familiar, like outdoor carpet or Astroturf.

Most of the leaves had been glued in place on top of the dyed Astroturf. Others had been scattered loosely. He followed the thin line all the way around and found that it made a rectangle more than large enough to swallow a car. The earth had a slight depression, leading him to believe that the road underneath the fake roof sloped downward.

Kristine Kathryn Rusch

He pictured the map of Gotham in his head. He stood on acres of publicly owned land that ended in a nature conservatory for migratory birds. Birds. Hmm. He remembered when the conservatory was formed. The main benefactor had asked to remain anonymous.

He pulled a small device from the belt around his waist. He pressed a few buttons and the device whirred and chugged, searching for the electronic pattern that ordered the rectangle to open. Such devices were illegal, since they often broke security codes, but he didn't care. He had to fight crime with its own weapons sometimes. He knew that the Penguin had this device, or else he wouldn't have been able to break into both the depository and the gallery.

Something creaked behind him. Batman turned. The rectangle stood open. It had raised to twice his height, and chill air came from the paved roadway below.

He put the device back on his belt, wrapped his cape around himself, and walked into the darkness.

The sound of a flushing toilet made Gordon look up. He had been studying the check. Wayne's signature had a flourish. And the amount. Gordon wasn't quite sure how to allocate the amount. He supposed it wasn't his problem. That was something the city had to decide.

The door to his private bath stood open. The couch was empty, the quilt pushed back against a bottom cushion. The towheaded kid came out of the bathroom, still clutching his blanket, thumb tucked in his mouth. He saw Gordon and stopped.

"Hi." The small voice trembled.

"Hi," Gordon said.

The little boy's black-and-blue eyes gave him the

round-eyed look of a raccoon. He walked with a slight limp. Gordon wondered what other bruises hid under the too-small clothes.

"My daddy coming?"

Gordon shook his head.

The little boy smiled, revealing a mouth only half full of teeth. "Good," he said, walking back to the couch. He sat down, letting his bare feet dangle off the edge. "Can I have something to eat? I know how to make a peanut butter sandwich."

The comment made Gordon's heart ache. He didn't know how to make his own food at that small age. The child had offered his ability like a shield to deflect anger. Gordon stuck the check in his wallet. Its dispersement had just become his responsibility. He was going to make sure the funds went to the right place.

The air got colder as Batman followed the road. The darkness had lessened. Fluorescent lights appeared on the ceiling—a few at first, and more as he continued walking. When he could no longer see the entrance, he noted frost had formed on the rock-slab walls. Just ahead, water dripped.

He had walked almost three miles before the road turned to the right. He could see his breath, and small patches of black ice had covered the roadway. If he hadn't been expecting it, he would have had a nasty fall.

To his left, a small fleet of cars were parked behind a rock. He walked over to them. The car he had followed was there, along with several others of the same make and model. He noted the license plates, but he doubted they would tell him anything.

Kristine Kathryn Rusch

The cold had seeped in through his cape. He usually didn't feel temperatures. He wondered just what the temperature was down here.

He left the cars and followed the sound of dripping water. He rounded another corner, and what he saw took his breath away.

A large underground lake opened into the distance. Chunks of ice floated on its surface. Miniature icebergs. Most looked solid. The road ended at the water's edge.

If he hadn't known before who was behind all this, he knew now. He doubted that the area around Gotham naturally supported this kind of environment. When he reached the surface again, if he hadn't found the children, he would not only check those license plates, he would check on the land ownership and the power bills. Someone had to know about the extensive deep freeze down here.

A splash made him turn. A group of penguins—real penguins—stood at the end of an ice floe. Their little bodies quivered, wings flapping with excitement. One of them was in the water. Then it emerged with a fish in its mouth. This place was even more elaborate than he'd thought.

He couldn't see the end of the lake. He had to find a way across it, though. He knew that what he was looking for rested on the other side.

Gordon found a small stain on the center of his couch. Someone had tried to wipe it away, and the leather was turning white. He touched the spot and brought his fingers to his nose. Ammonia. He smiled, not angry at all.

Little Scotty had already been checked out by the doctor. *Clear case of abuse,* the doctor said. *I'll testify to it, and the kid's young enough. He might, too.*

The doctor took Scotty to the hospital for tests, to make sure there was no serious internal damages. Gordon had sent the police photographer to take pictures. He wanted to nail the parents in the most serious way.

The little boy couldn't have been more than three, and already he had known more pain than most people knew in a lifetime.

After the hospital was through with him, Scotty would move into foster care, and with luck—since he was young enough—he might find a permanent home with a family capable of loving him.

Gordon shook his head. He had had no clue . . .

A knock on his office door made him stand up. Before he could bid the person to enter, the door flew open. One of the rookies stood there, papers clutched in his hands.

"We found it, sir!" the young officer said. "It's a plant down on Fifty-ninth Street. Been there for years."

Gordon walked over to his desk, taking the papers out of the officer's hands as he passed. "Found what?"

"The toy factory. They're local. They assemble those penguins in-house. They got a special order about a month ago to make two thousand of the things. The owner almost said no, because they're not child-proof. They got one of those squeak boxes inside—you know, the kind young kids can swallow—and they have a tube leading to a hollow stomach. There's a little opening in the penguin's back where you can fill that stomach with water."

"Water." Gordon sat down on his desk. "And what happens when you squeeze the penguin?"

Kristine Kathryn Rusch

"It makes this awful noise, and water spurts out of its mouth."

"Water." Gordon said again. He templed his fingers and bounced them against his chin. "Have the stomachs of all those penguins we confiscated checked. Then bring in Abner and ask him if he noticed anything unusual about his sleep habits that night his gallery got broken into. And see if you can trace who placed that order."

"Yes, sir," the rookie said. He left the room, closing the door behind him.

Water. Those penguins hadn't been filled with water. They had something else in there. Something that probably rendered the person who squeezed the toy unconscious. Then the person could be moved with the minimum of fuss.

He wanted to contact Batman, to let him know about the latest discovery, but he didn't want to use the Bat-signal. If the Penguin didn't know that Batman was working on the case, so much the better.

They had taken a tiny, tiny step. But it made him feel better, all the same.

Boats were lined up like sentries on the edge of the lake.

They were small, three-person canoes, and they were all white, to blend in with the ice floes.

Batman pulled one higher on-shore and investigated it for alarms and tracking devices, but he found nothing. It bothered him that he couldn't find any security equipment on this side of the lake. Was the Penguins so cocky that he believed no one would find this place? Or did he think that people would stop at the lake and go no farther?

Or did he have a different plan?

Batman eased the canoe into the water and grabbed the paddle. He stroked the water with an ease born of experience, careful not to splash himself since water that cold was deadly.

The farther he went forward, the farther he went into a trap. Something this elaborate had to be guarded. But he was prepared. He would see what he could find.

He steered the canoe around the small icebergs and ice floes. The only sounds around him were the drip of water and the soft splashes his paddle made as he pushed his way along.

The penguins stood in cluttered rows, watching him as he passed. Their bright eyes shone in the reflected light. One of them chattered at him. He raised a hand and waved at it, wondering if such creatures could be happy here, away from the natural light and their traditional world.

Bats were happy in caves, but bats were creatures of the night. His creatures.

He wondered what kind of creatures these penguins really were.

The mayor stared at the check that Gordon had placed on his desk. He made no move to take it. "We've got to give the kids back," he said.

Gordon thought about the voices raised in laughter at the city building. The social workers had just begun their work. A few kids were being placed in the custody

Kristine Kathryn Rusch

of the state, but most didn't talk at all. Some said they wanted to go home.

"I don't think they're safe if they go home," Gordon said.

The mayor shrugged. "We have no legal grounds to hold them. One of the country's best-known lawyers just called me, said the parents are filing a class-action suit against the city. Something about breaking up homes without cause."

Gordon's stomach churned. "We have cause," he said. "Those kids—"

"Those kids belong with their families," the mayor said. "We haven't gone through the normal procedures to hold them. We can't farm them into foster care because we don't have the right. The parents have the law behind them on this one."

"We didn't pick them up because of the abuse," Gordon said.

"The hell we didn't! We chose those kids because they were the most likely to be abducted, and one of the things we looked for were signs of abuse."

"And poverty. Poverty's not a crime, is it? And homelessness. Homelessness isn't a crime in this city, either, last time I checked the books."

"We have vagrancy laws," the mayor mumbled.

"They've been on the books since the twenties and they haven't been enforced since the forties. No court would uphold those." Gordon was shaking. Through the large windows of the mayor's plush office, he could see the spirals of Gotham City. "Why don't you tell that attorney to lay off us? We're trying to protect people. Why don't you tell him to go after the real criminals so that we can return these people to their homes?"

Hide and Seek

"Because," the mayor said, "then he'll go after you."

Gordon sighed and sank into an upholstered chair near the mayor's desk. "We have some leads. We think we're going somewhere."

"And Batman?"

Gordon shook his head. "I haven't heard from him in almost two days. I'm thinking of using the Bat-signal, but I don't want the Penguin to know that Batman is on his trail."

"He probably already knows," the mayor said.

"Look," Gordon said. "We need a way to forestall those parents until we get this thing resolved. Can't you declare a state of emergency or something? We can't lose more kids to this man."

The mayor ran his hands through his hair. "I don't like being placed in this position, Gordon. If I send the kids back, and they get kidnapped, it's my neck. If I don't, those parents are going to cause trouble."

"Look, Bruce Wayne has given one hundred thousand dollars to feed and house those kids properly. If we hold a fund-raiser, I'm sure there are others in this community who would donate money, too. Declare a state of emergency. Let's protect these kids as best we can."

"And what happens if we don't catch him?" the mayor asked.

Gordon knew that the remark came out of fear, but it angered him nonetheless. "We'll catch him," he said. "We have to."

Max huddled in a corner of the dark room. Through the small, barred window, a thin ray of sunlight illumi-

Kristine Kathryn Rusch

nated the floor. He was cold, but then he was always cold. If he was lucky, his mom would give him something to eat today.

The room was empty except for the wood floors and the rough paneling covering the walls. He had been in here for almost a month now, leaving only to dump the Port-a-potty out once every two days. He couldn't even remember what he had done wrong. All the events blurred. Maybe he had said hi to the neighbor girl. Maybe he had picked his nose. Maybe he had spoken during dinner. The crime was long gone, but the punishment remained.

Something blocked the light at the window. He crouched, afraid someone would see him, afraid they were thinking he had done something wrong. Then he heard a loud crash, and glass tinkled all over the floor.

In the middle of the broken glass sat a stuffed penguin.

"Noooo," he wailed. It was some kind of trap. Now his mother would come in and think he had done this, he had caused the window to get broken. All he had done was sit there, but she would punish him just the same.

He listened, but heard nothing else. There was still light outside, so maybe his mother was at work. She usually stayed at work until after dark.

A chill breeze blowing in through the broken window made him shiver. If he could clean up the glass and hide it in his Port-a-potty, he could dump it the next time she let him outside. She rarely stayed in the room. She wouldn't notice the broken window or the cold. Not if he was careful.

He crawled across the floor, careful not to cut his

bare skin on any of the glass. He cupped one hand and picked up pieces with the other. When he reached the penguin, he stopped.

It was beautiful. Bits of glass were on top of its black head, and they shone in the thin sunlight. Its eyes seemed friendly and its fur looked soft. He wished he had a place to hide it, too. A place where it would be safe.

He reached out with his empty hand and knocked the pieces of glass off its head. The penguin seemed to smile at him. He wanted to take it against his bare chest and hold it there, to keep him warm, to have something to play with.

But maybe his mom was outside. Maybe she had thrown the penguin to him to test him. He glanced up at the window and saw nothing. Just the jagged bits of glass where the pane had broken.

He set the glass in his other hand down. He would hold it, just for a minute. For a minute, he would pretend he was a normal kid. For a minute, he would have something to love.

He pulled the penguin toward him, and it squawked. He screamed and dropped it, his heart hammering against his chest. She had trapped him. She had. He felt dizzy. He felt weak. He felt—

He slumped against the cold, glass-covered floor. As his eyes closed, he heard a door smack open.

He leaned forward on his umbrella, gloved hands clutching the gold handle. The security monitors sent black-and-white shadows in the darkened room. The guard, half hidden in the dim light, put her fingers over the control panel.

Kristine Kathryn Rusch

"You want me to warn the others?" she asked.

"No." He crouched a little, the tail of his tuxedo brushing against the black-and-white tile floor. The canoe looked small against the icebergs. Batman's dark uniform stood in perfect contrast to the white world around him. "I expected him."

"Sir?"

He sighed, not really wanting to explain, but not wanting the silence either. "When the city doesn't know what to do, they send for this man. He has caused me more problems over the years than anyone else. I think it's time we finally deal with him."

The guard put her hands on her black trousers. "You took those children to get at Batman?"

He put his pince-nez against his eye and stared at her coldly for a moment. "The children have nothing to do with him," he said.

"Then why—?"

He waved a white-gloved hand and silenced her. "Do you like your job?"

"Yes, sir."

"Does it pay you well?"

"Yes, sir."

"Do you have good benefits?"

"Yes, sir."

"Do you think I'm odd?"

"Sir?"

"Honesty," he said, clutching his umbrella closer, "is something I value in my employees."

"Eccentric, maybe, sir."

"And knowing that, why did you question me?"

"I was curious, sir."

He took two deep breaths to calm his anger. "I don't pay my employees to be curious." He got up, using his umbrella as a cane, and walked to the door. "Let me know when he finds the children," he said, and let himself out.

Underneath his gloves, his fingers had gone numb. Batman felt the cold seep under his clothing and into his skin. He had to stop soon, or go back for cold-weather gear.

He didn't want to go back.

He was close. He knew it.

The walls of the underground passage were covered in ice. Except for the floating icebergs, there was nothing solid to pull the canoe against. There had to be surveillance equipment somewhere inside this cavern—after all, the lighting continued, even though he went far into the cavern's depths—so he suspected someone knew about his arrival.

He didn't like not having the cover of darkness. Or the element of surprise. But sometimes going boldly into the face of an enemy had more power than any other action. He wondered if that would work with the Penguin.

Up ahead, he saw a row of additional lights. More penguins floated by on ice floes. They watched him like tiny sentries. He wondered if they were vicious birds, then decided it didn't matter. He would not provoke them.

He went around a slight corner and saw brown dirt extending up a long hill. If they had brought the children here, they had to do so one at a time. Unless they had other boats, more powerful boats, that held more people. And he doubted that those boats would be safe against the ice floes and icebergs.

Kristine Kathryn Rusch

He paddled the canoe toward what looked like a beach. The lights had grown brigher, illuminating the black water, reflecting off the ice. As he got closer to the rock beach, he noted doors built into the rock walls. He scanned the area for another entry and saw nothing.

If the surveillance equipment hadn't caught him already, it would catch him when he opened one of those doors.

For a moment, he toyed with going back. Since the doors were elevated from the lake, they probably had another entrance, one someone could get to from outside. If he used that entrance, he might be safer. But if he used that entrance, the Penguin might have the chance to hide everything.

Batman rowed to shore, then used his paddle to bring him in close. He got out, boots submerged in the frigid water, and pulled the canoe on the rock beach. Its bottom scraped against the rocks, making a squealing sound that echoed in the underground cavern. He glanced around, but saw no one else. The penguins continued staring at him from their perches on the ice.

He had never felt so alone before, on any of his cases. Something about this place made him feel as if he had no home, no place to return to. Something here made it feel as if time had stopped, and refused to take him with it.

With a sudden movement, he put the canoe behind a rock, in case he needed a quick escape. Perhaps someone would move it, or perhaps he would get lucky, and the canoe would stay in that place. He was loathe to leave it, as if it were an old and valued friend.

He flexed his fingers, made sure they had mobility despite the cold, and then he walked to the door. His footsteps crunched on the rocks, and his wet boots left prints on the brown surface.

The stairs to the door were cut small. He took little steps as he climbed them, noting that they had been built for a man much smaller than he was. Then he reached the center door. He turned the knob and pushed on it.

The door swung open, letting out a great and welcome warmth. The interior was dark after the brightness of the fluorescents on ice.

As he stepped into the darkness, he heard laughter.

Children's laughter.

Max jerked awake as cold air hit his skin. "Mom?" The word popped out of his mouth before he could stop it.

"He's awake," said a man whose voice Max didn't recognize.

He didn't open his eyes. Someone had wrapped him in a blanket, a thick quilt kind of blanket. It felt soft against his bruises. Only his face was cold.

"No, he's not." A woman's voice, deeper and gentler than Mom's.

Water dripped, the sound a constant one. He heard something scrape, then a splash. Arms slid underneath him and lifted him into the air. He didn't want to move. He hadn't realized how comfortable he had been.

"Got the extra blanket down?" the man asked.

"Yes," the woman replied, as if the man had asked a dumb question.

The arms put Max on another soft place and tucked him in carefully. Then the thing he was lying on rocked, as other people got in. There was another scrap-

Kristine Kathryn Rusch

ing, and the entire thing moved. Regular splashes sounded around him.

He opened his eyes just a little and looked through his lashes. The world around him was white. He was in a small boat, with two other people. The man, at his feet, was using a paddle on the left side, and the woman, just above his head, was using a paddle on the right. The boat moved almost silently through the water.

The people didn't look scary. In fact, they looked kinda nice. They had given him blankets, which was more than Mom had done in a long time. He snuggled deeper into the warmth and closed his eyes. He didn't care where the couple took him. Anyplace was better than where he had been.

"The mayor doesn't like the negative publicity," Darleen, Gordon's secretary, said. "He was calling to complain about our department's comments to the press. He says we're anti-family."

Downstairs, kids' voices rose as they were being herded to their new locations. Wayne's money had come in handy for sheltering and feeding the kids. Maybe more money would be forthcoming. Gordon ran a hand over his face.

"Anti-family?" he repeated.

"The mayor's office has received complaints from a wide variety of groups. Parents, not unified, say that the police's action is breaking up the family. That families can't protect their own kids. Your comments about the wide rate of child abuse in this city sparked a heated debate, and one of the groups over at the college says the police are using this as a way to remove children of the poor. They're saying that abuse occurs in rich families, too." She was reading off a list, her red painted nail keeping her place.

Gordon stood in front of her desk like a supplicant. "I suppose the mayor wants me to do something."

"He wants you to make a statement about the American family, saying it's not the bed of abuse and hatred that your previous statements made it sound like."

Gordon looked out the door. Down the marble staircase, police officers kept children in a straight line as they headed to the vans. "I don't recall saying anything like that."

"Personally, I agree with you," Darleen said, "but an outside observer, looking at this situation, might think we believe that the family is dead. And we have only protected the children of the poor and homeless."

"Oh, for heaven's sake." Gordon snatched the paper off her desk, crumpled it into a small ball, and tossed it into the wastebasket. "We took poor and homeless kids because the Penguin is kidnapping them. Or has everyone forgotten that in this mess? He doesn't target abused wealthy or middle class kids. He doesn't go after poor kids with happy families. We're just trying to do our job."

He was surprised at the amount of anger inside him. He unclenched his fists and headed for his office. "Set up that press conference. I'll clean up this mess for the mayor. Even though he might wish I hadn't."

Batman followed the laughter. The corridor smelled of peppermint and hot cocoa. Relaxing smells.

But he didn't relax. The corridor was dark, but clean. It looked as if it was used often.

Kristine Kathryn Rusch

His boots made no noise on the carpeted floor. He saw the red-eye blink of a security camera, but ignored it. The Penguin wanted him to go in, wanted him to go as far as he could. And Batman would. Sure, he might trap himself, but he might also set the children free.

Ahead, light reflected off the corridor's white walls. As he rounded a corner, he saw one-way observation windows. Inside, a large group of children sat in an oversized room. The room was decorated in black and white check, and the children's clothing complemented it. He recognized most of the faces from the Commissioner's files, but they had a different aspect to them now. They looked fuller, not as pale. No bruises and lots of smiles.

A woman was going through the room, passing out mugs of a hot drink—the cocoa he smelled, probably— and the kids were taking them eagerly. A few kids backed away from the others, as if they expected the treat to get taken from them.

He watched the children for a minute, saw how clean they were, how bright their eyes were, how animated their expressions were. Then he saw the little boy that the thugs had taken from the alley. He sat off in a corner, the stuffed penguin at his side, his mug of hot cocoa on a lap table beside him. He was playing with a computer game and he was humming to himself.

For a moment, Batman's vision blurred and he remembered—*standing in an alley, blood spattering his clothing, a bag of popcorn still clutched in his hand. His mother's screams echoed in his ears, and the footsteps of the murderers still rang on the pavement. He looked at his parents, crumpled like used candy wrappers on the concrete, and knew they were dead.*

*He would be alone forever, stuck in that alley, without
anyone to love him—*

He shook himself free of the memory, but the sound
of footsteps remained, ringing on concrete. He glanced
at the children—there were too many of them to gather
together and run with—then at the ceiling. No place
to hide, not really, and what was the point? They already knew he was here.

Still, he couldn't just stand and wait. He walked
past the observation window to the door leading into
the children's room. He opened it and stepped inside.

Children screamed and backed up in fright. The
cocoa woman hit a buzzer on the far wall. He sat on
the stairs leading into the room and extended one leg.
"You don't have to be frightened of me," he said in his
softest voice. "The cocoa looked good. Do you mind
sharing?"

The children stopped screaming, but their expressions were wary. The little boy in the corner clutched
his penguin and it continued squawking. One of the
older boys, a black youth with an elaborate cornrow
and a faceful of scars, crept close to him.

"You're the Batman, aren't you?" he asked.

Batman nodded and accepted the cup of cocoa the
woman offered him. "I came to see if you all were
happy."

A chorus of "yesses" greeted him, their force so
strong that he had to sit back just a little. He pretended
to sip the cocoa, smelling nothing unusual in its contents. A few children didn't answer. They just watched
him with wide eyes.

He turned to one of those children, an eight-year-old
boy with a scrawny, clean-scrubbed face. "What about
you?" he asked. "You happy?"

Kristine Kathryn Rusch

The boy swallowed, then nodded.

"You don't look happy," Batman said.

The boy licked his upper lip. "My mom," he said. "Do you think you could tell her I'm okay?"

"She doesn't know where you are?"

The boy shook his head. "I sure wish she could come here, too."

The little girl next to him hugged a corn-haired doll. She came forward and sat beside Batman, head buried in the doll's hair. "My daddy was hitting Mommy," she said in a soft voice. "She was screaming."

"Are you worried about her?" Batman asked.

The little girl nodded.

Then the door behind them burst open. A short, rotund man stood there. He wore a tuxedo, white gloves, and a top hat. A pince-nez hung around his neck, and he clung to an ornate umbrella. "Well, Batman," he said. "What do you think of my children?"

Batman stood and found himself towering over the little man. "Why are they here?"

The Penguin waved a gloved hand. "To be cared for. All the food they need, all the toys they want, a warm place to sleep, a place where no one will hurt them. All the things the big, bad world out there failed to provide."

"Why?"

The Penguin smiled. "Because I can afford to."

Batman shook his head. "No. What are your plans for these kids? What do you want them to be?"

The Penguin put his pince-nez on his nose and peered at Batman. Then he pointed his umbrella at the woman with the cocoa. "Take the children to the play area. I would like to talk with our tall friend here."

The woman scooped the children around her, then

led them out through a side door. The little girl looked back, her face half hidden by doll.

Batman watched the door close. "Planning to raise them in a life of crime?"

The Penguin laughed. "What a Dickensian imagination you have! I'm trying to save them from a life of crime. The good citizens of Gotham ignore children like this, and so these kids must steal to survive. Or they learn how to use their fists to get what they want."

"The homeless children maybe."

"And the poor children." The Penguin leaned against the doorframe. "The children of the middle class suffer different expectations. No matter how badly they get hurt, they must perform well—get a job, raise their children. And children of the rich, well, they can afford to run away. But children of the poor, and the homeless, usually turn to a life of crime.

"Since when did you become so altruistic?"

The Penguin let his pince-nez slip off his nose. "I never said I was being altruistic. I'm simply being smart, Batman. If I give these children what they need, than they'll become bankers and lawyers and politicians, just like children of the middle class."

"I need to take them back," Batman said.

"To what? A life of poverty and aimlessness? Such heroism, Batman." The Penguin turned and started to walk out the door. Batman grabbed the little man's arm. The Penguin looked down at Batman's hand. "I was actually thinking of letting you go," he said. "But since you insist—"

The doors opened and black-and-white-clad guards rushed in. Batman knocked the Penguin aside and pushed his way to the door, only to discover more guards coming in. He kicked a few aside, then dove

Kristine Kathryn Rusch

through the observation window into the corridor. He rolled on the glass-covered carpet, then glanced down the hall. If he went back to the ice floes, he was trapped. He got up and hurried down the hall, pushing open the door at the end. Inside was a circular staircase that climbed over fifteen stories. He took his Bat-clip, sent it shooting up and up, until it wrapped on the railing near the top. Then he pushed the button and rose as the guards flooded the stairway. They started shooting at him. A few hit his body armor, knocking the breath out of him, but he continued to rise.

A few stories from the top, he saw daylight flooding in windows, and he felt a thin relief. He reached the top floor, vaulted over the railing, and found himself staring at a dozen uniformed guards, all holding guns.

Gordon started down the marble stairway, dreading the press conference. He hated the political aspect of his job. He felt as if it hindered rather than helped his effort as Commissioner. Anti-family, indeed. Couldn't they see that he was trying to prevent someone from breaking up the family?

"Commissioner?" The voice echoed in the great hall.

He looked down. A young officer was running up the stairs toward him.

Gordon stopped and waited. Anything to delay the conference a moment longer. "What is it?"

"We finally got an address. A driver for the toy warehouse told us that he was ordered one night to take the shipment to a weird place. It's an abandoned mansion just outside the city limits. Only, on the way, one of the squads passed the Batmobile. It looks like it's been there awhile, sir."

Hide and Seek

Gordon felt tension rise in his body. "And the mansion?"

"We sent two squads, and they report that it looks inhabited, sir. They're asking for backup before going in."

"I trust it was sent."

"Yes, sir, but dispatch thought you should know." The officer stopped in front of Gordon, panting, as if he had run quite a distance. "Here's the address, sir."

Gordon took the paper and pocketed it. He thanked the officer and walked the rest of the way down the stairs. City hall seemed empty without all the young voices filling its hallways. He walked across the marble floor, noting that the scuff marks had disappeared. Even the presence of the kids had been wiped away. He pushed open the glass double-doors and faced the press.

He wasn't going to let them know anything was up. He would keep them occupied, answer their questions, and then go to the scene. That would give his officers a chance to find those children, without anyone getting in the way.

Max snoozed as the canoe made its way across the water. He would wake on occasion to cover a cold limb or to bury his face deeper in the blankets. The air here smelled good to him. Rich, fresh, and cold, not like the room he had been in for so long.

He didn't want the boatride to end, but it did, with the sound of wood scraping against rock. He opened his eyes and watched as the man bent down to pick him up.

Kristine Kathryn Rusch

"Where are we?" he asked.

"Somewhere safe," the man said. His voice was soft.

"He awake?" the woman asked. She had pulled the boat on the rocks. Max snuggled closer to the man's chest, away from the woman's voice.

"Yep."

"I'm done here," she said. "Let's get him inside."

They crossed the rocks in a hurry. Max saw the blur of lights above him. Long lights, like the ones in the gym at his old school—the school he'd attended when his dad was still alive. So they weren't outside, not really. They were in a building, even though it felt like outside. So dreamlike, but he accepted it. The dream was better than being at home.

"Hear that?" the woman asked.

Max strained, but heard nothing. The man walked even faster. The woman pulled a door open, and then Max heard it—popping sounds, followed by shouting.

"Oh, no," the man said. He started to run. Max jostled with him, clinging to the blankets so that they wouldn't fall.

"Let's put him in the rec room—oh, God." The woman stopped in front of a broken window. Glass covered the carpet, but inside the room were toys and soft chairs and mugs of hot cocoa. "Something's gone wrong."

Max's heart began to ache. Just when he thought he was safe, something went wrong. That always happened to him. Nothing went well.

"I'm going to put you in this room for a minute," the man said. "You stay tight and don't do anything, you hear?"

He didn't wait for Max's answer, but put him on a

Hide and Seek

couch just inside the window. Then the man ran down the hall. There were more pops, followed by shouting, and a scream.

Max looked around the room. It was a nice room, with furniture. He liked all the black and white colors. But he couldn't stay here. Not even when the man asked him to. He couldn't stay in any room too long. Someone would come back and seal up the window, and then he would be trapped here, just like he had been trapped at home.

"Sorry," he whispered, in case anyone was watching. He took his blanket and threw it over the glass on the carpet. Then he left the room and started down the corridor. His legs were shaky, but he saw a door up ahead. An open door. He would go for that. He wouldn't escape so much as find sunlight, find the way outside. If he knew where that was, he could come back and sit in the room, and wait for the man to come back.

He stood at the base of the stairs, looking up, oblivious to the bullets flying around him. He clutched his umbrella in one hand, and a gun in the other, but he wasn't firing. He had seen a bullet hit Batman, and yet the man had vaulted over the railing easily. He could still see Batman's cape, swinging back and forth. His guards were up there, holding him, but they wouldn't hold him for long.

He glanced at the stairs. He wanted to kill Batman himself, but he didn't want to walk all those flights of stairs. Perhaps he could share the glory. Perhaps someone else could shoot him—

Then Batman vaulted off the landing back into midair. Gunfire sprayed around him. He swung toward

Kristine Kathryn Rusch

the fourteenth floor, where there were no guards, where no one was there to stop him.

Penguin pulled his gun, aimed, and was about to shoot when something crashed into him.

"Imbecile!" he cried as he turned—and saw a little boy, so thin that his bones stood out in his skin, bruises covering his tiny body, staring at the guns all around him.

Robbie huddled in the playroom, the other children gathered around him. He knew that sound. Gunfire. He had heard it on the street.

"Something's wrong," he said. The other kids were cowering, too. They all knew how to hide. That's what they did best. But they had it good here, and he didn't want anything to happen to anyone, not the other kids, not the Penguin, who had been good to them, not the Batman, who was going to find his mother. They had to stop all of this, somehow. He had sat back too many times, waiting for someone else to do something. This time he would act.

"Guys,'" he said to the other kids, "we've got to make them stop."

The world froze for a split second. Batman swinging overhead. Bullets spraying around them. Guards on all sides, focusing on killing. And a little boy, the kind Penguin wanted to save, in the middle of it all.

"Get him out of here!" Penguin cried.

Someone grabbed the kid's arm, then Batman swooped down, and scooped the kid up with one hand.

Hide and Seek

He held the kid against his chest and went back up to the fourteenth floor.

The guards continued shooting. Bullets ricocheted around the small space. They could all get killed. The little boy would get killed and Penguin would lose his one and only chance to be benevolent.

"Stop firing!" he called.

Batman vaulted over the railing on the fourteenth floor and disappeared.

The man's skin was cold, but his cape was warm. Max clung to him as hard as he could. He could see the man's eyes through his hood. They were blue and concerned. The man held him, protected him against the noise and bullets. They vaulted over the railing, and in front of them was a door. A paneled door with windows. Through the windows, Max could see lights—red and blue—turning round and round lazily.

The man opened the door and pushed him forward. "Run!" he said. "Run as fast as you can. You have to get away from here."

Max didn't have to be told twice. His bare feet hit the cold, wet grass, and he ran to the cars, seeking warmth.

Gordon's black car pulled up behind the squads. He got out without even bothering to shut off the ignition. The men had surrounded the building as if they were going after a group of terrorists. Gordon hurried to the officer in charge.

"You going in?" he asked.

"There's gunfire inside. I'm afraid if we move too fast, the kids will die. We're scoping the building now."

Gordon stared at it. He had driven past it a hundred times. A five-story wreck of a place, with boards falling off the front and windows reflecting a vacant interior. Doors on all floors opened to porches, except on the first floor, where the door opened directly onto the lawn.

As he watched, the door burst open, and a child ran from inside the house, arms pinwheeling, eyes wide with fright. He bounded across the yard and straight into one of the officers.

"We have to go in," Gordon said. "We have no choice now."

Batman whirled and headed back for the stairs. He would get the Penguin. He had to.

For a moment, he had almost been sucked in by Penguin's explanations, by his obvious commitment to those kids. But two things stuck: Penguin was going to use them, after all, convince them to work with him ten, twenty years down the road when they were bankers and lawyers. He would blackmail them, test them, make them pay for this care. Then there was something the little girl had said, about her mother.

No matter what material possessions Penguin had, he could never give those kids love.

Batman swung back over the railing, heading for the bottom. As he descended, he saw police officers running across the lawn.

The gunfire was beginning again. He would have to swoop as he had done before, grab Penguin, and bring him up. That was the only solution.

Hide and Seek

The guards had started up the stairs, but Penguin had stayed down in the basement, alone. He looked up, saw Batman leap off the rail, cape flying, making him look like the giant winged-creature that had given him his name. Behind him a bevy of police officers crowded the door.

His guards were gone. Penguin was alone.

It had happened too quickly. And it wasn't fair. This time he was trying to do something right. This time, he was trying to give back some of what he had received.

He turned and bolted out of the room. He only had one chance for escape.

He was going to take it.

Robbie led them to the door of the playroom and stopped. The big mirror had been broken, showing a corridor outside. Someone had placed a blanket on the floor.

The shouts had grown fainter, and there were no more gun pops. Still, he had to see what had happened.

He turned to the other kids and beckoned them to follow him, to do what he did. Their black-and-white clothing would make them blend with the decor. He would keep them hidden as best he could.

As he crossed the room, he saw the Penguin run past the window. Little legs flying, umbrella trailing behind him.

Robbie was about to call out to him when he heard more footsteps. Batman was running behind him, cape flying like wings.

Kristine Kathryn Rusch

Something awful was happening. The safe world that Penguin had brought them to was going away.

Robbie climbed out the mirror onto the blanket. The other children followed.

Almost there. Almost there. Just a few more feet and then the door. The Penguin heard Batman's footfalls behind him.

Almost there, he repeated to himself. Almost there.

The door stood open and he vaulted out of it into the cold winter of his underground cavern. Penguins stood on the ice, watching him, as if this were all a show put on for their inspection.

He hurried across the rocks, grabbed a boat, and started to drag it to the water when he heard someone behind him.

"You're done, Penguin," Batman said.

The little man hovered over the canoe for a second longer, looking ridiculous against the world he'd made. Batman waited for the Penguin to turn, to say something, to justify himself, but the little man pushed the canoe and jumped in.

Batman lunged down the beach, grabbed the edge of the canoe, and pulled Penguin from it. For a man so short, he was heavy. He kicked his spats at Batman, the sharp pointy toes slamming against the body armor.

"I wonder how long you would survive in the cold water," Batman said. "You're not a true penguin, not like your little friends there."

The little man's gaze darted over Batman's shoulder, giving him a half-second of warning. Then a myriad of little arms clutched his legs, voices raised in fear.

"Let him go!"

"Don't hurt him!"

"Put him down!"

Batman struggled forward. Penguin kicked again, and Batman lost his grip. Little bodies slammed against his and he fell, face forward in the rocks. Penguin scrambled to his feet and ran to the canoe. It was floating in a few inches of water, and he splashed his way to the wooden sides, then jumped in.

Batman rolled away from the children, only to have them catch him again.

"No!" one of the little boys cried. "Don't hurt him."

The little girl with her dolly stood at the door, tears running down her cheeks. *My daddy was hitting Mommy,* she had said to him. *She was screaming.*

He couldn't attack Penguin in front of the children. That would make him as bad, or worse, than the people they had already known.

"All right, kids," he said, getting to his feet. "I'll let him go."

He could always catch him on the other side.

Penguin watched as Batman herded the children inside. He had been so close. He felt as if he had actually done something right. Now he was paddling a canoe as fast as he could to get away from Gotham City, to get away from the police and the winged man who haunted him.

He headed the canoe behind an iceberg to a smaller cavern that only he and the cave's designers knew about. He would have to paddle farther than he had planned, but at least he would get away.

But he would be back. They would forget about the children, as they had before, and he would be back. He would do it differently next time. He would do it better.

They would never know that he was wooing their children away from them.

Two days. It had been two days, and they had searched every inch of that ice cave. They had found the side panel and the abandoned canoe. The Penguin had escaped them again.

Gordon sat back in his leather chair. Most of the children were still in protective custody—ostensibly to see if Penguin had done any damage to them. But soon Gordon would have to return them to their homes—if they had homes.

He felt as if they had lost this one. There was little the city could do to protect these children once they returned to their old lives. He closed his eyes and thought of little Scotty. At least he was safe, as were Max and a few of the others. Those where the physical abuse was so bad, the police actually had a case for removal. But all the kids who had good parents, and were starving. The kids who wouldn't speak up. They were still trapped.

The Penguin had shown the city that it had a problem, a problem that it now had to deal with. It wasn't about increasing security at Gotham Night Depository or returning the goods to Markowitz's Gallery. It was something more complex than that. Something for which Gordon, and the mayor, and the city council had no glimmering of a solution.

Hide and Seek

His intercom buzzed, making him start. He pushed
the button. "Yeah?"

"Mr. Wayne here to see you, sir."

Gordon wiped his hand over his face, trying to hide
the exhaustion in his features. "Send him in."

The door opened, and Bruce Wayne stood there. The
light from Darleen's office hid his face in shadow and,
for a moment, he looked tall and strong and almost
menacing. Then he stepped forward, and the illusion
disappeared.

"I'm heading over to see the mayor in a few minutes,"
Wayne said, sinking into one of the chairs across from
Gordon's desk. "But I wanted to talk with you first.
What's going to happen to all the children?"

"The ones we rounded up are already back at home
or in temporary shelters," Gordon said. "We'll be doing
the same with the kids that the Penguin took in a day
or so."

Wayne frowned. "You have names of the kids and
records, don't you?"

"What are you getting at?"

"I've been doing some thinking over the past few
days," he said, "and a bit of research. Every place has
these kinds of problems, and most of them are cyclical.
Once poor, most people remain poor. Abuse also travels
in families, unless someone learns how to parent properly. There are people all over the country who train
parents how to discipline their kids without hurting
them, and programs for people who have chemical de-
pendence, as well as for the kids living with them."

"I know, Wayne. We can't just farm all these people
off to some special program."

Wayne stood. "I thought about that. But you're right.
It's not feasible. It is feasible, however, to bring the

experts here. I'll throw the opening money at it. I'll set up the fund-raising programs. We can become the first place in the nation that pays attention to its ignored children. But I need your help."

"My help?" Gordon tried not to let a feeling of hope rise in his chest.

"I want us to figure out ways to get families involved without condemning them. Without making it seem like a punishment. And I need your help convincing the mayor."

Mention of the mayor made the hope turn into acid indigestion. "This isn't something we can do overnight, Wayne."

"We can start," Wayne said. "Keep those shelters open. Get some of the programs underway. Protect the kids we can. We have to, Commissioner. Or we open ourselves up to this same kind of attack again."

Gordon glanced at his couch, with its little white stain. He never again wanted to feel the helplessness he had felt the last few weeks. "All right," he said, taking a deep breath, "let's go see the mayor."

A few weeks later, Max sat on a swing in the backyard of the large house that was home to him and ten other children. He pumped his legs, riding higher and higher, feeling the sunlight on his face. . . .

. . . Scotty sat in the police commissioner's office, playing with a notebook. Mr. Gordon had said he could visit once a week. . . .

. . . Robbie made a peanut butter sandwich, and offered it to his mom. They both sat in front of a small black-and-white TV in their new apartment. His mom had gotten the rooms, along with a job cleaning the halls and the basement of the apartment complex. . . .

. . . Tyson tugged a new flannel shirt tighter to his body, loving the soft feel of the fabric. He sat in a classroom for kids like him, without much education, and he was beginning to realize how much he loved computers. . . .

. . . Stacy sat next to her mom at a talk about drinking. The man on the stage was saying that even nice people can get mean when they drink. "Oh, baby," Stacy's mom whispered. "I didn't know. . . ."

. . . Ellen had a new room. It was smaller than her old one, but she felt safer. No one yelled at her here. No one hurt her. She even had other kids to play with. . . .

. . . Jack kept an eye on the other kids. It felt good to have a place to live, even if it was in a kind of a home. He let the other kids know what life was like on the streets. And if one of them started to go wrong, he would sit down and explain it again. After all, here they got three meals a day. . . .

Kristine Kathryn Rusch

. . . Lisbet sat on the porch, arms around her knees. The screendoor slammed, and her daddy came out. He sat beside her. She leaned as far away from him as she could.

"I'm going to go away for a little while, honey," he said. "To a place where they'll make me better. But first, I have something for you."

He took his hand from behind his back and handed her a doll. It was soft and pretty with long dark hair. "I'm sorry I hurt your other one," he said. "And I'm sorry I hurt you. . . ."

And Bruce Wayne stood on a rain-slicked street in a deserted alley. The street light barely dispelled the darkness. He crouched and set a rose on the pavement. For a moment, the clatter of pearls echoed, followed by gunshots, his mother's scream—

Too well, he remembered that feeling of loss, of loneliness, of never being loved again.

He could fight crime, but he never thought he could fight those feelings. Until now. With the Thomas Wayne Memorial Children's Foundation.

He stood. The city had started to turn the mess around. If the Penguin ever returned, he would find nothing he could use in Gotham.

The rose looked pretty there, in the light. Wayne smiled, then stepped into the darkness, letting it enfold him, as if something large and powerful were wrapping him in loving arms.

ABOUT THE EDITOR

MARTIN H. GREENBERG has edited more than 700 fiction and nonfiction books. He is also a Member of the Board of Advisors of the Sci-Fi Channel and CEO of TEKNO-BOOKS, the book packaging division of BIG Entertainment. He has received Lifetime Achievement Awards in both the science fiction and, most recently, the mystery field.

ABOUT THE AUTHORS

EDWARD BRYANT began writing professionally in 1968, and has since published more than a dozen books. His latest short story collection, *Flirting with Death*, will be published in mid-1995. His work has appeared in such anthologies as *Orbit, Night Visions,* and *Blood Is Not Enough*, as well as such magazines as Omni, Writer's Digest, and Locus. He's won the Nebula Award (twice) and is currently living in North Denver finishing his next novel.

MORT CASTLE has published more than 300 shorter works, including novellas and short stories in such magazines and anthologies as *The Twilight Zone, Mike Shayne Mystery Magazine, Voices from the Night,* and *The Secret Prophecies of Nostradamus*. Active in the comics field since 1989, Castle is currently scripting celebrity biographies for Pop Comics.

MAX ALLAN COLLINS is two-time winner of the Shamus Best Novel Award for his historical thrillers *True Detective* (1938) and *Stolen Away* (1991), both featuring Chicago P.I. Nate Heller. He scripted the Dick Tracy comic strip from 1977–1993, and his comic book credits include *Batman* and his own *Ms. Tree*.

NANCY COLLINS-LINHART is the author of *Paint It Black, Walking Wolf, Wild Blood, In the Blood, Tempter,* and *Sunglasses After Dark*. Her short fiction has appeared in such venues as *Year's Best Fantasy & Horror, Definitive Best of the Horrorshow, Splatterpunks I & II,* and *The Best of Pulphouse*. She is currently working on the 4th installment of the Sonja Blue cycle, *A Dozen Black Roses*. She resides in New York City with her husband and their dog.

GEORGE ALEC EFFINGER has written more than twenty books and 250 pieces of short fiction. His best-known novels include *When Gravity Fails, The Wolves of Memory,* and *What Entropy Means to Me*. His novella, "Schrodinger's Kitten," won the Hugo and Nebula awards in 1989. He currently lives in New Orleans.

ED GORMAN has published several novels and three collections of short stories. The *San Diego Union* calls him "One of the most distinctive voices in today's crime fiction."

KAREN HABER's short fiction has appeared in *Isaac Asimov's Science Fiction Magazine, After the King, Women of Darkness* and other anthologies. Her newest novel, *The Woman Without a Shadow,* appeared from DAW books in March 1995, the first of a three-book series.

JON HAMMER and KAREN McBURNIE live in New York City. They do not own any cats.

ANDREW HELFER was born and raised in Brooklyn, New York. He attended prestigious New York City public schools, and later he went to college and did graduate work in journalism at New York University. Still later, he discovered the joy of comic books and has spent the last thirteen years writing and editing them for DC Comics. In his spare time, Andrew has written many illustrated children's books, branching storybooks, and novelizations, and has co-authored fifteen episodes of the syndicated *Adventures of Superboy* television series. Andrew lives in New York City.

STUART M. KAMINSKY is well known for his tales of 1930's Hollywood and the author of the Toby Peters and Porfiry Petrovich mystery series. *A Cold Red Surprise*, the latest novel in the Rostnikov series, won the Edgar Award for Best Novel in 1988. Born in 1934, he is Professor of Radio, Television, and Film at Northwestern University.

PAUL KUPPERBERG is an editor at DC Comics and a veteran writer in the comic book field with over 500 stories to his credit in the U.S. and U.K. He has also written both the *Superman* and *Tom & Jerry* syndicated newspaper strips and his short stories have appeared recently in the anthologies *Superheroes* and *Fear Itself*. He lives in Connecticut with his wife Robin and cat Cassie, both of whom contributed to the story in this volume.

JOE R. LANSDALE is best known as a writer of horror and suspense, with over a hundred short stories and eleven novels to his credit. His latest novel, *The Two Bear Mambo*, was published by Mysterious Press. He has been referred to as the "cult king of the horror and crime fiction underground," and his stories consistently appear in Year's Best volumes and reprints. In addition to writing the teleplays for three episodes of the Emmy Award-winning *Batman: The Animated Series*, he is also the writer of DC Comics' *Jonah Hex: Two-Gun Mojo*, recently nominated for a Bram Stoker Award. Mr. Lansdale lives and works with his wife and children in Nacodoches, Texas.

WILLIAM F. NOLAN's most famous creation is *Logan's Run* (3 bestselling novels, MGM film, CBS television series, audio cassette, etc.), but he has another 60 books to his credit, along with 700 stories and articles and 40 TV and film scripts. His latest novel, *The Marble Orchard*, is due out from St. Martin's Press in November 1995.

GARFIELD REEVES-STEVENS is a Canadian-born writer whose writing credits include *Bloodshift*, *Dreamland*, and *Children of the Shroud*. He currently resides in California.

KRISTINE KATHRYN RUSCH's novel *Alien Influences* has been nominated for the Arthur C. Clarke Award for Best Science Fiction Novel first published in England. Her novel *Sins of the Blood* is on the preliminary Stoker ballot for Best Horror Novel here in the United States. Last August, she won the Hugo Award for the Best Editor for her work at *The Magazine of Fantasy and Science Fiction*.

ROBERT SILVERBERG is the author of over 100 books and an uncounted number of essays and short stories. He has also edited numerous anthologies and collections, and is the winner of four Hugo awards, five Nebulas, as well as most of the other significant science fiction honors. His latest book, *Hot Sky at Midnight*, was published by Bantam Books. Born in New York City, Mr. Silverberg is a graduate of Columbia University. He currently lives and works in California.

DAN SIMMONS is the author of five novels: *Song of Kali*, *Carrion Comfort*, *Phases of Gravity*, *Hyperion*, and *The Fall of Hyperion*. Winner of *Twilight Zone* magazine's Rod Serling Memorial Award for best new writer in 1982, he currently resides in Colorado.

HENRY SLESAR's credits include almost 500 short stories, 7 novels, 30 collections, more than 100 prime time teleplays, 5 movies, 50 radio plays and 19 productions of six plays. He has been headwriter of five daytime serials, received two Edgars and one Emmy. He threatens to write a great deal more.

ROBERT WEINBERG sold his first short story in 1967 and hasn't stopped writing since. He is the author of sixteen books and numerous short stories and has edited over one hundred anthologies and story collections. His recent novel, *Vampire Diary: The Embrace*, written with Mark Rein-Hagen, was a hardcover best seller. He lives in Chicago's south suburbs with his wife Phyllis, son Matt, and over twenty thousand books.